Decade of Decisions

American Policy Toward the Arab-Israeli Conflict

1967~1976

William B. Quandt

DECADE OF
DECISIONS

DECADE OF DECISIONS

American Policy Toward the
Arab-Israeli Conflict, 1967–1976

WILLIAM B. QUANDT

UNIVERSITY OF CALIFORNIA PRESS
Berkeley / Los Angeles / London

University of California Press
Berkeley and Los Angeles, California

University of California Press, Ltd.
London, England

Copyright © 1977 by
The Regents of the University of California

ISBN: 0–520–03536–4
Library of Congress Catalog Card Number: 77–73499
Printed in the United States of America

6 7 8 9

Contents

Acknowledgments

                    For much of the period covered by this book, I have been trying to learn about, and to explain as well as I could, American foreign policy toward the Arab-Israeli conflict. The complexity of the subject and the emotions surrounding it continue to impress me. I have nonetheless tried to make sense out of the record, and I have tried to do so without partisanship.

Needless to say, I have been assisted in this effort by many friends and colleagues. Scholars have shared with me their insights, and policy makers have talked candidly of their experiences. I cannot even begin to name all those who have been helpful.

I would, however, like to pay special tribute to Harold H. Saunders. For two years, from 1972 to 1974, I worked as his deputy in the Middle East office of the National Security Council staff. His analytical skill, his understanding of issues, and his sense of the human dimensions of the Arab-Israeli conflict made a great impression on me and significantly influenced my approach to the topic of this book.

This study was mostly written during the summer of 1976. To carry on my research and writing during that period, I received grants from the Middle East Center and from the International Relations Program at the University of Pennsylvania. I am grateful to Professors

vii

Thomas Naff and Frederick Frey for their support. The grants permitted me to engage the research assistance of Sidney R. Jones, without whose help and encouragement I would have found it difficult to complete this work.

In January 1977, shortly after submitting the manuscript for publication, I returned to the National Security Council staff to work on Middle Eastern affairs. I have made no substantive changes in the text since then and I have deliberately refrained from any speculation about future policy, which I might have been tempted to do in other circumstances. I hope it will be clearly understood that the book as it stands is a product of my academic work and reflects only my own views, not those of the U.S. government or of President Carter's administration.

Washington, D.C.
July 1977

Introduction

THE DECADE from 1967 through 1976 was punctuated by four acute international crises in the Middle East: the June 1967 Arab-Israeli war, the September 1970 Jordan crisis, the October 1973 war, and the Lebanon civil war of 1975–76. On the first three of these occasions, the United States was caught by surprise by events over which it seemed to have little control. Two American presidents, Lyndon Johnson and Richard Nixon, faced the awesome danger of a nuclear confrontation with the Soviet Union because of crises that had their origin in the conflict between Israel and her Arab neighbors.

Few issues have been considered more critical to American foreign-policy makers than the Arab-Israeli dispute. It is not simply the risk of nuclear war that rivets the attention of Americans to the Middle East. There is also a deeply felt commitment to Israel, a commitment that political leaders take seriously, not only in election years. It would hardly be an exaggeration to say that for a significant number of Americans, Israel's security and well-being are top-priority concerns.

In recent years, however, other aspects of the Middle East have entered the consciousness of thoughtful Americans. Increasingly, the dependence of the United States on foreign petroleum, much of it from the Arab world, has been viewed as a serious problem. The cost of United States oil imports alone should be cause for concern. In the

1

late 1970s, the United States will probably spend annually between $25 and $30 billion for imported oil, a figure that dwarfs the controversial sums allotted to foreign aid each year. Even if the economic costs of oil imports can be borne with equanimity, there is fear of political costs. Despite all the brave talk of increasing "interdependence" among nations, many Americans seem uncomfortable when interdependence takes the form of reliance upon Arab oil for a substantial portion of the energy required to maintain a modern industrialized society. Some Americans clearly fear that the United States is opening itself to Arab "blackmail," and that the commitment to Israel will be diluted by oil politics.

The Middle East, then, appears to be a region where American national security is threatened, where our economic well-being can be directly affected, and where our basic commitments as a nation are in jeopardy. Little wonder that the Arab-Israeli conflict, in its various aspects, is constantly in the headlines. For all the importance attributed to that region, however, there is a dearth of public discussion of issues, of reasoned debate, and of consistent interest. Emotionalism and sloganeering often replace serious analysis. Politicians can rarely resist the temptation to appeal to voters in overly simplified terms, playing upon their genuine fears and concerns by offering shallow formulas. Once in office, however, they frequently behave quite differently from their promises. The president who pledges unstinting support for Israel may also favor arms sales to Saudi Arabia and to Egypt. Although this may be a perfectly defensible posture, he will stress the former policy and try to minimize the latter until elections are safely behind him.

The Arab-Israeli conflict will no doubt remain a major preoccupation in United States foreign policy in the years ahead. If the past decade is any guide, we can anticipate severe crises that may draw the superpowers to the brink of confrontation; the use of oil as a political weapon; and ambivalence and vacillation on the part of American policy makers as they try to cope with the intricate, perhaps intractable, problems of the Middle East.

An understanding of the past is no guarantee that future policy will be more enlightened or effective. But the history of American foreign policy toward the Arab-Israeli conflict from 1967 to 1976 has a fascination apart from its possible utility. The events and individuals, the dangers and the hopes of this period make up a particularly exciting phase of the American experience in world affairs.

Beyond the description of events, however, lies the need for understanding, for explanation, for analysis. Foreign-policy making is a complex process, rarely more so than with regard to the Middle East. The process by which policy is formulated involves efforts to make sense out of the jumble of events, to mobilize resources on behalf of purposes, and to translate values into concrete decisions. Policy making is disorderly and often less than inspirational, but the process must be understood if the results are ever to be improved upon.

Fortunately, the way in which American foreign policy usually is made is not a total mystery. Policy makers, through their memoirs and other writings, as well as policy analysts, through their academic studies, have done much to lift the veil of secrecy that surrounds the great and less great decisions of the recent past. The American press has been vigilant and diligent in uncovering facts, and presidents and secretaries of state have been cross-examined in public. Documents on key issues have been published or leaked, often providing vital bits of information on policy.

The obstacles to understanding American policy in the Middle East stem less from a paucity of data or information than from the failure to ask the appropriate questions. Too frequently, the complexities of decisions have been reduced to simplistic notions of whether someone was pro-Arab or pro-Israeli, or whether the oil lobby succeeded in influencing the president. An individualistic bias may attribute policies to the personality of one man, whereas a crude Marxism may point to some obscure economic "fact."

Several alternative ways of explaining American foreign policy toward the Arab-Israeli conflict offer useful insights into the process and substance of decision making. Each approach is limited, however, by the assumptions on which it is based, by the questions it asks, and by the range of answers it provides. Hence, before analyzing the policies of the United States in the Middle East between 1967 and 1976, it is essential to clarify these various perspectives on policy making.

Four distinctive, though often complementary, approaches, deserve attention:

First is the strategic, or national-interests, perspective. This is most commonly employed by decision makers in justifying their policies and by analysts who view Middle East developments from a global or systemic vantage point.

Second is the domestic-politics perspective, which emphasizes the role of interest groups, public opinion, and Congress in shaping foreign policy. Both apologists for and critics of policies will often refer to "the Zionist lobby" or "an unresponsive Congress" to explain some aspect of policy that does not fit the national-interests approach.

Third is the bureaucratic-politics perspective, which focuses on the functioning of the executive branch in shaping and implementing policies. Actions otherwise inexplicable may be traced to bureaucratic rivalries, organizational routines, or negotiations between powerful factions within the government. Anyone who has worked in a vast bureaucracy is likely to appreciate the importance of this approach.

Fourth is the presidential-leadership perspective. In the American political system, the president and a few of his closest advisers typically make high-level policy. It is thus extremely important to know how they view issues, the way in which they reason, and the guidelines they rely upon for reducing the complexity of day-to-day events into stable patterns. This approach assumes that policy is the product of individuals, not of abstract forces, and that an understanding of how key policy makers define issues will provide insights into the intellectual processes by which policy is made.

THE STRATEGIC, OR NATIONAL-INTERESTS, PERSPECTIVE

In its simplest form, this approach is based on the assumption that foreign policy is essentially a rational adaptation of means (resources) to ends (national interests). Nation-states seek security, well-being, and prestige, and to attain these goals they employ power, whether in its military or its economic form. Policy making is primarily a calculation of the costs and benefits accruing from alternative courses of action. That course of action which is best suited to enhance national interests at a given cost will be selected by decision makers, barring irrationality or error.

Viewed from this perspective, American policy toward the Arab-Israeli conflict is best understood as part of a global strategy in which superpower rivalry is a dominant reality. Starting with the structure of the international system as a whole, a strategic analyst will emphasize the nature of the nuclear balance, the pattern of alliances, and perhaps the economic transactions among nations. Stanley Hoffmann, for example, has discussed the consequences for American foreign policy toward Europe of the erosion of "bipolarity" and the emergence of a more complex international order in which the dispersion of nuclear weapons and the weakening of alliances are essential elements.[1] The "rules of the game" that were applicable to the bipolar world of the 1950s can no longer guide policy makers in the multipolar, polycentric world of the late 1960s and the 1970s.

Applied to the Middle East, this point of view focuses on American reactions to Soviet moves into the area. During the early period of the Cold War, the United States sought bases and allies in the Middle East as part of its global defense system against the Soviet Union. Turkey and Greece were drawn into the NATO alliance; Iran was prevented from turning to a neutralist course; moderate Arab states were supported; and U.S.-Israeli relations remained uncharacteristically cool. But as the Soviet Union became involved in Egypt from 1955 onward, American policy began to vacillate between bidding against the Soviet Union for Egypt's favors and trying to punish Egypt by aid to anti-Egyptian regional forces, including Israel. Neither policy worked particularly well, and with the waning of the Cold War in the mid-1960s, Washington's interest in playing this game seemed to recede.

It was in this atmosphere that the June 1967 Arab-Israeli war erupted, revealing the fragility of the regional balance, the continued danger of superpower confrontation, and, eventually, the danger of polarization of the area between the United States and Israel, on the one hand, and the Soviet Union with the radical Arabs on the other. The September 1970 civil war in Jordan was the highpoint of U.S.-U.S.S.R. rivalry, and was followed by a move toward détente at the global level. That move had only minimal impact on the Arab-Israeli region, as the October 1973 war demonstrated. Then, with the oil crisis taking its toll of the American economy, the United States

1. Stanley Hoffmann, *Gulliver's Troubles, or The Setting of American Foreign Policy* (New York: McGraw-Hill, 1968), pt. I; also, Raymond Aron, *The Imperial Republic: The United States and the World, 1945–1973* (Englewood Cliffs, N.J.: Prentice-Hall, 1974), pt. I.

launched an intense diplomatic effort to neutralize Arab pressures, reduce Soviet influence, and regain control over the strategic dimensions of the Arab-Israeli conflict.

This, in brief, would be the broad outline of a strategic, systemic view of United States policy in the Middle East. The emphasis on the U.S.-Soviet relationship is well taken, along with the stress on linkages between global developments and their regional consequences. The anti-Soviet theme has certainly been a dominant one in American foreign policy in the area, but it does change in accordance with the overall U.S.-Soviet relationship. The focus on oil as an interest is also valid. But the complexities of U.S.-Israeli and U.S.-Egyptian relations are not easily captured by this perspective. Only after the fact can the analyst portray aid to Israel or Egypt as fitting the strategic purposes of the United States; the withholding of such aid is just as plausibly accounted for in terms of United States national interests.

The Marxist-Leninist variant of the strategic perspective also takes a comprehensive approach to United States policy in the Middle East. United States behavior in the area is likely to be seen as a manifestation of the broader strategy of imperialism, which aims at preserving the capitalist economic system by exploiting Third World resources, weakening national liberation movements, and using Middle East countries as forward military and intelligence-gathering bases from which to attack the leading antiimperialist "progressive" countries.

Marxists are often more concerned with the internal logic of their theories than with evidence, but the best Marxist analysts strive for a sophisticated blend of fact and theory. Some incidents seem ready-made for their approach. For example, in 1951 the prime minister of Iran nationalized the holdings of British oil companies in his country. During the next two years, the international oil companies refused to purchase Iranian oil, causing great harm to the economy. In August 1953, the Shah tried to dismiss his prime minister, but instead was forced to flee the·country in the face of mob demonstrations. Then, with the help of the Central Intelligence Agency, the Shah was returned to power. Shortly thereafter, negotiations were begun to establish a consortium of western oil companies, including for the first time American companies, in Iran. The negotiations were successful, Iranian oil production increased, the Shah established his power firmly, banned the communist Tudeh party, entered into alliance with the United States, and generally presented Iran to the world as a guardian of western interests against the forces of disorder and subversion. A Marxist interpretation might seem to fit the picture quite well. The only flaw is that the CIA's role in restoring the Shah to power was unrelated to the subsequent developments concerning oil.[2] Marxist interpretations, by overemphasizing economics, often fail to address adequately the question of motivation. In this case, ideology, in the form of anticommunism, seems to have played a much greater role than the desire for oil profits. Marxists appear, however, to have great difficulty in dealing with ideology.

United States support for Israel has also been difficult for Marxists to explain. At first glance, it seems obvious that the concrete economic interests of the United States in the Middle East lie in the Arab world, not in Israel. It is from the Arabian peninsula, the Persian Gulf, and North Africa that oil flows to the capitalist world. And most Arab oil producers are militantly anti-Zionist and are angered by United States support for Israel. The logical American response might seem to be to try to minimize the United States relationship with Israel and to concentrate its attention on the Arab oil-producing states instead. Indeed, American policy throughout the 1950s followed this pattern rather closely. From 1967 on, however, despite the growing importance of Arab oil, United States support for Israel increased enormously. A new explanation is therefore called for. Israel, according to Marxists, has become an agent of United States imperialism, a guardian of its economic interests, and an antirevolutionary force in the area. For evidence, they point to the 1967 war, arguing that the United States encouraged Israel to attack Egypt in order to weaken President Nasser, whose antiimperialist tendencies were well-developed. By defeating Nasser, Israel opened the way for the conservative Arab countries such as Saudi Arabia, Libya, and Kuwait to use their financial resources to neutralize the threat to their societies from Nasser's Egypt.

Turning to the post-1967 period, Marxists would single out the role played by Israel and by Jordan, another American client, in crushing the Palestinian resistance movement. During the September 1970 civil war in Jordan, the United States and Israel openly supported King Hussein against the Palestinian *fedayeen* and the "progressive" Syrian regime, which sought to aid the Palestinians. Again

2. Sidney R. Jones, "American Intervention in Iran, 1953," unpublished manuscript, University of Pennsylvania, spring 1975.

in 1975–76, Marxists would argue, the United States, Israel, and Syria conspired to eliminate the PLO as a "progressive" force in Lebanon. Once again, Israel appears as a key factor in an "imperialist counter-revolutionary" strategy. In the Marxist argument, American military aid to Israel is thus perfectly comprehensible, because it serves to extend the reach of American military power. If the Arab oil producers were ever to withhold oil from the capitalist world for a prolonged period, Israel could be expected to help break the embargo by military force.

Marxist theories exhibit the same virtues as other systemic approaches. They look for interrelations, for nonobvious connections, for the "real causes" behind events. From the standpoint of science and psychology, however, Marxist approaches often fail lamentably. They typically look at consequences and interpret them as causes. This form of teleology, in which, for example, the fact that Nasser was weakened by the 1967 war is used to explain United States and Israeli policy during the war, is simply indefensible on empirical grounds. And because reality does not conform to the theory, the theory is constantly having to be adjusted. Only the categories remain the same. Syria passes from being a "progressive" regime to being a lackey of imperialism because of its role in the Lebanese civil war in 1976. A simplistic form of Marxism is attractive to many because it so readily offers explanations of apparent plots and conspiracies. And conspiracy theories have a wide following in the Middle East among Marxists and non-Marxists alike.

One other group of strategic analysts should be mentioned: the military thinkers who worry about fleet movements, outflanking maneuvers, and the global balance of power. Inevitably they must also think systemically, concentrating upon the global military equation, of which the Middle East is only a small part. Shortly after World War II, the American military strategists were greatly worried by the threat of Soviet military expansion, especially into important areas such as the Middle East. Some of them opposed United States support for Israel on the ground that it would provide the Soviet Union with opportunities to "leap over" the northern tier (Turkey, Iran, Pakistan) and to "penetrate" the Arab world. In this way, Moscow would succeed in "outflanking NATO," could turn off the "oil tap of the Persian Gulf," and could pose a threat to "NATO's soft underbelly."

After 1967, some military strategists came to see Israel as a strategic asset for the United States. Israel's presence in Sinai kept the Suez Canal shut, which made it difficult for the Soviet Union to send naval units to the Indian Ocean. Israel's military victory over Egypt yielded valuable Soviet weaponry, some of which was being used against American forces in Vietnam. In exchange for the opportunity to examine the SAM II surface-to-air missiles, some American military strategists were happy to recommend the sale of sophisticated United States arms to Israel. Moreover, Israeli intelligence capabilities were reputed to be superb, and in return for aid the Israelis might share some of their information on Soviet activities in the Middle East and elsewhere. Finally, the Israelis were unusually skillful in handling American military equipment, and their suggestions and advice were helpful in modifying the design of the F-4 Phantom jet, the mainstay of the tactical wing of the United States Air Force. With all of these military virtues, Israel deserved to be treated as an ally.

As with the Marxist views, those of the military strategists contain some important elements of truth. On the other hand, they also result in vast oversimplifications and simply do not accord well with the full range of evidence. In particular, how can this view account for the periodic crises in U.S.-Israeli relations over arms supply? Why did the United States acquiesce so readily in the reopening of the Suez Canal in 1975? If the military strategists were correct in their assessment, they must somehow have failed to convince American policy makers.

How, one may ask, have American policy makers in fact viewed United States interests in the Middle East? And how have they seen those interests being affected by the Arab-Israeli conflict, especially during the crisis-ridden period from 1967 to 1976? Three sets of interests have generally been of concern to policy makers. First is a preoccupation with the Soviet presence and influence in the area. Second is the commitment to Israel's security and well-being. Third is the fact that the Middle East contains nearly two-thirds of the known reserves of petroleum in the world.

The simplest version of the American interest regarding the Soviet Union in the Middle East is derived from the "containment" doctrine. Conceived after World War II, the policy of containment sought to prevent the expansion of Soviet influence into any part of the "free world." This proved to be a losing battle in the Middle

East in the 1950s, but the concern with minimizing the Soviet role in the area has persisted.

In the mid-1960s, with the Soviet Union strongly involved on the side of several "radical" Arab states, a new dimension of the Soviet presence preoccupied policy makers. This was the fear of confrontation between the two nuclear superpowers. It was believed that the nature of United States and Soviet interests and involvements in the Arab-Israeli conflict was such that the two powers might inadvertently be drawn into a local war. The military intervention of one superpower on behalf of its client would almost certainly be met by counterintervention by the other superpower. Consequently, the risk of nuclear war seemed especially acute in the event of an outbreak of hostilities between the Arabs and Israel.

The interest in avoiding confrontation thus emerged as a major preoccupation, for after all, the only threat to the vital security interests of the United States stemmed from the risk of nuclear war. Even if the probability of confrontation was low, its consequences were considered so dangerous that its prevention became a prime objective. The problem was how to achieve the end sought. One way might have been to withdraw entirely from the Middle East, but no one favored such a strategy. Instead, an effort was made to strike a balance between limiting Soviet influence and avoiding a confrontation. The means to be used would be diplomacy, to remove the sources of local conflicts, and arms shipments, to bring about a regional balance of power. In addition, a United States military presence would be maintained in the area.

Virtually everyone in the American foreign-policy establishment could agree on the importance of the first set of interests, but there was much less agreement on how it related to the second and third interests, Israel and oil. Nor was there a clear understanding of how the latter two interests could be reconciled.

The concern for Israel's security was taken for granted as a basic commitment of United States foreign policy. Although no formal treaty bound the two countries, American presidents and the Congress had repeatedly spoken of an undefined commitment to Israel's survival. And certainly after 1967, the United States did more than any other country in the world to make good on that commitment.

The unanimity concerning Israel's security, however, concealed important areas of ambiguity and disagreement. For example, did the commitment apply to any specific territory? If so, did it include territory beyond the 1967 armistice lines? Did the commitment to Israel as a predominantly Jewish state imply that the United States would not support the repatriation of Palestinian refugees? Did the commitment mean that the United States would intervene to offset any Soviet military threat, regardless of how it came about? Americans tended to prefer to leave such awkward questions unanswered, whereas Israelis tried to obtain precise answers, usually with only partial success.

Apart from confusion over the nature of the commitment to Israel, there was a remarkable degree of uncertainty as to its origins. Some argued that the commitment was basically a moral one. The survivors of the holocaust, the remnant of the Jewish people, had a right to a state within their historic homeland. It was perhaps unfortunate that the Jewish right conflicted with that of the Palestinian Arabs, but in light of recent history the need for a place of refuge for the Jews was simply more compelling than the need to establish a Palestinian Arab state. In addition, Israel was a democracy which shared many of the same values as the United States. For these reasons, Israel's safety and prosperity were properly of interest to the United States. The fact that the interest stemmed from moral concerns in a world of power politics simply made it that much more worth protecting.

Others took a less lofty view of the American interest in Israel, ascribing it to domestic politics and to the existence of a well-organized, effective Zionist lobby in the United States. Somewhat more generously, it was noted that public opinion in the United States was much more pro-Israeli than pro-Arab and that, in a democracy, foreign-policy interests were defined in large measure by public sentiment.[3] Consequently, a commitment to Israel growing out of domestic political realities was no more remarkable than a commitment to England or opposition to the white-supremacist regimes in southern Africa. In each case, the policy was at least in part a function of American public opinion.

A third view of the U.S.-Israeli connection centered upon the

3. See Hazel Erskine, "The Polls: Western Partisanship in the Middle East," *Public Opinion Quarterly*, winter 1969–70, pp. 627–40.

classical notion of national interest. Clearly the United States would
not spend billions of dollars in military and economic aid merely out
of a sense of moral obligation or because of the pressures of 2 percent
of its population. Something more tangible and concrete must be at
stake. Israel must be a strategic asset to the United States, and its
power must be capable of counterbalancing Soviet influence. According to this concept, Israel is the only reliable ally of the United States
in the area. In extremis, Israel could use its power to protect United
States interests, perhaps even offering bases for American military
operations. Under less dire circumstances, Israel was valuable as an
anti-Soviet bastion in a sea of radical Arab states. If Soviet arms were
allowed to tip the scales against Israel, United States prestige would
suffer. If Israel were defeated by the Arabs, American commitments
around the world would be questioned. Thus, United States aid to
Israel could be justified in terms of self-interest. Somewhat surprisingly, many Israelis seemed to prefer this view of the American commitment to Israel rather than the moral argument. Hard-headed
realists will always prefer concrete national-security arguments to im-
precise moral or political rationales for policies.

If the United States interest in Israel is widely accepted but poorly
understood, the same can be said of the interest in Middle East oil.
The basic facts of Middle East oil are well enough known—it is abun-
dant, it costs little to produce, it is predominantly in Arab hands,
and American companies are deeply involved in its production and
marketing. But what does all this mean for the United States? Here
the confusion begins.

Immediately after World War II, experts believed that the United
States would soon exhaust its reserves of petroleum. Some drew the
conclusion that Middle East oil would be vital to American security,
and that therefore the United States should do nothing to jeopardize
friendly relations with the Arab states. Above all, the United States
should try to keep its distance from Israel. During the 1950s and
1960s, however, the predicted oil shortage did not occur. Instead, oil
was available in the world market at comparatively low prices. American production covered most domestic needs. Embargoes in 1956
and 1967 proved ineffective and short-lived. American oil companies
continued to earn respectable, if not excessive, profits from their
Middle East operations. True, American allies in Europe and Japan
were heavily dependent on Middle East oil and thus theoretically

vulnerable to blackmail and pressure, but the mood of the late 1960s was one of comparative optimism regarding oil.

For the United States, the oil interest was viewed as having two dimensions. First, the flow of Middle East oil to Europe and Japan should not be endangered, hence Soviet control of Saudi Arabia, Iran, or Libya would be viewed as a serious threat. Moreover, any regional conflict that might disrupt the flow of oil would pose dangers for the western alliance. This was an additional reason for trying to prevent the outbreak of local hostilities. The second tangible United States interest in Middle East oil was strictly commercial. American oil companies earned and repatriated at least $2 billion annually in the late 1960s from their Middle East operations.[4] This benefited the American economy as well as the balance of payments.

In 1971, the petroleum picture began to change drastically. United States production seemed to be leveling off, and at the same time demand was soaring. The oil-producing states were becoming more assertive on prices and control of production. Libya took the lead in increasing prices and Iran followed quickly behind. Once again, the American response was ambivalent. Higher oil prices were passed along to consumers, thus reducing their economic well-being, but the higher prices also served to restrain the demand for oil and to provide incentives for new exploration and production. Increased expenditures for imports were bad for the balance of payments, but the United States was hurt less than other industrialized countries, so that prices rose without provoking a governmental response. The companies were not suffering, and consumers seemed to be voiceless.

Only with the Arab embargo of oil to the United States in October 1973 and the fourfold price increases of that year did the United States begin to show concern about Middle East oil developments.[5] Even then, the United States interest was not clearly perceived. Some emphasized the need to lower prices by breaking the monopoly power of the OPEC (Organization of Petroleum-Exporting Countries) cartel.

4. A further American economic interest in the Middle East involved trade. In the late 1960s, the United States sold about $1 billion worth of goods annually to Arab countries, a figure that enormously increased as a result of sudden increases in oil revenues after 1973. Saudi Arabia was by far the largest customer.
5. A few lone voices warning of an impending oil crisis were raised before the war, but were generally not treated seriously. See James E. Atkins, "The Oil Crisis: This Time the Wolf Is Here," *Foreign Affairs*, April 1973; and an earlier article from an opposite viewpoint by M. A. Adelman, "Is the Oil Shortage Real? Oil Companies as OPEC Tax Collectors," *Foreign Policy*, fall 1972.

Others were more concerned with the physical supply of oil and felt that U.S.-Arab relations should be strengthened as a means of guaranteeing the flow of oil to the West. The link between oil, the Arab-Israeli conflict and American national security was hotly debated.[6] What emerged from the confusion was a conviction that oil prices should be brought down to a "reasonable level," that the United States should reduce its dependence on foreign sources of oil, that oil consumers in the OECD (Organization for Economic Cooperation and Development)[7] should band together to weaken the leverage of OPEC, and that the embargo must be lifted. Needless to say, it was easier to state these goals than to attain them. At least by the mid-1970s, however, no one was claiming that the American interest in Middle East oil developments was not important.

The strategic and national-interest approaches to the understanding of American policy in the Middle East together account for several broad developments. The fact that the United States has been actively involved in Middle East affairs since World War II is clearly traceable to U.S.-Soviet rivalry, a commitment to Israel, and oil. By the very nature of these interests, however, the United States cannot hope to find a single policy that maximizes all three sets of interests.[8] At best, a catalogue of United States national interests alerts policy makers to issues to which they should pay special attention. Developments concerning Soviet influence, Israel, and oil will be monitored more closely than other issues. Likewise, a strategic or systemic perspective will alert a policy maker to linkages between regional and global concerns. A crude empiricist might fail to appreciate these points. Continuities in policies can be accounted for by interests and the nature of the international system.

The strengths of this perspective should not be minimized. But, as used by policy makers, ideas of national interest often have the ring of post-facto justifications for action. Policy does not flow directly from interests, nor do interests remain constant. Interests as concrete realities of a situation may impress the foreign-policy analyst, but the

6. William B. Quandt, "U.S. Energy Policy and the Arab Israeli Conflict," in *Arab Oil: Impact on the Arab Countries and Global Implications*, ed. Naiem A. Sherbiny and Mark A. Tessler (New York: Praeger, 1976).

7. The OECD consists of Western European countries, Turkey, Greece, Japan, the United States, Canada, Australia, and New Zealand.

8. This point is discussed in greater detail in William B. Quandt, "United States Policy in the Middle East: Constraints and Choices," in *Political Dynamics in the Middle East*, ed. Paul Y. Hammond and Sidney S. Alexander (New York: American Elsevier, 1972).

policy maker operates in a much more subjective environment, where it is the perception of national interests that matters, and, more important, it is the way in which conflicting interests are resolved and policies devised that is crucial to outcomes. Insofar as policies seem invariant, one can perhaps argue that they are clearly based on a stable national interest, as understood accurately by policy makers. But how can one account for inconsistencies, vacillation, and reversals of policy? Do the interests change? Or is it the change in the international system? To get a clearer understanding of the nuances of policy, however, we must turn to politics. Strategic calculations often take place in a political vacuum, but policy is an eminently political phenomenon.

THE DOMESTIC-POLITICS PERSPECTIVE

In a democratic polity, foreign policy is inevitably influenced by domestic realities. Even the most tough-minded practitioner of realpolitik would acknowledge that perceptions of national interests and values are shaped by public opinion in a democracy. Elitists may regret the intrusion of "politics" into policy making, but realists have always known that American foreign policy was deeply rooted in the nature of the political system. This is not to say that domestic politics determines United States behavior in the Middle East or elsewhere. Nevertheless, it does provide the immediate context for decisions, it sets some of the rules of the game, and it defines in large measure who will be responsible for the decisions made.

Several features of American politics have a particularly important bearing on policy toward the Arab-Israeli conflict. These involve matters of both style and structure. By tradition and habit, Americans tend to approach foreign policy in a distinctive manner. By convention and law, the political system is competitive, open to the persuasive efforts of organized minorities and voting majorities. Congress often becomes the vehicle through which domestic groups try to achieve their goals, and lobbying, electoral battles, and struggles between the legislative and executive branches of government are part of the foreign-policy process.

The notion of an American national style is both elusive and important. The American past conditions the approach to the future. Generally speaking, Americans retain an optimistic, pragmatic view of the world, often tinged with moralism and self-righteousness. A tragic sense of historical inevitability is far from the thoughts of most American policy makers. Instead, there is likely to be a belief in the possibility of finding solutions to problems, particularly through economic and technological means. Differences of opinion may be inevitable, but conciliation and compromise are traditional remedies. An international political order based on peaceful resolution of disputes and moderate regimes would produce the type of stability that Americans value highly. When challenged or frustrated, however, Americans are capable of strong reactions: self-righteous withdrawal from international affairs and aggressive use of force are parts of the American past. Some observers have noted a dangerous tendency for Americans to vacillate between these two orientations.[9] A sustained involvement in balance-of-power politics, with the necessary concomitants of restraint and amorality, seems unusually difficult for the United States.

Assuming that this caricature bears some resemblance to the broad cultural trends that shape American foreign policy, how do they affect United States action in the Middle East? First, there is a clear preference for supporting regimes that are viewed as moderate, status quo powers. Radical challengers of the status quo such as Egypt's President Nasser are viewed with distrust and distaste. Nasser's successor, Anwar Sadat, is definitely a more congenial figure in the view of most Americans.

The bond between the United States and Israel is unquestionably strengthened because of the presumed congruence of values between the two nations. Americans can identify with Israel's national style— the pioneering spirit, the commitment to western-style democracy, the ideals of individualism and freedom—in a way that has no parallel on the Arab side. Neither the ideal of the well-ordered Muslim community nor that of a modernizing autocracy evokes much sympathy among Americans. Consequently, a predisposition no doubt exists in American political culture that works to the advantage of the Israelis.

A second result of the American national style is a certain impatience with intractable conflicts, with ideologically tinged rhetoric, and with ingratitude for assistance. However much one may know, on an intellectual level, that the Arab-Israeli dispute is based on pro-

9. Hoffmann, op. cit. chaps. 4–6.

found fears and grievances, however much one may recognize that radical rhetoric must be seen in the Arab cultural context, and however much one is conscious that aid never produces gratitude, it is nonetheless irritating to find Arabs and Israelis being "unreasonable" and "intransigent"; it is frustrating to be attacked as an imperialist and to have one's motives questioned by those who seek one's help; and it is galling to be rebuffed by those who profit from one's generosity. The net effect is to produce an unsteadiness in American policy in the Middle East, a tendency to react angrily and emotionally to events in the area. This may produce sudden shifts in policy, periods of withdrawal and reassessment. United States policy therefore often seems erratic and unpredictable to Arabs and Israelis alike.

The classic example of this characteristic of American Middle East policy comes from the tumultuous period of the mid-1950s. Secretary of State John Foster Dulles condemned Egypt's President Nasser after the announcement in September 1955 of an arms deal with the Soviet Union, then tried to bribe him with the offer to finance the Aswan high dam, and then attempted to embarrass him by precipitately withdrawing the offer. Dulles subsequently opposed Nasser's nationalization of the Suez Canal Company in July 1956, but supported Egypt against the British, French, and Israeli military attack in October. A few months later, in January 1957, Dulles tried to limit Nasser's influence with the enunciation of the Eisenhower Doctrine. Of course, the reasons for each of these decisions were more complex than suggested here, but the overall pattern reflects some important aspects of the American national style.

If national style is a nebulous term, public opinion is somewhat more tangible. As revealed in countless surveys and polls, as reflected in the press, and as played out in electoral contests, American public opinion does influence foreign policy, but often in very indirect ways.[10] Politicians are more likely to be responsive to the public mood than to public preferences on specific issues, and the American mood concerning international affairs is remarkably volatile.[11] Anticommunism and belief in the need for a strong military establishment

10. Bernard C. Cohen, *The Public's Impact on Foreign Policy* (Boston: Little, Brown, 1973).
11. Gabriel Almond, *The American People and Foreign Policy* (New York: Praeger, 1960).

have alternated with periods of idealistic belief in collective security, the United Nations, negotiations, and détente. Public support for American involvement in both the Korean and Vietnamese wars was initially very high, but later began to drop as casualties rose. Ultimately public opinion played an important role in bringing American involvement in both wars to an end.[12]

Public opinion concerning the Arab-Israeli conflict appears to be somewhat more stable than is true in regard to other such problems. Americans in general consistently say that they sympathize more with Israel than with the Arabs.[13] American Jews are overwhelmingly pro-Israeli, but non-Jews also tend to support Israel, though with considerably less enthusiasm. And the commitment does seem to have limits. Only 14 percent of the adult population in late 1970 said they would have favored sending American troops to help Israel if she were being overrun by Arab forces.[14]

Nonetheless, the Israelis enjoy a high level of general support in American public opinion, and the press both reflects and reinforces this tendency. News on Israel is widely reported, whereas the Arab world is poorly covered in most newspapers. Editorials tend to favor Israel over the Arabs, although since 1973 there has been a tendency to take into account Arab views as well. On the whole, however, the public and the press are oriented more toward Israel than to the Arabs. This tends to reinforce the pro-Israeli orientation already derived from the American national style.

The translation of style and sentiment into policy involves political processes and institutions. In particular, the activities of interest groups, electoral campaigns, and congressional behavior serve to sharpen general public opinion into specific policy choices.

Interest groups are often portrayed as sinister forces in the making of American policy in the Middle East. Zionist and oil "lobbies" are reputed to be powerful advocates of their different perspectives. Both are vastly overrated by their adversaries, whereas each group denies its own influence over policy. The analytical task of carefully amassing

---

12. John E. Mueller, *War, Presidents and Public Opinion* (New York: John Wiley, 1973).

13. See the evidence summarized by David Garnham, "The Oil Crisis and U.S. Attitudes Toward Israel," in Sherbiny and Tessler (ed.), op. cit., p. 298. About 50 percent of Americans since the 1967 war have identified themselves as pro-Israel, about 5 to 7 percent as pro-Arab, and the rest are indifferent or have no opinion.

14. *Newsweek*, Dec. 14, 1970. Elite opinion appears to be more interventionist. See Garnham, op. cit., p. 302.

evidence to demonstrate the alleged effectiveness of the Zionists or the oil companies has rarely been undertaken.[15] Instead, an otherwise inexplicable outcome is attributed to the activities of pressure groups.

The interest group approach to the understanding of policy has respectable origins, however much it may be abused in practice.[16] In pluralistic, competitive political systems, organized groups do strive to influence decisions, and evidence abounds that they often succeed. The stronger the group, the more likely its success. Policy is seen as the result of conflicting group pressures. Seemingly irrational policies may merely reflect compromises based on a particular balance of forces. Although overly mechanistic, this view does have the virtue of focusing on the competitive struggle to influence policy makers dealing with the Middle East. It is also true that organized groups with specific goals are more likely to be effective in shaping policy than unorganized public opinion.

Numerous pro-Israeli groups exist in the United States, one of the most important being the American Israel Public Affairs Committee (AIPAC). Although Jews make up less than 3 percent of the American population, through effective organization they have succeeded in making their voice heard on an astonishingly wide scale. There is no question that American pro-Israeli groups are among the best organized, best financed, and most active of all interest groups. Nevertheless, the question remains: do they influence policy? If so, how?

Interest groups typically suffer from a number of disadvantages in trying to influence foreign policy. First, there may be internal divisions that weaken their effectiveness. Second, they are unlikely to have the resources, in money and information, that would allow them to present their case effectively. Third, lobbyists have a strong tendency to seek out those who already agree with them rather than trying to make converts. Fourth, lobbyists are vulnerable to counterpressures, especially from the powerful federal bureaucracy.

Not all of these drawbacks affect pro-Israeli groups. They seem to

15. An exception is Robert H. Trice, "Domestic Political Interests and American Policy in the Middle East: Pro-Israel, Pro-Arab and Corporate Non-Governmental Actors and the Making of American Foreign Policy, 1966–1971" (Ph.D. thesis in political science, University of Wisconsin, 1974).

16. For example, see Arthur Bentley, *The Process of Government: A Study of Social Pressures* (Chicago: University of Chicago Press, 1908), and David Truman, *The Governmental Process* (New York: Knopf, 1951), for two of the classical studies of the group basis of politics.

show a high degree of unity on key issues of aid and diplomatic support for Israel. But they may at times be unsubtle in their approach,
poorly informed, heavy-handed, and therefore ineffective. Their actions, however, are likely to make issues more prominent, to define
possible political costs of a given course of action, and to set outer
limits beyond which policy makers will venture only at their peril.[17]
Nevertheless, they do not dictate policy, and it is only a weak or
dissembling policy maker who will attribute his decisions to the activities of interest groups. More often, interest groups provide a useful
excuse for a policy maker to do what he intended to do for other
reasons.

A careful study of interest groups and foreign policy has concluded that the net effect of their activities is to raise the salience of
issues. By doing so, they may provoke a response on the part of Congress or the president, but that response will have more to do with
preexisting beliefs than with the preferences of the interest groups.
Consequently, the danger of provoking actions contrary to their intentions hangs over interest groups.[18] In the Israeli case, however, the
predispositions that exist in Congress and the White House generally
minimize such dangers.

Pro-Israeli groups are often most influential when they do nothing at all to influence policy. Their mere existence is enough to con-
strain the actions of policy makers. The "law of anticipated reaction"
governs here, as elsewhere,[19] and alternative courses of action are
frequently rejected because of the expectation of negative reaction
from pro-Israeli groups and their supporters in Congress. Caution
may result in internal vetoes over policy, based on the untested assumption that the proposed action would be too controversial. Real
tests of strength are rare, so the "anticipated reaction" is often as
effective in shaping policy as the mobilization of support in a confrontation would be.

The oil and pro-Arab interest groups are considerably less vocal
and less effective than the pro-Israeli groups. Oil companies operating

17. William B. Quandt, "Domestic Influences on U.S. Foreign Policy in the Middle
East: The View from Washington," in *The Middle East: Quest for an American Policy,* ed.
William A. Beling (Albany: State University of New York Press, 1973).

18. Raymond A. Bauer, Ithiel de Sola Pool, and Lewis A. Dexter, *American Business
and Public Policy: The Politics of Foreign Trade* (New York: Atherton Press, 1963), pp. 466–89.

19. Carl J. Friedrich, *Man and His Government* (New York: McGraw-Hill, 1963),
chap. 11.

in the Middle East do worry about the possible outbreak of war and about the Arab reaction to America's pro-Israeli policies. They are fearful, however, of publicly taking a stand on the Arab-Israeli conflict, preferring to concentrate more narrowly on oil-import policy, tax allowances, and bilateral U.S.-Arab relations. For such a powerful industry, oil has little voice with respect to basic Arab-Israeli issues. This is not to say that policy makers do not think about Arab oil. They do think about it, and they frequently speak with oil-company representatives. However, they do not discuss diplomacy or arms sales, or, if this occurs, it is in a very private setting. Deprived of their public voice on this issue, the oil companies tend to be ineffectual as lobbyists. The perceived interest in oil is enough to keep policy makers attentive to some of their concerns without constant pressure.

If the oil companies are afraid of going public with their views on the Arab-Israeli conflict, the same cannot be said for other pro-Arab groups, such as the Arab-American University Graduates and Americans for Near Eastern Refugee Aid. These, however, speak for comparatively small constituencies, and, although their sophistication and funding has been increasing, they as yet offer little competition to the Zionists.

Interest groups cannot be dismissed as unimportant in the policy-making process, but to be effective they need allies. These are most readily found in Congress, where the promise of money, campaign support, or votes has a way of working wonders. Lobbyists have generally viewed Congress as the most accessible part of the foreign-policy-making apparatus. By contrast, the State Department and the White House are considerably more difficult to reach and to cultivate. Congressmen, on the other hand, often value the services of lobbyists, for they provide information, alert representatives and senators to possible controversial issues, and can provide very concrete material services as well.

Over the years, Congress has been much more responsive to pro-Israeli groups than to oil or Arab interests. In part, this reflects an accurate political judgment concerning public sentiment, but it also demonstrates that pro-Israeli efforts on Capitol Hill are generally better organized than those of other groups. The Israeli embassy supplements the efforts of the lobbyists and pro-Israeli spokesmen, and the combination often proves to be unusually effective in producing support on vital issues.

In recent years, about three-fourths of all senators, and a sizable majority of representatives, have put their names to pro-Israeli statements. The depth of commitment no doubt varies, as does the motivation, but when it comes time to vote on aid bills, for example, Israel can usually count on support. The game has become so predictable, in fact, that the administration may request less aid for Israel than it expects to provide, in the full knowledge that Congress will probably increase the amount substantially. In an area where Congress has effective control, for example, such as over the budget, Israel is the beneficiary. One need only compare the nature of congressional action when it comes to providing aid to Israel with that of sending arms to Jordan or Egypt. On occasion, the administration has even tried to enlist the support of pro-Israeli spokesmen on behalf of aid to "moderate" Arab regimes, hoping that this would ease passage of the bill in Congress.

Control over expenditures is the most important tangible congressional role in the conduct of foreign policy. Elsewhere Congress is likely to be less effective. As a body, it is unable to develop diplomatic initiatives, to conduct negotiations, to make commitments, or to handle the day-to-day relations with the states of the Middle East. At best, Congress provides an arena for individual senators or representatives to articulate alternative policies, to hold hearings on various topics, and to make recommendations to the executive branch in the form of resolutions. Legislation can also provide restrictions on the ability of the president to act. For example, Congress can write into law conditions that will prohibit the granting of aid to certain countries, and it can reserve the right to veto proposed arms sales.

The net effect of congressional action is to set limits on presidential authority, and to ensure in the Middle East context that Israel's interests will be carefully respected. Nevertheless, Congress is far from omnipotent. With rare exceptions, it does not make policy, nor does it usually ignore presidential requests that are buttressed by arguments of national security. Especially in crises, Congress tends to be both deferential and cautious, as at the time of the 1967 Arab-Israeli war, when it was extremely worried about possible American involvement in a Middle East war. It was not certain that Israel's desire for a strong commitment from the United States would have been supported by the normally pro-Israeli Congress.

One way in which Congress and the president are made attentive to public opinion and to interest groups is through the electoral process. Every two years, the members of the House of Representatives must stand for election, along with one-third of the senators. Every four years, presidential elections dominate American political life. This imparts a predictable rhythm to American political life and to its foreign policy. In presidential-election years, particularly when the competition is severe, much of the year is devoted to domestic politics. Foreign-policy initiatives that might prove controversial are delayed, although the incumbent may seek some visible triumph to underscore his suitability for office. Middle East policy being nearly always controversial, it tends to fade into the background in election years. Such was the case in 1968, 1972, and 1976. Candidates and incumbents feel obliged to outbid each other in terms of their commitment to Israel. A few votes may be won this way, along with other forms of support, but, more important, no votes are lost.

Whereas formerly most American Jews supported the Democratic Party's candidate, this is now less axiomatic than in the past. In 1972 President Nixon reportedly won nearly 40 percent of the "Jewish vote." Still, Democrats are inclined to be more pro-Israeli, whereas Republicans tend to be more solicitous of business interests, which predisposes them to a less pro-Israeli orientation. The difference, however, is not overwhelming, and supporters of Israel are increasingly uncertain as to which party or candidate will pursue the most desirable policies in the Middle East.

Once elected, presidents tend to use their first year in office to launch new moves in foreign policy. (This happened with respect to the Arab-Israeli conflict in both 1969 and 1973.) The congressional elections the following year may or may not slow the process, but once again the tendency is to raise the costs of a controversial policy, while rewarding success and support for Israel. The president's third year may offer new opportunities for diplomatic initiatives, depending upon his expectations concerning the upcoming elections. In early 1971, Nixon authorized a serious effort to reach an "interim settlement," but brought it to an abrupt end in the summer when it seemed unlikely to succeed and was becoming politically costly.

It is in their timing that diplomatic initiatives concerning the Middle East are chiefly affected by elections. In addition, elections raise the risk of going against prevailing public opinion or congressional views. A strong president with a broad popular base can afford to take stands that are controversial, as President Eisenhower did at the time of the Suez crisis in 1956, but a weak president is inevitably more susceptible to the pressures of domestic politics.

Having surveyed the numerous ways in which domestic politics influences the conduct of foreign policy, one is forced to conclude that American foreign policy toward the Arab-Israeli conflict is generally constrained, but not determined, by domestic realities. Public opinion, interest groups, Congress, and elections all serve to set outer limits on presidential discretion. No president is likely to be overtly anti-Israeli; no president would support the creation of a secular democratic state in Palestine, as some Arabs demand; no president would allow Israel to remain defenseless against a substantial arms buildup by the Arabs and the Soviets. This does not mean that Israel can count on complete support or that it will receive everything that it wants. Nor will it be immune to American pressure. Nevertheless, that country's vital security interests and well-being will not be knowingly jeopardized by any American president.

A substantial area of choice still exists after all domestic factors influencing American policy toward the Arab-Israeli conflict have been taken into account. Within that sphere of maneuver, the way in which choices are presented, decided, and ultimately acted upon may be closely related to the functioning of the foreign-affairs bureaucracy of the executive branch.

THE BUREAUCRATIC-POLITICS PERSPECTIVE

If indeed foreign policy making, especially toward the Arab-Israeli conflict, is a political process, there is no reason to believe that politics stops at the door of the chief executive. In fact, some analysts have emphasized the importance, for policy outcomes, of the rivalries and divergent perspectives within and among the various bureaucracies that share responsibility in the field of foreign affairs.[20] In this view, the Departments of State and Defense, the CIA, and the White House are likely to support different policies because of the nature of

20. See especially Graham Allison, *Essence of Decision* (Boston: Little, Brown, 1971), and Morton Halperin, *Bureaucratic Politics and Foreign Policy* (Washington: Brookings Institution, 1974). For a critique, see Robert Art, "Bureaucratic Politics and American Foreign Policy: A Critique," *Policy Sciences* 40 (1973).

their responsibilities and their habitual approaches to issues. The resolution of these bureaucratically rooted divergences is likely to come through bargaining, compromise, power plays, or some other political tactic, often producing results that are not favored by any of the participants.

Those who have labored deep within a bureaucratic organization often find this perspective compelling. After all, what comes out as policy at the top of the organization often bears little resemblance to what went in at their level. The State Department country expert lives with the perpetual feeling that his expertise counts for little in the formulation of policy, inasmuch as domestic politics or bureaucratic compromise will thwart his most valiant efforts. Morale in the middle ranks of large bureaucracies is therefore often low. Performance suffers. Innovation is stifled. Routine wins out over originality, and routine is basically conservative and geared to short-term organizational interests.

With regard to the Middle East, the classic bureaucratic rivalry has been that between the State Department and the White House, with the Defense Department occasionally joining the fray. President Truman, for example, was opposed by both the secretary of defense and the secretary of state on his policy of recognition of Israel in 1948. Their reasons were consistent with the bureaucratic perspectives of the two departments. Defense worried about strategic access to oil and bases; State was concerned with political relations between the United States and the Arab world, as well as with oil. Truman, of course, made the decision to recognize Israel despite the opposition of several of his key advisers.

The State Department has often been thought of as a bastion of pro-Arab, anti-Israeli sentiment, especially in contrast to Congress and public opinion generally. Within State, the Bureau of Near Eastern and South Asian Affairs houses the "Arabists," those who presumably urge a more "evenhanded" or pro-Arab policy on their superiors. Two questions arise. Do the "Arabists" exist as a cohesive group, and if so, why? Do they influence policy?

Arabists, of course, do exist in the State Department, in the sense of career diplomats who have served in the Arab world and who in many cases have learned Arabic. With nearly twenty embassies situated in Arab countries, the State Department inevitably produces more Arabists than it does specialists on Israeli affairs. In a general way, too, the experience of living in Arab countries and studying Arabic seems to make foreign-service officers more, rather than less, sympathetic to Arab concerns. This is perhaps not astonishing. Diplomats see their job as "improving relations" between the United States and the countries to which they are assigned, and this requires a degree of empathy and openness to other cultures and their concerns. Some of this stays with diplomats long after they have left the Arab world.

Arabists in the State Department do not, however, all agree with one another. For example, Arabists were strongly divided over the proper policy toward Nasser's Egypt. Furthermore, virtually all accept the United States commitment to Israel's security as unalterable. They disagree quite often with the particulars of United States aid to Israel, ascribing it to domestic politics, but they do not challenge the basic policy.

In recent years, those responsible for dealing with the Middle East have not always been Arabists. Assistant Secretary Joseph Sisco, for example, was not an Arabist, nor were all of those who dealt with Arab affairs after the 1967 war. Moreover, as a result of a desire to produce well-rounded generalists in the State Department, it is increasingly common to find ambassadors and other diplomats dealing with the Arab world who have little or no experience there. A few cases also exist of foreign-service officers who have served in both Israel and the Arab world and who know both Hebrew and Arabic.

Despite these qualifications, it is probably fair to say that the Near East bureau tends to favor what might be called an "evenhanded" policy. Occasionally it succeeds in having its recommendations adopted, as was the case with the Rogers proposals in 1969 and 1970. More often, however, its views are offset by others that take Israeli concerns into account. Certainly no president has ever become a captive of the Arabists in the State Department, although on occasion the White House may complain about State's tilt in a predictably pro-Arab direction.

The Defense Department is less consistent than the State Department on the Arab-Israeli issue. Some military men have genuinely admired the Israelis for their skill on the battlefield. Others have argued that, on strategic grounds, the United States has a greater interest in the Arab world than in Israel and that its policies should reflect this fact. Finally, in recent years there has been some resentment among American military men over the large transfers of equipment from United States stocks to Israel.

During the October 1973 war, it was widely rumored that the Defense Department was obstructing the delivery of arms to Israel. As the Israelis protested delay after delay, they were told that the cause lay in bureaucratic rivalries. Only when President Nixon intervened with a direct order did the arms start to flow, according to this version. If true, this would be an important example of the effect of "bureaucratic politics" on the implementation of policy. As we shall see, however, that was not in fact the case.

The bureaucratic perspective, upon careful examination, is of limited help in understanding the policy-making process. It is most useful in accounting for the often bland and predictable quality of analytical papers that emerge from the bureaucracy. Insofar as bureaucratic routines and narrow organizational interests thwart creativity, which they appear to do, senior decision makers, including the president, may be deprived of useful ideas and important pieces of information. This may have the effect of narrowing the range of perceived choices, of stifling unpopular views, and of suppressing information that might have a bearing on policy.[21]

These deficiencies are most acute, though least dangerous, when one is dealing with low-priority issues in noncrisis periods. They are particularly a feature of the behavior of low- and middle-ranking "experts," who tend to view problems from a narrow perspective and who are particularly vulnerable to career pressures.

The other area in which bureaucratic routines and rivalries may affect policy is that of implementation. A president or a secretary of state may decide on a policy, but he rarely has the time or the resources to ensure that it is being carried out precisely as he wants. At a cost, presidents may be able to get their way, but on innumerable occasions the implementation of policy is left to the responsible agency (or, worse yet, agencies). At that point, the best policy could theoretically be sabotaged by poor implementation. For example, in the 1967 war, some State Department officials thought that the

21. Alexander L. George, "The Case for Multiple Advocacy in Making Foreign Policy," *American Political Science Review* 66, no. 3 (September 1972).

Defense Department was organizing a multinational naval fleet to open the Strait of Tiran. Their recommendations to the president were predicated on the availability of this option. The Defense Department, however, apparently did not share the same enthusiasm for the idea or the sense of urgency, and the president was left without the option recommended by his secretary of state. Of course, if President Johnson had taken a more pressing interest in the matter, he almost certainly would have gotten his way, but he had other things on his mind. Thus, bureaucratic breakdowns or rivalries on low-level matters can, in some settings, become a serious constraint on presidential choices.

This brings us to the key issue, which is not adequately dealt with by the bureaucratic-politics model. And that is precisely the realm of choice. Presidents and their advisers do make a difference in foreign policy, and they are not mere creatures of their organizational affiliations. When all the constraints stemming from the nature of the international system and from domestic and bureaucratic politics are taken into account, presidents still have to make decisions. How they reach these decisions, how they and their advisers reason, and how they develop new policy orientations is the essence of leadership, and it is this perspective that ultimately yields the greatest insight into American policy toward the Arab-Israeli conflict.

THE PRESIDENTIAL-LEADERSHIP PERSPECTIVE

In American politics, there is a strong presumption that who is president matters. Vast sums are spent on electoral campaigns to select the president. That office is shown immense respect and deference, and much of American political history is written from the implied viewpoint that the man occupying the White House is capable of shaping events. Does this merely reflect an individualism rooted in American culture, or does it contain a profound truth?

One can easily imagine situations in which it would be meaningless to explain a policy by looking at the individuals responsible for making the decisions. If no real margin for choice exists, then individuals do not count for much. Other factors take precedence. For example, to predict the voting behavior of senators from New York on aid to Israel, it is probably not necessary to consider the identity of the incumbent. It is enough to know something about his constituency, the overwhelming support for Israel among New Yorkers, and the lack of countervailing pressures. In this case, an understanding of the broad political context is all that is needed to know with virtual certainty the policy choice of the individual senator.

If context can account for behavior, so can the nature of perceived interests or objectives. If we were studying Japan's policies toward the Arab-Israeli conflict, we would not be especially concerned with who was prime minister at any given moment. It would make more sense to look at the dependency of Japan on Arab oil and the complete lack of any significant cultural or economic ties to Israel to predict that Japan will adopt a generally pro-Arab policy. When interests easily converge on a single policy, individual choice can be relegated to the background.

Finally, if a nation has no capability to act in foreign policy, we will not be particularly interested in the views of its leaders. To ask why a small European country does not assume a more active role in promoting an Arab-Israeli settlement does not require that we examine who is in charge of policy. Instead, the lack of significant means to affect the behavior of Arabs and Israelis is about all that we need to know. A country without important economic, military, or diplomatic assets has virtually no choices to make in foreign policy.

It is evident that none of these conditions holds for the United States in its approach to the Arab-Israeli conflict. Capabilities for action do exist. The nature of American interests, as generally understood by policy makers, does not predetermine a single course of action. And despite the obvious constraints that are imposed by the nature of the international system and domestic politics, choices do exist on most issues, even though at times the margin may be narrow.

We therefore come back to the need for a perspective on policy making that incorporates the psychology of decision making, and in particular the perceptions and understanding of issues by the president and his closest advisers. This is not the same as saying that a profound understanding of the personality and motivations of the president is essential to the study of foreign policy. However desirable such insights might be, they are neither necessary for most questions nor easy to come by.

It is less the personality of the president that must be understood than the way he and his advisers view the world and how they reason.

Policy making is an intellectual process embedded in a social context.[22] It is not merely an acting out of one's deepest fears, anxieties, and aspirations. Two points can be made to clarify the ambiguous link between personality and policy making.

First, individuals with remarkably different personal backgrounds are typically found supporting similar policies. In fact, it is rare that serious arguments over policy take place at high levels in government. The tendency is toward consensus and toward reinforcement of prevailing views. Discussions of policy behind closed doors seem not to be characterized by deep disagreements among strong, idiosyncratic personalities.[23] More often, a shared perspective quickly emerges, group dynamics operate so as to suppress dissent, and policies come to be supported by most participants.

Second, the same individual, with no noteworthy alteration in his personality or his psychodynamics, may very well change position on given policy issues. Particularly when dealing with complex events and ambiguous choices, individuals may shift their stances quite suddenly, without altering the more invariant aspects of their approaches to policy, which may have to do more with style than with substance. As Raymond Bauer has said, "policy problems are sufficiently complex that for the vast majority of individuals or organizations it is conceivable—given the objective features of the situation—to imagine them ending up on *any* side of the issue."[24]

Why, one might ask, cannot issues be decided "on their merits"? This, after all, is what a rational decision maker is expected to do. He should weigh all the pros and cons, assess costs and benefits, and then select the course of action that best suits his interests. The difficulty is not merely that "policy making is not simply a pursuit of objectives but is rather an expenditure of some values to achieve others," but also that "our minds determine what is relevant and irrelevant, by imposing a structure upon the problem situation."[25]

The question to be asked is not whether policy decisions are

22. Raymond Bauer, in *The Study of Policy Formulation,* ed. Raymond Bauer and Kenneth Gergen (New York: The Free Press, 1968), states this slightly differently (p. 5): ". . . policy formulation is a social process in which an intellectual process is embedded."
23. Robert Axelrod, "Argumentation in Foreign Policy Decision Making: Britain in 1918, Munich in 1938, and Japan in 1970," paper delivered to the 1976 annual meeting of the American Political Science Association, Chicago, Sept. 2-5, 1976.
24. Bauer, op. cit., p. 15.
25. David Braybrooke and Charles E. Lindblom, *A Strategy of Decision* (New York: The Free Press, 1970), pp. 24, 43.

rational or irrational, but rather what kind of calculation goes into them. Decision makers do try to relate their actions to purposes. Unlike the computer, they link means to ends,[26] but the way in which this is done is imperfect, at least according to the rules of economic rationality.

Some would argue for a broader concept of "political rationality." As Paul Diesing expresses it,

> In a political decision . . . action never is based on the merits of a proposal but always on who makes it and who opposes it. Action should be designed to avoid complete identification with any proposal and any point of view, no matter how good or popular it might be. The best available proposal should never be accepted because it is best; it should be deferred, objected to, discussed, until major opposition disappears. Compromise is always a rational procedure, even when the compromise is between a good and a bad proposal.[27]

For policy makers, however, the problem is often that of recognizing the difference between a good and a bad proposal. Bargaining and compromise may indeed be rational courses for a politician, but this assumes that issues have been defined according to some criteria. It is precisely what these criteria are in a given situation that holds the clue to how key decisions are made.

On most issues of importance, policy makers operate in an environment in which uncertainty and complexity are the dominant realities.[28] Addressing an unknowable future with imperfect information about the past and present, policy makers must act on the basis of guidelines and simplifications drawn from their own experience, the "lessons of history," or the consensus of their colleagues. The result is often a cautious style of decision making that strives merely to make incremental changes in existing policies.[29] At times,

26. John D. Steinbruner, *The Cybernetic Theory of Decision* (Princeton: Princeton University Press, 1974), describes the "cybernetic paradigm" as one that avoids the calculation of outcomes. His more valuable contribution comes in his discussion in chap. 4 of the "cognitive processes" that underlie decision making.

27. Paul Diesing, *Reason in Society* (Urbana, Ill.: University of Illinois Press, 1962), as cited by Aaron Wildavsky, *The Politics of the Budgetary Process,* 2d ed. (Boston: Little, Brown, 1974), p. 190. Wildavsky's own definition of rational man is "one who manipulates the few variables under his control to good effect," ibid., p. 229.

28. Steinbruner, op. cit., pp. 15–18.

29. Charles E. Lindblom, "The Science of 'Muddling Through,' " *Public Administration Review* 19, spring 1959; and Wildavsky, op. cit., pp. 6–16.

however, very sudden shifts in policy may also take place. How can one account for both of these outcomes?

Leadership is only rarely the task of selecting between good and bad policies. Instead, the anguish and challenge of leadership is to choose between equally plausible arguments about how best to achieve one's goals. For example, most presidents and their advisers have placed a very high value on achieving peace in the Middle East. But values do not easily translate into policy. Instead, several reasonable alternatives are likely to compete for presidential attention, such as the following:

—If Israel is to feel sufficiently secure to make the territorial concessions necessary to gain Arab acceptance of the terms of a peace agreement, she must continue to receive large quantities of American military and economic aid.

—If Israel feels too strong and self-confident, she will not see the need for any change in the status quo. United States aid must therefore be withheld as a form of pressure.

Presidents Nixon and Ford have subscribed to both of the foregoing views at different times.

Similarly, consider the following propositions:

—The Soviet Union has no interest in peace in the Middle East because it would lose influence unless it could exploit tensions in the area. Hence, the United States cannot expect cooperation from the Soviet Union in the search for a settlement.

—The Soviets, like outselves, have mixed interests in the Middle East. They fear a confrontation, and therefore are prepared to reach a settlement, provided they be allowed to participate in the diplomatic process. By leaving the Soviet Union out, the United States provides it with an incentive to sabotage the peacemaking effort. Therefore, U.S.-Soviet agreement will be essential to reaching peace in the Middle East.

Concerning the Arabs, one may also hear diverse opinions:

—Only when the Arabs have regained their self-respect and feel strong will they be prepared to make peace with Israel.

—When the Arabs feel that time is on their side, they increase their demands and become more extreme. Only a decisive military defeat will convince them that Israel is here to stay and that they can regain their territory only by political means.

Each of these propositions has been seriously entertained by recent American presidents and secretaries of state. One could almost say that all of them have been believed at various times by some individuals. The key element in selecting among these plausible interpretations of reality is not merely whether one is pro-Israeli or pro-Arab. A more complex psychology is at work.

In selecting among plausible, but imperfectly understood, courses of action, policy makers inevitably resort to simplifications. Guidelines emerge from recent experiences, historical analogies, wishful thinking, and group consensus.[30] Categorical inferences are thus made; confusing events are placed in comprehensible structures; reality is given a definition that allows purposive action to take place.

Recent experience is a particularly potent source of guidance for the future. If a policy has worked in one setting, there is likely to be a strong disposition to try it in another context as well. It appears that Secretary of State Kissinger, for example, consciously relied on his experiences in negotiating with the Chinese, Russians, and Vietnamese in approaching negotiations with the Arabs and Israelis. Step-by-step diplomacy was the result.

More general historical "lessons" may loom large in the thinking of policy makers as they confront new problems.[31] President Truman was especially inclined to invoke historical analogies. He well understood that the essence of presidential leadership was the ability to make decisions in the face of uncertainty and to live with their consequences. By relying on history, he was able to reassure himself that his decisions were well-founded.[32]

Several historical analogies have been notably effective in structuring American views of reality. The lessons of Munich, for example, have been pointed to repeatedly over the years. In brief, the lesson is that appeasement of dictators only serves to whet their appetite for further conquest, hence a firm, resolute opposition to aggression is required. The "domino theory" is a direct descendant of this perspective, as was the policy of containment.

A second set of guidelines for policy has been derived from

30. Steinbruner, op. cit., pp. 109–24.
31. Ernest May, *"Lessons" of the Past: The Use and Misuse of History in American Foreign Policy* (New York: Oxford University Press, 1973).
32. Merle Miller, *Plain Speaking: An Oral Biography of Harry S. Truman* (New York: Berkeley Publishing Corporation, 1973).

President Wilson's fourteen points after World War I, especially the emphasis on self-determination and opposition to spheres of influence. As embodied in the Atlantic Charter in 1941, these principles strongly influenced American policy during the Second World War.[33]

Since the failure of American policy in Southeast Asia, new "lessons" have been drawn, which warn against overinvolvement, commitments in marginal areas, excessive reliance on force, and pretensions of playing the role of world policeman. Whether these will prove as durable as the examples of Munich and of Wilsonian idealism remains to be seen, but American policy in the 1970s probably will be tested against these historical guidelines as well as others from earlier periods.

When recent experience and historical analogies fail to resolve dilemmas of choice, other psychological mechanisms come to the rescue. Wishful thinking is a particularly potent means of resolving uncertainty.[34] When in doubt, choose the course that seems least painful, that fits best with one's hopes and expectations; perhaps it will turn out all right after all. In any event, it is almost always possible to rationalize one's choice after making it. Good reasons can be found even for bad policies, and often the ability to come up with a convincing rationale will help to overcome uncertainties.

Apart from these well-known but poorly understood aspects of individual psychology, there are social dynamics in most decision settings that help to resolve uncertainty. If through discussion a group can reach consensus on the proper course of action, individuals are likely to suppress their private doubts. Above all, when a president participates in a group decision, a strong tendency toward consensus is likely. As some scholars have emphasized, presidents must go to considerable lengths to protect themselves from the stultifying effects of group conformity in their presence and the tendency to suppress divergent views.[35] Neither President Johnson's practice of inviting a large number of advisers to consult with him nor President Nixon's effort to use the National Security Council to channel alternatives to

33. Lynn E. Davis, *The Cold War Begins: Soviet-American Conflict Over Eastern Europe* (Princeton: Princeton University Press, 1974).

34. Steinbruner, op. cit., pp. 116–17.

35. George, op. cit.; and Irving L. Janis, *Victims of Groupthink: A Psychological Study of Foreign Policy Decisions and Fiascoes* (Boston: Houghton-Mifflin, 1972).

him are guarantees against the distortions of group consensus, in part because presidents value consensus as a means of resolving doubts.

At any given moment, presidents and their key advisers tend to share relatively similar and stable definitions of reality. However this definition emerges, whether through reference to experience or to history, through wishful thinking and rationalization, or through group consensus, it will provide guidelines for action in the face of uncertainty. Complexity will be simplified by reference to a few key criteria. In the Arab-Israeli setting, these will usually have to do with the saliency of issues, their amenability to solution, the role of the Soviet Union, and the value of economic and military assistance to various parties.

Crises play an extremely important role in the development of these guidelines. By definition, crises involve surprise, threat, and enhanced uncertainty. Previous policies may well be exposed as flawed or bankrupt. Reality no longer accords with previous expectations. In such a situation, a new structure of perceptions is likely to emerge, one that will reflect presidential perspectives to the degree that the president becomes involved in handling the crisis. If the crisis is satisfactorily resolved, a new and often quite durable set of assumptions will guide policy for some time.

It is important to note that crises can produce significant policy changes without causing a sweeping reassessment of a decision maker's views. It may only be a greater sense of urgency that brings into play a new policy. Or it may be a slight shift in assumptions concerning the Soviet role, for example, or the advantages of pursuing a more conciliatory policy toward Egypt. Small adjustments in one's perceptions, in the weight accorded to one issue as opposed to another, can lead to substantial shifts of emphasis, of nuance, and therefore of action. Again, it is not the case that policy makers change from being pro-Israeli to pro-Arab overnight, but rather that crises may bring into focus new relations among issues, or raise the importance of one interest, thus leading to changes in policy. Basic values will remain intact, but perceptions and understanding of relationships may quickly change.

In the case studies that follow, we shall see the important role of crises in defining issues for presidents and their advisers. We shall try to account for their views, to understand their reasoning, and to see situations from their standpoint. Between crises, we shall note how difficult it is to bring about changes in policies that derive from views that were forged in the midst of crises and that have the stamp of presidential approval. Starting, then, with the key role of the president and his advisers in shaping policy, particularly in moments of crisis, when domestic and bureaucratic constraints are least confining, we shall also see how politics and organizational routine affect both the formulation and implementation of policies in normal times. But it is those rare moments when policy makers try to make sense out of the confusing flow of events, when they strive to relate action to purposes, that will be at the center of this study, for it is on such occasions that the promises and limitations of leadership are most apparent. And if the Arab-Israeli conflict is ever to be resolved through the good offices of the United States, the quality and courage of presidential leadership will be an essential element.

CHAPTER II

The June 1967
Arab-Israeli War

LYNDON JOHNSON brought to the presidency a remarkable array of political talents. An activist and an intensely emotional man, Johnson seemed to enjoy exerting his power. As majority leader in the Senate, he had used the art of persuasion as few other leaders had; building consensus through delicately constructed compromises had been one of his strong suits. His political skills did not, however, extend to foreign policy making, an area that demanded urgent priority, especially as American involvement in Vietnam grew in late 1964 and early 1965.

Fortunately for the new president, one part of the world that was comparatively quiet in the early 1960s was the Middle East. Long-standing disputes still simmered, but in comparison to the turbulent 1950s, the situation seemed manageable. The U.S.-Israeli relationship had been strengthened by President Kennedy, and Johnson obviously was prepared to continue on this line. His personal sentiments toward Israel seemed warm and admiring. To all appearances, he genuinely liked the Israelis he had dealt with, many of his closest advisers were well-known friends of Israel, and his own contacts with the American Jewish community had been close throughout his political career.

Johnson's demonstrated fondness for Israel did not necessarily mean that he was in any sense anti-Arab, but it is fair to say that

Johnson showed little sympathy for the radical brand of Arab nationalism expounded by Egypt's President Nasser. Nor did he appear
insensitive to the fact that the Soviet Union was exploiting Arab
nationalism to weaken the influence of the West in the Middle
East. Like other American policy makers before him, Johnson seemed
to waver between a desire to try to come to terms with Nasser and
a belief that Nasser's prestige and regional ambitions had to be
trimmed. More important than his predispositions, however, was
the fact that Johnson treated Middle East issues as deserving of only
secondary priority.

U.S.-Egyptian relations deteriorated steadily between 1964 and
early 1967, in part because of the conflict in Yemen, in part because
of quarrels over aid. By 1967, of course, Vietnam was receiving most
of Johnson's attention, and problems of the Middle East were left
largely to the State Department to worry about. There the sense of
anxiety about increased tension between Israel and the surrounding
Arab states was growing after the Israeli raid on the Jordanian town
of As-Samuʿ in November 1966 and especially after the April 1967
Israeli-Syrian air battle. Under Secretary of State Eugene Rostow was
particularly concerned about the drift of events, suspecting as he did
that the Soviets were seeking to take advantage in the Middle East
of Washington's preoccupation with Vietnam.[1]

During the second week of May 1967, the Arab-Israeli conflict
suddenly took on a new dimension. Instead of the normal level of
tension along the armistice lines, the situation overnight became one
in which full-scale war seemed possible. President Johnson and his
key advisers were quick to sense the danger in the new challenge
posed to Israel by Nasser's remilitarization of the Sinai on May 14.
Because of his well-known sympathy for Israel and his forceful personality, one might have expected Johnson to take a strong and un-
ambiguous stand during the crisis, especially as such a stand might
help to prevent Arab miscalculations. Moreover, reassurances to Israel
would help to lessen pressures on Prime Minister Eshkol to resort to
preemptive military action. Finally, a strong stand in the Middle East
would signal the Soviet Union that it could not exploit tensions there
without confronting the United States.

1. The report prepared in the fall of 1966 by Ambassador Julius Holmes contained
this theme.

The reality of United States policy as the Middle East crisis unfolded in May was, however, quite different. American behavior was cautious, at times ambiguous, and ultimately insensitive to the danger that war might break out at Israel's instigation. Why was this the case? Was it just a matter of Vietnam? Or were the reasons more deeply rooted in Johnson's perceptions of the nature of the crisis? The greatest difficulty in understanding United States policy is to reconstruct how Johnson defined the issues and the stakes as the danger of war in the Middle East became apparent and to determine the reasons for the tentativeness and uncertainty with which he managed the crisis.

INITIAL REACTIONS TO THE CRISIS

Against a background of mounting tension between Syria and Israel, culminating in the second week of May with vague Israeli threats of action against the regime in Damascus if guerrilla raids continued, Nasser ordered his troops into Sinai on May 14. At the outset, this move was interpreted primarily in political terms. Nasser, who was under attack by the conservative monarchies of Jordan and Saudi Arabia for being soft on Israel, was attempting to regain prestige by appearing as the defender of the embattled and threatened radical regime in Syria. Middle East watchers in the State Department thought they recognized a familiar pattern. In February 1960, Nasser had sent troops into Sinai, asked for the withdrawal of the UN troops from the border, postured for a while, claimed victory by deterring alleged Israeli aggressive designs, and then backed down. All in all, a rather cheap victory, and not one that presented much of a danger to anyone. Consequently, the initial American reaction to Nasser's dispatch of troops was restrained. Even the Israelis did not appear to be particularly alarmed.

Two days later, however, the crisis took on a more serious aspect as the Egyptians requested the removal of UNEF from the border areas. This prompted President Johnson to sound out the Israelis as to their intentions and to consult with the British and French. On May 17, Johnson sent Eshkol the first of several letters exchanged during the crisis in which he urged restraint and specifically asked to be informed before Israel took any action. "I am sure you will understand . . . that I cannot accept any responsibilities on behalf of the

United States for situations which arise as the result of actions on which we are not consulted.''[2] Secretary Rusk followed this message with a query to the cosignatories of the tripartite declaration of 1950, which guaranteed the inviolability of existing frontiers in the Middle East, and found the French in a negative frame of mind and the British more cooperative.[3]

From the outset, then, Johnson seemed to want to avoid war, to restrain the Israelis, and to gain allied support for any action that might be taken. Two possible alternative courses of action seem not to have been seriously considered at this point. One might have been to stand aside and let the Israelis act as they saw fit, even to the extent of using force. The danger, of course, was that Israel might get into trouble and turn to the United States for help. Johnson seemed to fear this contingency throughout the crisis, despite all the intelligence predictions that Israel would easily win a war against Egypt alone or against all the surrounding Arab countries. The second alternative that was not considered at this point was bold unilateral United States action opposing Nasser's effort to change the status quo. Here the problems were twofold. A quarrel with Egypt might inflame the situation and weaken American influence throughout the Arab world. Nasser was not noted for backing down when challenged. Moreover, the United States did not have in place the instruments of coercion that a strong policy might require. Apart from the Sixth Fleet, which was understrength, United States military assets were deeply committed in Vietnam. Therefore, the initial United States effort, which colored the entire handling of the crisis, was directed toward restraining Israel and building a multilateral context for diplomatic action.

Eshkol's reply to Johnson's letter reached Washington the following day, May 18. The Israeli prime minister blamed Syria for the increase in tension and stated that Egypt must remove its troops from Sinai. Then, appealing directly to Johnson, Eshkol requested that the United States reaffirm its commitment to Israeli security and inform the Soviet Union in particular of this commitment. Johnson wrote to Kosygin the following day, affirming the American position of support for Israel as requested, but suggesting in addition a ''joint

---

2. Lyndon Baines Johnson, *The Vantage Point* (New York: Holt, Rinehart, & Winston, 1971), p. 290; M. Gilboa, *Six Years, Six Days* (in Hebrew) (Tel Aviv: Am Oved, 1968), p. 144.
3. Johnson, op. cit., p. 292.

initiative of the two powers to prevent the dispute between Israel and the U.A.R. and Syria from drifting into war.''[4]

Once Nasser had requested the partial withdrawal of UNEF on May 16, there was danger that he might overplay his hand by also closing the Strait of Tiran to the Israelis. The opening of the strait was the one tangible gain made by Israel in the 1956 war. American commitments concerning the international status of the strait were explicit and Israel felt that it could count on United States support for action to keep the strait open. UNEF had stationed troops at Sharm al-Shaykh since 1957, and shipping had not been impeded. If UNEF were to withdraw, however, Nasser would be under great pressures to return the situation to its pre-1956 status. Israel had long declared that such action would be considered a *casus belli*. In light of these dangers, one might have expected some action by the United States after May 16 aimed at preventing the complete removal of UNEF. After all, Nasser had not asked for withdrawal of the force from either of the two most sensitive zones, Gaza or Sharm al-Shaykh. But the record shows no sign of an urgent approach to U Thant on this matter, and by the evening of May 18 it was too late. The UN Secretary General had forced Nasser to choose between no withdrawal of UNEF and full withdrawal. Not surprisingly, Nasser opted for the latter.

The strait still remained open, however, and a strong warning by Israel or the United States about the consequences of its closure might have influenced Nasser's next move. From May 19 until the late evening of May 22, Nasser took no action to close the strait. Presumably he was waiting to see how Israel and the United States, among others, would react to UNEF's withdrawal. Once again, there is no sign of any direct American approach to Nasser until May 22, the day that Nasser finally announced the closure of the strait. No public statements were made reaffirming the United States view that the strait was an international waterway, nor did the reputedly pro-Israeli president respond to Eshkol's request for a public declaration of American commitment to Israel's security. Some Israelis feared that the cautious United States stand in this initial period might be seen by Nasser as an invitation to interfere with free passage in the strait.[5] At this point,

4. Gilboa, op. cit., p. 145; *Middle East Record* III (1967): 194, 196.
5. Michael Brecher, *Decisions in Israel's Foreign Policy* (New Haven: Yale University Press, 1975), p. 375, quoting Ambassador Harman to Assistant Secretary Battle.

however, the Israeli position was not particularly strong, as Eshkol's May 22 speech showed, and this made a restrained United States position easier to justify. Instead of spelling out its position on closure of the Strait of Tiran during this initial period between May 18 and May 22, the United States continued to warn Israel not to act unilaterally. A preference for working within a UN framework was conveyed to the Israelis, including a suggestion that UNEF troops be moved to the Israeli side of the armistice lines.[6]

The day before Nasser's speech at Bir Gifgafa announcing the closure of the strait to Israeli shipping, Johnson sent a second letter to Eshkol reassuring him that the Soviet Union understood the United States commitment to Israel. At the same time, however, Johnson sought to explain why he could not make a public statement on the consequences of a blockade of the Gulf of Aqaba. He did, however, refer to the need for "suitable measures either through the UN or independent of that international organization" to deal with the crisis.[7] Israeli Foreign Minister Eban reportedly felt that this letter did not reflect Johnson's real views and must have been drafted by a cautious bureaucrat.

On May 22, before Nasser's speech, Johnson finally sent a letter to the Egyptian leader. The thrust of the message was to assure Nasser of the friendship of the United States, while urging him to avoid any step that might lead to war. In addition, Johnson offered to send Vice President Humphrey to Cairo in a "new attempt to find a solution to old problems" in the Middle East. The message was not delivered by Ambassador-designate Richard Nolte until the following day, by which time the strait had already been declared closed.[8] Johnson informed Eshkol that same day that he was writing to the Egyptian and Syrian leaders warning them not to take actions that might lead to hostilities.[9]

Another message from Johnson to Kosygin was also sent on May 22. Reiterating his suggestion of joint action to calm the situation, Johnson went on to state that

6. Gilboa, op. cit., p. 123, quoting Rostow to Harman, May 20; Michel Bar Zohar, *Embassies in Crisis* (Englewood Cliffs, N.J.: Prentice Hall, 1970), p. 56, confirms this.

7. Gilboa, op. cit., p. 145; Brecher, op. cit., p. 375; Bar Zohar, op. cit., p. 68.

8. Mohamed Heikal, *The Cairo Documents* (New York: Doubleday, 1973), p. 243.

9. Rusk added a message to the Israelis suggesting that UNEF be transferred to the Israeli side of the border.

The increasing harassment of Israel by elements based in Syria, with attendant reactions within Israel and within the Arab world, has brought the area close to major violence. Your and our ties to nations of the area could bring us into difficulties which I am confident neither of us seeks. It would appear a time for each of us to use our influence to the full in the course of moderation, including our influence over action by the United Nations.[10]

These messages, which might have helped to calm the situation at an earlier date, were rendered meaningless by the next major escalation of the crisis.[11] The well-intentioned initiative of May 21–22 was too little and too late. Shortly after midnight May 22, Nasser's speech announcing the closure of the strait to Israeli ships and to strategic goods bound for Israel was broadcast.

THE CRISIS OVER THE STRAIT

If Johnson had feared that Israel might resort to force unilaterally before May 23, the danger now became acutely real. Therefore he requested that Israel not make any military move for at least forty-eight hours.[12] During the day of May 23, arrangements were made for Israeli Foreign Minister Eban to visit Washington for talks prior to any Israeli unilateral action.

American diplomacy went into high gear. Johnson issued a forceful public statement to the effect that "The United States considers the gulf to be an international waterway and feels that a blockade of Israeli shipping is illegal and potentially disastrous to the cause of peace. The right of free, innocent passage of the international waterway is a vital interest of the international community."[13]

In Tel Aviv, United States Ambassador Barbour repeated the request for a forty-eight-hour delay prior to unilateral Israeli action and raised the possibility of pursuing a British idea of a multinational naval force to protect maritime rights in the event that UN action failed to resolve the crisis. Eban's trip to Washington was designed in part to explore the feasibility of this idea.

10. Johnson, op. cit., pp. 290–91.
11. Johnson did take one step on May 22 that had continuing importance during the crisis: he ordered the Sixth Fleet, with two aircraft carriers, the *Saratoga* and the *America*, to the eastern Mediterranean.
12. Brecher, op. cit., p. 278.
13. *Department of State Bulletin*, June 12, 1967, p. 870.

In Washington, Israeli Ambassador Harman and Minister Evron met with Under Secretary Rostow and were told that "the United States had decided in favor of an appeal to the Security Council . . . The object is to call for restoring the status quo as it was before . . . the blockade announcement. Rostow explained that the congressional reaction compels a president to take this course."[14] Rostow reportedly referred to the realities created by the Vietnam war in describing Johnson's approach to the blockade.

As United States policy began to move toward consideration of multilateral action to break the blockade of the Gulf of Aqaba, Johnson understandably was concerned with congressional reaction. On May 23, Secretary Rusk briefed the members of the Senate Foreign Relations Committee and reported back to Johnson that Congress would support Israel, but was opposed to unilateral United States action.[15] In an effort to build public support for the administration, the president contacted former President Eisenhower, who confirmed that in 1957 the United States had recognized that if force were used to close the strait, Israel would be within her rights under article 51 of the UN Charter to respond with force.[16] George Meany was also asked to issue a statement in support of administration policy.

The basic elements of Johnson's approach to the crisis as of May 23 were the following:

—Try to prevent war by restraining Israel and warning the Egyptians and Soviets.

—Build public and congressional support for the idea of an international effort to reopen the Strait of Tiran. (Unilateral United States action was ruled out without much consideration.)

—Make an effort through the UN Security Council to open the strait; if that failed, as was anticipated, a multilateral declaration in support of free shipping would be drawn up; this would be followed, as the British had suggested, by a multinational naval force transiting the strait.

Noteworthy is the continuing reluctance either to consider unilateral United States action or to "unleash Israel," as a second option came to be known. These alternatives had been ruled out virtually

14. Brecher, op. cit., p. 381, quoting Evron cable of May 23.
15. Johnson, op. cit., pp. 291–92.
16. Ibid., pp. 259–60; Eugene Rostow, *Peace in the Balance* (New York: Simon & Schuster, 1972), p. 291.

from the beginning, and even the closure of the strait did not lead to a reevaluation of the initial policy. Instead, the two key elements of policy dating from May 17 were merely embellished as conditions changed. A complex multilateral plan was designed, which would surely be supported by Congress and public opinion, but could it produce results rapidly enough to ensure the other element in the United States approach—restraint of Israel? A dilemma clearly existed. In order to keep Israel from acting on her own, as even the United States acknowledged she had a right to do in order to reopen the strait, an acceptable alternative had to be presented. The stronger the stand of the United States and the firmer its commitment to action, the more likely it was that Israel could be restrained; by the same token, the less likely it was that Nasser would probe further. Yet a strong American stand was incompatible with the desire for multilateral action, which had to be tried, in Johnson's view, in order to ensure congressional and public support. Such support was essential at a time of controversy over the United States role in Vietnam.

Johnson was mindful of the furor over his handling of the Gulf of Tonkin incident in 1964. Then he had seized upon a small incident to broaden his power, with full congressional approval, to act in Vietnam. Subsequently, however, he had been charged with duplicity, with misleading Congress concerning the event, and with abusing the authority he had received. In mid-1967, Johnson was not about to lead the United States into another venture which might entail the use of force without full congressional and public backing. Consequently he insisted on trying the UN first, then seeking a multilateral maritime declaration, then sending ships through the strait. By moving slowly, cautiously, and with full support at home, Johnson would minimize the domestic political risks to his position.

The goals of restraining Israel and pursuing a multilateral solution were not necessarily incompatible, provided that sufficient time was available. For time to be available, perhaps as much as two to three weeks, the situation on the ground could not be allowed to change radically, nor could the balance of forces within Israel be permitted to shift toward those who favored war. At a minimum, then, Nasser had to sit tight, the Soviet Union had to remain on the sidelines, and Eshkol had to be given something with which to restrain his hawks. If any of these conditions should not be met, the assumptions of United States policy would be undermined and war would probably ensue.

One might have anticipated a careful monitoring of the regional situation to detect any changes in these areas, and rapid reevaluation of policy in the event of such changes. But, perhaps not surprisingly, once the basic policy was determined, and because it required time for successful implementation, officials from Johnson on down tended to ignore signs that time was running out. The lesson seems to be that once a crisis situation is initially defined, and a course of action is set, as it was on May 17 and again on May 23, it becomes extraordinarily difficult to redefine the stakes and the risks. This became amply evident in the last week of May.

EBAN'S VISIT TO WASHINGTON

The impending visit of Israel's foreign minister served as a catalyst for the further definition of an American plan of action for dealing with the closure of the Strait of Tiran. If Israel were to refrain from forceful action, a credible alternative to war must be presented. But the process of moving from general principles—restrain Israel, act within a multilateral context—to a more detailed proposal revealed inherent contradictions and ambiguities, as well as bureaucratically rooted differences of opinion. What had initially been a fairly widespread consensus among Johnson's top advisers on how to deal with the crisis began to fragment as the crisis grew more acute. When Johnson felt most in need of broad support for his cautious, restrained approach, the viability of that stance came under question.

The key to Johnson's policy on the eve of Eban's visit was the British idea of a multinational naval force. On May 24, Eugene Rostow met with the British minister of state for foreign affairs, George Thomson, and Admiral Henderson of the Royal Navy to discuss the British proposal. They agreed to try for a public declaration on freedom of shipping through the Strait of Tiran, to be signed by as many countries as possible; a multinational naval force would then be set up, composed of ships from as many maritime countries as were prepared to act; and a flotilla, soon to be known as the "Red Sea Regatta," would then pass through the strait.[17] Rostow talked to Johnson later in the day about the plan and found the president in a receptive frame of mind toward it.

Johnson was scheduled to make a trip to Canada on May 25, and

17. Johnson, op. cit., p. 292; Gilboa, op. cit., p. 143; Bar Zohar, op. cit., p. 98.

he used the occasion to seek Prime Minister Pearson's support for the multinational-fleet idea.[18] Meanwhile, the Pentagon was charged with coming up with a concrete plan for the formation of a naval force. At this point, consensus began to erode.[19] The overriding pre-occupation of Secretary of Defense McNamara and the Pentagon in mid-1967 was Vietnam. McNamara was reportedly apprehensive that American troops might be called upon to intervene in the Middle East. A second "McNamara's war" was not a particularly appealing prospect.

One might expect that professional military men would tend to favor the use of military force, but this was not the position emanating from the Pentagon during the Middle East crisis. In part, it was felt that Israel could take care of herself, and that American forces were not needed for military purposes. Moreover, the idea of a limited use of force, such as sending a few ships through the Strait of Tiran, encountered serious opposition from the military. What would happen, they argued, if the Egyptians fired on an American ship? Would the United States respond with force? Would Egyptian airfields be attacked? Would ground troops be required? If so, how many? If the Egyptians held their fire, but did not back down, the navy might find itself in the awkward position of having to patrol the strait indefinitely, under the guns of the Egyptians. Nothing would be solved politically, and the United States would simply find itself stuck with another commitment that diverted forces from other essential theaters. On balance, then, the military was not in favor of the use of American force. Bureaucratic self-interest and a professional attitude that dictated the use of force only when success was assured and when adequate power was available lay at the root of the opposition. The multinational fleet was a military man's nightmare. It was not the way the military would plan such an operation. It was "too political." Deeming it undesirable, the military did little to make it feasible. McNamara could scarcely hide his skepticism. Almost imperceptibly, Johnson was being deprived of his principal policy instrument because of the Pentagon's skepticism.

The State Department, at least at the top levels, was, by contrast, enthusiastic about the idea. Secretary Rusk endorsed it and Under Secretary Eugene Rostow became its chief advocate. From their point

18. Bar Zohar, op. cit., p. 123; Gilboa, op. cit., pp. 145–46; interview with Rostow.
19. Bar Zohar, op. cit., p. 125.

of view, the fact that it was a flawed military concept was less important than its politically attractive features. First, it would associate
other nations with the United States in defense of an important principle—freedom of navigation—and in the upholding of a commitment to Israel. Second, it would deflate Nasser's prestige, which was
once again on the rise, without putting him into an impossible position. If Nasser wanted to back down from confrontation with Israel,
the fleet would provide him with an honorable excuse to do so. The
State Department therefore set out to find cosigners of the maritime
declaration and donors of ships for the fleet. This essentially political
task was what State was best at performing; the planning of the fleet
was the province of Defense. Unfortunately, little coordination went
on between the two.

Foreign Minister Eban arrived in Washington on the afternoon
of May 25. His first talks were held at the State Department at 5:00
P.M. The result was to sow confusion among United States policy
makers, who had just adjusted to the crisis and thought they saw a
way out of it. Eban, who had left Israel with instructions to discuss
American plans to reopen the Strait of Tiran, arrived in the United
States to find new instructions awaiting him. No longer was he to
emphasize the issue of the strait. A more urgent danger, that of imminent Egyptian attack, had overshadowed the blockade. Eban was
instructed to inform the highest authorities of this new threat to
peace and to request an official statement from the United States
that an attack on Israel would be viewed as an attack on the United
States.[20] Despite his own skepticism, Eban followed his instructions
in his first meeting with Secretary Rusk, Under Secretary Rostow, and
Assistant Secretary Battle.

Rusk quickly ended the meeting so that he could confer with
Johnson about the new situation. The meeting with Eban resumed
at 6:00 P.M. for a working dinner, at which Eugene Rostow, Lucius
Battle, Foy Kohler, Joseph Sisco, Leonard Meeker (legal adviser), and
Townsend Hoopes were present among the American group. The
Israelis were told that United States sources could not confirm an
Egyptian plan to attack. Nonetheless, the Egyptians would be warned
against the use of force, and Moscow would be asked to make a
parallel démarche. Discussion then shifted to the British proposal,

20. Brecher, op. cit., p. 386; Bar Zohar, op. cit., p. 109; Moshe Dayan, *Moshe Dayan: Story of My Life* (New York: William Morrow, 1976), p. 329.

including the declaration of maritime powers, its endorsement by
the United Nations, and the multinational fleet. Israel was once again
warned not to preempt.[21] The opinion was put forward on the American side that Egypt would not resist the fleet when the time came;
but first the declaration must be issued, debate in the UN must
proceed, and only then could the ships move. American public opinion, it was stressed, must be convinced that all avenues had been
explored before force was used.

The conversation must have had an unreal quality about it, the
Israelis being preoccupied with reports of imminent Egyptian attack
and the Americans talking about declarations, the United Nations,
Congress, and hypothetical naval forces. After the talks ended, Israeli
Ambassador Harman returned to the State Department at about
midnight to reemphasize Israel's need for a concrete and precise statement of United States intentions.[22] He also warned that Israel could
not accept any plan in which the strait might be opened to all ships
except those of Israel.

American intelligence experts spent the night of May 25–26 analyzing the Israeli claim that an Egyptian attack was imminent. Several
specific items had been presented by the Israelis in making their case,
and by the morning of May 26 the intelligence community had ana-
lyzed each of these charges and concluded that an attack was not
pending.[23] The Israelis suffered a loss of credibility at an important
moment, and Johnson seems to have become suspicious that he was
being pressured to make commitments that he either could not make,
such as a statement that the United States would view an attack on
Israel as an attack on this country, or that he did not want to make
yet, such as a precise plan on the multinational fleet. According to
those who worked with him during this period, Johnson did not want
to be crowded, he disliked ultimata and deadlines, and he resented
the mounting pressures that he felt to adopt Israel's definition of the
situation. After all, as president he had to worry about the Soviet
Union, about Congress and public opinion, and about U.S.-Arab

21. Brecher, op. cit., pp. 386–87; Bar Zohar, op. cit., pp. 112–13. Eugene Rostow
called in Egyptian Ambassador Kemal and warned that Egypt must not attack Israel. The
Soviets were also asked to use their influence to restrain Nasser, which they reportedly did.
Heikal, op. cit., p. 244; Gilboa, op. cit., pp. 145–46; Brecher, op. cit., p. 387; Bar Zohar,
op. cit., pp. 111–12.
22. Brecher, op. cit., pp. 387–88. Harmon saw Eugene Rostow and Joseph Sisco.
23. Bar Zohar, op. cit., p. 114.

relations; he did not want to be stampeded, to use the imagery of his native Texas.[24]

Johnson was obviously reluctant to see Eban on Friday, May 26. He knew that it would be an important, perhaps crucial meeting. The Israeli cabinet was to meet on Sunday, and what he told Eban might make the difference between war and peace. The Israelis were pressing for a specific commitment, for a detailed plan, for promises to act, and for understanding in the event Israel were to take matters into her own hands. Faced with these pressures, Johnson tried to stall. Rusk called Harman early in the morning to find out whether Eban could stay in Washington through Saturday. This would allow Johnson to learn the results of U Thant's mission to Cairo. Eban, stressing the importance of the Sunday cabinet meeting, said that he had to leave Friday evening for Israel.[25]

During the morning of May 26, Eban went to the Pentagon, where he met with McNamara, Wheeler, CIA Director Helms, and Hoopes. There he was given the results of the intelligence review of the previous night. No evidence could be found that Egypt was planning to attack. In addition, Eban was told, both the CIA and the Pentagon were convinced that Israel would easily win if hostilities were to begin, no matter who struck first. The fighting would not last a week. This was probably more reassuring to the American military, which did not want to be called upon to intervene, than it was to the Israelis.[26]

Meanwhile, Secretary Rusk and Under Secretary Rostow had prepared a policy memorandum for the president. A meeting was scheduled for noon to discuss it and to plan for the Eban meeting. Walt Rostow called Evron during the morning to request a delay in Eban's meeting with the president, claiming that Johnson was busy studying the 1957 documents on the American commitment concerning the strait.

Rusk's memo to the president began with a review of his talk with Eban the previous evening, including the Israeli information that an Egyptian and Syrian attack was imminent and the request for a public statement of United States support for Israel against such aggression. Eban, it was stated, would not press this point with Johnson

24. See Tom Wicker, *JFK and LBJ* (New York: William Morrow, 1968), pp. 195–99.
25. Brecher, op. cit., pp. 389–90; Bar Zohar, op. cit., p. 115.
26. Gilboa, op. cit., pp. 146–47; Brecher op. cit., p. 390; Bar Zohar, op. cit., p. 117, claims that McNamara expressed his opposition to the multilateral naval fleet at this meeting.

and the president's talk could concentrate on the British proposal. Rusk then outlined two basic options:

—to let the Israelis decide how best to protect their own national interest, in light of the advice we have given them, i.e., to "unleash" them;

—to take a positive position, but not make a final commitment, on the British proposal.

Rusk recommended strongly against the first option. Noting that the British cabinet would meet on the multinational-fleet plan the following day, Rusk gave his endorsement to the second option, which he then reviewed in some detail. Included in his outline was the idea that a UN force should take a position along both sides of the Israeli-Egyptian frontier. If Egypt were to refuse, Israel might accept.

Eban's need for a strong commitment from Johnson was made clear in the Rusk memo. Congressional views were reviewed and the option of unilateral United States action was referred to with caution. A draft joint resolution of the Congress was being prepared to support international action on the strait. In closing, Rusk referred to the possibility of offering Israel economic and military aid to help offset the strains of continuing mobilization.

On May 26 at noon, President Johnson convened at the White House the first and only full-scale meeting of his advisers held during the crisis. Present were Vice President Humphrey, Secretary Rusk, Secretary McNamara, Under Secretary Rostow, Chairman of the Joint Chiefs of Staff Wheeler, CIA Director Helms, Assistant Secretary Battle, Assistant Secretary Sisco, and advisers Abe Fortas, Cyrus Vance, George Ball, and Clark Clifford. Wheeler began with a military briefing, which included the evidence available on each side's force postures. Wheeler expressed the judgment that Israel could stay at its present level of mobilization for two months without serious trouble. In a military sense, then, time did not seem to be running out. Rusk followed with a review of the diplomatic situation, especially his talks the previous night with Eban. McNamara then spoke of his morning session with Eban in which the Israeli foreign minister had raised the issue of United States commitments made in 1957 as part of the negotiations that resulted in Israel's withdrawal from Sinai. These consisted of an aide-mémoire of February 27, 1957, signed by Dulles, which stated that the United States considered the Strait of Tiran to be an international waterway. Eban was apparently trying to extend this and other statements made at the time into an American commitment to use force if necessary to reopen the strait. On the American side, the most that was acknowledged was that Dulles had said that the United States recognized Israel's right, under article 51 of the UN charter, to use force to open the strait if it was closed by force.

One by one, each of Johnson's advisers then expressed his views to the President. Discussion turned to the idea of a multinational fleet, with McNamara stating his disapproval of the idea on military grounds.[27] Rusk then reported on U Thant's talks in Cairo, which had elicited from Nasser a promise not to take preemptive action and had led to some discussion of how the blockade might be modified. He then introduced a phrase which was to be repeated to the Israelis frequently in the coming two weeks: "Israel will only be alone if it goes alone." To Rusk, it clearly mattered who opened fire first.[28] Johnson, who seemed to be reassured by the judgment that the military situation would not deteriorate suddenly, spoke of the maritime effort approvingly, terming it his "hole card" for his talk with Eban. But he realized that this might not be enough for Eban. He asked his advisers if they thought Eban would misinterpret this as a "cold shoulder." Johnson expressed his feeling that he could not make a clear commitment to use force, because of congressional sentiment. He wondered out loud if he would regret on Monday not having given Eban more today. Then he left the meeting.

By late afternoon, the Israelis were becoming anxious to set a definite time for Eban's meeting with the president.[29] Minister Evron called Walt Rostow and was invited to come to the White House to talk. Johnson, he was told, did not want any leaks to the press from the meeting and several details of the visit had to be discussed. While Evron was in his office, Rostow contacted Johnson, who, upon learning of Evron's presence, asked him in for an informal talk. Johnson knew and liked Evron, and presumably felt that it would be useful to convey his position through Evron prior to the more formal meeting

27. McNamara did not oppose the president's policy, however.

28. The view was expressed that no overt act of aggression had yet occurred. Until Egypt resorted to the use of armed force, according to this argument, the United States commitment to Israel would not be activated.

29. Jonathan Trumbull Howe, *Multicrises* (Cambridge, Mass.: MIT Press, 1971), pp. 362–67. Howe interviewed an unnamed White House source (John Roche) who stated that Johnson was stalling Eban because he had just been shown the memo of the Dulles-Eban talks of 1957 and wanted to check its authenticity.

with Eban. Johnson began by stressing that any American action would require congressional support of the president. He repeated this point several times. Talks in the UN, although not expected to produce anything, were an important part of the process of building support. On a more positive note, Johnson mentioned the multinational-fleet effort. He acknowledged that Israel, as a sovereign state, had the right to act alone; but in that case, the United States would feel no obligation for any consequences which might ensue. He stated that he did not believe Israel would carry out such unilateral action. In closing, Johnson stressed that he was not a coward, that he did not renege on his promises, but that he would not be rushed into a course of action that might endanger the United States simply because Israel had set Sunday as a deadline.[30]

Eban arrived at the White House unannounced while Evron was with the president. After some confusion, their meeting began shortly after 7:00 P.M. The Americans present included Johnson, McNamara, Rusk, Walt and Eugene Rostow, Sisco, and press secretary George Christian. In response to Eban's appeal that the United States live up to its explicit commitments, Johnson emphasized that he had termed the blockade illegal and that he was working on a plan to reopen the strait. He noted that he did not have the authority to say that an attack on Israel would be considered an attack on the United States. He again stressed the two basic premises of American policy: any action must have congressional support and it must be multilateral. Three times he repeated the phrase that Rusk had coined: "Israel will not be alone unless it decides to go alone." He said that he could not imagine Israel making a precipitate decision. In case Eban doubted his personal courage, Johnson stressed that he was "not a feeble mouse or a coward." Twice Eban asked the president if he could tell the cabinet that Johnson would do everything in his power to get the gulf open to all shipping, including that of Israel. Johnson said "yes."[31] Eban was given an aide-mémoire spelling out United States policy:

> The United States has its own Constitutional processes, which are basic to its actions on matters involving war and peace. The Secretary-General

30. Brecher, op. cit., pp. 390–91, provides the full text of Evron's official account of his meeting with Johnson.
31. Ibid., p. 392; Johnson, op. cit., p. 293, says he told Eban the United States would use "any and all means" to open the strait.

has not yet reported to the UN Security Council and the Council has not yet demonstrated what it may or may not be able or willing to do, although the United States will press for prompt action in the UN.

I have already publicly stated this week our views on the safety of Israel and on the Strait of Tiran. Regarding the Strait, we plan to pursue vigorously the measures which can be taken by maritime nations to assure that the Strait and the Gulf remain open to free and innocent passage of the vessels of all nations.

I must emphasize the necessity for Israel not to make itself responsible for the initiation of hostilities. Israel will not be alone unless it decides to go alone. We cannot imagine that it will make this decision.[32]

As Eban left the White House, Johnson turned to his advisers and stated: "I've failed. They'll go."[33]

PRELUDE TO THE JUNE 1967 WAR

Johnson obviously was aware of the awkwardness of the policy he was pursuing. The multinational fleet effort would take time, and even then might fall through for any number of reasons. The alternative of unilateral American action was not seriously considered. Congress was obviously a major concern, and behind Congress lay the realities of the Vietnam conflict. Johnson understood that Israel was subject to a different set of pressures and might be forced to go to war. But in that case, the United States, he said, would not be committed to act. He sincerely wanted to deter Israeli action, but he felt unable to provide the one thing that might prevent such a move—a firm guarantee to use force if necessary to reopen the strait. Eban had almost extracted such a promise, but in Johnson's mind it was clearly hedged by references to United States constitutional processes and "every means within my power."

What Johnson now needed most was time—time for the fleet idea to be explored, for passions to cool, for compromises to be explored. Therefore, his next action was to try to pin the Israelis down with a promise not to act for another two weeks. The occasion for such a demand came on May 27, when the Soviets informed Johnson that they had information that Israel was planning to attack. The president replied to Kosygin and sent a message to Eshkol repeating

32. Brecher, op. cit., pp. 392–93, gives a slightly different version of the aide-mémoire.
33. Interview with Eugene Rostow; Howe, op. cit., pp. 362–67. Howe quotes Roche to the effect that Johnson said after his meeting with Eban: "Israel is going to hit them."

the information from Moscow and warning Israel against starting hostilities.[34] Meanwhile, it was decided to initiate further contacts with Nasser and to that end Ambassador Charles Yost was sent to Cairo to assist Ambassador-designate Nolte in his dealings with the Egyptians, and Robert Anderson was requested to talk to Nasser privately in order to help set up an exchange of visits at the vice-presidential level. Rusk followed up Johnson's message to Eshkol with one of his own to Ambassador Barbour, for transmittal to the Israelis:[35] "With the assurance of international determination to make every effort to keep the strait open to the flags of all nations, unilateral action on the part of Israel would be irresponsible and catastrophic." Rusk also paralleled Johnson's message to Kosygin, which had called for a U.S.-U.S.S.R. effort to find a prompt solution to the Strait of Tiran issue, with a message to Gromyko calling for a two-week moratorium on the U.A.R. closure of the strait. The message to Eshkol had its intended effect. At the Sunday cabinet meeting the vote was split nine to nine on the issue of whether to go to war or not. Eshkol, reflecting on Johnson's letter and Eban's report of his talks, decided to accede to the president's request.

From this point on, Washington officials began to act as if they had at least two weeks in which to work toward a solution. The critical period, it was felt, would begin after Sunday, June 11. Although there was reason to believe that the Israelis would stay their hand until that date, as Johnson had requested, it was clear that such a pledge would lose validity if the situation on the ground or within Israel were to change substantially. And in ensuing days, changes did indeed occur, but Johnson and his advisers stuck to their definition of the situation. In part this was out of wishful thinking, in part for lack of any better alternative. To the Israelis, however, the lack of a new policy from Washington in the light of the new circumstances was tantamount to saying: "We've tried all of our alternatives and have nothing new to offer." The Israelis began to scrutinize Johnson's messages for indications that he really wanted Israel to act unilaterally, provided

34. Brecher, op. cit., pp. 399–400, provides the text of this message: "The Soviets stated that if Israel starts military action, the Soviet Union will extend help to the attacked state. . . . As your friend, I repeat even more strongly what I said yesterday to Mr. Eban: Israel just must not take pre-emptive military action and thereby make itself responsible for the initiation of hostilities." Johnson then requested a two- to three-week delay before Israel would resort to force to open the strait.
35. Ibid., p. 400.

the United States would not be drawn in. After all, what was really meant by the curious oft-repeated phrase: "Israel will only be alone if it decides to go alone." It was not quite an absolute prohibition. It did not require a Talmudist to read into the phrase the hint of a "green light" to Israel—and there were plenty of Talmudists in Israel who were convinced that United States policy was precisely that. The multinational fleet was simply not plausible; and, besides, there were some reports that Eban had missed the point of Johnson's talk, assuming a stronger commitment than was intended. To check on these impressions and to follow up on earlier suggestions that intelligence liaison should be improved, the head of Israeli intelligence, Meir Amit, flew to Washington under an assumed name on May 30.

Just before Amit's departure for Washington, one major change took place in the situation. King Hussein, under great pressure to join the Arab-nationalist mainstream, had flown to Cairo and signed a mutual-defense pact with Nasser. He returned to Jordan with an Egyptian general in tow who would head the joint military command.

In Washington on May 30 and 31, confusion began to emerge concerning the depth of the American commitment to act. A proposed joint declaration of maritime powers had been shown to the Israeli ambassador, but it made no mention of the use of force, if necessary, to break the blockade.

Eshkol replied to Johnson's letter of May 28 on May 30, noting that United States assurances to take "any and all measures to open the straits" had played a role in Israel's decisions not to go to war and to agree to wait for "a week or two."[36] Within that time frame, Eshkol urged, a naval escort must move through the strait. Apprised of this message on May 31, Johnson became angry, claiming that he had not given Israel a blank check in the form of a promise to use "any and all means," but rather had stressed that he would make every effort within his constitutional authority. Walt Rostow was told to contact Evron to ensure that there should be no misunderstanding on this point. Evron replied by warning of the implications of what seemed to be a weakening of the United States commitment.[37]

From Cairo, Yost reported his impression that Egypt would not

36. Johnson, op. cit., pp. 2–4; Bar Zohar, op. cit., pp. 159–60; Brecher, op. cit., pp. 338, 413.
37. Brecher, op. cit., p. 414; Gilboa, op. cit., p. 197; Bar Zohar, op. cit., p. 160.

back down and that any American effort to force the strait would have grave consequences in the Arab world. The following day, Anderson met with Nasser to arrange for Zakariyya Muhieddin to visit Washington on June 7.[38] It was suspected by some in Washington that Nasser might propose referring the dispute over the strait to the International Court of Justice to be resolved. The United States might find such a proposal difficult to refuse; Israel would certainly find it impossible to accept.

Rumors began to circulate in Washington on May 31 that the United States was looking for possible compromises to end the crisis.[39] In fact, some consideration was being given in the State Department to such steps. This was the atmosphere that Amit found when he filed his first report on his soundings in Washington. His advice was to wait a few more days, but he observed that the mood was beginning to change. In his opinion, the fleet idea was increasingly seen as bankrupt. If Israel were to act on her own, and win decisively, no one in Washington would be upset. The source for these impressions, it is worth noting, was not the State Department or the White House. Amit's talks were confined to the Pentagon, where he saw McNamara, and CIA, where he talked with Helms. Little wonder that he was able to report a feeling of skepticism in regard to the fleet.[40] That same day, the Israelis picked up a report that Rusk had told a journalist that "I don't think it is our business to restrain anyone," when asked if the United States were trying to restrain Israel.[41]

On June 1, the simmering political crisis in Israel broke, and Moshe Dayan, hero of the 1956 Suez campaign, was brought into the cabinet as minister of defense. War now seemed likely in the near future. News from Cairo was not encouraging either, as Yost reported on a meeting with Foreign Minister Riad in which it was made clear that Egypt would not reopen the strait. Faced with these new indications that war was imminent, Johnson stuck to his announced position, but a sense that war might be inevitable began to spread through Washington. No one could see any easy way out.

June 2 was the last occasion for serious diplomatic efforts prior to Israel's decision to fight. The Israeli ambassador was scheduled to

---

38. Heikal, op. cit., p. 245; Brecher, op. cit., p. 420; Bar Zohar, op. cit., p. 168.
39. Bar Zohar, op. cit., pp. 160–61.
40. Brecher, op. cit., p. 417.
41. Bar Zohar, op. cit., p. 157, states that on May 30, after Jordan threw in its lot with Egypt, Walt Rostow expressed the opinion that he no longer saw a political solution.

leave for Israel on June 3, and another "fateful" cabinet meeting would be held on June 4. At about 11:00 A.M. on June 2, Minister Evron called on Walt Rostow at the White House. He wanted to make sure that Johnson understood that time was very short and that Israel might have to go to war. He was seeking further confirmation of Amit's impression that the United States would not object too strenuously if Israel acted on its own. Evron stressed that he was not conveying an official communication from his government, but his points were taken seriously. First he emphasized that time was working against Israel and that the military cost of war with Egypt was rising every day. He then asked what the American response would be if an Israeli ship were to try to break the blockade, drew Egyptian fire, and then Israel responded with an attack on Sharm al-Shaykh. Would the United States see this as a case of Israel asserting its legitimate right of self-defense? What if the Soviet Union were to intervene? Rostow said he would seek Johnson's views. He then asked Evron how much time remained, in reply to which Evron referred to June 11, although he stressed that there was nothing ironclad about that date.[42] Evron then mentioned the 1957 commitment, emphasizing that it had two parts: an American commitment to assert the right of free passage in the strait; and acknowledgment of Israel's right to act with force if the strait were closed. It was this second track that he was now exploring, the former having been discussed with Eban. Among other things, he noted, it would be better for U.S.-Arab and U.S.-Soviet relations if Israel acted alone rather than relying on the United States to use force to open the strait.[43] This was a point that several American ambassadors in Arab countries had also made and it was not lost on Rostow.

Johnson's reaction to Evron's ideas is unknown, although he reportedly discussed them with Rusk. There is no reason to believe that Johnson ever wavered from his statement to Eban. Certainly in the letter he sent to Eshkol later that day there is no hint of a new approach. Instead, the letter, a reply to Eshkol's message of May 30, largely repeated what Eban had already been told. The text of the aide-mémoire was quoted in full. Johnson promised to "provide as

42. Johnson, op. cit., p. 294, without naming Evron, reveals part of this incident. The rest is based on interviews with participants.
43. Interview with Evron, Dec. 30, 1974.

effective American support as possible to preserve the peace and freedom of your nation and of the area." He again referred to the need for the backing of Congress and for working through the UN. The maritime-powers declaration and the naval escort were mentioned, and Johnson added that "Our leadership is unanimous that the United States should not move in isolation."[44]

Ambassador Harman had a last talk on June 2 with Secretary Rusk before departing for Israel. Rusk had little new to report. Efforts to gain adherents to the maritime declaration were continuing. The necessary multilateral context for action in the Gulf of Aqaba did not yet exist. The question as to which side fired first would be extremely important, and Rusk cautioned Harman against Israeli action.

The following day, June 3, it was announced in Cairo that Muhieddin would visit the United States for talks on June 7. The Israelis had not been informed of this and were obviously irritated. Such a visit could only work to their disadvantage. In Israel, both Harman and Amit, who had returned together, reported that there was no chance of unilateral United States action nor of successful multilateral action. The conclusion was inescapable: Israel was on her own. Amit judged that the United States could not object if Israel opened the blockade in her own way.[45] Sensing that time was running out, Rusk cabled ambassadors in the Arab world with the warning that Israel might act soon, urging that they send in any ideas on how to avoid war, and that they remain "evenhanded" if hostilities did begin.

On Sunday, June 4, Israel decided to go to war. Washington was not informed of the decision. The day passed quietly, and in some quarters there was even a distinct feeling that the peak of the crisis was past. With Muhieddin's upcoming visit, with arrangements under way for aid to Israel, with Eshkol's promise not to act for a week or two, war no longer seemed quite so likely. The next day, June 5, at 7:45 A.M. local time, the Israeli airforce went into action, and within hours the Egyptian and Syrian air forces had been virtually destroyed. The third Arab-Israeli war had begun.

44. Brecher, op. cit., p. 419; Gilboa, op. cit., pp. 200–01, contains a partial text of this letter in Hebrew translation; Bar Zohar, op. cit., p. 175, also printed part of this text. Dayan, op. cit., pp. 345–46, states that a letter from Johnson reached Israel on June 4 during the ministerial defense committee meeting at which the decision for war was made. This must have been the Johnson letter of June 2.

45. Gilboa, op. cit., p. 199.

THE PRESIDENT AT WAR

The outbreak of war on June 5 created a profoundly changed situation for United States policy makers. The premises of the preceding three weeks were invalidated overnight, and new issues assumed priority. How would President Johnson cope with the urgent problems that now confronted him? The president had gone to great lengths to warn the Israelis against preemptive action; he had urged them to consult before moving on their own; he had extracted a virtual promise of no action before June 11. As late as May 26, the opinion had been expressed in Johnson's presence that Egypt had committed no overt act of aggression that could justify the use of force, either by the United States or Israel. Secretary Rusk had repeatedly told the Israelis that it would matter who opened fire. Would Johnson now conclude that Israel, by defying him and by starting a war, was the aggressor? Had this been his definition of the new circumstances, American policy would have been much different. Unlike French President de Gaulle, however, Johnson did not brand Israel as the aggressor, although he did express "disappointment" that the Israelis had not taken his advice.[46]

Why was Johnson prepared to support Israel so strongly once the war had begun, especially in view of his firm expression, before June 5, of his opposition to war? Was he responding to pressures from pro-Israeli opinion in the United States, or to his own sympathy for the Jewish state? Or from the outset had he subtly been urging the Israelis to act, provided that there be no hint of collusion with the United States? Many Israelis, not being able to reconcile Johnson's prewar opposition to Israel's use of force and his postwar support of Israel, assumed that Johnson had all along been trying to signal Israel to act on her own. In this view, the multinational-fleet idea was not meant seriously. But this interpretation seems clearly wrong. Johnson was opposed to an Israeli resort to force; he did support the multilateral-fleet idea; and still he was prepared to support Israel after the war had begun. Only a simplistic version of rational decision-making would insist that these positions were inherently self-contradictory.

The key to understanding Johnson's position was his fear that the United States would be drawn into another war, possibly even involving a confrontation with the Soviet Union. Vietnam was bad enough,

46. Johnson, op. cit., p. 303.

but Vietnam plus the Middle East, plus a possible showdown with the Soviet Union, was virtually unthinkable. True, Johnson's top advisers were unanimous that Israel would win if war began and that the United States would not be called upon to help. But what if this judgment proved to be false? Could Johnson afford to ignore the remote possibility that Israel might get into trouble and call on the United States for assistance? Or what if the Soviet Union were to intervene, on the assumption that the United States was so bogged down in Vietnam that it could not respond effectively? These seem to have been the genuine fears that lay behind Johnson's advice to the Israelis not to attack. What he was trying to say to the Israelis was not to count on the United States if they got into trouble. Within hours of the beginning of the war, it was clear that the Israelis would prevail. Johnson's main fear therefore vanished and he was able to deal with the new situation from a different vantage point.[47]

If Israel was in no danger of defeat by the Arabs, then the United States could concentrate its efforts on obtaining a cease-fire and ensuring that the Soviet Union would not intervene. The question of how the war had begun, which excited some interest in the early hours, was quickly overtaken by events. (Eban told Barbour that Egypt had attacked first. By the time it was known that Israel had struck the first blow, it no longer seemed to matter.) The United States, for the moment, was "off the hook," as one top-level policy maker expressed it.

Johnson obviously was anxious to convey the impression that the United States was not involved in the fighting. This might help to minimize the danger to United States interests in the Arab world, to reduce the likelihood of Soviet intervention, and to facilitate a cease-fire. When the war began, the Marine Battalion Landing Team which was part of the Sixth Fleet was deliberately on shore leave in Malta.[48] Two carriers were on station near Crete, but they were not moved closer to the area of conflict.

The first news of the fighting reached Johnson early on the morning of June 5. Three hours after the start of hostilities, Secretary Rusk, after consultations with the president, sent a message through normal channels to Moscow expressing surprise at the outbreak of war and

47. As a politician, Johnson probably had some understanding of the domestic political pressures that obliged Israel to act.
48. Howe, op. cit., p. 70.

calling for an early end to the fighting.[49] At about 8:00 A.M., Premier
Kosygin replied over the "hot line"—the first use of this channel of
communication in a crisis. He referred to the dangerous situation
and the need for U.S.-Soviet cooperation in bringing about a cease-
fire. Johnson's answer, sent by the hot line at 8:47 A.M., stated that
both superpowers should stay out of the conflict and encourage a
cease-fire. The American position very quickly became one of support
for a cease-fire, but there was ambiguity as to whether it would be
linked to a provision for return to the prehostilities borders. Restoration of the immediate status quo ante of June 4 was clearly ruled out,
inasmuch as that would have left the strait closed; but withdrawal of
Israeli forces in conjunction with a lifting of the blockade probably
would have found support in Washington if the Soviets or the Arabs
had pressed the issue on the first day.

By June 6, however, the United States came out in favor of a
simple cease-fire in place.[50] Kosygin had communicated with Johnson
during the day on the need for a cease-fire coupled with Israeli withdrawal, but by the end of the day the Soviets supported a simple end
to the fighting. The Egyptians, however, rejected a cease-fire in place.
By that time, Johnson was not in a mood to help Nasser, who that
day had falsely accused the United States of directly participating in
the war alongside Israel. The result of his charge was that several Arab
states broke off diplomatic relations with Washington and considerable bitterness was created toward Nasser, even among the State
Department Arabists.

Apart from denying Nasser's accusations and continuing to support a cease-fire, the United States did little on the next day of the
war, June 7. On the 8th, however, an American intelligence ship
stationed off the Sinai coast, the *Liberty*, was attacked by unidenti-
fied aircraft, which proved later to be Israeli. When news of the attack
was flashed to Washington, McNamara and Johnson both feared that
the Soviet Union might be responsible, and dark predictions of
"World War III" were briefly heard in the White House situation
room. The identity of the attackers was quickly clarified, and Johnson
informed Moscow by the "hot line" of the incident and the dispatch
of aircraft from the Sixth Fleet to the scene of the attack. The incident

49. Ibid., p. 90, interview with Rusk.
50. Ibid., pp. 91, 93, where Rusk states that an immediate cease-fire, favored by the
United States, would have left Israel only 50 miles inside Sinai.

is primarily of interest as an indication of the extraordinary degree to which Johnson was attuned to Soviet behavior once the war actually began. If during the May crisis he had been prepared to see the conflict primarily in terms of Arabs and Israelis, once hostilities were under way the main focus of his attention was the Soviet Union. With Israel secure from defeat by the Arabs, only Soviet behavior could trigger a direct American military response. The regional dispute paled in significance before the danger of superpower confrontation.

The risk of Soviet intervention appeared once again before an effective cease-fire on all fronts went into effect on the sixth day, June 10. On the Syrian front, where fighting was particularly intense on June 9 and 10, the Israelis seemed capable of threatening Damascus. Although American officials were quite sure that Israel was on the verge of agreeing to a cease-fire once the Golan Heights had been secured, the Soviets apparently were less sanguine. At about 9:00 A.M. Washington time, they sent a hot-line message to Johnson warning that they would take necessary actions, "including military," if Israel did not stop its advance.[51] Johnson responded by assuring the Soviets that Israel was prepared to stop and by instructing McNamara to turn the Sixth Fleet toward the Syrian coast to make certain that the Soviet Union would not underestimate Johnson's determination to meet any Soviet military move with one of his own. By noon the crisis was nearly over, a cease-fire soon went into effect, and the Sixth Fleet stopped its eastward movement. The war was over. Once again, a new situation existed and new policies were called for.

POSTWAR DIPLOMACY

Johnson and his advisers were mindful of how Eisenhower had dealt with the Israelis after the Suez war. They were determined not to adopt the same strategy of forcing Israel to withdraw from conquered territories in return for little in the way of Arab concessions. This did not mean that the United States endorsed Israel's indefinite hold on the occupied territories, but rather that the territories should be exchanged for a genuine peace agreement, something that had been missing in the Middle East ever since Israel's creation. This would take time, obviously, but time seemed to be on Israel's side. And the Israelis had officially made it clear that they did not intend

51. Johnson, op. cit., pp. 301–02. Other participants in the events have judged Johnson's version overly dramatic.

to enlarge their borders as a result of the war.[52] The need, as American officials saw it, was to establish a diplomatic framework for a peace settlement, and then to allow time to pass until the Arabs were prepared to negotiate to recover their territories. Apart from helping to establish the diplomatic framework, the United States need only ensure that the military balance not shift against Israel. This was not very likely in the near future, however, because the Egyptian, Syrian, and Jordanian armed forces lay in ruins.

Johnson apparently did not believe that the United States should launch a high-level, intensive peacemaking effort immediately. Either he considered that such a move could not succeed, given the minimal influence of the United States in Arab capitals, or he did not feel that he could sustain such an effort at a time when Vietnam was demanding so much of his attention. In either event, the option never seems to have been considered seriously. Instead, a general outline of a settlement was suggested by Johnson in a major policy statement on June 19, on the eve of his meeting with Soviet Premier Kosygin at Glassboro.

Johnson clearly placed the major responsibility for the war on Egypt, terming the closure of the Strait of Tiran an "act of folly." He then stated that the United States would not press Israel to withdraw in the absence of peace. Five principles essential to such a peace were spelled out: the recognized right to national life; justice for the refugees; innocent maritime passage; limits on the arms race; and political independence and territorial integrity for all. In brief, a full settlement of all the issues stemming from 1947–49 and 1967 was contemplated.

In the course of the next five months, American diplomatic efforts were aimed at achieving a UN Security Council resolution that would incorporate Johnson's five points. The key areas of disagreement between Israel and the Arabs, as well as between the United States and the Soviet Union, rapidly emerged. The Arabs insisted upon full Israeli withdrawal from newly occupied territory prior to the end of belligerency. Israel, on the other hand, held out for direct negotiations and a "package settlement" in which withdrawal would occur only after the conclusion of a peace agreement. The Soviet Union generally backed the Arab position, whereas the United States agreed

52. Evron conveyed this to Walt Rostow on June 5.

with Israel on the "package" approach, but was less insistent on direct negotiations.

As to the withdrawal of Israeli forces, the American position changed between June and November. Initially, the United States was prepared to support a Latin American draft resolution which called on Israel to "withdraw all its forces from all territories occupied by it as a result of the recent conflict." The resolution was defeated, as was a tentative joint U.S.-Soviet draft in mid-July that was never considered because of radical Arab objections to provisions calling for an end of war with Israel. In late August, the Arab position hardened further at the Khartoum conference, where Nasser and Hussein, in return for subsidies from the oil-producing Arab countries, were obliged to subscribe to guidelines for a political settlement with Israel based on no recognition, no negotiations, no peace agreement, and no abandonment of Palestinian rights.[53]

When the UN debate resumed in late October, the United States position had shifted to support for "withdrawal of armed forces from occupied territories." The ambiguity was intentional and represented the maximum that Israel was prepared to accept. Finally, on November 22, 1967, UN Resolution 242 was passed.[54] It incorporated all of Johnson's five points, along with a delicately balanced call for "withdrawal of Israeli armed forces from territories occupied in the recent conflict" and "termination of all claims of belligerency and respect for and acknowledgement of the sovereignty, territorial integrity, and political independence of every state in the area and their right to live in peace within secure and recognized boundaries free from threats or acts of force." In brief, the resolution fell just short of calling on Israel to withdraw from all territories and on the Arabs to make "full peace" with Israel. Much of the diplomacy of the subsequent years revolved around efforts to make more precise and binding the deliberately vague language of Resolution 242. The resolution called for a UN-appointed representative to work with the parties to

53. See Arthur S. Lall, *The UN and the Middle East Crisis, 1967* (New York: Columbia University Press, 1968).

54. In order to obtain their acceptance of the resolution, the American ambassador to the UN, Arthur Goldberg, gave assurances to the Jordanians that the United States would work for the return of the west bank to Jordanian authority. When George Ball, who became United States ambassador to the UN in June 1968, visited the Middle East in mid-July, he was authorized by the Israelis to convey to King Hussein that they were prepared to return the west bank, with minor modifications, to his authority in return for peace.

find a solution, a task which fell to Gunnar Jarring, a Swedish diplomat who had had considerable diplomatic experience in the Middle East.

During most of 1968, the Johnson administration assumed a comparatively low profile in Arab-Israeli diplomacy, leaving the main task to Jarring. In private, American officials consistently told the Israelis that a peace settlement would have to be based on virtually complete Israeli withdrawal, but in public, nothing was said to modify the language of Resolution 242. Johnson was clearly preoccupied with Vietnam, especially after the Tet offensive in February, and in late March he announced his intention not to seek the presidency for another term, a decision which set off an intense political campaign within his own party and, after Hubert Humphrey's nomination, between the two parties. In this atmosphere, major initiatives for peace in the Middle East could not be expected. Instead, Johnson acted to ensure that the post-1967 status quo would not be disrupted by Soviet arms shipments to Syria and Egypt. With a war on his hands in Vietnam, he was not anxious to see a resumption of fighting in the Middle East. In January 1968, the American embargo on new arms shipments to the region was ended.[55] Both Jordan and Israel were the beneficiaries, although on quite different scales.[56]

Johnson met with Prime Minister Eshkol in January 1968 to discuss Israeli arms requests. Topping the Israeli list was the high-performance F-4 Phantom jet. Before 1967, the United States had not been a primary supplier of military equipment to Israel. The Israeli air force was of French origin, but France, because of de Gaulle's Arab policy, was no longer a reliable arms supplier, hence the need for American arms.

Johnson reportedly assured Eshkol that Phantoms would be provided, but the terms, the timing, and possible conditions were left unspecified.[57] Within the bureaucracy, many officials felt that the

55. On Oct. 25, 1967, the State Department announced that 48 A-4 Skyhawk jets, agreed on in February 1966, would be delivered to Israel. This came one day after the Egyptian sinking of the Israeli naval ship *Elath*. Eventually, the Johnson administration agreed to sell a total of 100 A-4s to Israel.

56. Israeli Prime Minister Eshkol stated in *Davar*, Jan. 24, 1969, that Johnson had effectively given him a veto over whether the United States should sell tanks to Jordan.

57. Johnson reportedly delayed announcing his tentative decision on the F-4s in the hope of interesting the Soviets in an arms-limitation agreement for the Middle East. The Soviet position was consistent and negative: prior to a political settlement, there could be no agreement to limit arms to the area.

United States should use the furnishing of F-4s to extract some concessions from Israel. Two possibilities were considered. First, in order to reverse Israel's growing appetite for territory, some felt that Israel should be asked to agree to the principle of full withdrawal in the context of peace in exchange for the jets. Others, who were fearful of Israeli nuclear development, argued that Israel should be required to sign the nonproliferation treaty (NPT) before receiving U.S. arms.

The NPT issue was discussed at length with Israeli representatives. The most the Israelis would say was that they would not be the first ones to "introduce" nuclear weapons in the Middle East. In trying to clarify what this meant, United States officials discovered that it was understood by Israeli Ambassador Rabin to mean that Israel would not be the first to "test" such weapons or to reveal their existence publicly. Paul Warnke, Assistant Secretary of Defense, then sent a letter to Rabin spelling out the American understanding of what nonintroduction of nuclear weapons meant: no production of a nuclear device. Before the issue was ever resolved, Johnson ordered the bureaucracy to end the search for a quid pro quo on the F-4s. Pressures were mounting for an affirmative United States response to the Israeli request; political candidates were all endorsing the Israeli position; in July the Senate passed a resolution calling for the sale of F-4s to Israel. Finally, on October 9, Johnson publicly announced that Israel would be allowed to purchase the Phantoms.[58] A deal for fifty F-4s was signed in late December, providing for delivery of sixteen aircraft late in 1969 and the rest in 1970.

Perhaps in the hope of offsetting negative Arab reactions to the Phantom deal, Secretary of State Dean Rusk informed the Egyptians on November 2 that the United States favored full Israeli withdrawal from Sinai as part of a peace settlement. A year later, this position was publicly disclosed in the "Rogers Plan," but in fact it had consistently been part of the American official consensus on the terms of an Israeli-Egyptian agreement. It did little, however, to win the confidence of the Israelis, and the last months of the Johnson administration were marked by a perceptible chill between the two countries.

58. The announcement came after unsuccessful talks earlier in October between Rusk and Gromyko on limiting arms to the Middle East. The atmosphere created by the Soviet invasion of Czechoslovakia in August had made agreement in such talks unlikely. In addition, on Oct. 8, Israeli Foreign Minister Eban presented a nine-point "peace plan" to the UN. Eban, consistent with American preferences, subsequently downplayed the need for direct negotiations and endorsed Resolution 242 as a useful set of principles "which can help the parties and guide them in their search for a solution."

In December, with the Nixon administration on the verge of taking office, the Soviet Union sent the United States a diplomatic note urging a more active search for an Arab-Israeli settlement. Britain and France were also pushing for a role in any Middle East peace talks. But time had run out on the Johnson presidency, and these issues would be passed on to Richard Nixon, against a background of escalating violence and mounting guerilla activity on the part of the Palestinian fedayeen.

ANALYZING JOHNSON'S MIDDLE EAST POLICY

The development of American policy before, during, and after the June 1967 Arab-Israeli war highlights the importance of a few key assumptions held by top decision makers, especially the president, at each stage of the crisis. The reality of the situation in the Middle East in May and June 1967 was extraordinarily complex. To make sense out of the flow of events, some guidelines, some simplifying assumptions, were essential for decision makers. They were found, not surprisingly, among the "lessons of the past" and the categorical inferences that had served well in other circumstances. An element of wishful thinking also existed. Together, several key principles provided a gyroscope of sorts for the decision-making process; order was perceived where it might have otherwise been missing.

The basic principles from which policy flowed in each of the phases of the crisis can be summarized as follows:

—*Pre-war imperatives*: No unilateral use of American force; therefore try to prevent hostilities and develop a multilateral context to end the blockade of the Strait of Tiran.

—*Wartime policy*: Deter Soviet intervention; seek a cease-fire (but not a return to the status quo ante, which had been dangerous and unstable).

—*Postwar policy*: Try for "full peace"; territory would ultimately be traded for peace; keep Israel strong through arms shipments.

Several things about the decision-making process during the crisis are noteworthy. First is the obvious preeminence of the president. Crises, by their very nature, bring the president to the center of the policy-making arena. His perceptions tend to define the situation for others; his needs tend to dominate the process. In May and June, this meant a great sensitivity to congressional views, a desire not to become involved in a second war, and a hope that time could be found to pursue the more cumbersome, but politically preferable, multi-lateral alternative. When this policy failed on June 5, it was primarily the president again who defined the stakes in the new game, as he did once more after the cease-fire went into effect on June 10.

Although there was not complete agreement on policy among Johnson's advisers during the crisis, there was nonetheless a remarkable degree of consensus. No one made a case for unilateral United States action; only a few voices were raised on behalf of "unleashing Israel"; little debate occurred over policy on a cease-fire in place as opposed to a cease-fire plus withdrawal; nor did anyone challenge the "package settlement" approach that emerged almost imperceptibly after the war. When divergent perceptions did appear, they seem to have been more deeply rooted in bureaucratic rivalries than anything else. For example, on political-diplomatic grounds, both Secretary Rusk and Under Secretary Rostow strongly favored the multinational fleet. McNamara and the professional military men were skeptical of the fleet on military grounds and were doubtless not anxious to see forces diverted from Vietnam or NATO for use in the Middle East. Small, politically motivated uses of force are not exactly what the Pentagon tends to favor.

Advisers did not split along pro-Israeli or pro-Arab lines. In fact, it would be hard to say what course of action might be most dangerous for American interests in the Arab world. Some American ambassadors in the Arab countries, sensing that war was inevitable, hoped that Israel would act quickly, but on a limited scale, to break the blockade without involving the United States. This came very close to being the "unleash Israel" option that the Israelis were seeking by late May. The State Department, however, normally thought to "tilt" toward the Arabs, did not favor this option, at least not at the policy-making level of Rusk and Rostow.

An important lesson of the crisis, and one that is often encountered in Middle Eastern policy making, is that American policy choices rarely come to be seen in simple pro-Israeli or pro-Arab terms. Thus, individuals, whatever their particular sympathies, may find themselves in support of policies which to the outside observer seem inconsistent with their sympathies. In a crisis, however, policy evolves in complex circumstances, is defined under presidential directive, and comes to be rationalized in terms of principles that are easily supported by high-level policy makers.

What seems to have been missing from the policy-making process during the crisis was an explicit effort to relate policies to outcomes, as the rational decision maker is supposed to do. To a limited degree, of course, outcomes are discussed. But no one seems to have thought through the full implications of Israel's going to war, especially the problems that this might cause in the long run. The future is indeed unknowable, but policy makers do have to consider consequences. They do so, however, in fairly simple ways. For example, the extremely low-probability event of Israel's being militarily defeated by the Arabs was given serious consideration by Johnson, to the point of becoming one of the chief reasons for his effort to restrain Israel. The more likely outcome, as predicted by the intelligence community, of rapid Israeli victory was acknowledged, but its consequences were not thought through in detail. No one asked what Israel would do with Sinai, the West Bank, and the Golan Heights after the war was over. Would east Jerusalem ever be returned to Jordan once it had been conquered in war? What would happen to the Palestinians on the West Bank? These were all important questions, and came to be seen as such after 1967, but they paled in comparison with the overriding question of what would happen if Israel were to face defeat.

Noteworthy by their unimportance during the crisis were the allegedly powerful pro-Israeli interest groups and the oil lobby. Johnson was sympathetic to Israel already and did not need to be reminded of the United States interest in supporting the Jewish state. But the president showed no sign of being preoccupied with the "Jewish vote" or the pro-Israeli lobby during the prewar crisis. His political concerns focused on Congress, where he feared lack of support for actions that he might want to take on Israel's behalf. The normally pro-Israeli Congress was in a hesitant frame of mind, and this induced Johnson to use caution in dealing with the crisis. Once the war had begun, and especially in its aftermath, the extremely pro-Israeli tone of American public opinion, coupled with Nasser's hostility, probably did make it easier for Johnson to maintain a policy of support for Israel. Lobbying, however, was not a significant factor.

Oil was of only marginal significance to the formulation of policy. It was clear to some policy makers that any increase in Nasser's prestige would eventually bring pressure to bear on the oil-rich Arab countries, such as Saudi Arabia and Libya. This was undesirable and added an incentive to the other reasons for trying to force Nasser to back down from the closure of the strait. In addition, there was some recognition that unilateral American use of force to open the strait could damage United States interests in the oil-producing Arab countries. There was some fear, too, that an oil embargo as part of an Arab-Israeli war might have dangerous consequences for NATO allies and Japan. But, on balance, oil was very much a secondary factor in presidential policy considerations in 1967.[59]

Finally, an important lesson of the policy-making process in the 1967 Arab-Israeli crisis is that the initial definition of a situation tends to endure unless subjected to overwhelming disconfirming evidence from external sources. Between May 16 and June 5, Johnson and his key aides maintained essentially the same basic perceptions, adding details to a framework created in the initial stages of the crisis but not basically altering policy until the outbreak of war. At that point a new definition was required and was quickly provided. Not surprisingly, the Soviet Union assumed a much greater salience once war had begun.[60] Then, with the cease-fire achieved, the third basic policy framework emerged, which emphasized the need to pursue a full peace agreement. This last policy was largely a reaction to the 1956–57 approach of pressing Israel for immediate withdrawal. The war of 1967 had shown that the Eisenhower decision had not brought peace; Johnson had opposed it at the time and now he had the chance to try an alternative approach. With little discussion and no apparent dissent, the United States found itself supporting Israel's hold on the newly conquered territories pending Arab willingness to make peace. It would not be long before the dilemmas of such a policy would become evident.

59. The United States was not heavily dependent in 1967 on Arab oil. Walter Levy, acting as adviser to the State Department, correctly predicted that an Arab oil embargo would not be very effective.

60. Some new faces were added to the circle of Johnson's advisers once war broke out—in particular, McGeorge Bundy.

CHAPTER III

The Rogers Initiatives
of 1969–70

RICHARD M. NIXON was, to say the least, an unusual president. By the time he resigned from office in disgrace on August 9, 1974, his domestic support had virtually disappeared. The Watergate scandal, exposed in exquisite detail by the press, Congress, and the tapes of the president's conversations, revealed a man in the White House who lied, who was vindictive, and who appeared to be strangely indecisive and incoherent when it came to dealing with important policy issues. Many Americans, as well as foreigners, had difficulty reconciling this image with that of the Richard Nixon who was overwhelmingly reelected in 1972 to a second term in office, a man whose achievements in the realm of foreign policy won him the grudging support of many former opponents.

These two faces of President Nixon were no doubt part of the same complex, unhappy personality, but it is Nixon as foreign-policy strategist who is of primary concern here. Nixon viewed his experience in international affairs as one of his strongest assets and foreign relations as a particularly important arena for presidential action. As Eisenhower's vice-president for eight years, Nixon had been on the margins of key foreign-policy decisions of the 1950s. He had earned a reputation as a tough-minded anticommunist and an advocate of a strong international role for the United States.

During his period of exile from elective politics, from 1960 to 1968, Nixon had traveled widely and had met many heads of state.

These trips must have made an impression on him, for he spoke of them frequently in later years. In discussions of the Middle East, he would refer to his talks with Israeli, Egyptian, and Saudi leaders, emphasizing his personal knowledge of key individuals and their countries. His experience in foreign affairs, such as it was, came large-ly through his own first-hand experience and discussions. He had little patience with academic studies or lengthy briefing materials.

Unlike President Johnson, Nixon never betrayed a strong desire to immerse himself in the day-to-day flow of events and information. He prided himself instead on his detachment and his analytical ability to see problems in their broad strategic context. He admired strength and toughness, and firmly believed that foreign policy should be formulated in secret, with only minimal contributions from Congress and public opinion. During the Watergate crisis, Nixon used the "national security" argument so frequently in his attempts to limit the investigation that his genuine concern for the need for confiden-tiality was no longer taken seriously. But in his early years, Nixon played his foreign-policy cards very close to his chest. The circle of his advisers was small. Few ever knew what the president was thinking.

THE NIXON TEAM

From the outset it was clear that President Nixon intended to make the basic decisions in foreign policy. To ensure his control of the vast foreign-policy bureaucracy—which he distrusted as being a bastion of the Democrats—he decided to reinvigorate the National Security Council system.[1] Nixon's NSC evolved substantially over the years, but at the outset it was designed for two purposes: to provide the president with genuine policy alternatives, or options; and to educate the bureaucracy concerning the new themes in Nixon's foreign policy. Toward both of these ends, Nixon requested an un-precedented number of policy studies in his first few months in of-fice, mostly in the form of National Security Study Memoranda (NSSM). These were to be discussed by a Senior Review Group (SRG),[2] then referred to the full NSC for decision, after which a National Security Decision Memorandum (NSDM) would be issued. Overseeing this elaborate system was a former Harvard professor, Henry A. Kissinger, Nixon's national security affairs adviser.

---

1. See I. M. Destler, *Presidents, Bureaucrats and Foreign Policy* (Princeton: Princeton University Press, 1972), pp. 121-27, for a description of the NSC under Nixon.
2. Initially, this was called the Interdepartmental Group (IG).

Kissinger was a well-known foreign-policy analyst. He first gained public recognition with the publication of an influential book in 1957, *Nuclear Weapons and Foreign Policy*. Subsequently he became a consultant to both the Kennedy and Johnson administrations, but his closest ties were with his earliest patron, Nelson Rockefeller. Kissinger's acceptance of the national security affairs position was as unexpected as Nixon's offer. The two men seemed fundamentally different in temperament and character, but they quickly recognized in each other a remarkable intellectual compatibility. Nixon was instinctual and decisive; Kissinger was analytical and subtle. Nevertheless, they held similar views of the international role of the United States, of the need for strength wedded to diplomacy, of the intimate links between domestic and foreign policy, and of the danger of nuclear war. Within a short time, the Nixon-Kissinger team was working smoothly, and Kissinger had ascended from the obscurity of the White House basement to a well-appointed office on the first floor of the west wing.[3] Nixon and Kissinger both had a keen sense for the symbols as well as the realities of power.

For the position of secretary of state, Nixon named a close personal friend, William P. Rogers, a lawyer by profession, who had served as attorney general in Eisenhower's cabinet. He was not particularly experienced in foreign policy, nor was his a strong, assertive personality. He did, however, have an affable, reassuring style and a dignified bearing. Given the modest role that Nixon envisaged for him, this was perhaps enough.

If Rogers seemed unlikely to be a particularly aggressive secretary of state, some of his subordinates in the department were men of considerable talent, energy, and ambition. Elliot Richardson, during his brief tenure as under secretary, played an important role in the running of the department and in keeping lines open to the White House. Unlike Rogers, Richardson quickly developed a close working relationship with Kissinger.

The new assistant secretary of state for the Near East and South Asia was a controversial figure. Joseph Sisco, formerly assistant secretary of state for international organizations, was a Democrat and

---

3. Kissinger's staff consisted of several close personal assistants as well as specialists in certain geographic and functional areas. Those who participated in Middle East policy included his deputy, Alexander Haig, two special assistants, Peter Rodman and Winston Lord, and his senior Middle East specialist, Harold H. Saunders, who had been on the NSC staff since the Kennedy administration.

had never served overseas in his long career in the State Department. His knowledge of the Middle East came from his years in Washington. He was a consummate bureaucratic politician; he knew the ins and the outs of the State Department; he was a man of drive, a skillful speaker, and a shrewd tactician. Working closely with him was Alfred ("Roy") Atherton, first as office director for Israel and Arab-Israeli affairs and later as deputy assistant secretary for the Near East. Atherton represented continuity, experience, professional expertise. He was cool when Sisco was hot. The two were a formidable pair in Middle East policy-making circles.[4]

Nixon's other appointees in the foreign-policy arena had less direct influence on Middle East policy. Melvin Laird, secretary of defense, was preoccupied with Vietnam, the defense budget, and relations with his former colleagues in Congress. The chairman of the joint chiefs of staff, General Earl Wheeler, played little part in decisions affecting the Middle East. CIA Director Richard Helms occupied a particularly sensitive position, for the CIA was directly responsible to the NSC and was used by Nixon as a source of alternative views and channels of communication to those provided by the State Department. He was not, however, a strong advocate of specific policies in the Middle East.[5]

Finally, Nixon surrounded himself with a number of advisers, assistants, and colleagues who were primarily concerned with domestic affairs but who inevitably had some influence on foreign policy as well. Chief among these were John Mitchell, the attorney general; H.R. Haldeman, Nixon's chief of staff; and John Ehrlichman, personal counsel to the president and later head of the Domestic Council. Although rarely involved in policy making on the Middle East, these men seem to have played an important role in reinforcing Nixon's view of the world as divided into friends and enemies, and

4. Two other office directors were influential in the shaping of Middle East policy during this period: Richard Parker, in charge of Egyptian affairs, and Talcott Seelye, office director for Arab Republic Affairs (ARA), which covered Jordan, Lebanon, Syria, and Iraq. Deputy Assistant Secretary Rodger Davies was also involved in most of the policy deliberations during this period. These three men were all "Arabists," in the sense of being familiar with the Arab world and knowing Arabic fluently.

5. The CIA was organized in a peculiar way with respect to the Middle East. The division normally responsible for the region did not cover Israel. That was handled by James Angleton, nicknamed "mother," a curious personality whose other function consisted of heading counterintelligence operations. He finally resigned under pressure in 1974 and Israeli affairs returned to the responsibility of the national intelligence officer in charge of the Middle East.

they doubtless emphasized in private talks with the president the links they saw between foreign policy and the president's domestic support.

NIXON'S FOREIGN POLICY

President Nixon, with the assistance of Henry Kissinger and some parts of the State Department, quickly established a set of priorities and guidelines for American foreign policy. Some represented new departures; others reflected continuities and standard responses to long-standing problems.

Inevitably, Vietnam stood at the top of Nixon's agenda of foreign-policy issues. Domestic dissent over Vietnam had destroyed Lyndon Johnson's chances for reelection and had produced a grave crisis of confidence and of conscience within the United States. Nixon was no doubt less tempted by the prospects of "victory" in Vietnam than Johnson had been, but at the same time he was strongly opposed to a sudden withdrawal of American forces. Kissinger, before being named to his White House post, had spelled out a middle-of-the-road strategy for negotiations and the disengagement of American troops from Vietnam. In an article published in January 1969, he expressed a concern that was to haunt the Nixon administration throughout its first term: ". . . what is involved now is confidence in American promises. However fashionable it is to ridicule the terms 'credibility' and 'prestige,' they are not empty phrases; other nations can gear their actions to ours only if they can count on our steadiness."[6] In private, Nixon and Kissinger expressed the fear that a precipitate withdrawal from Vietnam, followed by a communist victory, might provoke a right-wing McCarthyite backlash in the United States and would reinforce latent isolationist sentiments. The art of managing the Vietnam commitment was to disengage United States troops in such a way that, domestically and internationally, the United States would still be able to conduct an effective foreign policy in other parts of the world, such as the Middle East, where important interests were at stake.

Apart from Vietnam, Nixon and Kissinger were primarily concerned with the other major powers, especially the Soviet Union. Both men were preoccupied with the dangers of nuclear war; both were intrigued by the possibility of establishing a new relationship with

6. Henry A. Kissinger, "The Viet Nam Negotiations," *Foreign Affairs* 47, no. 2 (January 1969), pp. 211–34.

the Soviet Union that would help to ensure global stability and to minimize the risks of confrontation; both were prepared to transcend the ideological rivalry of the Cold War and to establish ties with adversaries based on mutual interest.

Part of Nixon's strategy of restructuring the relations between the superpowers involved China. In October 1967, Nixon had published an article entitled "Asia After Viet Nam."[7] In it he wrote: "Any American policy toward Asia must come urgently to grips with the reality of China." Little public notice was taken of China during Nixon's first two years in office, but it is clear in retrospect that the president and Kissinger were already laying the ground work for a dramatic opening to Peking. Apart from intrinsic benefits in opening U.S.-Chinese relations after a generation of hostility, Nixon recognized that an American-Chinese connection could have a moderating effect on Soviet foreign policy. In addition, improved ties to Moscow and Peking might help bring about a Vietnam settlement and ensure that the post-Vietnam era in Asia would be comparatively free of conflict. Consequently, Vietnam, the Soviet Union, and China came to be linked as priority concerns to the Nixon Administration. Significantly, each was managed almost exclusively from the White House, the President providing general guidance and Kissinger and his staff working on the details of the new policies and overseeing their implementation.

One priority area remained for the State Department to deal with: the Middle East. The Arab-Israeli conflict was recognized as dangerous, although hopelessly complex and perhaps less urgent than the other tasks facing the administration. Some momentum had already been established under Johnson, and around it a modified policy might be constructed. The State Department was anxious to play a leading role and was able to call on impressive expertise. Thus, with some skepticism about the likelihood of results, Nixon authorized the State Department to develop and carry forward a new American policy toward the Arab-Israeli conflict. If it should succeed, there would be credit enough for everyone; if it were to fail, Nixon and Kissinger would be relatively free of blame.

With these priorities—Vietnam, the Soviet Union, China, and the Middle East—in mind, Nixon articulated several themes that would become code words of his foreign policy. First was his emphasis

7. Richard M. Nixon, "Asia After Viet Nam," *Foreign Affairs* 46, no. 1 (October 1967), pp. 111-25.

on the concept of "linkage." Linkage meant that issues would not be negotiated in isolation from one another. Rather, the United States in its talks with the Soviet Union would aim for a global settlement of issues. Progress should be made across the board on Vietnam, strategic-arms talks, and the Middle East. Simultaneous negotiations in each of these areas would mean that trade-offs could be made, thus adding flexibility and nuance to the negotiations. A Soviet concession on Vietnam might be reciprocated by an American move in the Middle East. As an intellectual construct, it made sense; in practice, it rarely worked. Nevertheless, throughout 1969, linkage was one of the key concepts of the Nixon foreign policy.

"Negotiations" became another theme of the Nixon diplomacy. Nixon and Kissinger shared the view that force and diplomacy must go hand in hand, which meant that negotiation with adversaries was not incompatible with threats or the actual use of military might. Kissinger in particular was fascinated by the process of negotiations and proved to be an astonishingly successful negotiator in his own right. Soon after Nixon took office, negotiations on a wide range of issues—the Middle East, Vietnam, China, and strategic arms—were begun or accelerated. The objective of the negotiations was to create, in the Nixon-Kissinger jargon, a "structure of peace," the main components of which would be U.S.-Soviet "détente," arms limitations, and eventually a normalization of U.S.-Chinese relations. All of this was to be accomplished without detriment to traditional allies—the NATO partners and Japan—and without much regard for the Third World, where détente would serve to limit the dangers to global peace inherent in local conflicts.

In order to pursue such an ambitious foreign policy at a time of great popular disenchantment, President Nixon sought to meet the demand that America no longer play the role of "world policeman," while at the same time avoiding the extreme of isolationism. This delicately balanced posture of restrained internationalism came to be known as the "Nixon Doctrine," one manifestation of which was Vietnamization—the gradual disengagement of American combat troops from Vietnam, coupled with high levels of aid to the Saigon regime and an active search for a political settlement.[8]

8. The "Nixon Doctrine" was outlined by the president on July 25, 1969, during a news conference on Guam. The first practical manifestation of the policy, "Vietnamization," was announced by Nixon in a speech delivered Nov. 3, 1969.

Nixon's great hope during his first term was that he would be able to recreate a domestic consensus on behalf of his foreign-policy goals. The style and timing of each major foreign-policy step was taken with an eye toward domestic public opinion. Vietnamization and the end of the draft helped to ease the divisions created by the war, and the prospect of a peace agreement during 1972 greatly enhanced Nixon's popularity. The spectacular opening to China, carried out in total secrecy and with high drama, also strengthened the Nixon-Kissinger team. Finally, the SALT agreement of May 1972 seemed to hold out the promise of an end to the nuclear-arms race. Against these successes, the lack of progress in the Middle East counted for comparatively little. Yet, for our purposes, it is extremely important to understand how the Nixon administration approached the Arab-Israeli conflict, how policy evolved as time went on, and why it failed.

MIDDLE-EAST INTERESTS

Two sets of concerns dominated the thinking of policy makers in early 1969 as the administration undertook its first review of the situation in the Middle East. The president and Kissinger seemed to be chiefly worried by the global ramifications of the Arab-Israeli conflict. Nixon repeatedly used highly colored and explosive imagery in describing the area. Again and again the theme of confrontation between the superpowers was mentioned in discussions of the Middle East. This, it was said, was what made the Arab-Israeli conflict even more dangerous than Vietnam.

The State Department professionals tended to agree that the situation in the Middle East was dangerous, but their perceptions were more affected by the threats to United States interests arising from trends in the area. At State, one heard of the "erosion" of American influence, of "deterioration" of the American position, of "radicalization," and of "polarization." The region was viewed in stark, sometimes simplistic terms: the United States, with Israel and the "moderate" Arabs, aligned against the Soviet Union and the "radical" Arabs. It was widely believed that the continuation of the Arab-Israeli conflict would work to the advantage of the Soviet Union, resulting in the isolation of the United States and Israel in a sea of radical, anti-American Arabs. The rise of the militant Palestinian fedayeen movement during 1968 was a harbinger of things to come:

increased violence and terrorism, direct threats to American lives and
interests, mounting instability, and eventually another war.[9] The
White House and the Departments of State and Defense were all
concerned with one other issue involving the Middle East: the possibility that Israel would develop, or possibly already had developed,
nuclear weapons. This fear brought together those who worried about
regional trends and those who were preoccupied by global, strategic
issues. No one knew quite what to do about the Israeli nuclear option,
but it added to the sense that the Middle East was too dangerous to
ignore.[10]

The combination of these preoccupations led to several related
policy guidelines that shaped the American approach to the Middle
East from early 1969 until August 1970. Most important was the
broad consensus that the United States should adopt an active diplomatic role in promoting a political settlement based on the principles
embodied in UN Resolution 242. The efforts of the Johnson administration were judged as having been too passive, those of UN Ambassador Gunnar Jarring as too cautious. The United States, in concert
with the other major powers, and in particular the Soviet Union,
should therefore seek to engage the regional parties in a negotiating
process, the first step of which would be a refinement of the principles
of a settlement to be worked out in talks between the two superpowers. The hoped-for result would be considerably less than an imposed settlement, which the administration rejected, but would be
something other than the directly negotiated peace agreement that
the Israelis desired.[11] Both the White House and State were in basic
agreement on this point.

The State Department had long advocated an "even-handed"
approach to the Arab-Israeli conflict. In essence, this meant adopting
a posture which was neither overtly pro-Arab nor openly pro-Israeli.
With respect to arms deliveries to Israel, the even-handed approach

9. Middle East oil was, of course, an important concern, but United States dependence
on Arab oil was still virtually nil in 1969–70; prices were comparatively low; alternative sources
seemed available. The main worry was continued supply of oil to Europe and Japan and, to a
lesser degree, the repatriation of profits of American oil companies and their favorable
contribution to the United States balance of payments.
10. It was feared that excessive pressure on Israel, such as withholding conventional
arms, might accelerate Israel's search for a nuclear option. Indifference, on the other hand,
might also encourage the Israelis to go ahead with their program.
11. The administration's opposition to an imposed settlement was twofold: it probably
would not last for long, because the parties would have little sense of commitment to its terms
and outside powers would tire of trying to enforce it; and it would be unfavorably received
in this country.

urged restraint, and on territorial withdrawal, it favored a clear statement opposing Israeli acquisition of territory from the 1967 war. As to the quality of the peace agreement, the standards to be applied to Arab commitments were not overly rigorous. From the Israeli perspective, an "even-handed" American policy was tantamount to being pro-Arab. When President-elect Nixon's special emissary to the Middle East, Governor William Scranton, used the word "even-handed" in December 1968, it set off shock waves in Israel.

Fortunately for the Israelis, the White House was less committed to "even-handedness" than State, and at an early date the Israelis began to bypass Rogers in favor of direct dealing with Nixon and Kissinger. Both men were primarily concerned with the outbreak of war in the Middle East and the danger of nuclear confrontation. If the Arabs were to lose again, the Soviets might feel obliged to intervene; if the Israelis were under severe military pressure, the Americans could not stand aside. The intervention by one superpower would almost automatically trigger a reaction from the other. Detailed scenarios of confrontation were not developed, but the possibility was nonetheless taken seriously. The conclusion reached was that the military balance—however defined—must be maintained in Israel's favor. Otherwise the Arabs might be tempted to resort to force. Johnson having already agreed to the sale of 100 A-4s and 50 F-4s, there was no immediate pressure on the president to provide new arms to Israel, but the military balance would bear careful watching. Soviet arms aid to the Arabs would not go unchecked for long by comparable deliveries to Israel. In principle, this perspective was significantly different from that of the proponents of an "even-handed" policy, but during most of 1969 the contradiction was dormant. It was not until 1970 that the two views came into conflict, with serious results for United States policy in the area.

POLICY MAKING

In January 1969, President Nixon clearly viewed the Middle East situation as potentially dangerous. His thinking is best reflected in his answers to questions posed during a press conference on January 27, 1969, just one week after he took office:

> What I want to do is to see to it that we have strategic-arms talks in a way and at a time that will promote, if possible, progress on outstanding political problems at the same time—for example, on the problem

of the Mideast and on other outstanding problems in which the United States and the Soviet Union, acting together, can serve the cause of peace. . . . I believe we need new initiatives and new leadership on the part of the United States in order to cool off the situation in the Mideast. I consider it a powder keg, very explosive. It needs to be defused. I am open to any suggestions that may cool it off and reduce the possibility of another explosion, because the next explosion in the Mideast, I think, could involve very well a confrontation between the nuclear powers, which we want to avoid.[12]

On February 1, the National Security Council met for an exhaustive review of Middle East policy. Three basic alternatives, each discussed at length in NSSM 2, were considered:
—Leave the search for a settlement of the Arab-Israeli conflict to the parties and to Ambassador Jarring.
—Pursue a more active United States policy, involving U.S.-U.S.S.R. talks.
—Assume that no settlement is possible and concentrate efforts on objectives short of a settlement.
The second alternative was decided upon, the third remaining available as a fall-back position in the event of failure. The NSC discussions identified several principles that should guide United States policy.
—The parties to the dispute must participate in the negotiations at some point in the process. Although the United States would not hesitate to move somewhat ahead of Israel, any final agreement would be reached only with Israel's participation and consent.
—The objective of a settlement would be a binding agreement, not necessarily in the form of a peace treaty, but involving some form of contractual commitments. The administration was concerned about the imbalance in the concessions to be sought from each side. The Israelis would give up territory; the Arabs would give promises to respect Israel's sovereignty.
—Withdrawal of Israeli forces should take place back to the international frontier between Israel and Egypt, with a special arrangement for Gaza. There should be Israeli evacuation of the West Bank of Jordan, with only minor border changes.
—Some critical areas should be demilitarized.

12. President Nixon, news conference on Jan. 27, 1969, *Department of State Bulletin*, Feb. 17, 1969, pp. 142–43.

—Jordan should have a civilian and religious role within a unified city of Jerusalem.

—There should be a settlement of the refugee problem.

Issues of a guarantee to Israel and assurances of arms were also discussed. Then the NSC considered two possible diplomatic strategies. First, the United States could unilaterally present a peace plan. This was rejected. Second, the United States could follow a "step-by-step" approach whereby specific elements of a settlement would be gradually injected into the negotiations. It was recognized that withdrawal and the nature of the peace agreement would be the most critical issues. Primacy would be given to developing common ground in the U.S.-Soviet talks, with the aim of producing a joint document that could then be approved by the four powers and given to Jarring to present to the local parties.[13]

On February 4, Nixon again met with the NSC to discuss the Middle East. This time he asked for a study that would describe a peace settlement, assess its acceptability to the parties, and discuss the role of outside guarantees. He also asked what the links would be between the two-power and four-power talks. Finally, he asked what the United States should plan to do if a general settlement was impossible. The following day, Nixon announced that the United States was preparing a new initiative in the Middle East on a multilateral basis in order to head off a "major war." For the remainder of the year, United States policy adhered closely to the guidelines laid down in February. The eventual result was the "Rogers Plan."

LAUNCHING THE ROGERS PLAN

During the last week of February, President Nixon traveled to Europe. In France, he spoke with President de Gaulle about four-power talks on the Middle East involving the United States, the Soviet Union, Great Britain, and France. He also told de Gaulle of his hope that a U.S.-China dialogue might begin. De Gaulle promised to help. By coincidence, the Soviet-Chinese relationship was at that moment at a particularly low ebb, and military clashes were taking place along the Ussuri River.

Shortly after his return from Europe, Nixon and Rogers met with Soviet Ambassador Anatoly Dobrynin. At a news conference on

13. This account was obtained in interviews with participants in the first NSC policy review of the Middle East.

March 4, the president stated: "We have had encouraging talks with
the Soviet ambassador—the secretary of state and I have both talked
with the Soviet ambassador—with regard to the Mideast. We will
continue these bilateral consultations, and if they continue at their
present rate of progress, it seems likely that there will be four-power
discussions at the UN on the Middle East."[14]

In effect, several simultaneous rounds of negotiations were soon
underway. U.S.-Israeli meetings were frequent, as the administration
tried to allay the apprehensions of the Israeli government, now
headed by Prime Minister Golda Meir.[15] Once the U.S.-Soviet talks
began in earnest, Israel was initially kept closely informed of the
progress in the talks, although by the fall this pattern of consultations
had weakened. Finally, the four-power talks proceeded simultaneously with the U.S.-Soviet ones.

Although each set of negotiations was important, it was the U.S.-
Soviet talks that took center stage. Between March 18 and April 22,
Assistant Secretary Sisco met for substantive talks with Soviet Ambassador Dobrynin on nine occasions. The objective of this round was
to determine whether there was sufficient agreement on general principles to justify trying to reach a joint proposal. During this phase,
the United States spelled out its basic position on a settlement in a
document presented to the participants in the four-power talks on
March 24. The main points of this document were the following:

—Final borders would be agreed upon by the parties. Minor adjustments in the 1967 lines were possible.

—There would be no imposed settlement.

—The four powers would work closely with and through Ambassador Jarring.

—A final agreement would take the form of a contract signed by
all parties.

—Peace would be achieved as part of a package settlement.[16]

The last point, on the need for a package settlement, was of
fundamental importance. It meant that there would be no Israeli
withdrawal until all elements of a peace agreement on all fronts had
been achieved. This stood in stark contrast to the insistence of the

14. *New York Times*, Mar. 5, 1969.
15. Prime Minister Eshkol died on Feb. 25. Golda Meir was sworn in as head of government on Mar. 17.
16. *New York Times*, Mar. 26, 1969.

Soviets and the Arabs that Israel should withdraw first, after which an end to belligerency and other issues could be discussed.

During March and April, the situation in the Middle East began to deteriorate significantly. Fighting broke out along the Suez Canal; fedayeen attacks mounted in severity, as did Israeli retaliation; and in early April Nasser announced the abrogation of the cease-fire, initiating what came to be known as the "war of attrition." In Lebanon, a state of emergency was declared in April after clashes with the fedayeen, and for months Lebanon was virtually without a government.

Against this background, the pace of diplomacy quickened. The four powers—the United States, the Soviet Union, Great Britain and France—held their first meeting on April 3. These talks continued at regular intervals into June. Meanwhile, the United States began to talk directly with two of the Arab parties to the conflict, Jordan and Egypt. King Hussein met with Nixon and Rogers on April 8. The administration was sympathetic to Jordan, but realized that the king was unable to move on a settlement without Nasser. To help Jordan, it would also be necessary to help Egypt. Hussein did bring with him a concession from Nasser that might smooth the path of U.S.-Egyptian relations. The king publicly declared that he was authorized to state that, as part of a settlement, there would be freedom of navigation in the Suez Canal for all nations. Several days later, Nixon met with a top aide of Nasser, Mahmoud Fawzi, who confirmed this point and added privately that Egypt would not feel constrained by Syria's opposition to a political settlement. In short, Egypt and Jordan indicated that they were prepared for a settlement, even if Syria were not.

In order to assess the results of this first phase of Middle East talks, Nixon held a meeting of the NSC on April 25. The major question to be discussed was whether the United States should put forward more specific proposals for a settlement. Secretary Rogers took the position that the talks had not yet reached the "cutting edge." He noted that Nasser was an "enigma" and that the Israelis were showing a growing tendency to define security in terms of territory. It was decided that Sisco should resume his talks with Dobrynin, introducing more specific proposals as appropriate.

The American position in April on the terms of a settlement had been summarized in nine points and given to Ambassador Jarring.

These were expanded upon subsequently, but in essence they covered the major issues:

—Agreement on the full package was necessary before implementation of any part.

—The parties must engage in more direct contact at later stages of the talks.

—There must be a contractually binding peace with international participation.

—Security considerations on both sides must be taken into account and final boundaries must not reflect the weight of conquest.

—Special arrangements would be required in Gaza.

—There should be a Jordanian economic, civil, and religious role in a unified city of Jerusalem.

—The refugee problem should be settled through negotiation, with controls and conditions, to take place over a long period, or through compensation and resettlement.

—There should be free navigation in the Suez Canal and the Gulf of Aqaba.

—Special security arrangements would be necessary at Sharm al-Shaykh.

Between May 6 and May 12, Sisco conveyed the main points of the United States proposal on an Egyptian-Israeli settlement to Ambassador Dobrynin. The Soviet position had evolved somewhat, the most important change being acceptance of the idea of a package settlement.[17] In the American view, it was now up to the Soviet Union to bring pressure to bear on the Egyptians to accept these points. In return, the United States would be prepared to use its influence with Israel to gain Israeli adherence to the basic principles agreed upon by the superpowers.

A crucial debate within the American administration concerned the role of the Soviet Union. Some felt that the Soviet Union, for global-strategy reasons, would be prepared to cooperate with the United States in the Middle East, even if this might cause Moscow some strain in its relations with Nasser. In fact, it was privately hoped that the Soviets might weaken their position in Egypt by trying to force Nasser to accept the U.S.-Soviet proposals. Others doubted that the Soviets would be prepared to sacrifice regional interests for the

17. This was revealed by Secretary Rogers in a news conference on June 5, 1969; ibid., June 6, 1969, p. 5.

sake of improved U.S.-Soviet relations. They argued that the Soviet Union had worked hard to build a position of influence in the Middle East; to maintain that position, it depended chiefly on providing arms to key clients; and if peace were established, these arms would no longer be needed in large quantities. The Soviets therefore had an interest in preventing a real peace agreement, preferring instead a state of "controlled tension." From this perspective, the U.S.-Soviet talks had one purpose, as seen by Moscow and Cairo: to get the United States to pressure Israel to withdraw from Arab territory in return for only minimal Arab concessions.

An early test of Soviet intentions was provided by Soviet Foreign Minister Gromyko's trip to Cairo from June 10 to 13. After high-level talks in Moscow, which included Ambassador Dobrynin, the Soviets on June 17 made a formal counterproposal to the United States position presented to them in May by Sisco. Although the Soviet position was still not entirely compatible with the United States proposal, there was agreement on the need for a lasting peace agreement and on a package settlement. In addition, the Soviets reported that they had persuaded Nasser to accept informal direct talks with the Israelis, patterned on the Rhodes armistice negotiations in 1949.

The Soviet proposal was sufficiently encouraging to prompt further discussions. From July 14 to 17, Sisco met in Moscow with Soviet leaders, and on July 15 he presented a document to them that embodied the earlier United States proposals, which had been modified to correspond to the Soviet points of June 17. By now, the United States position on several issues was more explicit:[18]

—All territories evacuated by Israel should be demilitarized.

—The status of Gaza should be settled by negotiations including Israel, Egypt, and Jordan.

—The parties to a peace agreement would be responsible for preventing acts of force by military or paramilitary forces on their territory (e.g., Egypt and Jordan would have to control the fedayeen).

—The state of war would end on the date the accord went into effect.

—The international frontier between Egypt and Israel would "not necessarily be excluded" as the final peace border.

With the completion of Sisco's talks in Moscow, the positions of

18. See the summary of the United States and Soviet proposals in the *New York Times,* Oct. 19, 1969.

the two superpowers were fairly well defined. Each pleaded its inability to move further in the absence of concessions from the other side. In particular, the Soviet Union urged the United States to be more explicit on the final border between Egypt and Israel. Sisco had said in Moscow that a more concrete United States position might be possible on the final border if the Soviets could be more specific on Egyptian commitments to peace and on direct negotiations. In particular, the United States insisted that the state of war should end with the signing of an agreement, not with the completion of Israeli withdrawal, and also was adamant that peace was incompatible with continued fedayeen activity.

For the remainder of the summer, the positions of the superpowers remained essentially frozen,[19] but the situation in the Middle East did not. Fighting along the canal intensified; Israel informally approached the United States in July with a request for an additional 100 A-4 Skyhawks and 25 F-4 Phantoms to make up for the Mirages that France was refusing to sell.[20] Then, on September 1, one of the most conservative and pro-Western of the Arab governments, that of King Idris of Libya, was overthrown in a surprise coup d'état led by young Nasserist army officers. Coupled with the "radical" coup in Sudan the previous May, this seemed to confirm the fears of those who saw a trend toward extremism and violence in the Arab world in the absence of progress toward a peace agreement.

Early in September, the first F-4 Phantom jets (the furnishing of which had been agreed to the previous December) reached Israel. They soon became a potent symbol to the Arabs of American support for Israel, and an intensive campaign began in the Arab world to prevent further such agreements.

On September 11, another NSC meeting on the Middle East was held. The questions discussed were whether the United States should move to its fall-back position on Israeli withdrawal to the Israeli-Egyptian international frontier; whether this would alienate Israel unnecessarily and appear hypocritical to the Arabs; and whether the United States should stick to its strategy of according priority to the Israeli-Egyptian front at the expense of Jordan. It was decided that

19. Between July 31 and Aug. 25, the Soviets commented on Sisco's July 15 proposals in talks held in Moscow with Ambassador Beam. No new Soviet position was forthcoming, however.

20. Prime Minister Meir made the formal request for the 100 A-4s and 25 F-4s on Sept. 15, 1969.

the United States would continue to press for a joint U.S.-Soviet draft of principles and that the fall-back position on territory should be revealed, conditional upon satisfactory security arrangements for Gaza and Sharm al-Shaykh.

Between September 22 and 30, Rogers and Sisco met with Gromyko and Dobrynin in New York at the United Nations. President Nixon, in his speech to the UN General Assembly on September 18, had emphasized the need for "binding, irrevocable commitments" as part of a peace agreement in the Middle East. The question now was whether the Soviets would be able or willing to elicit such commitments from Egypt.

Unfortunately, the signs were not promising. On October 10, Egypt denied that it had ever agreed to the Rhodes formula for negotiations. Meanwhile, attacks on United States policy in the Middle East were mounting, especially in Lebanon, where serious fighting was going on and Syria seemed to be on the verge of intervention. Nonetheless, on October 28, Sisco handed Dobrynin the final paragraph of a proposed joint document containing the United States fall-back position on Israeli withdrawal.

THE ROGERS PLAN AND ITS RECEPTION

The Rogers Plan, as it came to be known, consisted of a short preamble calling for the conclusion of a final and reciprocally binding accord between Egypt and Israel, to be negotiated under the auspices of UN Ambassador Jarring following procedures used at Rhodes in 1949, along with the following ten points:

1. The United Arab Republic (U.A.R.) and Israel will agree on a timetable for withdrawal of Israeli forces from U.A.R. territory occupied during the war.

2. The state of war between the U.A.R. and Israel will end officially and both sides will abstain from any activity inconsistent with the state of peace between them. This will involve refraining from any acts of aggression and ensuring that such acts by private organizations will not be carried out from their territory. The two sides will refrain from interfering in the internal affairs of each other and will agree that their mutual relationship will be governed by provisions 3 and 4 of article 2 of the UN Charter.

3. Both sides will agree to establish secure and recognized borders specified on maps. The agreement will include the establishment of

demilitarized zones and taking effective measures in the Sharm al-Shaykh area to guarantee freedom of navigation in the Strait of Tiran. Within this framework, secure borders will be established at the international frontier that existed between Egypt and Palestine at the time of the British mandate.

4. The two sides, through Rhodes-type indirect talks, will formulate agreement on areas to be demilitarized, measures to guarantee freedom of passage through the Strait of Tiran, and effective security measures and a final settlement of the Gaza Strip.

5. The two sides will agree that the Strait of Tiran is an international waterway, and the principle of free navigation will apply to all states, including Israel.

6. In exercising sovereignty over the Suez Canal, the U.A.R. will acknowledge the right of ships of all nations, including Israel, to pass freely through the canal without discrimination or interference.

7. The two sides will agree to submit to conditions for a fair settlement of the refugee problem similar to the final agreement between Jordan and Israel.

8. The U.A.R. and Israel will agree to recognize each other's sovereignty, political independence, and the right to live in peace within secure boundaries free from threats of force.

9. The final agreement will be included in a document signed by the two sides and filed with the UN, the agreement going into effect once the document has been deposited with the secretary-general. The final agreement will provide that any major violation of the agreement by either side will give the other the right to suspend implementation of the agreement, either partially or totally, until the violation has been ended.

10. The two sides will agree to submit the final agreement to the UN Security Council for ratification. The United States, the Soviet Union, Great Britain, and France will promise to exert their efforts to help the two sides adhere to the provisions of the agreement.[21]

On November 10, both the United States and the Soviet Union presented the text of the plan to Egypt. After nearly a month with no reply from either Egypt or the Soviet Union, Secretary Rogers, on

21. The exact English text of the Oct. 29 document has not been publicly released. A generally accurate, although somewhat abridged, Arabic translation appeared in *An-Nahar* (Beirut), Dec. 9, 1969, and has been retranslated into English in *Arab Report and Record*, Dec. 1–15, 1969, pp. 521–22.

December 9, outlined the basic elements of the plan in a public speech.[22] The following day, Israel rejected Rogers's proposals; the NSC met on the Middle East, against the background of warnings of worsening trends in the area conveyed the previous day to Nixon by David Rockefeller, John McCloy, and Robert Anderson.

On December 18, the United States presented a parallel plan for a Jordan-Israel settlement to the four powers. It was hoped that this would strengthen King Hussein at the Arab summit meeting that was to open in Rabat the following day. The plan contained many of the same points as the October 28 document, adding or modifying a few points to fit the special circumstances on the Jordanian front.[23] The permanent border, for example, would "approximate" the armistice demarcation line existing before the 1967 war, but would allow for modifications based on "administrative or economic convenience." In addition, point four of the December 18 document stressed that Israel and Jordan would settle the problem of Jerusalem, recognizing that the city would be unified, with both countries sharing the civic and economic responsibilities of city government. Point eight provided guidelines for a settlement of the refugee problem that would allow for repatriation or resettlement with compensation. An annual quota of refugees to be repatriated would be agreed upon between the parties.[24] King Hussein was reported to be pleased with the American proposal.

On December 22, the Israeli cabinet issued a statement saying that "Israel will not be sacrificed by any power or interpower policy and will reject any attempt to impose a forced solution on her. . . . The proposal by the U.S.A. cannot but be interpreted by the Arab

22. The Dec. 9, 1969, speech by Rogers contained most of the points in the Oct. 28 document. He described United States policy as "balanced," emphasizing friendly ties to both Arabs and Israelis. He referred to three principal elements of an agreement:

—binding commitments by the parties to peace, including the obligation to prevent hostile acts originating from their respective territories.

—Rhodes-style negotiations to work out details of an agreement. Issues to be negotiated between Egypt and Israel would include safeguards in the area of Sharm al-Shaykh, the establishment of demilitarized zones, and final arrangements in Gaza.

—in the context of peace and agreements on security, Israeli forces would be required to withdraw to the international border between Egypt and Israel.

The full text of the speech can be found in the *New York Times*, Dec. 11, 1969.

23. Points 1, 2, 4, 5, 7, 8, 9, and 10 of the Oct. 28 document were essentially repeated in the Dec. 18 proposal.

24. A summary of the text of the Dec. 18 document appears in *Arab Report and Record*, Dec. 16-31, 1969.

parties as an attempt to appease them at the expense of Israel."[25]
As Rogers was deploring the Israeli use of the word "appease" the
following day, the Soviets delivered an official note rejecting the
Rogers proposals virtually in their entirety.[26]

The Israeli and Soviet rejection of the Rogers Plan put a sudden
end to the first Middle East initiative of the Nixon Administration.
With it died the hope that "linkage" diplomacy would help provide
the key to peace in the Middle East. Not for the first time, a basic
reassessment of policy toward the Arab-Israeli conflict was undertaken. And although the Rogers proposals remained the most explicit
statement of a preferred American peace settlement, little was to be
heard of them in subsequent years.

REASSESSMENT

When foreign policies have fallen short of expectations or have
spectacularly failed, previously held images that buttressed those
policies may be rapidly revised. New "definitions of the situation"
are likely to emerge in short order, reflecting both the "lessons
learned" from the preceding phase of policy formulation and the
assessment of the new situation to be dealt with.

The Rogers initiative of 1969 had clearly failed, at least for the
time being. Apart from Jordan, there were simply no takers, and the
Israeli reaction in particular was extremely hostile. What had gone
wrong? Most policy makers agreed in retrospect that it had been naive
to assume that the United States would be able to separate the Soviet
Union from Egypt during the process of negotiations. The justification for the two-power talks had been that the United States and the
Soviet Union would find it easier to reach agreement on principles
than Israel and Egypt, and that they could both use their influence
constructively to moderate the positions of their "clients." The concept fit nicely with Nixon's emphasis on "linkage," "détente," and
"negotiations." But the implied symmetry was lacking, as was the
ability of either power to "deliver" its respective client. The United
States was indeed willing to take its distance somewhat from Israel,
but this was not reciprocated by the Soviet Union. Even if it had

25. *Arab Report and Record*, Dec. 16–31, 1969, no. 24, p. 549. Israel's opposition to
the Rogers Plan was as much procedural as it was substantive. Israel had been prepared for
the plan's content, but not for the way it would be presented publicly.

26. The Soviet note was published in the *New York Times*, Jan. 13, 1970.

been, it is not clear how the superpowers could have moved forward to bring the local parties into line.

A second mistake, in the view of some officials, was the marginal involvement of the White House in the formulation and execution of the Rogers Plan. Perhaps a "Nixon Plan" would have had better chances of success. Not that the president was opposed to the initiative—he had approved each of the major steps—but he had not engaged his full prestige, nor had his increasingly visible adviser, Henry Kissinger, lent his weight to the effort. Instead, Kissinger was preoccupied with Vietnam and SALT—the important issues—and with the secret diplomacy aimed at China.

A third error of the bureaucracy, according to Kissinger, was its underestimation of Israel's will and ability to resist American pressure. Not only did he and Nixon respect the strength of Israel's support in Congress and in public opinion generally, but they also found it misguided and possibly dangerous for the United States to try to improve its relations with adversaries—the Soviet Union and Egypt—by pressuring one's own friend, Israel. While such things might be done in the interest of achieving a genuine peace agreement, they should not become part of the standard American negotiating repertoire. The Soviets and Arabs should instead learn that United States influence with Israel was conditional upon their restraint and moderation.

The lessons drawn from the failure of the Rogers Plan of 1969 were fairly obvious by early 1970. First, since it was impossible to separate the Soviet Union from Egypt, it would be preferable for the United States to talk directly to Nasser rather than through Moscow. Second, since American concessions had not been reciprocated, the next move would have to come from the Soviets or Egyptians. No further unilateral United States concessions would be made. The United States and Israel could afford to sit tight until the "other side" had completed its own reassessment and concluded that a resumption of serious negotiations was needed. Third, any future United States initiative would be less legalistic in tone, less public, and perhaps less ambitious. The package-settlement approach, though appealing in theory, was simply too complicated. Failure on one issue would prevent progress anywhere. More modest approaches would henceforth be considered.

Two developments threatened this new consensus almost as rapidly as it emerged. First, the fighting in the Middle East escalated sharply during the spring of 1970, particularly with the introduction of Soviet SAM III surface-to-air missiles in Egypt, Israeli deep-penetration bombing attacks near Cairo, the dispatch of ten thousand or more Soviet advisers to Egypt, and the appearance of Soviet combat pilots flying air cover over the Egyptian heartland. Second, the domestic pressures on the Nixon administration to abandon the Rogers Plan and to accede to an Israeli request for 100 A-4 and 25 F-4 jets mounted rapidly. With congressional elections on the horizon, members of both the House and Senate became particularly vocal in support of Israel.

The administration now faced two urgent problems in the Arab-Israeli dispute. One was to take some type of political initiative to end the fighting and to begin talks on a settlement. The other was to respond to Israeli arms requests, especially as Soviet involvement grew. A dilemma, however, was acutely perceived. In order to pursue a credible political initiative aimed at Nasser, the United States would have to appear to be nonpartisan. This was particularly difficult at a time when American-made Phantom jets were bombing the outskirts of Cairo with impunity and the Israelis were virtually declaring that their goal was to topple the Nasser regime. At the same time, the United States could not indefinitely stand by and watch Soviet arms and personnel flow into Egypt without some response. This had as much to do with global politics as with the Middle East. The State Department was concerned above all with the first issue; the White House worried more about the second. The somewhat schizophrenic nature of United States policy during the next seven months was rooted in this bureaucratic and conceptual dualism.

RESUMPTION OF DIPLOMACY AND ARMS FOR ISRAEL

The first signs of a new tone in American Middle East policy after the abortive Rogers effort came in January 1970. President Nixon, in several public statements, tried to mend the U.S.-Israeli relationship and warn the Soviet Union about the consequences of its uncooperative policy in the area. For example, on January 25, the president sent a message to an emergency meeting of the conference of presidents of American Jewish organizations in which he reaffirmed his support for Arab-Israeli negotiations and stated that the United States was carefully watching the military balance. Then, in a press conference on January 30, Nixon surprised his staff and the Israelis by stating that he would announce his decision on Israel's pending arms requests within thirty days. The issue of arms to Israel had become particularly acute in the aftermath of the French decision to sell Libya more than 100 Mirage jets, some of which had originally been earmarked for Israel.

While Nixon was seeking to mend fences with the Israelis, President Nasser was seeking arms and aid from the Soviet Union. Early in January the Israelis had begun an intensified bombing campaign in Egypt's heartland, ostensibly designed to force Nasser to divert some of his forces from the sensitive canal area, but also aimed at exposing his weakness to his own people.[27] An Egyptian delegation had gone to Moscow in December, presumably in search of more arms, and now Nasser himself decided that there was need for a secret visit to the Soviet capital. According to Egyptian sources, Nasser pleaded not only for an effective missile defense against the Israeli Phantoms but also for Soviet personnel and pilots to ensure that the system should operate effectively while Egyptians were being trained for the new equipment.[28] The Soviet reply was affirmative, and by March large quantities of arms and advisers were arriving in Egypt. In mid-April, the first Soviet pilots were observed flying combat sorties in response to Israeli raids.

The stepped-up Soviet role in the conflict did not come as a total surprise in Washington. In a very frank letter to President Nixon dated January 31, Premier Kosygin had stated:

27. Dayan was quoted in the *New York Times,* Jan. 29, 1970, as saying that one of the purposes of the bombing raids against Egypt was to bring home to the Egyptian people the truth about the war. "We are saying, 'Now look here. Your leaders are not doing you any good.'" The same theme is picked up in comments by Prime Minister Meir, *Le Monde,* Jan. 18–19, 1970.

28. See Mohamed Heikal, *The Road to Ramadan* (New York: Quadrangle Books, 1975), pp. 83–90. Israeli sources have generally argued that the Soviets decided to increase their military support for Egypt during the December 1969 talks in Moscow, if not earlier. This version relieves Israel of the responsibility for provoking the Soviet response by engaging in deep-bombing raids near Cairo in early January, using the newly acquired Phantom jets. See Uri Ra'anan, "The USSR and the Middle East: Some Reflections on the Soviet Decision-making Process," *ORBIS* 17, no. 3 (fall 1973), for evidence in support of this view. Whatever the truth of the Egyptian-Soviet arms negotiations, few officials in Washington were prepared to accept the Israeli version. This view accounts for their hesitance to agree to more F-4s during the spring, despite the Soviet buildup. Many officials felt that Israel had brought on the Soviet response by a reckless bombing campaign and irresponsible rhetoric aimed at the Nasser regime's existence.

There is danger that in the immediate future the military actions may become wide scale. . . . We consider it our duty, however, to draw your attention, Mr. President, to the highly risky consequences the course chosen by the Israeli leaders may have both from the point of view of the situation in the Middle East and international relations as a whole. . . . We would like to tell you in all frankness that if Israel continues its adventurism, to bomb the territory of the U.A.R. and other Arab states, the Soviet Union will be forced to see to it that the Arab states have the means at their disposal with the help of which due rebuff to the arrogant aggressor could be made.[29]

In his reply on February 4, President Nixon rejected the Soviet effort to place the blame for the fighting on Israel alone and called for the prompt restoration of the cease-fire and an understanding on limitations of arms shipments into the area. In concluding, the president noted:

It is a matter of regret that Soviet unresponsiveness to these proposals [of October 28 and December 18, 1969] is holding up this process [of negotiations]; a more constructive Soviet reply is required if progress toward a settlement is to be made.

We note your desire to work with us in bringing peace to this area. We do not believe peace can come if either side seeks unilateral advantage.[30]

This last point was stated even more forcefully in the president's "State of the World" message, released on February 18.

This Administration has shown its readiness to work alongside the Soviet Union in cooperation with nations in the area in pursuit of peace. But the United States would view any effort by the Soviet Union to seek predominance in the Middle East as a matter of grave concern. Any effort by an outside power to exploit local conflict for its own advantage or to seek a special position of its own would be contrary to [the freedom of other nations to determine their own futures].

For these reasons, this Administration has not only pressed the effort to restore observance of the cease-fire and to help begin the process of negotiating a genuine peace. It has also urged an agreement to limit the shipment of arms to the Middle East as a step which could help stabilize the situation in the absence of a settlement. In the meantime, however,

29. The full text of the Soviet note appears in *Arab Report and Record*, Mar. 1–15, 1970, p. 167.

30. Ibid., pp. 167–68.

I now reaffirm our stated intention to maintain careful watch on the balance of military forces and to provide arms to friendly states as the need arises.[31]

Here are to be seen the strands of American policy over the next months: a warning to the Soviets, a call for restoration of the cease-fire and for the beginning of negotiations, and an ambiguous policy on arms for Israel, refusing a posture of unilateral restraint and promising to watch military developments closely.

On balance, Nixon seemed to be leaning toward a positive response on Israel's arms requests. The rest of the bureaucracy was generally opposed to the supply of more Phantom jets, arguing that Israeli military superiority was still unquestioned and that Soviet arms shipments were a response to Israel's reckless campaign of deep-penetration bombing using the Phantoms.[32]

The president's thirty-day self-imposed deadline for making a decision on the F-4s came and went with no announcement. Several factors seem to have dictated continued restraint. First, and perhaps most important, was Nixon's displeasure at the way in which the American Jewish community had treated French President Pompidou during his visit in late February.[33] According to numerous sources, the president was so incensed at the demonstrations and discourtesies during the Pompidou visit that he ordered that routine messages to pro-Israeli groups be suspended. Second, the four-power talks were resumed in late February and the Soviets hinted at a more flexible posture. In a secret meeting with Rogers on March 11, Ambassador Dobrynin stated that the Soviet Union had managed to obtain political concessions from Nasser in return for the new arms shipments that were just beginning to reach Egypt.[34] Third, the situation in Jordan was unstable and a United States decision on arms to Israel might further weaken the king.

31. "U.S. Foreign Policy for the 1970s," *Department of State Bulletin*, Feb. 18, 1970, p. 304.
32. The chairman of the JCS took the position that the 100 A-4s should be sold, but not the F-4s.
33. See Robert H. Trice, Jr., "Domestic Political Interests and American Policy in the Middle East: Pro-Israel, Pro-Arab and Corporate Non-Governmental Actors and the Making of American Foreign Policy, 1966–1971" (Ph.D. thesis in political science, University of Wisconsin, 1974), pp. 274 ff.
34. *New York Times*, Mar. 26, 1970. In addition, there was a lull in the fighting along the canal in early March which was interpreted in some quarters as the result of Soviet pressure on Nasser; *New York Times*, Mar. 12, 1970.

Finally, on March 23 Secretary Rogers announced that the president had decided to hold Israel's request for 100 A-4s and 25 F-4s in abeyance pending further developments in the area. As a consolation, economic credits of $100 million were offered.[35]

AN APPROACH TO EGYPT

In an effort to build on the limited credibility with the Arabs generated by the decision on the Phantoms, the administration decided to send Sisco to Cairo for direct talks with Nasser. The Soviets had said that Nasser was prepared to make concessions. The Americans would try to find out for themselves. During his stay in Cairo from April 10 to 14, Sisco essentially invited Nasser to try dealing with the United States as an honest broker. Although Nasser had little reason to hope for much from the United States, he was experiencing great losses in the continuing fighting with Israel; his dependence on the Soviet Union was growing; and perhaps a positive approach to the Americans would prevent new shipments of Phantoms to Israel. Nasser's reply to Sisco came in his May 1 speech in which he invited the United States to take a new political initiative.[36]

The Sisco visit and the Nasser speech marked the turning point of one aspect of American diplomacy. This led the State Department during the following three months to pursue an intensive effort to restore the cease-fire. A parallel, partly related, strand of policy involved both arms to Israel and the growing Soviet involvement in Egypt. The White House assumed control of this area. Nixon had denied that arms supply would be used as a form of leverage over Israel, but in the ensuing months that fiction was dropped.

35. Also, Nasser had warned in mid-February that the United States would lose its economic interests in the Arab world within two years if it agreed to sell additional Phantom jets to Israel. Interview with James Reston, *New York Times,* Feb. 15, 1970.

36. Nasser's "final" appeal, repeated in a letter to President Nixon the following day, stated:

The U.S.A., in taking one more step on the path of securing military superiority for Israel, will impose on the Arab nations an irrevocable course from which we must draw the necessary conclusions. This will affect the relations of the U.S.A. and the Arab nation for decades, and, maybe, for hundreds of years. . . . We will not close the door finally on the U.S.A., in spite of the offenses against us, in spite of the bombs, the napalm and the Phantoms. . . . I say to President Nixon that there is a forthcoming decisive moment in Arab-American relations. There will be either rupture forever, or there will be another serious and defined beginning. The forthcoming developments will not only affect Arab-American relations alone, but will have wider and more far-reaching effects.

Part of the text appears in *Arab Report and Record,* May 1–15, 1970, p. 276.

The last half of April was a very important period in the Middle East and for American foreign policy generally. Within the region, riots in Jordan prevented Sisco from visiting Amman and King Hussein requested the withdrawal of the American ambassador there. In Egypt, Soviet pilots were first noted flying combat patrols on April 18. Several days later, President Nixon began planning for a bold, and very controversial, military move into Cambodia. The operation began on April 30; violence flared on university campuses; and several of Kissinger's closest aides resigned their positions. The atmosphere in Washington was extraordinarily tense. In the midst of it all, Nixon, long preoccupied by other issues, finally ordered a full investigation of the expanded Soviet role in Egypt. A policy of restraint and dialogue would clearly be difficult to maintain much longer. In addition to incurring hostility to his Southeast Asia policy, the president was earning precious little support for his policy in the Middle East.

On May 21, President Nixon met with Israeli Foreign Minister Eban. The president assured him that the flow of military equipment to Israel would be quietly resumed, but he urged that no publicity be given to this. He made no specific commitment on the A-4s and F-4s, but made it clear that the jets that remained to be delivered from the December 1968 agreement would be delivered without conditions.[37] In return, Nixon asked for a public Israeli statement that would indicate a degree of flexibility on terms of a settlement. This was forthcoming on May 26, when Prime Minister Meir formally announced that Israel continued to accept UN Resolution 242 as the basis for a settlement and would agree to something akin to the Rhodes formula for talks.

The next move came from the Soviet Union. On June 2, Dobrynin met with Rogers and Sisco. The Soviet Union, he claimed, had won two important concessions from Nasser. First, Egypt would agree to control fedayeen activities from Egyptian territory if a cease-fire went into effect. Second, Egypt would agree that the state of war would end with the signing of an agreement.

The American response was to ignore the Soviet bid for a joint initiative and to press forward instead with its own unilateral call for a cease-fire and renewed talks. The NSC met on June 10 and 18 to

37. This was repeated in a letter from President Nixon to Mrs. Meir dated June 20, 1970, just after the second Rogers initiative had been launched.

discuss the Middle East.[38] The president authorized Rogers in NSDM 62 to request the parties to agree to a cease-fire of at least three months' duration and renewed talks under Ambassador Jarring's auspices. This was done on June 19.[39] Rogers publicly revealed the initiative on June 25.

Israel's immediate reaction was to reject the appeal. Ambassador Rabin, however, refused to deliver the note of official rejection and during the next month the White House devoted considerable energy to persuading the Israelis to accept the new initiatives.[40]

The first step in the campaign was to reassure the Israelis on continuing arms deliveries. This was done in a letter from Nixon to Golda Meir dated June 20. Next, Henry Kissinger was quoted on June 26 as saying: "We are trying to get a settlement in such a way that the moderate regimes are strengthened and not the radical regimes. We are trying to expel the Soviet military presence, not so much the advisers, but the combat pilots and the combat personnel, before they become so firmly entrenched."[41]

In an interview on television on July 1, President Nixon spoke at length on the Middle East. Referring to the U.A.R. and Syria as Israel's "aggressive neighbors," the president went on to state:

> I think the Middle East now is terribly dangerous. It is like the Balkans before World War I—where the two superpowers, the United States and the Soviet Union, could be drawn into a confrontation that neither of them wants because of the differences there. . . . Now, what should U.S. policy be? I will summarize it in a word. One, our interest is in peace and integrity of every country in the area. Two, we recognize that Israel is not desirous of driving any of the other countries into the sea. The other countries do want to drive Israel into the sea. Three, then, once the balance of power shifts where Israel is weaker than its neighbors, there will be a war. . . . We will do what is necessary to maintain Israel's strength vis-à-vis its neighbors, not because we want Israel to be in a position to wage war—that is not it—but because that is what will deter its neighbors from attacking it.

38. During the second week of June, a minicrisis erupted in Jordan as the PFLP, led by George Habash, seized hostages, including Americans, in two Amman hotels. On June 12, President Nixon ordered the 82d Airborne Division on alert.

39. See the text of Rogers's letter to Egyptian Foreign Minister Riad, dated June 19, 1970, *New York Times*, July 23, 1970, and *Department of State Bulletin*, Aug. 10, 1970, pp. 178–79.

40. See Michael Brecher, *Decisions in Israel's Foreign Policy* (New Haven: Yale University Press, 1975), chap. 8, for details of the Israeli response.

41. Marvin and Bernard Kalb, *Kissinger* (Boston: Little, Brown, 1974), p. 193.

And then we get to the diplomacy. The diplomacy is terribly difficult, because Israel's neighbors, of course, have to recognize Israel's right to exist. Israel must withdraw to borders, borders that are defensible. And when we consider all these factors and then put into the equation the fact that the Russians seem to have an interest in moving into the Mediterranean, it shows you why this subject is so complex and so difficult.[42]

Several days later, on July 4, the president authorized the shipment of electronic-counter-measure (ECM) equipment to be used against the SAMs in the canal zone.[43] Although still holding back on new commitments on aircraft, the administration was now prepared to help Israel attack the SAMs with new sophisticated equipment. On July 10, the president also ordered that the remaining A-4s and F-4s under the existing contract be shipped to Israel at an accelerated pace.[44]

President Nasser had left for Moscow on June 29, primarily for a health cure. While there, he discussed the American proposal with the Soviet leaders and reportedly informed them that he intended to accept it.[45] At a minimum, it would provide him a breathing space to complete the construction of the "missile wall." Accordingly, shortly after his return from Moscow, on July 22, Nasser accepted unconditionally the Rogers initiative of June 19.[46] On July 26, Jordan also accepted.[47]

The United States now had to bring about a positive Israeli response or risk the collapse of its Middle East diplomacy. President

42. Text of President Nixon's interview, July 1, 1970, *Department of State Bulletin*, July 27, 1970, pp. 112–13.

43. This decision was made in response to a letter from Prime Minister Meir dated July 2, 1970, in which she appealed for help in dealing with the threat posed by the SAMs that were being moved closer to the canal. The ECM equipment was first used by the Israeli Air Force on July 18.

44. All of the jets under the December 1968 contract had been delivered by the end of August 1970. According to the *New York Times*, June 26, 1970, the Israelis were reassured that they would be allowed to purchase additional aircraft if the cease-fire proposal of June 19 were to fail or to break down.

45. Heikal, op. cit., pp. 93–95.

46. Egypt orally accepted the United States proposal "unconditionally." The subsequent formal written reply was somewhat more guarded.

47. Inasmuch as Jordan and Israel were formally respecting the cease-fire, one might ask why Jordan was included in the second Rogers initiative. The answer seems to be that the United States wanted to ensure that both Egypt and Jordan would be committed to controlling the *fedayeen*, who were expected to oppose any political settlement based on the Rogers Plan. In accepting the Rogers proposal of June 19, King Hussein clearly understood that he would be held responsible for preventing all acts of force from his territory. He informed his cabinet before his acceptance that this might mean further military clashes with the *fedayeen*.

Nixon wrote to Prime Minister Meir on July 23, urging that Israel accept the proposal and making several important commitments. First, the United States would not insist that Israel agree to the Arab definition of Resolution 242. Second, Israel would not be forced to accept a refugee settlement that would fundamentally alter the Jewish character of the state or jeopardize its security. Third, and most important at the moment for the Israelis, Israel would not be asked to withdraw any of its troops from the occupied areas "until a binding contractual peace agreement satisfactory to you has been achieved." This was merely the standard American position on the "package settlement," but the Israelis apparently saw it as a significant step away from the Rogers plan of 1969.[48] In addition, Nixon promised to continue the supply of arms to Israel.

In reply, Prime Minister Meir sought assurances that Israel would be allowed to purchase Shrike missiles and Phantom jets, that the Rogers Plan would be withdrawn, and that the United States would veto any anti-Israeli resolutions in the United Nations.[49] Israel received a commitment only on arms, but that was apparently enough for Meir to accept, with clear reservations,[50] the American initiative on July 31, one day after an air battle between Israeli and Soviet pilots in which four Soviet MIG-21s were shot down.

The formal Israeli written reply was not forthcoming until August 6, and included some changes in the language that Jarring was authorized to use in announcing the cease-fire. The United States ignored the Israeli changes, to Prime Minister Meir's great displeasure, and on August 7 a three-month cease-fire, with a provision for a complete military stand-still in a zone fifty kilometers wide on each side of the Suez Canal, went into effect. In the State Department, the mood was one of elation. It was not to last for long.[51]

48. Brecher, op. cit., p. 494; *Yedi'ot Aharonot,* July 31, 1970, p. 4, "The Message that Tipped the Balance," by Ariyeh Tsimaqi. The letter reached Israel July 24.
49. Brecher, op. cit., p. 495. In addition, President Nixon stated at a news conference on July 30 that the United States was committed to "maintaining the balance of power in the Mideast. Seventy-one Senators have endorsed that proposition in a letter to me which I received today." Nixon further reassured Israel that she would face no risk of a military buildup during the cease-fire, because there would be a military standstill during that period. Text of the interview in *Department of State Bulletin,* Aug. 17, 1970, p. 185. A letter signed by seventy-three Senators had been sent to Secretary Rogers on June 1, 1970, urging the sale of 100 A-4s and F-4s. The text of that letter and the signatures appear in *Congressional Quarterly* XXVIII, no. 23, June 5, 1970, p. 1475.
50. See Prime Minister Meir's speech to the Knesset, Aug. 4, 1970, printed in *The Jerusalem Post,* Aug. 5, 1970.
51. See the text of the cease-fire agreement in *Arab Report and Record,* Aug. 1–15, 1970,

CONCLUSION

Between January 1969 and August 1970, the Middle East policy of the Nixon administration passed through two stages. During the first year, a consensus existed that the State Department should take the lead in negotiating with the Soviet Union to produce a set of principles that would spell out in some detail the terms of an Arab-Israeli settlement. As part of this policy, the administration adopted a restrained position on new arms agreements with Israel.

Two potentially divergent concepts underlay this policy. The first saw the Middle East as primarily an issue in global politics, and was characteristic of Nixon and Kissinger. They underscored the danger of superpower confrontation and the desirability of U.S.-Soviet talks. The second viewpoint stressed regional trends more than global "linkages." It emphasized that the United States position in the Middle East was eroding and that radicalization of the area was inevitable in the absence of a peace agreement. So long as the Soviets seemed cooperative and the regional conflict remained within manageable limits, these two perspectives were compatible with a single policy. The result was a year-long initiative which ended with the Rogers Plan of October 28 and December 18.

The second stage of policy toward the Middle East began with the failure of the Rogers Plan and the escalation of Soviet involvement in Egypt early in 1970. The shift in policy was not primarily the result of bureaucratic politics, of the White House winning out over the State Department. Rather, the new situation confronting the administration in the spring of 1970 required a more complex, differentiated response. The growing Soviet role made the fear of confrontation increasingly real. This was what the White House had most dreaded. One way of meeting the Soviet shipment of arms to Egypt, and of demonstrating that lack of Soviet restraint in the Middle East would not pass unnoticed, was to provide arms to Israel. This decision was made in principle in May and was set in motion on a large scale during the remainder of the year.

The intensified fighting along the canal and the increasingly important role of the Palestinian fedayeen in Jordan confirmed the worst fears of the State Department specialists. In their view, the best way to reverse the trends was with a new diplomatic initiative, this

p. 457, and the Egyptian, Jordanian, and Israeli replies to Rogers's proposal of June 19, ibid., pp. 458-60.

time less ambitious in scope than the Rogers Plan and less dependent
on Soviet cooperation. A simple "stop shooting, start talking" formulation was therefore proposed directly to each party on June 19.

These two perspectives risked collision on one issue, namely, arms
to Israel. New U.S.-Israeli arms agreements might lead Nasser to
reject the American initiative and might provide the "radical" Arabs
with strong arguments to use against the United States. Nixon recognized the danger and therefore dealt with the arms issue circumspectly.[52] Above all, he tried to ensure that arms for Israel should be
coupled with Israeli acceptance of the new American initiative.

On August 7, as the cease-fire went into effect, it seemed as if
both the State Department and the White House could feel satisfied
that their preferred policies had produced a successful outcome.
Within days, however, the provisions of the cease-fire were being
violated and a new crisis was in the making. The tenuous, delicate
balance between the State Department and the White House concerning the Middle East was also shattered. By the time the next
crisis was over, the views of Nixon and Kissinger had prevailed, and
those in the State Department who had urged "even-handedness"
were virtually banished from center stage. The Jordan crisis of September 1970 was thus a fitting culmination of the first two stages of
the Nixon diplomacy in the Middle East.

52. For example, in his news conference on July 20, 1970, Nixon emphasized the importance of the peace initiative then under way, stating: "That is why we have not announced
any sale of planes or delivery of planes to Israel at this time because we want to give that peace
initiative every chance to succeed." *New York Times,* July 21, 1970.

CHAPTER IV

The Jordan Crisis:
September 1970

As THE GUNS along the Suez Canal fell silent on August 7, 1970, a new phase of the Arab-Israeli conflict opened. A few optimists held out the hope that talks might soon begin that would lead to a resolution of at least some of the issues stemming from the 1967 war. Nasser had hinted that he was prepared to consider a political settlement. King Hussein, despite erosion of his authority within Jordan, could be expected to play his part. The United States seemed anxious that the Jarring mission be resumed.

The cease-fire, however, unleashed forces that quickly undermined the prospects for peace talks and instead led to a crisis of unprecedented danger for the Nixon administration. Regional in its origin, the Jordan crisis at its peak had much more to do with U.S.-Soviet relations than with the Arab-Israeli conflict or the Palestinians. At any rate, that was the view in Washington. To understand this dramatic episode in American policy, one must look beyond the ostensible issues in dispute between Israel, Egypt, Jordan and the Palestinians. As the Jordan crisis erupted in September 1970, Nixon was approaching an important moment in his presidency, the congressional elections of November. His popularity had been hurt by the worsening crisis in Southeast Asia during the spring. His foreign policy was still more rhetoric than realization. United States relations with the Soviet Union were strained, the Vietnam war was continuing to take American lives, the strategic arms race went on unchecked, and the Arab-Israeli conflict had reached an extremely critical point. The State Department had labored to bring about a cease-fire between Egypt and Israel, which had gone into effect, but almost immediately, it threatened to collapse.

During August and September, Nixon and Kissinger were increasingly preoccupied with the crisis in the Middle East. They held a particularly stark view of Soviet intentions, and as they began to reshape American policy in the midst of the Jordan civil war, it was the U.S.-Soviet perspective that dominated their thinking. The result was a new definition of issues in the Middle East, a revised understanding of the political dynamics of the region, in which the U.S.-Israeli relationship came to be seen as the key to combating Soviet influence in the Arab world and attaining stability.

From the standpoint of the Nixon administration, the Jordan crisis was successfully handled: King Hussein remained in power; the militant fedayeen were crushed; U.S.-Israeli relations were strengthened; and the Soviet Union was forced to back down, reining in its Syrian clients under U.S.-Israeli pressure. Finally, Nasser's death, just as the crisis was ending, seemed to open the door to a more moderate Egyptian foreign policy. The image, of course, proved to be flawed in many respects, but for nearly three years it served as justification for an American policy aimed at reducing Soviet influence in Egypt, mainly through a generous provision of United States arms to Israel. This proved to be a costly policy in many ways, as the October 1973 war was to demonstrate.

PRELUDE TO CRISIS: THE AUGUST CEASE-FIRE CONTROVERSY

The achievement of the cease-fire on August 7 created a breach in U.S.-Israeli confidence that continued to widen in subsequent weeks. Before Prime Minister Meir had time to recover from her anger at the way in which the United States had ignored Israel's efforts to qualify the terms of the cease-fire, a new issue of dispute had arisen. Israeli sources maintained that Egypt was not adhering to the standstill provisions of the cease-fire agreement. Missiles were being moved into the canal zone, new sites were being prepared, and missiles were being rotated from active sites to previously inactive ones.

Unfortunately, no one in Washington had thought about the problem of how to verify compliance with the agreement. Normal

United States intelligence activities did eventually detect major changes, but the issue now was whether Egypt had moved new equipment into the canal zone immediately after the cease-fire had gone into effect. A base-line measure was needed to establish what was allowed and what was not. No one, however, apparently had thought to order a U-2 reconnaissance plane to fly over the area to take photographs precisely at the moment of the cease-fire. Satellite photographs had been taken the previous week, but could not serve as a point of comparison, because a very rapid build-up on both sides of the canal had gone on in the days just before the cease-fire. It was not until August 10 that a U-2 finally flew over the canal, providing a reference point for judging any subsequent changes in military deployments.

Nixon and Kissinger were angry at the State Department and the CIA for not anticipating the problem of determining violations. The Israelis were producing evidence of Egyptian movement of missiles. State was dismissing it as inconclusive and was urging the Israelis to stop making such a fuss and to get on with the Jarring talks.[1] Israel's credibility at the White House was by now greater than State's, and soon Nixon and Kissinger were beginning to alter the thrust of United States policy.

On August 14, before American intelligence had confirmed Egyptian violations, Nixon authorized a $7-million arms package for Israel, consisting of equipment to be used against the missile sites along the canal in the event the cease-fire broke down. Deputy Secretary of Defense Packard met with Ambassador Rabin to try to work out an understanding on how the arms might be used and to ensure total secrecy. Nixon still did not want to provoke Nasser needlessly, but Israel would receive sophisticated electronic equipment, Shrike missiles, and cluster-bomb units (CBUs) that could be used to attack missile sites.

Gradually the United States was able to piece together a picture of what had happened along the canal after August 7. On August 19, State acknowledged that there had been some forward deployment of Egyptian missiles, but that hard evidence of numbers and locations

---

1. On Aug. 12, 1970, the Department of State termed Israeli evidence of Egyptian violations "inconclusive." Several days later, on Aug. 19, Ambassador Barbour urged the Israelis to end the public discussion of cease-fire violations and to name a representative to the Jarring talks.

was still difficult to obtain. Three days later, Egypt and the Soviet Union were informed that the United States had "incontrovertible evidence of clear-cut violations" of the standstill cease-fire agreement. Egypt replied on August 24, claiming the right to rotate missiles within the zone and denying that any new missiles had been introduced. Finally, on September 3, the United States made a strong démarche to Egypt and the Soviet Union concerning the violations, presenting evidence that at least fourteen missile sites had been modified during August. There was little evidence of completely new sites—these were constructed later in September—but a number of technical violations had been confirmed: incomplete sites had been finished; dummy sites had been activated, and some live sites had been abandoned; and a few new missiles appeared in the canal zone.[2]

The military significance of the violations was difficult to assess, but the political consequences were very important. At a minimum, they showed bad faith on Nasser's part and added weight to Israeli demands for compensation through new American arms deliveries. In retrospect, it does appear as if Nasser had accepted the cease-fire mainly in order to be able to complete construction of his missile defenses. But Nixon and Kissinger read an even more sinister design into the violations: Egypt was not acting alone. Those were Soviet missiles that were being installed, with the help of Soviet technicians. Therefore the Soviet Union was clearly aiding and abetting Nasser in violating the cease-fire agreement. Beyond that, it was trying to sabotage the Rogers initiative, which had aimed at getting talks started to settle the conflict. The Soviets, or so it seemed, were afraid that peace in the Middle East would hurt their position, hence they were doing all they could to sabotage it.

One might have wondered what obligation the Soviet Union had to respect the terms of an American-arranged cease-fire to which it had not been a party. The Soviet bid for a cooperative approach had been rebuffed in early June, and the United States had proceeded unilaterally. The Soviet Union was not violating any agreement to which it was a party. But such legal technicalities counted for little. Nixon and Kissinger were unhappy with the Soviets for a whole host of reasons—Southeast Asia, arms talks, the Middle East.[3] They felt

2. According to the *New York Times*, Sept. 17, 1970, Israel had also technically violated the standstill provision of the cease-fire by reinforcing near the canal.

3. In early September 1970, United States intelligence sources detected what appeared to be preparations for a Soviet submarine base in Cienfuegos, Cuba. Secretary Rogers tended

that the time had come to stand up to Moscow. Events in the Middle East were about to provide an unexpected opportunity for just that.

Perhaps the Soviets thought that Nixon was too preoccupied with Vietnam to act elsewhere; perhaps they misread the public reaction against the Cambodian invasion as a lack of will to use power; perhaps they misunderstood American restraint in arming Israel. If this were the case, they would have to be taught otherwise. Equally important, the Chinese, with whom Nixon hoped to open a new relationship, must recognize that the United States had the will and the capability to resist aggressive Soviet actions. Otherwise Mao would see little reason to compromise his ideological purity by tacit alignment with the United States against the Soviet Union. Only a strong America would be of interest to the Peking leadership.

Nixon was also aware that his domestic base of support would be affected by any signs of weakness toward the Soviet Union. If detente were seen as appeasement, Nixon's foreign policy would be in trouble. Munich had not been forgotten, nor had the Cold War. The running quarrel with Israel over arms had already taken its toll. Nixon had been prepared to put up with that if peace talks could begin. Now, however, Israel was in a morally justified position, for Egypt had violated the cease-fire agreement, with apparent Soviet connivance. Public and congressional support for Israel was strong. It was evident that a new policy on arms supply was needed.

Throughout his first year and a half in office, Nixon had exercised considerable restraint in responding to Israeli arms requests. But he had failed to convince the Soviet Union that it should observe comparable limits, as its behavior from January to August 1970 had unmistakably shown. Nor had American restraint served its purpose with Nasser. He, like the Soviets, seemed to be taking advantage of the cease-fire at Israel's expense. Consequently, on September 1, 1970, Nixon met with Rogers, Kissinger, and Sisco in San Clemente to review Middle East policy. The decision was made to sell Israel at least eighteen F-4 Phantom jets. Egypt would be told of the sale, and it would be explained in the context of the violations of the cease-fire agreement. On September 3, Nasser was so informed.

---

to dismiss the report as unimportant, but Kissinger treated it very seriously, alluding to it in a briefing in Chicago on Sept. 16, just on the eve of the acute phase of the Jordan crisis. The story became public in the *New York Times,* Sept. 25, 1970. It seems clear that the Cienfuegos incident accentuated Nixon's and Kissinger's distrust of Soviet intentions during this period. See Marvin and Bernard Kalb, *Kissinger* (Boston: Little, Brown, 1974), pp. 209–12.

Meanwhile, the previous day the Senate had approved a military authorization bill with an amendment sponsored by Senator Jackson that gave Nixon virtually unlimited authority to provide arms to Israel with United States financing.

On September 6, Israel announced that it was unable to participate in the Jarring talks so long as the Egyptian violations of the standstill cease-fire had not been rectified. That same day the Popular Front for the Liberation of Palestine (PFLP) astonished the world by hijacking three international airplanes, two of which were flown to a desert airstrip in Jordan, where their passengers were held as hostages, while the other was flown to Cairo, where it was blown up minutes after the passengers debarked.[4] Suddenly the Jarring talks and the cease-fire violations along the canal were overshadowed by a new situation, one which soon provided Nixon and Kissinger with an opportunity to confront the Soviet Union.

THE HIJACKINGS

When Egypt, Jordan, and Israel agreed to a U.S.-sponsored cease-fire in late July 1970, a danger signal went out to the Palestinian fedayeen. From February 1970 on, the fedayeen had succeeded in undercutting King Hussein's authority to the point of virtually becoming a state within a state. Now their position was endangered as President Nasser, their most prestigious backer, was apparently joining Hussein in a political settlement that could only be at their expense. The PLO energetically opposed the Rogers initiative, and because of their efforts Nasser suspended their right to use Radio Cairo for their inflammatory broadcasts.

The fedayeen movement had reached a decisive crossroads in late August 1970 when it convened an emergency session of the National Council in Amman.[5] Some of the more radical groups called for the overthrow of the Hashemite monarchy, but Fatah contrived to temporize. Before any consensus could emerge, however, the maverick PFLP, led by George Habash, carried out the hijackings on September 6. On September 9, another plane was hijacked and flown to Dawson

4. A fourth hijack attempt, led by Leila Khaled of the PFLP, against an El Al plane in London, failed.
5. See William B. Quandt et al., *The Politics of Palestinian Nationalism* (Berkeley: University of California Press, 1973), pp. 124–28.

field in the Jordanian desert.[6] Altogether, the PFLP held nearly 500 hostages, many of whom were Americans.

The PFLP's announced objective was to force Israel to release fedayeen prisoners held in Israel. Beyond that, the PFLP sought to upstage other Palestinian groups by appearing more militant than they. Most dangerous of all, the PFLP sought to provoke a confrontation between Hussein and the fedayeen movement, with Iraq and Syria throwing their weight behind the Palestinians. Iraq had nearly 20,000 troops in Jordan, and the Syrian army was just across the border within an easy two-day march of Amman.

The United States had been concerned about Hussein's weakened position for some time. The situation in Lebanon was also worrisome. These two moderate Arab states might well be taken over by radicals, just as Nasser seemed ready to move toward a settlement with Israel. In July, a high-level group had met in Washington to discuss contingencies for United States military intervention if Lebanon or Jordan should be threatened. The conclusion was a somber one: without access to bases in the eastern Mediterranean, the United States would find it difficult to send a sizable ground force into the area. The Sixth Fleet could provide some air support if it were on station, but otherwise American military capabilities were not impressive. If a serious military option were required, Israel was far better placed to provide both ground forces and air cover, particularly on short notice, but that, of course, was politically sensitive. No Arab regime would want to be rescued by Israel if there were any alternative. Hussein was a realist, however, and had gone so far as to query the United States early in August on the full range of options available if Iraqi troops were to move against him.

When faced with the hijacking challenge, Hussein militarily played for time. His choices were not very attractive. If he did nothing, the Jordanian army might move on its own against the fedayeen, thus destroying his authority. If he acted, Syria or Iraq might intervene. Hussein knew his army could handle the fedayeen alone, but what about their friends? Hussein therefore was forced to look for possible support against outside intervention, and that meant the United States and Israel.

6. The PLO temporarily suspended the PFLP from the Central Committee because of the unauthorized hijackings, but welcomed it back once the fighting broke out on Sept. 16.

The initial American response to the hijacking was cautious. At a minimum, it might prove necessary to evacuate the several hundred Americans in Amman. Perhaps an opportunity to rescue the hostages would present itself. Looking a bit further ahead, Nixon could see the need for a strong show of American force in the eastern Mediterranean as a deterrent to Soviet, Syrian, or Iraqi moves.

The Egyptians and Soviets were acting circumspectly, and were not openly supporting the fedayeen in Jordan. On September 9, Nasser had gone out of his way to inform the United States that he was still interested in the American peace initiative. If this were true, perhaps the crisis in Jordan could be contained and resolved without igniting a broader conflict. Nixon was determined, however, that the crisis should not be settled on terms set by the fedayeen. He would not pressure the Israelis to release prisoners as the price of recovering the hostages, and he urged the British to adopt the same tough attitude. This was Nixon at his law-and-order, no-capitulation-to-blackmail best.

Instead of acceding to the PFLP demands, Nixon urged a strong response. The United States contribution was a steadily escalating series of military moves meant to demonstrate Nixon's determination to act forcefully if necessary, and to provide a modest intervention capability if needed. On September 10, the 82d Airborne Division at Fort Bragg, North Carolina, was placed on "semialert"; six C-130 transport planes were also flown from Europe to Inçirlik air base in Turkey, where they could be available for evacuation of Americans from Jordan. The following day, units of the Sixth Fleet began to leave port as part of what the White House termed "routine precautions in such a situation for evacuation purposes." Four more C-130s, escorted by twenty-five F-4 jets, were flown to Turkey. That same day, the fedayeen blew up the aircraft and moved the remaining fifty-four hostages in their hands, thirty-four of whom were Americans, to an undisclosed location.

On September 15, King Hussein informed the British, who then informed the United States, that he was forming a military government with the intention of moving against the fedayeen. He indicated that he might need to call on the United States and others for help. When the news reached Washington, Kissinger quickly convened a meeting of the Washington Special Action Group (WSAG) at 9:30 p.m. Further military moves were ordered. The aircraft carrier

Saratoga would proceed to the eastern Mediterranean, where it would join the *Independence* off the Lebanese coast; airborne units in West Germany would be placed on semialert; additional C-130s would fly to Turkey. Despite these preparations, it was decided that the United States would not unilaterally try to rescue the hostages.[7]

CIVIL WAR IN JORDAN

With the outbreak of heavy fighting in Jordan between the army and the fedayeen on September 16 and 17, the United States suddenly faced a new set of dangers in the Middle East. At one extreme, the conflict in Jordan might ignite an Arab-Israeli war if Israel were to intervene directly. Egypt and the Soviet Union could then be drawn in, which might lead to a U.S.-Soviet confrontation, the fear that all along had haunted Nixon and Kissinger. Almost as dangerous would be Hussein's overthrow. A close friend of the United States would have been defeated by radical forces armed with Soviet weapons. Even if the Soviet Union were not directly involved, the symbolism of a fedayeen victory would be to its advantage. Nixon clearly wanted Hussein to crush the fedayeen, but he also wanted the conflict contained within Jordan. His role, as he saw it, was to encourage Hussein to act, while restraining the Israelis from precipitate military moves. At the same time, an American and Israeli show of force might help to deter the Syrians, Iraqis, and Soviets. The balance between restraint and belligerence would be difficult to establish; too much of either on the part of the United States or Israel could be counterproductive. Timing and a close monitoring of events on the ground were essential, and a high degree of coordination among Jordan, the United States, and Israel would be vital.

Nixon's first moves were to warn against outside intervention. At Kansas State University on September 16, he gave a tough law-and-order speech in which he denounced the fedayeen. He then flew to Chicago, where he met with Kissinger and Sisco for an update on the crisis. There were conflicting views in the intelligence community on the likelihood of Syrian or Iraqi intervention. On the whole, it was discounted as a possibility.

Nixon thought otherwise, however, and on September 17 he met twice with editors of Chicago newspapers to discuss the crisis in

7. M. and B. Kalb, op. cit., p. 197; Brandon, op. cit., p. 133; Frank Van der Linden, *Nixon's Quest for Peace* (New York: Robert B. Luce, 1972), p. 77.

Jordan. The *Sun-Times* rushed into print that evening with a story summarizing Nixon's views. The United States was reportedly "prepared to intervene directly in the Jordanian war should Syria and Iraq enter the conflict and tip the military balance against government forces loyal to Hussein."[8] Hussein's survival was judged by Nixon to be essential to the American peace-settlement effort. Israeli intervention against the fedayeen would be dangerous, and if Syria or Iraq were to enter the battle, it would be necessary for the United States to intervene. Nixon reportedly also told the editors that it would not be such a bad thing if the Soviets believed he was capable of irrational or reckless action.[9] This was vintage Nixon—be tough; keep your opponents off balance; remain mysterious and unpredictable. With luck, no one will then test to see if you are bluffing.

Returning to Washington the evening of September 17, Nixon met with his advisers again. A third aircraft carrier, the *John F. Kennedy*, was ordered to move from the Atlantic into the Mediterranean, and the *Guam*, a helicopter carrier with fifteen hundred marines on board, was ordered to proceed as rapidly as possible from Norfolk to the Mediterranean. Nixon also discussed the meeting that he was scheduled to have with Prime Minister Meir the following day. The time had clearly come to mend U.S.-Israeli relations, because the two might have to work closely during this crisis. Nixon therefore authorized $500 million in military aid for Israel and agreed to accelerate the delivery of eighteen F-4s.

Nixon and Meir met on September 18 for what the *New York Times* termed the most important talks between the United States and Israel in twenty-two years. Relations were judged to be at an "extremely low ebb" because of the quarrel over the cease-fire and restraint in providing arms.[10] The reality actually was less stark, and Nixon's promise to give Israel's aid requests his "sympathetic attention" helped set the stage for a remarkable improvement in the ties between the two countries during the next few days. In view of subsequent developments, it seems odd that Nixon apparently did not discuss the possibility of intervention in the Jordan civil war with Meir. This was left to Rogers, Sisco, and Kissinger; it still seemed a remote contingency.

8. *Chicago Sun-Times*, Sept. 17, 1970; *New York Times*, Sept. 19, 1970.

9. Henry Brandon, *The Retreat of American Power* (New York: Doubleday, 1973), p. 134.

10. *New York Times*, Sept. 18, 1970.

It was not until later that evening that the first reports of a Syrian armored probe into Jordan reached Washington.[11] The Soviet Union was quick to warn against outside intervention in Jordan and joined President Nasser in a call for a cease-fire. The Soviet chargé in Washington, Yuli Vorontsov, informed the State Department that the Soviets were urging restraint on the Syrians and were themselves in no way involved in the attack. Kissinger relayed this news to Nixon at Camp David. Nixon was unimpressed and skeptical. The Soviets, after all, had denied complicity in the standstill cease-fire violations along the Suez Canal. And now their client, Syria, was sending tanks into Jordan. Could this really be done without the Soviets at least giving their tacit blessing? More likely, the Soviets were urging the Syrians on.[12] Whatever the truth, United States diplomatic and military moves would thenceforth be aimed at getting the Soviets to pressure the Syrians to withdraw their forces.

CRISIS MANAGEMENT

It was not until the next day, September 19, that the Syrian intervention became ominous. While Secretary of Defense Laird was denying any need for United States intervention, Nixon was preparing for precisely that contingency. This was his crisis, not Laird's or Rogers's. Only Kissinger would be fully involved with the president's decisions.

The WSAG met more or less continuously throughout the day of September 19. Nixon ordered the 82d Airborne and units in West Germany to be placed on high alert, and the Sixth Fleet was ordered farther east.[13] In addition to these signals to the Soviet Union, Sisco conveyed a warning to Vorontsov in the morning, stressing that both Israel and the United States might be forced to intervene unless the Syrians pulled back. Rogers publicly denounced the Syrian "invasion."[14]

Besides these developments, United States diplomacy was engaged in two other vital tasks that day. First came King Hussein's

11. The Syrians went to considerable lengths to make their intervention appear to consist of units of the Palestine Liberation Army. Tanks were hastily painted with PLA symbols.

12. The most damaging evidence of Soviet complicity in the intervention was reports that Soviet military advisers had accompanied Syrian tank units as far as the Jordanian border.

13. M. and B. Kalb, op. cit., pp. 200–01.

14. *New York Times*, Sept. 21, 1970. M. and B. Kalb, op. cit., p. 202. Rogers's personal views were less hawkish. He reputedly favored a joint U.S.-Soviet effort to end the fighting but was rebuffed by Nixon and Kissinger.

urgent request through his trusted aide, Zaid Rifai, to the American ambassador for American help against the Syrians. The situation in Amman was under control, but in the north it was very threatening. Late in the evening in Jordan, King Hussein ordered Rifai to send United States Ambassador L. Dean Brown a request by radio for intervention by air and land from any quarter against the Syrian tanks.[15]

In Washington, the WSAG met at 7:00 P.M. to consider the King's extraordinary appeal. Nixon joined the group at 7:45. As the talks were ending, General Haig entered the situation room with the sobering news that the town of Irbid had fallen to the Syrians.[16] The time had come to contact the Israelis with Hussein's request.[17] Golda Meir and Ambassador Rabin happened to be in New York at that moment at a fund-raising dinner. At 10:00 P.M., Kissinger managed to reach Rabin by phone to convey the king's appeal for intervention. Rabin consulted with the prime minister and then again with Kissinger. It was agreed that Rabin would fly to Washington for further talks and that Prime Minister Meir would immediately return to Israel to take charge of matters there. The next day would clearly be a momentous one.[18]

Monday, September 21, was indeed a critical day in the Middle East. King Hussein had called for help, but had made it clear that Jordan must have the final say on the kind of intervention. He preferred that the United States or Great Britain be involved, not just the Israelis. In the course of the day, as the situation on the ground changed, the king frequently modified his initial request. During the morning, Rifai indicated that the king preferred air strikes alone, but that ground intervention would be acceptable without further approval if communications were to break down. Later that afternoon Rifai requested an immediate air strike to check the advancing Syrian tanks. In the evening, Hussein shifted position once again, urging Israeli ground action into Syria, but ruling out Israeli armored intervention in Jordan.

15. Communications in Amman between the American embassy and the royal palace were extremely difficult. Radio and walkie-talkie were used, and the *fedayeen* often eavesdropped on sensitive conversations.

16. Van der Linden, op. cit., pp. 81 ff.

17. The message was also passed to the British.

18. See M. and B. Kalb, op. cit., pp. 202–07, for the most accurate account of this period. See also the *New York Times*, Oct. 8, 1970.

Meanwhile the president had to consider possible United States action and to develop a combined strategy with Israel for dealing with the king's frantic and sometimes confusing appeals. The WSAG principals met at 8:30 A.M. Present were Laird, Rogers, Packard, Moorer, and Kissinger. The chairman of the joint chiefs was opposed to United States ground intervention, because the capability simply was not there. Hence, if ground action were needed, Israel would have to act. Intelligence estimates from Israel claimed that 250 to 300 Syrian tanks were in the Irbid area.[19] The Israelis doubted that air strikes alone would be enough to deal with the threat.

In view of the critical situation in Jordan and the apparent need for Israeli action, Nixon authorized Kissinger to work out a plan for intervention with Rabin.[20] Israel was prepared to move. A plan existed for sending 200 tanks toward Irbid, combined with air strikes. Israel would guarantee that her forces would be withdrawn from Jordan once the military operation was over. Kissinger and Sisco relayed to Rabin the king's preference for Israeli ground action inside Syria, not Jordan. This was considerably more risky for the Israelis, and might even provoke a Soviet response. Rabin therefore sought an American commitment to prevent Soviet intervention against Israel, as well as a promise of aid if Egypt were to attack.

By the end of the day, Rabin conveyed to Kissinger the cabinet's decision to intervene if Syrian tanks continued to advance on Tuesday. The Israeli air force would attack first, but, if this were insufficient, a tank force would also be sent into Jordan, and perhaps into Syria as well. Rabin insisted, however, on an American "umbrella," a presidential commitment to use force if necessary to prevent a Soviet attack on Israel. During the evening, Hussein again appealed for help as Syrian reinforcements entered Jordan. Nixon now decided to approve the Israeli plan.[21] The United States agreed in principle to an Israeli air and land strike, subject to review at the last moment. The United States would not be just an onlooker.[22]

As these negotiations were going on, Israel began to move its

19. The United States had no independent aerial intelligence-collection capabilities to follow the course of the battle. It had to rely on Israeli reconnaissance flights and Israeli and Jordanian accounts of what was happening on the ground.

20. M. and B. Kalb, op. cit., pp. 204–06.

21. Israel asked for clarification of the United States position on seven points. This was given orally. Both sides relied on these oral undertakings in planning their subsequent moves.

22. M. and B. Kalb, op. cit., p. 206, and interviews with American officials.

forces ostentatiously toward Jordan. As a symbol of commitment to the Israeli action, the United States ordered a plane to fly from an aircraft carrier of the Sixth Fleet to Tel Aviv for the announced purpose of coordinating targeting information. Presumably Moscow took note of these moves. A moderate message was conveyed by Vorontsov during the evening, which stressed that the Soviet Union was opposed to all outside intervention in Jordan. He appealed to the United States to restrain Israel.

The next day, Tuesday, September 22, was decisive. Israel, with United States backing, was poised to act. Hussein, with the assurance that Israel and the United States were behind him, finally ordered his own small air force to attack the Syrian tanks around Irbid, which it did with satisfactory results.[23] By afternoon, Syrian tanks were beginning to withdraw from Jordan. The need for Israeli intervention was less urgent. The king, speaking in code, informed Ambassador Brown that Israeli intervention was all right "up high," but should be directed elsewhere "down below."[24] An Israeli air strike would still be welcome, but land intervention should be only against Syria. Israel did not wish to undertake ground action only in Syria, and by the end of the day the prospects for Israeli or American intervention had virtually passed.

Kissinger and Nixon had met that day several times. They were acutely aware of how difficult it would be for the United States to intervene. Even with access to British bases in Cyprus, only 50 sorties daily over Jordan could be flown. Aircraft from the Sixth Fleet would be able to carry out 200 sorties per day, but even that could not compare with what the Israelis were capable of providing. It was with considerable relief, then, that the president learned that Syrian tanks were beginning to withdraw. Just to make sure the Soviet Union did not change its position, Kissinger went out of his way that evening to tell Vorontsov at an Egyptian reception that it was up to the Soviets to rein in their friends. "You and your client started it, and you have to end it."[25] The State Department had already announced that day that the Soviets were claiming to be restraining the Syrians, but

23. The Syrian Air Force did not intervene, nor did the Iraqi troops in Jordan, confronted as they were by a full division of the Jordanian army.
24. M. and B. Kalb, op. cit., p. 204, misinterpret the meaning of this message.
25. Ibid., p. 207; Brandon, op. cit., p. 137. Kissinger decided to attend the Egyptian reception in part to improve his image with the Arabs.

Kissinger seemed to feel that a few added tough words could do no harm.

By Wednesday, the acute phase of the Jordan crisis had passed. Shortly after noon, Nixon met with Rogers and Kissinger in the Oval Office. While discussing the crisis, they received news that all Syrian tanks had left Jordan. A statement was soon released from the White House welcoming the Syrian withdrawal, and Sisco was asked to contact Rabin to obtain his assurance that Israel would make no military move. The Jordanians had the situation under control and no longer wanted outside intervention. For the United States and Israel, the crisis was over. Nixon celebrated on Thursday by playing golf at Burning Tree Country Club with Rogers, Mitchell, and AFL-CIO president George Meany. The following day, a cease-fire was announced in Jordan.

Nixon was proud of the way he had handled the Jordan crisis. He compared his restrained, yet forceful, use of military power with Kennedy's behavior in the Cuban missile crisis of October 1962. To underscore the role of the Sixth Fleet in helping to resolve the crisis, Nixon flew to Rome on September 26, and from there to the aircraft carrier *Saratoga*, where he spent the night of September 27.

Meanwhile, President Nasser of Egypt was trying to arrange a stable cease-fire and a new modus vivendi between Jordan and the PLO. Nasser had differed with the fedayeen in their opposition to the Rogers initiative and in their desire to bring down King Hussein, but he did not want to see the PLO crushed by Hussein's troops. He therefore summoned Hussein, Arafat, and other Arab leaders to Cairo to work out an agreement that would govern the PLO presence in Jordan and prevent further clashes. The agreement was signed on September 27. The following day, while seeing off his last guests at the airport, President Nasser fell ill. He returned home, where, several hours later, he died of a heart attack. With Nasser's death, an era in Arab politics came to an end. By chance, it coincided with the beginning of a new U.S.-Israeli strategic relationship.

THE AFTERMATH

The outcome of the Jordan crisis was widely considered a successful result of American policy. Certainly Nixon and Kissinger portrayed it as such, and in terms of declared American objectives, the claim seemed justified. King Hussein was securely in power. The fedayeen had been badly weakened, and the hostages had all been rescued. The Syrian military intervention had been turned back by Jordan without Israeli or American involvement. The Soviet Union had refrained from direct intervention once the United States made a strong show of force. And U.S.-Israeli relations were stronger than ever. The outcome of the crisis being consistent with United States goals, few bothered to ask whether it had been American actions that had accounted for these developments, nor were the premises of American policy closely examined. Apparently successful policies are spared the type of critical scrutiny reserved for failures.

Nixon and Kissinger were therefore able to take credit for successfully handling a major international crisis. Jordan was the first in a series of foreign-policy spectaculars that boosted Nixon's prestige and popularity and made Kissinger's name a household word. After Jordan came the opening to China, the SALT agreement, and the Vietnam negotiations. Each of these achievements looks a bit tattered from the perspective of several years, but at the time they contributed immensely to the reelection of Richard Nixon in November 1972. The theses of his foreign policy—negotiations, détente, a new structure of peace based on a multipolar power balance—all appeared to take on substance in the period after the Jordan crisis.

U.S.-Israeli relations, which had reached a low point in mid-1970, were quickly brought to an unprecedented high level by the Jordan crisis. There had been a long-standing debate within the bureaucracy concerning policy toward Israel. The conventional wisdom, especially in the State Department, was that American support for Israel was an impediment to U.S.-Arab relations. By granting economic and military aid to the enemy of the Arabs, the United States was providing the Soviet Union with an opportunity to extend its influence in the Middle East. Although few questioned that Israel's existence should be defended by the United States in an extreme case, many felt that an "even-handed" policy, whereby the United States would not always align itself with Israel and would not become her primary arms supplier, was the best guarantee of United States interests in the region. In this view, Israel was more of an embarrassment for United States policy than a strategic asset. Even if Israel was an impressive military power, that power could be used only to defend Israel, not to advance American interests elsewhere in the region.

Israelis have generally resented the idea that American support is rooted primarily in domestic politics or in some vaguely felt moral commitment. They reject the reasoning of the proponents of "even-handedness," who regard Israel as a burden on United States diplomacy in the Middle East. Particularly after the spectacular military victory of June 1967, Israelis began to argue that a strong Israel was in America's strategic interest.

The Israeli argument was less than fully convincing, especially to the seasoned Middle East specialists in the bureaucracy. Apart from appearing overly self-serving, the argument did not fit the facts of the post–June 1967 situation very well. Soviet influence in the region did not decline; instead, it attained new levels, especially in Egypt, Syria and Iraq. Radical forces in the Arab world gained strength, particularly with the rise of the fedayeen, the coup in Iraq in July 1968, and the overthrow of the conservative monarchy in Libya in September 1969. If King Faisal was grateful to Israel for having checked Nasser's ambitions, he had a curious way of showing it. He was among the harshest critics of American support for Israel, arguing that such support played into the hands of radicals, communists, Zionists, and other dangerous elements. Even King Hussein, who, more than any other Arab leader, saw Israel as an important element in the regional balance of power, was angered by American aid to Israel and continuing Israeli occupation of formerly Jordanian territory. He shared Faisal's view that Israel's 1967 military victory, and subsequent American support for Israel, would polarize and radicalize the area. Only the Soviets and their friends would profit.

Nixon and Kissinger had been prepared to allow the State Department to pursue the logic of an "even-handed" approach to the Arab-Israeli conflict, and this had led to the Rogers Plan and the August 1970 cease-fire. But both efforts had been flawed. The Soviet Union had failed to cooperate; U.S.-Israeli relations had been badly strained, with little to show for it; and the Arabs displayed little gratitude for United States restraint in providing arms to Israel.

As the Soviet dimensions of the Arab-Israeli conflict grew during the spring of 1970, Nixon and Kissinger began to accept parts of the Israeli argument that only a strong Israel could deal with the growing Soviet presence in Egypt. If the Soviet Union were allowed to succeed in helping Nasser recover Sinai by force of arms, Soviet aid would be sought throughout the region. Only by frustrating the Soviet-Egyptian scheme would American interests be protected. Arms to Israel would therefore serve an important global interest of the United States.

The August cease-fire violations created the necessary emotional climate for Nixon and Kissinger to turn to Israel as a strategic ally. The Soviets and Egyptians appeared to be double-dealing and were trying to exploit the American policy of restraint and to drive a wedge between Israel and the United States. Even without the Jordan crisis, Nixon would have agreed to new arms aid to Israel, but the crisis provided a convincing rationale for a policy based on arming Israel as a strategic asset for American policy in the Middle East. In an emergency, Israeli forces had been prepared to protect King Hussein, a task which would have been much more difficult for United States forces. By its mere presence, Israel had deterred the Syrian air force from entering the battle; Israeli armor massed in the Golan Heights must have helped convince the Syrians that they should withdraw. Then, too, by forcing Syria to back down, Israel and the United States had further tarnished the Soviet image in the region, while demonstrating that moderate Arab regimes could count on effective American support. The agreement hastily negotiated between Kissinger and Rabin on September 21 was a remarkable testimony to the new strategic relationship that existed between the two countries.

For the next three years, U.S.-Israeli relations flourished. Unprecedented levels of aid were provided by Washington. To both parties' satisfaction, the region remained comparatively calm, and Soviet influence seemed to be declining. When President Sadat precipitately expelled over ten thousand Soviet military advisers in July 1972, Nixon, Kissinger, Meir, and Rabin must all have congratulated themselves on the success of their joint policy.

The aftermath of the Jordan crisis did indeed comprise a momentary period of comparative stability. The cease-fire remained in force on all fronts. King Hussein successfully reestablished his authority in Jordan, from which the remnants of the fedayeen were expelled in July 1971. U.S.-Jordanian relations flourished, reaching substantial levels of economic and military aid. Jordan came to be treated as another regional partner of the United States, along with Israel, Iran, and a few others. Jordan's special task on behalf of American interests, in King Hussein's view, would be to promote stability in the small oil-producing Arab states of the gulf after the British departure at the end of 1971. Nixon and Kissinger gave the king some encouragement and boosted aid to Jordan accordingly. In true Nixon-doctrine style, Israel, Jordan, and Iran were emerging in official Washington's view as regional peacekeepers. Aid and arms to these United States partners would serve as a substitute for a costly American military presence in the region or unpopular military intervention.

Elsewhere in the Middle East, post-Jordan-crisis trends also seemed favorable. In Syria, the faction of the Baath party most closely associated with the intervention in Jordan was ousted by General Hafiz al-Asad in November 1970. Syria's new leaders were reportedly more moderate, or at least more cautious, than the former regime. Egypt's president, Anwar-al-Sadat, was also viewed in Washington as a considerable improvement over Nasser. Sadat, at any rate, had less prestige in the Arab world than Nasser, and therefore less trouble-making potential. Perhaps he would turn to Egypt's domestic problems instead of promoting revolution elsewhere. This had long been the hope of American policy makers, and had served as a major justification for aid programs in the early 1960s.

In foreign policy, Sadat was something of an enigma at first. His feelings toward the Soviet Union were unknown, but by spring 1971, after he successfully survived a coup attempt organized by Nasser's closest aides, Sadat's anti-Soviet colors became more evident. Even in Egypt, therefore, the trend seemed to be encouraging.

LESSONS LEARNED

The net effect of the regional developments that grew out of the Jordan crisis was to breed a sense of complacency in Israel and the United States. The fears of radicalization, polarization, and confrontation that had haunted policy makers from 1967 to 1970 all but disappeared in the aftermath of September 1970. Now the region appeared to be relatively stable, and the key to this stability was a military balance that unquestionably favored Israel. The chief remaining threat came from the continuing Soviet military presence in Egypt and Syria. It thus became a prime objective of U.S.-Israeli policy to demonstrate to Sadat that the Soviet military presence in his country was an obstacle to his recovering Sinai. Soviet arms to Egypt would be matched by American arms to Israel, thus ruling out Sadat's military option. And so long as a Soviet military presence remained in Egypt, United States diplomacy would make only half-hearted attempts to promote a settlement.

The roots of this view, which dominated American policy during the next three years, can be traced to the Jordan crisis. Nixon and Kissinger had convinced themselves that Israel had played a vital role in helping to check the Soviet-inspired Syrian invasion of Jordan and might play a comparable role in thwarting Soviet designs in Egypt. It would be useful to examine other explanations of what happened in September 1970, for the lessons drawn by Nixon and Kissinger seem to have had little to do with the crisis per se. Instead, they seem to have reflected predispositions established in an earlier period.

Nixon and Kissinger failed to grasp two critical dimensions of the Jordan crisis. On the regional level, they misinterpreted the Syrian invasion, overemphasizing the Soviet role and minimizing the degree to which it grew out of internal Syrian politics. The difference was a significant one. If Syrian action were primarily rooted in domestic Syrian politics, then a policy directed at the Soviet Union was unlikely to have much effect. Syrian withdrawal from Jordan may well have had little to do with Soviet pressure, and much more to do with the refusal of General Asad to commit the Syrian air force to an adventure planned by his rival, Salah Jadid. Jordanian power, along with the obvious danger of Israeli intervention, was probably the key to the Syrian retreat, not Soviet démarches made in response to United States threats. In short, American policy in the crisis may well have had very little effect on the Syrian decision to withdraw its armor.

The second related flaw in Nixon's and Kissinger's view was to overemphasize the global U.S.-Soviet dimension of the crisis. The Soviets had comparatively little at stake in Jordan. They were not on particularly good terms with the PLO, which was criticizing their primary client in the area, President Nasser. Syria was receiving military aid, but was refusing to follow the Soviet political line on a settlement. In addition, Syria was faction-ridden and unstable, was quarreling with Egypt and Iraq, and was essentially unpredictable. Once Syrian units did enter Jordan in the September crisis, the Soviets adopted a cautious policy. They made no threats. Instead, they warned against all outside intervention in Jordan, called for a ceasefire, and pointedly took credit subsequently for making démarches in Damascus to bring the fighting to an end.[26] If the Soviet stand had been primarily a function of the strong position taken by the United States, and if Soviet pressures had significantly influenced Syria's behavior in the crisis, then Nixon and Kissinger might have rightly concluded that the combination of United States and Israeli threats to act had produced the desired outcome. However, no evidence can be found that such was the case. This is not to say that Nixon and Kissinger were wrong to make a strong show of force in the Jordan crisis. Among other things, it might have been a useful signal to the Soviets and the Chinese. The error was to conclude that the outcome of the crisis was mainly due to United States action. That was at least a debatable proposition, but instead it became something of an axiom in subsequent policy debates.

Nixon and Kissinger were wrong in the significance they attributed to American behavior in the Jordan crisis, but this does not imply that the United States role was unimportant. On at least two counts, the American contribution may well have been essential to the regional outcome. First, King Hussein needed encouragement to draw fully on his own military resources. He seemed to be afraid of committing his own air force without assurances that outside help would be available if he got into trouble. His willingness to order the successful counterattack on September 22, which removed the need for United States or Israeli action, may well have been a result of the assurances he received from the United States.

The second essential role filled by the United States was that of coordinator of the Israeli response. Left to their own devices, Israeli leaders might have responded to the Jordan crisis differently. By working closely with the United States, Israel made its power available on terms that King Hussein was able to accept. Because direct communication between Israel and Jordan did not exist during the crisis, serious miscalculations could have resulted. The United States was in close and continuous contact with both parties, however, and could urge restraint on Israel at the beginning and end of the crisis, while ensuring that Israel was prepared to act at the critical moment on September 22. To play this role effectively, the United States had

26. Speech by President Podgorny, Sept. 23, 1970. See Mohamed Heikal, *The Road to Ramadan* (New York: Quadrangle Books, 1975), pp. 98–100, for evidence that the Soviets urged "utmost restraint" on Egypt during the Jordan crisis.

to place its own forces on the line as a possible backstop to the Israeli operation.

Seen in this light, United States action in the Jordan crisis still appears as relatively successful. Hussein took the necessary risks on September 22 because he knew that assistance would be available if needed. He succeeded thereby in removing the need for United States or Israeli intervention. The lesson of the crisis, from this perspective, was that American diplomacy, through a mixture of subtlety and restraint combined with visible force, had helped to create a situation in which Jordan was able to cope with its own problems. It had been a close call, however, involving a number of imponderables, such as factional balances in Syria and King Hussein's shifting moods. It would be hard to repeat the Jordan experience elsewhere, especially in situations where United States and Israeli interests might not overlap so clearly with that of any other Arab regime.

What guidelines could this crisis provide for dealing with the serious problems of the Egyptian-Israeli conflict or with broader issues of the Soviet presence in the Middle East? What was the lesson regarding the role of American threats to use force in the crisis? Had they really been effective? Against whom? After all, the Syrian intervention came after Nixon's widely publicized threat on September 17 and after the visible movement of American military forces to the eastern Mediterranean. Was it possible that the Syrians had not taken the threats seriously, or that they came to their senses only when confronted with Soviet pressure and Israel's might? These were legitimate questions, well worth asking, but it was much easier for Nixon and Kissinger to see American power and diplomacy as responsible for the favorable outcome. Israel was regarded as the helpful junior partner in the successful management of a grave global test of superpower wills.

The result of these misperceptions was a United States policy in subsequent years that was too narrowly focused on Israel, Jordan, and the Soviet Union. The military balance was seen as the key to stability, if not to peace. Arms to Israel and Jordan were of higher priority than new peace initiatives. Too little attention was paid to political developments in the region, to the mounting frustrations in Egypt and Syria and among the Palestinians, and to the growing activism of the Arabs, who had begun to recognize the potential power they possessed because of their petroleum resources.

In short, American policy became a captive of the perceived success in handling the Jordan crisis. The global dimension of the conflict was virtually all that Nixon and Kissinger seemed to care about. By ignoring regional trends, they misjudged the very forces that would lead within three years to a much more dangerous outbreak of war in October 1973. During the interval, several ineffectual diplomatic efforts were launched by the State Department, but Nixon and Kissinger, having taken charge of Middle East policy during the Jordan crisis, were reluctant to relinquish it to Rogers and Sisco. The White House was unwilling to give the State Department the type of support that had been available in 1969 and early 1970. The result was a series of half-hearted initiatives that simply raised the level of Arab frustrations while reinforcing the sense of complacency felt in Israel and in Washington.

Several important opportunities to pursue a political settlement of the conflict may have been missed during this period. Caught in a perceptual trap largely of their own making, Nixon and Kissinger failed to notice them. The period of "standstill diplomacy" from 1970 to 1973 will not go down in the annals of American foreign policy as one of the more enlightened. In many ways, the success in Jordan in 1970 resulted in a series of failures in the succeeding years, culminating in the October 1973 war.

CHAPTER V

Standstill Diplomacy: 1971–73

WITH THE continuation of a cease-fire along the Suez Canal, the restoration of King Hussein's authority in Jordan, and the death of Egypt's President Nasser, the situation in the Middle East appeared to American policy makers to be less dangerous and more manageable than at any time since the 1967 war. The danger of U.S.-Soviet confrontation had passed. United States interests had survived intact through a difficult period, and less urgency was now attached to new American diplomatic initiatives.

Prior to the Jordan crisis, the State Department had been primarily responsible for the formulation and conduct of policy toward the Arab-Israeli conflict. Thereafter, Nixon and Kissinger were to play a more important role, chiefly through their emphasis on the Soviet dimension of the regional conflict and their desire for a close relationship with Israel. Over the next three years, the White House refrained from day-to-day involvement in Middle East diplomacy, but a careful eye was kept on the State Department to ensure against excessive activism. Ultimately, Nixon and Kissinger succeeded in undermining State Department initiatives and in gaining virtually complete control over policy toward the Middle East.

The State Department understandably was loath to surrender this last remaining area of substantive responsibility. Instead, for nearly a year Secretary Rogers and Assistant Secretary Sisco tried to revive

American diplomatic efforts. Initially the emphasis was on resumption of talks through Ambassador Jarring. As that effort faltered in February 1971, a conceptually different approach based on the idea of an "interim settlement" between Egypt and Israel was explored. By August 1971, this too had failed. For the next two years, the Arab-Israeli conflict was absent from the headlines, American diplomats remained uncharacteristically quiet and passive, and Arab frustrations mounted in direct proportion to the warmth of the U.S.-Israeli relationship. Even President Sadat's bold move in expelling more than ten thousand Soviet advisers from Egypt in July 1972 was not enough to lead to a major reassessment of American policy. Instead, United States diplomacy continued to aim at what Kissinger was later to term the "complete frustration" of the Arabs, a policy which he admitted was short-sighted and may have contributed to the October 1973 war.

The period from 1971 to 1973 thus seems to have been one of lost opportunities to prevent war and move toward a settlement. With the advantage of hindsight, it appears that the type of agreement arrived at between Israel and Egypt in January 1974 could have been reached three years earlier at much less cost. But hindsight may distort more than it illuminates, for it fails to reconstruct events as they were perceived at the time. Context disappears, along with nuance, when one looks back at what might have been.

To understand this uninspiring chapter in American diplomacy between the Jordan crisis and the October 1973 war, one must recall the administration's intense preoccupation with other areas of the world. It was with relief that policy makers turned away from the Middle East to areas of higher priority. The Vietnam war was still raging, but in May 1971 Kissinger began a series of secret talks with top-level North Vietnamese representatives to try to reach a negotiated settlement. In parallel to these important talks, Nixon and Kissinger were planning a momentous opening toward Peking, symbolized by Kissinger's secret trip to China in July 1971. Finally, serious negotiations with the Soviet Union on limiting strategic armaments were under way.

Each of these three issues was so handled that in 1972, the presidential election year, Nixon would be able to point to visible achievements—visits to Peking and Moscow, and, it was hoped, an end to the war in Vietnam. The same election-year imperatives

dictated a very low profile in the Middle East. In the absence of any
chance for a negotiated agreement there, Nixon focused instead on
maintaining the military balance in Israel's favor, thereby preventing
an unwelcome outbreak of fighting and no doubt earning the gratitude of Israel's many supporters in the United States.

In many ways, the period from 1971 to 1973 is rich in lessons. It
demonstrates the way in which Middle East issues can be influenced
by global developments and by American domestic politics. Particularly in noncrisis periods, United States foreign policy tends to be
insensitive to regional developments, responding instead to strategic
concepts, bureaucratic rivalries, and electoral necessity. The vacillation that so often seems to characterize American policy, especially
in the Middle East, is likely to be especially intense at such times.
The president is less involved than during crisis periods, and the
bureaucracy therefore is left to devise policies that may ultimately
fail for lack of presidential support.

Only one new policy concept concerning the Arab-Israeli conflict
emerged during this period. Responding to Israeli and Egyptian
suggestions, the United States backed away from the "package
settlement" approach and began to emphasize the desirability of
partial agreements unlinked to a final peace plan. A serious, but
flawed, initiative was launched in the spring of 1971; several months
later it came to an inglorious end. However, the concept of "interim
steps" was eventually revived in a new setting by Henry Kissinger,
the very person who opposed the 1971 effort. And it was he who
made "step-by-step" diplomacy famous. By then, of course, Rogers
was no longer secretary of state, and Sisco, the architect of the 1971
initiative, was serving as Kissinger's under secretary of state and chief
adviser on Middle East policy.

THE JARRING TALKS AND U.S.-ISRAELI RELATIONS

During the post-Jordan-crisis policy reviews on the Middle East,
American officials considered several alternative approaches, including one dealing more directly with the Palestinians, before deciding
to resume the interrupted Rogers initiative of the preceding June.[1]

1. On Oct. 12, 1970, Kissinger and Sisco gave a background briefing to the press on
the post-Jordan-crisis situation in the Middle East. Sisco addressed the question of the
Palestinians in the following terms:

   . . . more and more the Palestinians are thinking in terms of a given entity, wherever that
may be. . . . So that if I were to look ahead over the next five years, assuming that we can

This time, however, the U.S.-Israeli relationship would remain close. Kissinger in particular felt that if Israel were ever going to make concessions it would be from a position of strength and self-confidence, not under American pressure. Consequently, a two-stage policy was adopted: first, an understanding would be reached with Israel on the terms of reference for the Jarring talks and on United States military assistance; second, Jarring would be encouraged to take a more active role than previously in seeking agreement on basic principles of a peace agreement. The United States would support Jarring's efforts through bilateral talks with Israel, Egypt, and Jordan. The State Department was anxious for Jarring to try to establish the principle that Israel would withdraw from the occupied territories in return for Arab commitments to peace. That, after all, had been the essence of the original Rogers Plan.

The first step in the new American initiative was to bring Israel back into the Jarring talks and to extend the cease-fire beyond its expiration in early November. On October 15, Nixon approved an arms package of $90 million for Israel. It consisted of antitank weapons, reconnaissance aircraft, and other minor items.[2] In addition, the administration decided to seek a $500 million supplemental appropriation for Israel in the current fiscal year to cover arms expenditures.[3] Israel was particularly anxious to receive a guarantee for the supply of high-performance aircraft in 1971 and had requested 54 F-4s and 120 A-4s. The Israelis were also beginning to press for long-term military agreements that would prevent the periodic supply disruptions and quarrels that had marked the previous two years.

Despite the American decision to send substantial quantities of arms to Israel, Egypt's new president, Anwar al-Sadat, agreed to a three-month extension of the cease-fire in early November. During this period, he expected the Jarring talks to resume and to produce results. Egypt and the Soviet Union also began to show interest in outside guarantees as part of a peace settlement. If the United States adopted the idea, it might be prepared to pressure Israel to abandon

stabilize this area, it would be on the basis of the Arabs having adopted a live and let live attitude, that is, willing to live alongside of Israel; Israel's meeting at least part of the Arab demands insofar as the occupied territories are concerned; and, lastly, giving expression to the Palestinian movement and very likely in the form of some entity.

2. The administration sought an understanding on the conditions under which Israel might use the new weapons.

3. *New York Times*, Oct. 24, 1970. The supplemental defense appropriation, including $500 million in credits for Israel, was signed by Nixon on Jan. 11, 1971.

Arab territory in return for guarantees from the major powers. In any event, this was an idea that might appeal to the Americans.[4]

Nixon's immediate problem, however, was to get the Israelis to return to the Jarring talks. The memory of the August cease-fire violations and the American vacillation was strong in Israel, and Prime Minister Meir decided to exact a high price for resuming the Jarring talks. Israeli Foreign Minister Eban informed Rogers on November 7 that Israel might return to the Jarring talks in the near future, but that assurances from the United States were first required.

On December 1, Prime Minister Meir wrote to Nixon, asking for explicit commitments on aircraft deliveries after the end of the year; on freedom for Israel from United States pressure in future negotiations; on support for Israel against Soviet intervention in the Middle East; and on the use of the United States veto against any anti-Israeli resolutions introduced at the United Nations.[5] Two days later, Nixon replied with general reassurances and a strong bid to Israel to return to the Jarring talks. Israel would not be allowed, said Nixon, to be put at a diplomatic or military disadvantage if talks were resumed.

Prime Minister Meir pressed for further clarifications. In particular, she wanted the United States to drop its support for the idea of full withdrawal on the Egyptian front and from all but "insubstantial" portions of the other captured territories.[6] Dayan, who arrived in Washington for talks in mid-December, raised the issue of long-term military commitments. In return, he was told that the United States was prepared to participate in a multilateral UN-sponsored peace-keeping force as part of a settlement.[7]

This new twist in American policy was hardly what the Israelis wanted to hear. On December 17, Nixon replied to the Israeli prime minister's plea for further clarifications. The United States could not make any formal promise to use the veto at the UN, but it could offer more general assurances that Israel's security would not be endangered. In addition, the United States promised to deliver twelve F-4s and twenty A-4s during the first six months of 1971. Not inclined to let the Americans off quite so inexpensively, the prime minister

4. Senator William Fulbright, chairman of the Senate Foreign Relations Committee, and not known as a particularly close friend of Israel, publicly endorsed the idea of a U.S.-Israeli security treaty as part of a settlement involving full Israeli withdrawal.

5. New York Times, Dec. 2, 1970.

6. Ibid., Dec. 7 and 8, 1970.

7. Ibid., Dec. 15, 1970.

termed this a "step backward," one of the "greatest blows" from the United States. Soon her emotions calmed, however, and on December 28 she announced that Israel would return to the Jarring talks.

According to Prime Minister Meir, the United States had made commitments to preserve the balance of power in the Middle East. Israel would be allowed to negotiate freely, without fear that the United States would be a party to any UN effort to determine borders or the terms of a refugee settlement. The United States, she claimed, upheld the principle that Israel should have defensible borders, that Israel should be strong, that Israel should not be forced to withdraw to the June 5 lines, and that Israel would not be obliged to accept the Arab version of a refugee settlement. Furthermore, the conflict must be ended by a binding, contractual commitment to peace. Until that was achieved, not a single Israeli soldier would be expected to withdraw from the cease-fire lines. And finally, Jarring's terms of reference should not be altered.[8]

If indeed this represented United States policy, it was hard to see why Mrs. Meir had been so upset at Nixon's December 17 letter. Perhaps she sensed the impending crisis over the Jarring mission and the American bureaucracy's reluctance to offer a blank check on arms. Perhaps she also realized that her insistence on no Israeli withdrawal without peace was being undermined by her own defense minister, who had begun to hint as early as November that it might be wise for Israel and Egypt to thin out their forces along the canal, perhaps even to withdraw them to a certain distance and to allow the canal to reopen.[9]

THE EGYPTIAN REACTION

While Nixon's exchanges with the Israelis were going on, he and Rogers had been in contact with Sadat as well. Sadat had sent Nixon a letter dated November 23, which reached him on December 14, indicating Egypt's interest in the Jarring talks. Nixon had replied orally through Mahmoud Fawzi on December 22, and Sadat sent word two days later through Donald Bergus, the American minister

8. Meir speech to the Knesset, as cited in Lawrence L. Whetten, *The Canal War: Four Power Conflict in the Middle East* (Cambridge, Mass.: The MIT Press, 1974), p. 142; and *New York Times*, Jan. 1, 1971.

9. The idea of a mutual thinning out of forces along the canal had first been officially raised in Washington on Sept. 19, 1970, by Israeli Ambassador Rabin and General Aharon Yariv.

in Cairo, that he was genuinely interested in peace. Sadat, who had
originally been viewed as something of a lightweight by Washington
officials, was beginning to be taken more seriously.[10]

On January 5, 1971, Jarring met at the UN with representatives
of Israel, Jordan, and Egypt. The next day he departed for the Middle
East. The Israelis presented him with a statement of their position,
emphasizing the need for explicit and binding commitments to
peace.[11] Jarring conveyed this to the Egyptians, who replied with
their own draft on January 15.[12] As might have been expected, Egypt
stressed the need for Israeli withdrawal from all territory captured in
1967. Jarring redrafted the Egyptian document somewhat and presented it to the Israelis on January 18. The Israelis responded with a
new draft on January 27.

At this point the United States began to urge Jarring to take a
more aggressive approach, abandoning his role as message carrier and
putting forward ideas of his own. The Israelis were opposed to such
a procedure, but the State Department strongly favored it, particularly as time seemed to be running out. Sadat had agreed in November to a three-month renewal of the cease-fire, which therefore would
expire on February 7.

Rogers had been in contact with the Egyptian foreign minister,
Mahmoud Riad, earlier in the month. The Egyptians were clearly
more interested in knowing what role the United States was prepared
to play and what type of settlement it envisaged than they were in
receiving Israeli proposals through Jarring. They had long believed
that Israel was little more than an extension of the United States, so
that if Washington favored full Israeli withdrawal, Israel would have
to comply.

On January 27, Rogers sent Riad an oral message through Bergus.
He appealed for an extension of the cease-fire, promising that Israel
would submit new "substantive ideas" for a peace settlement immediately thereafter. Rogers confirmed that the views that he expressed in his December 9, 1969, speech were still valid and that the

10. Little was known in Washington about Sadat when he became president. The
biography prepared by the CIA was less than flattering. It prominently mentioned that Sadat
had gone to the cinema on the night of the Egyptian revolution in 1952, implying that this
was typical of his political style. Sadat openly discusses the incident in his book, *Revolt on
the Nile*.

11. The Israeli position was outlined accurately in *Jeune Afrique*, Jan. 19, 1971, and
Arab Report and Record, Jan. 16–31, 1971, p. 75.

12. *Arab Report and Record*, January 16–31, 1971, p. 75.

United States was prepared to make an "all out effort to help the parties reach a settlement this year." He took credit for having gotten Israel to drop the demand for face-to-face talks and denied that Israel had a veto over United States policy.[13]

With these assurances in hand, Sadat announced on February 4 that he would agree to a one-month extension of the cease-fire. Although he castigated the United States for its "full alignment with Israel," Sadat nonetheless presented a "new Egyptian initiative, compliance with which we shall consider as a true yardstick of the desire to implement the UN Security Council resolution."

> We demand that during the period when we refrain from opening fire that a partial withdrawal of the Israeli forces on the east bank of the Suez Canal be achieved as the first stage of a timetable which will be prepared later to implement the other provisions of the Security Council resolution. If this is achieved within this period, we shall be prepared to begin immediately to clear the Suez Canal and reopen it to international navigation to serve the world economy.
>
> We believe that by this initiative, we shall be turning envoy Jarring's efforts from ambiguous words into definite measures. . . .[14]

In fact, Sadat's initiative was soon to supersede Jarring's mission, but not before Jarring had made one last effort. On February 8, Jarring presented a memorandum to Egypt and Israel in which he asked both parties for "parallel and simultaneous commitments." Israel was asked to agree in principle to withdraw to the former international boundary between Egypt and the British mandate of Palestine, subject to practical security arrangements and freedom of navigation in the Suez Canal and the Strait of Tiran. Egypt was asked to enter into a peace agreement with Israel, including an end to belligerency, respect for Israel's independence and right to live in peace within secure and recognized boundaries, and noninterference in Israel's domestic affairs.

On February 15, Egypt replied, accepting all of Jarring's points and adding a number of others. Israel's reply was not forthcoming until February 26. Israel welcomed Egypt's unprecedented expression of readiness to enter into a peace agreement with Israel, but on the crucial issue of withdrawal the reply was blunt: "Israel will not

13. *New York Times*, Feb. 2, 1971.
14. The text of Sadat's Feb. 4, 1971, speech can be found in *New Middle East*, March 1971, pp. 32–35.

withdraw to the pre-June 5, 1967, lines." Instead, Israel offered to negotiate without prior conditions. Egypt, however, viewed Israel's refusal to accept the principle of full withdrawal as an unacceptable prior condition. Under these circumstances, the Jarring talks came to an abrupt end.[15]

THE INTERIM CANAL-AGREEMENT INITIATIVE

As Jarring was making his last effort to get the parties to agree to the outlines of an overall settlement, an alternative approach based on a partial agreement involving the Suez Canal was gaining increasing attention. Thus the collapse of the Jarring talks did not leave the diplomatic field empty. In fact, the idea of an "interim agreement," which had been in the wings for some time, was now to move to center stage.

Israeli Defense Minister Dayan had publicly spoken in November 1970 of the possibility of a mutual Egyptian and Israeli thinning out of forces along the Suez Canal, thereby permitting its clearing and eventual reopening to international trade. In Dayan's view, such a step would help to stabilize the situation along the canal and to reinforce the cease-fire then in effect. If the canal were open and the cities along its banks were rebuilt, Sadat could obviously not resume hostilities without paying a high cost. Besides, such a small step might relieve Israel from the continuing international pressures to accept the principle of full withdrawal from Arab territory.

Within Israel, Dayan's ideas received a mixed reaction. The prime minister seemed unenthusiastic, and others were overtly hostile. The concept apparently did have some appeal, however, to the Egyptian leadership. Shortly after the resumption of the Jarring initiative, a high-ranking Egyptian official approached an American diplomat in Cairo on January 11, 1971, and expressed interest in Dayan's idea of a mutual thinning out of forces and a reopening of the canal. Several days later, Assistant Secretary Sisco informed Israeli Ambassador Rabin of this communication. Then, on February 4, Sadat publicly announced his initiative: in return for a partial Israeli withdrawal from the canal, Egypt would begin to clear and then reopen it. No mention was made of a mutual thinning out of forces, nor were specifics concerning the line of Israeli withdrawal mentioned.

15. For Jarring's memorandum, along with the Egyptian and Israeli replies, see *Arab Report and Record,* Mar. 1–15, 1971, pp. 158–59. The United States had strongly urged Israel not to include the sentence on refusing to withdraw to the pre-June 5, 1967, lines.

The Israelis were immediately urged by Washington to take Sadat's proposal seriously. Egypt was pressing for a rapid reply. On February 9, Golda Meir stated that Israel was prepared to consider the idea of reopening the canal, but that Israeli troops would not withdraw from the existing cease-fire lines until an overall settlement had been reached. In passing, she criticized the Americans for emphasizing international guarantees, which she implied might be substitutes for peace.[16] Three days later, Israel asked the United States to convey a message to Egypt reiterating Israel's interest in discussing the reopening of the canal. This was done on February 14, along with an expression of hope that Egypt would respond positively to Jarring's initiative, which was done the following day.

In an interview with *Newsweek* on February 15, Sadat spelled out in more detail his concept of an interim agreement. If Israel were prepared to withdraw to a line running from Al-Arish to Ras Muhammad, nearly two-thirds of the way across Sinai, he would reopen the canal within six months, extend the cease-fire, and allow international forces to remain at Sharm al-Shaykh to ensure freedom of navigation. Sadat's concept of a partial agreement was very far removed from Dayan's initial idea, but it could be assumed that this opening definition of the line of Israeli withdrawal might be softened with time.

Sadat seemed to realize that Israel would not agree to his terms, but perhaps he could enlist the United States on his side. Over the next several weeks, he repeatedly queried Washington on its attitude to his February initiatives and encouraged Nixon to take an active diplomatic role in the search for a settlement.

Nixon's own views, as articulated by Kissinger, were only partly in tune with Sadat's. In his report to the Congress on United States foreign policy on February 25, 1971, Nixon termed the Middle East the most dangerous region in the world, chiefly because of the potential for superpower confrontation. After describing earlier American peace initiatives in 1969 and 1970, the report called for negotiations among the parties to determine the shape of peace. The United States would not impose a settlement. No specific mention was made of the interim canal-settlement idea. Instead, a lengthy analysis of the "great-power contest" ensued. In a direct warning to the Soviet Union, Nixon declared that "Any effort by any major power to

16. Mrs. Meir's Feb. 9, 1971, speech is reproduced in *New Middle East*, March 1971.

secure a dominant position [in the Middle East] could exacerbate
local disputes, affect Europe's security and increase the danger to
world peace. We seek no such position; we cannot allow others to
establish one."[17]

In contrast to Sadat's insistence on a major United States initiative
and a partial agreement between Egypt and Israel, Nixon placed
greater emphasis on the U.S.-Soviet relationship in the area and the
responsibility of the local parties to negotiate their own terms of
settlement within a comprehensive framework. Sadat was not discouraged, however, and continued to try to draw the United States
toward his own views, suggesting at one point that it was up to the
United States to "squeeze Israel."[18]

Following a secret two-day trip to Moscow on March 1 and 2,
Sadat sent Nixon a long letter on March 5. In it, he set forward his
reasons for not renewing the cease-fire upon its expiration two days
later. More important, he appealed to Nixon to launch an initiative
to bring about an interim agreement along the lines of his February 4
speech. Nixon took Sadat's bid seriously, and the State Department
was instructed to begin work on the interim canal-settlement idea.

Israel was not particularly pleased to see the signs of American
activism. The Nixon report to Congress, with its emphasis on the
Soviet presence in the Middle East, had been welcomed, but now the
State Department was showing signs of vacillation. Israeli leaders
were distrustful of Rogers, suspecting that he would be prepared to
pressure Israel for concessions as a way of conciliating the Arabs.
Whether Nixon and Kissinger would support such a move was an
open question. After the close working relationship established with
the White House during the Jordan crisis, the Israelis had reason to
hope that Rogers was not reflecting Nixon's true feelings.

As the American initiative began to get under way, the Israelis
complained that arms agreements were being delayed as a form of
pressure.[19] Reacting to questions about Israel's peace map, Prime
Minister Meir publicly stated on March 13 that Israel must retain Sharm
al-Shaykh and an access road to it, that Sinai must be demilitarized,
that the border around Eilat must be changed, that the Egyptians

17. *U.S. Foreign Policy for the 1970s, "Building for Peace,"* A Report to the Congress
by Richard Nixon, Feb. 25, 1971.
18. *Al-Ahram* editor Mohamed Heikal soon began a series of articles on the need to
"neutralize" the United States.
19. *New York Times*, Mar. 10, 1971.

must not return to Gaza, that the Golan Heights would remain under Israeli control, that Jerusalem must remain united, and that border changes on the West Bank would be necessary.[20] In talks with Foreign Minister Eban a few days later, Rogers urged Israel to rely on guarantees instead of territory for security.

As these exchanges suggest, it was difficult to keep the diplomacy focused on a limited, partial agreement involving the Suez Canal and a thinning out of forces. Both sides wanted to know the other's position on broader issues, and when those were raised the gap was enormous, especially on the issue of territory.

Nonetheless, on March 31, Nixon wrote to Sadat, welcoming the canal proposal. This led to an intensified exchange of positions, with Sadat conveying to the American minister in Cairo, Donald Bergus, his opinion of the terms for a final settlement on April 1. His frame of reference was Prime Minister Meir's statement of March 13. He would not accept the complete demilitarization of Sinai, nor could Israel remain at Sharm al-Shaykh. Limited demilitarized zones would be acceptable only if they were on both sides of the frontier.[21]

In an effort to get the talks back to the issue of the Suez Canal and a partial agreement, the United States encouraged the Israelis to set forth their position in writing. As an inducement, it was announced on April 19 that twelve more F-4s would be sent to Israel.[22] That same day, Israel offered a proposal containing the following terms:

—After the reopening of the canal, Israeli ships and cargoes should be allowed through.

—A cease-fire of unlimited duration should be part of any future agreement.

—Israel would retain control of the Bar Lev line along the canal.

—Egypt would thin out its forces to the west of the canal.

—The line of withdrawal established in the interim agreement would not be considered a final border.

In addition, Israel asked for full United States support for its position and a reaffirmation of the assurances contained in Nixon's letters of July 23, 1970, and December 3, 1970. Two days later Nixon

20. Meir interview in *The London Times*, Mar. 13, 1971. Mrs. Meir's comments set off a lively debate within Israel. The right-wing Gahal party accused her of being too conciliatory.
21. *New York Times*, Apr. 2, 1971.
22. Ibid., Apr. 20, 1971.

conveyed the desired assurances, but declined to offer full support. The Egyptians were told that an Israeli proposal had been received, but its content was not immediately disclosed.

Reacting to press reports of the Israeli proposal, Sadat met with Donald Bergus and Michael Sterner, the Egyptian-desk officer from the State Department, on April 23. Egyptian forces, he said, must be allowed to cross the canal; Egypt must control the strategically important Mitla and Giddi passes; demilitarized zones could be established; Israel could retain Sharm al-Shaykh in the first stage, but within six months a full settlement must be reached. If Israel were not prepared to give up the passes, said Sadat, then the United States should end its initiative.

Sadat's statement, if taken literally, would have brought the American effort to a halt. Israel was obviously not prepared to accept these terms. At the White House, the conclusion was drawn that there was little chance of agreement, but State was not prepared to give up so easily. Instead, hoping that Sadat would moderate his position, Rogers decided to travel to the Middle East, the first secretary of state since 1953 to visit Egypt and Israel.

By the time Rogers reached Cairo on May 4, it was apparent that Sadat's domestic political situation was somewhat shaky. Two days earlier he had dismissed the powerful secretary general of the Arab Socialist Union, Ali Sabri. Since Sabri had a reputation for being pro-Soviet, his removal was welcomed by the Americans, and in this atmosphere, the talks with Sadat went well. Sadat was polite, charming, and apparently willing to be flexible. Rogers reportedly praised his moderation and implied that the United States had nothing more to ask of him—or so Sadat later said.[23]

It was in Israel that Rogers encountered more difficulty. The Israelis were cool to Rogers personally and suspected him of being pro-Arab. Nonetheless, the discussions were detailed and quickly hit upon the key issues. How would an interim agreement be linked to an overall peace settlement? Israel wanted no linkage, whereas Sadat wanted a timetable for full Israeli withdrawal, of which the interim agreement would merely be the first step. How long would the cease-fire last? Israel wanted an indefinite extension, whereas Egypt preferred a short renewal. How far would Israel withdraw from the canal? A few kilometers, or halfway or more across Sinai? How would the

23. *Newsweek*, Dec. 13, 1971.

agreement be supervised? Would Egyptian troops be allowed across the canal? Would Israel's ships be allowed to use the canal after its opening? On each of these points, the parties were far apart. Defense Minister Dayan sensed the danger of deadlock, and in talks with Sisco he outlined some modifications of the Israeli position. Israel would be prepared to accept Egyptian civilians and technicians on the east bank of the canal, but no military forces. Once the canal was re-opened, Israel would agree to talk about withdrawal of her forces.[24] Sisco was authorized to return to Egypt to discuss these ideas with Sadat and to report on the talks in Israel.

In Cairo, Sisco offered a number of ideas that he hoped might bridge the gap between the two parties.[25] Sadat indicated a willing-ness to consider only a limited Egyptian force on the canal's east bank and promised to send his trusted aide, Mahmoud Fawzi, to Washing-ton with a reply to Sisco's other suggestions. A few days later, having just deposed some of his key ministers for having plotted against him,[26] Sadat asked for clarification on the points raised by Sisco. Was it correct to assume that the Israelis might consider a line of withdrawal east of the passes? Sisco replied on May 18 that such a line was not precluded, that there was some flexibility in the Israeli position.

Rogers and Sisco must have realized that they were in a very deli-cate position. With the Egyptians, they were trying to present Israeli proposals as more forthcoming than they actually were. With the Israelis, the Egyptian statements were recast in the best possible light. But instead of succeeding in convincing either party of the other's good intentions, Rogers and Sisco seemed instead to lose credibility, especially with the Israelis. With the Egyptians it took a bit longer, but ultimately the sense of deception was equally great. At the White House, meanwhile, support for Rogers and Sisco was quickly fading.

On May 20, Egyptian Foreign Minister Mahmoud Riad met with Bergus to present Egypt's reply to Sisco's points of May 9. Bergus was sure that the Egyptian statement was so negative in tone that the

---

24. Whetten, op. cit., pp. 182–83; *New York Times*, May 10, 1971; Meir speech of June 9, 1971, reported in *New York Times*, June 10, 1971.

25. Sadat claimed subsequently, in his interview in *Newsweek*, Dec. 13, 1971, that Sisco had illustratively sketched lines on a map of Sinai indicating the depth of Israeli withdrawal. Sadat suggested that UN peacekeeping forces should be stationed between the Egyptian and Israeli lines.

26. Including Sami Sharaf, in charge of presidential security; Sharawi Guma, minister of interior; General Mohammed Fawzi, minister of defense.

diplomatic effort would collapse. Riad was known to be opposed to
an interim settlement in any event, but perhaps Sadat would agree
to a softer statement of the Egyptian position. Bergus returned to
see Riad's deputy three days later with a redraft of the foreign minister's paper, which he offered as a suggestion of how Egypt could
present its position in a more positive light. He emphasized that he
was doing this on his own initiative and that his government had not
been informed. At the top of the paper, Riad's deputy wrote in
Arabic that these were points suggested unofficially by Donald
Bergus.

Meanwhile, Sadat was trying to consolidate his shaky hold on
power in the aftermath of the internal shake-ups of May. The Soviet
Union was uneasy because of the disappearance of some of its friends
from key positions. On May 25, Soviet President Podgorny arrived
in Cairo with a draft treaty in hand for Sadat's signature. After two
days of talks, Sadat agreed, and on May 27 an Egyptian-Soviet treaty
of friendship, to last for fifteen years, was signed.

Sadat hastened to inform the Americans that the treaty changed
nothing, and to demonstrate his continuing interest in an interim
agreement, he called in Bergus on May 30 to discuss Egypt's terms
for a settlement. He still insisted on obtaining the passes and on
sending tanks across the canal. Then, on June 4, Sadat handed Bergus
a formal Egyptian proposal that included these and other points,
and which was virtually identical to the paper Bergus had prepared
on May 23.

Sadat must have expected an early and positive reply to his proposal. After all, it was very close to Bergus's paper, and Sadat thought
that Bergus must have been reflecting official American thinking.
Bergus carried Sadat's June 4 document to Rogers immediately. However, there was no reaction.[27] A month passed with no American
reply. Rogers had asked Nixon if he would relaunch his initiative,
but Nixon had demurred. There simply did not appear to be grounds
for an agreement. A quarrel with Israel at this time would serve no
purpose, and it could only hurt the administration. Moreover, this
was a time when Nixon needed all the support he could muster.

27. Sadat later complained on numerous occasions that he had accepted 90 percent of
the United States proposal in the Bergus paper, and that the United States had then ignored
his reply. There seems to be little doubt that Sadat viewed the paper as an official statement
of United States policy. See Mohamed Heikal, *The Road to Ramadan* (New York: Quadrangle
Books, 1975), p. 146.

Unknown to the general public, Kissinger had begun to hold secret talks with the North Vietnamese in Paris, and Nixon wanted to concentrate on big issues like Vietnam. He had one other surprise in store as well. On July 9, Kissinger secretly flew to Peking from Pakistan, and this opening to China was made public a few days later. Compared with these dramatic developments, the Middle East was a tiresome distraction.

Meeting in San Clemente for a review of foreign policy after Kissinger's China trip, Nixon, Rogers, and Sisco discussed the Middle East. Sadat was apparently still interested in a limited agreement, but his patience was wearing thin. Nixon agreed that Sisco should travel to Israel to learn whether the Israelis would drop their objection to a token Egyptian force on the east bank of the canal. He pointedly refused, however, to promise that he would exert pressure on Israel if Sisco encountered difficulty. In brief, Sisco was on his own.

Sisco's talks in Israel dragged on from the end of July through the first week of August.[28] Israel would not budge, and Sisco could do nothing but admit defeat. He did not even stop in Cairo, so that it was left to Bergus to brief Mohamed Heikal on the talks.

To say the least, the Egyptians were disappointed. At worst, the Americans had played Sadat for a fool. He had announced that 1971 would be a "year of decision," either war or peace.[29] He had made unprecedented concessions in February, and had again tried to meet American expectations in June. He had risked his relations with the Soviet Union by moving against its supporters and by helping to crush a communist coup in Sudan in July. Not only had he failed to win the Americans to his side, but the Americans were considering new arms agreements with Israel. Frustrated and humiliated, Sadat decided to abandon the interim-settlement idea. The result was a two-year diplomatic stalemate.

KISSINGER TAKES CHARGE

The failure of the interim canal settlement effectively ended the predominance of Rogers and Sisco as Middle East policy makers. If there were to be any new American initiatives, Nixon and Kissinger would be in charge.

28. Sisco tried to persuade the Israelis to accept a two-stage agreement, with only a token Egyptian force crossing the canal. *New York Times,* Aug. 7, 1971.

29. Rogers seems to have first termed 1971 the "year of decision" in the Middle East. See *Department of State Bulletin,* Jan. 11, 1971, p. 43.

Kissinger was critical of the way the State Department had handled the Middle East from the beginning. He had little admiration for Secretary Rogers and was unenthusiastic about the plan that bore his name. His attitude toward Sisco was more complex. He genuinely admired the assistant secretary's energy and intelligence, but felt that he was too much of an activist, a tactician more than a strategist, and more interested in procedure than in substance. Perhaps Sisco's worst fault, however, was that he did not defer sufficiently to Kissinger's authority.

With respect to the interim-settlement effort, Kissinger drew a number of lessons that later guided his own diplomacy after the October 1973 war. The United States, he thought, had become involved too quickly in the substance of the negotiations. Once this happened, the role of impartial negotiator was in jeopardy. Only when the parties were near agreement was it appropriate for the United States to make substantive recommendations. Kissinger also felt that Rogers and Sisco had not been fully candid with Egypt and Israel. They had tried to soften the real positions of the two sides, but had only succeeded in raising false hopes, especially on the part of Sadat. Whatever their motivations, Rogers and Sisco should have represented each party's negotiating position accurately.

Kissinger strongly believed that negotiations, to be successful, had to be carried out in secret. This was difficult with both the Arabs and the Israelis, but Rogers and Sisco had conducted too much of the negotiations in the glare of publicity. And when secrecy was maintained, as during Rogers's talks in Cairo, it was the White House that was kept in the dark! Kissinger never knew exactly what Rogers told Sadat, nor did he know of the Bergus memorandum until it was publicly revealed at the end of June.[30]

The idea of an interim agreement unlinked to the final terms of settlement very much appealed to Kissinger. He was particularly anxious for such an accord if it would ensure the departure of the Soviet military advisers from Egypt. In practice, however, the interim-agreement approach had very quickly drifted back to the package-settlement concept, with the canal pullback as only the initial stage of a comprehensive accord. Therefore, Kissinger's initial interest in the approach began to fade by April, and by summer he was prepared

30. *New York Times*, June 30, 1971.

STANDSTILL DIPLOMACY: 1971-73

to see it die an ignominious death, even at some risk to United States-Egyptian relations.

Kissinger also disagreed with the State Department's contention that Israel could be persuaded to moderate her negotiating stance if arms were withheld. Kissinger argued that this would simply make the Israelis feel more insecure and therefore intransigent. It would raise the hopes of the Arabs, particularly in view of the fact that Soviet arms were being delivered to Egypt and Syria in large quantities. Only if Israel felt strong would she be reasonable in negotiations, and only if the Arabs saw that Soviet arms did not hold the promise of a military solution would they turn to diplomacy in a serious way. Finally, Kissinger felt that the Israelis were on firm ground in refusing to make concessions to Egypt while the Soviet military presence there remained so large. Let Sadat expel the Soviets; then peace talks could begin.

Kissinger's hope that the Soviet position in the Middle East might be undercut had been strengthened since the Jordan civil war. First, Sadat had moved against his allegedly pro-Soviet advisers in May, then Jordan had eliminated the remnants of the PLO remaining in the country. Even more important, a communist coup d'état in Sudan in July had been reversed by the combined intervention of Egypt and Libya.

Offsetting these desirable developments, however, was the Egyptian-Soviet treaty and an increase in the flow of Soviet arms to Egypt and Syria. Sadat had, on several occasions, stated that the Soviet advisers in his country would leave after the first stage of Israeli withdrawal, but until then he was anxious to keep his military ties intact. Kissinger now hoped to convince Sadat that the removal of the Soviet advisers would have to precede the first stage of withdrawal.

Sadat soon realized that it was not worth dealing with Rogers and Sisco any longer. Following talks between Rogers and Riad in September 1971, Sadat thereafter communicated with Kissinger or Nixon through his adviser on national security, Hafiz Ismail.[31] This link, which bypassed the State Department by relying on each country's intelligence channels, was rarely used in the following months, but it was available when needed.

31. According to Heikal, op. cit., pp. 140, 152-55. My own sources date the initiation of communications through this "back channel" as July 1972, just after Sadat's expulsion of the Soviet advisers, but it may have been in existence earlier, as Heikal contends.

The State Department nonetheless continued to try to promote an Egyptian-Israeli agreement. On October 14, 1971, Rogers spoke at the United Nations, outlining six areas of disagreement between the two parties that had emerged in the interim-canal-settlement talks. Now Rogers proposed that Egypt and Israel send high-ranking officials to the United States to engage in "proximity talks," with Sisco acting as mediator and "catalyst."[32] Sadat accepted, apparently still hoping for some progress before the end of the "year of decision."

Israel was less enthusiastic about proximity talks. Before returning to such a forum, Israel wanted a basic understanding with the United States on arms supply and on the United States and Soviet roles in future negotiations. On November 1, 1971, the United States and Israel signed a significant memorandum of understanding regarding American aid to Israel to enhance her military self-sufficiency.[33] Israel was planning to build a jet fighter modeled on the French Mirage. A complete set of blueprints for the plane had been smuggled out through Switzerland.[34] Israel could not produce the engine, however, hence the United States agreed in principle to provide the missing component.

Since mid-year the United States had refrained from signing any new arms agreements with Israel. This was done out of a conviction that the military balance remained in Israel's favor and in the hope of gaining leverage over Israeli policy. Moreover, the State Department did not want to undercut Sadat's position during the interim canal negotiations.

Prime Minister Meir visited Washington in early December 1971 to discuss a new arms agreement. She argued that Israel needed to be assured of a continuing flow of aircraft and other equipment well into the 1970s. The Soviets had no hesitation in helping their friends. Why did the Americans insist on punishing Israel by withholding arms? That only increased Arab intransigence. A long-term agreement would convince the Soviets and the Arabs that they could not separate the United States from Israel and that a military solution was impossible, and such an agreement would allow Israel to negotiate from strength.

Nixon and Kissinger were basically in agreement with Mrs. Meir's

32. Sadat interview, *Newsweek*, Dec. 13, 1971.   33. *New York Times*, Jan. 14, 1972.
34. *New York*, Aug. 30, 1976.

points. In addition, a long-term agreement would help to avoid periodic squabbles over new arms agreements. Each time a new arms package was requested, the United States and Israel argued over the terms and the timing. The Arabs saw the quarrels as encouraging signs, but then felt disillusioned when the United States eventually provided the arms. In an election year, especially, Nixon had no desire to confront Israel over arms. Should an initiative prove to be possible after the elections, it would not be marred by publicity over a new arms agreement if a long-term accord were reached now. Consequently, on December 31 it was announced that the United States had agreed in principle to resume shipments of F-4s to Israel.

Much of January 1972 was spent in discussing the terms of the new arms deal with the Israelis. In addition, Sisco and Rabin met frequently to establish the ground rules for proximity talks. The result was another memorandum of understanding on February 2, 1972, whereby the United States agreed to sell Israel forty-two F-4s and eighty-two A-4s over the coming years. In the proximity talks, the Soviet Union would play no substantive role. Most significant of all, the United States would take no initiative in the talks that had not first been fully discussed with the Israelis. If the memorandum were taken literally, the United States had tied itself almost completely to the Israeli position.[35] Four days later, the Israeli cabinet agreed to the idea of proximity talks, but Egypt now refused, and no further diplomatic progress was made.

U.S.-Israeli relations, however, were stronger than ever. Throughout 1972, Nixon was able to portray his administration as a firm supporter of Israel. All the old disputes were forgotten, and Ambassador Rabin came very close to endorsing Nixon's bid for the presidency against the Democratic contender.

During 1972, United States Middle East policy consisted of little more than open support for Israel. The White House explicitly told the State Department not to consider any new initiatives until after the elections. Meanwhile, Nixon set out to reap the rewards of Kissinger's negotiations with the Chinese and the Soviets. A successful foreign policy was clearly going to be a major theme in his reelection campaign.

35. *New York Times*, Feb. 3, 1972; according to Ambassador Rabin, in *Maariv*, Dec. 1, 1972, the memorandum of understanding also acknowledged that Israel would not be expected to make a commitment on full withdrawal as part of an interim agreement.

In his survey of foreign policy presented to the Congress on February 9, 1972, Nixon highlighted the Soviet role in the Middle East. He quoted himself to the effect that U.S.-Soviet interests were "very diametrically opposed" in the Middle East, except for the desire to avoid a confrontation.[36] He then reviewed earlier United States initiatives, emphasizing the obstacles to an Arab-Israeli agreement. The shortcomings of both the package-agreement and the interim-settlement approaches were candidly discussed, but the major theme of his remarks was the need for great power restraint:

> . . . the Soviet Union's effort to use the Arab-Israeli conflict to perpetuate and expand its own military position in Egypt has been a matter of concern to the United States. The U.S.S.R. has taken advantage of Egypt's increasing dependence on Soviet military supply to gain the use of naval and air facilities in Egypt. This has serious implications for the stability of the balance of power locally, regionally in the eastern Mediterranean, and globally. The Atlantic Alliance cannot ignore the possible implications of this move for the stability of the East-West relationship. . . .
>
> We hope the Soviet Union understands that it can serve this interest [of avoiding a major conflict in the Middle East] best by restraint in its arms supply, refraining from the use of the dispute to enhance its own military position, and encouraging the negotiation of a peace.

Aside from urging the parties to begin serious negotiations, Nixon made no suggestions as to how the conflict might be resolved. He did, however, add: "Injecting the global strategic rivalry into the region is incompatible with Middle East peace and with détente in U.S.-Soviet relations."[37]

SUMMITRY

In the last week of February 1972, President Nixon traveled to Peking for talks with Chairman Mao Tse-tung and Prime Minister Chou En-lai. The occasion was historic in terms of U.S.-Chinese relations, but also carried broader significance. Nixon and Kissinger were attempting to alter relations among the major powers in the interests of stability and the avoidance of nuclear war. It was assumed that the

36. From a media briefing on June 18, 1971.
37. *U.S. Foreign Policy for the 1970s,* "*The Emerging Structure of Peace,*" A Report to the Congress by Richard Nixon, Feb. 9, 1972.

Soviet Union would remain the principal adversary of the United States and the greatest threat to United States interests. To help induce restraint on the part of the Soviet Union, the United States was prepared to develop ties with Moscow's main rival, the leadership in Peking. This was a classic stroke of balance-of-power politics, and if successful it would lend substance to the policy of détente which Nixon and Kissinger had widely promoted. Peking was thus an important way-station on the road to Moscow, where Nixon was expected in May.

Between the Peking and Moscow summits, developments in Vietnam took an alarming turn for the worse. The North Vietnamese sent troops across the demilitarized zone on March 30, and for several weeks the communist forces made impressive gains. The United States responded with intensified bombing, and with a major concession to the North Vietnamese during Kissinger's talks in Moscow in late April.[38] On May 8, Nixon made a controversial decision to resume heavy bombing of North Vietnam and to mine the harbor of Haiphong, hoping by those actions to cut the flow of arms to Hanoi. He realized that this might bring the United States into open conflict with both the Soviet Union and China. Many of his advisers were sure that Brezhnev would feel compelled to cancel the upcoming summit conference. Nixon held firm, however, and the Soviets swallowed their price and received Nixon in Moscow on May 22.

One of the great hopes of the Nixon-Kissinger foreign policy had been that détente between the superpowers would have benefits for American policy elsewhere. The summits seemed to confirm their belief that neither the Chinese nor the Soviets would allow developments in Vietnam to stand in the way of their interests in dealing with the United States. Perhaps Moscow could also be persuaded to subordinate its Middle East policies to the requirements of détente. In any event, Nixon and Kissinger were prepared to explore the possibility as one means of reducing the chances of superpower confrontation in the Middle East and, they hoped, of undercutting Soviet influence in Egypt.

In essence, this was a return to the "linkage" concept that had guided the Rogers-Sisco initiative of 1969, but now there was more to build on in the U.S.-Soviet relationship, particularly with the

38. Tad Szulc, "Behind the Vietnam Ceasefire Agreement," *Foreign Policy* 15 (summer 1974), pp. 34–41.

achievement of a treaty limiting strategic nuclear arms. Equally important, from Kissinger's point of view, was the fact that he, not Rogers or Sisco, would handle the talks with the Russians on the Middle East.

Kissinger's objective was to reach agreement with the Soviet leadership on a set of principles that would serve as a framework for an Arab-Israeli peace settlement. Next, he would enlist their support for beginning a "step-by-step" negotiating process based on those principles, but leaving key issues such as final borders to be negotiated by the parties themselves.

Unbeknownst to the State Department, Kissinger and Gromyko reached a tentative working agreement on eight principles. In essence, the two superpowers were in accord on the following points:

—The agreement should be comprehensive, but could be implemented in steps.

—The agreement should contain provisions for withdrawal of Israeli forces from Arab territories occupied in 1967.

—Any border changes should result from voluntary agreement among the parties.

—Security arrangements could include demilitarized zones, UN forces at Sharm al-Shaykh, and international guarantees with the participation of the United States and the Soviet Union.

—The agreement should lead to an end of the state of belligerency and to the establishment of peace.

—Freedom of navigation through the Strait of Tiran and the Suez Canal should be assured. This would be consistent with Egyptian sovereignty over the canal.

—The agreement must include recognition of the independence and sovereignty of all states in the Middle East, including Israel.

—The Palestinian refugee problem should be solved on a just basis in accordance with appropriate UN decisions. (The United States reserved its position on this.)

Finally, the United States maintained that completion of the agreement should involve negotiations between the parties. The Soviet Union did not take a position on this point.

Although this tentative agreement remained secret, the United States and the Soviet Union did announce agreement on a set of basic principles.[39] The two superpowers committed themselves to

39. "Basic Principles of Relations Between the United States of America and the Union of Soviet Socialist Republics," May 29, 1972.

conducting their relations on the basis of peaceful coexistence (article 1) and to "preventing situations capable of causing a dangerous exacerbation of their relations. . . . They will always exercise restraint in their mutual relations, and will be prepared to negotiate and settle differences by peaceful means." (Article 2.) "The U.S.A. and the U.S.S.R. have a special responsibility . . . to do everything in their power so that conflicts or situations will not arise which would serve to increase international tensions." (Article 3.)

In the joint communiqué issued on May 29, the United States and the Soviet Union reaffirmed their support of UN Resolution 242 and of the Jarring mission. A settlement of the Arab-Israeli conflict "would open prospects for the normalization of the Middle East situation and would permit, in particular, consideration of further steps to bring about a military relaxation in that area."[40]

Read in Cairo, the basic principles and the joint communiqué seemed to confirm Sadat's worst fears. Both the United States and the Soviet Union had agreed to freeze the Middle East situation for fear of damaging their own relations. Under the guise of détente, the United States had persuaded the Soviets to reduce their support for the Arabs. This would explain the Soviet reluctance to provide advanced weaponry and the delays in deliveries that had been irritating Sadat for months.

Sadat was well aware that the Americans viewed the Soviet presence in Egypt as an obstacle to a peace settlement. Rogers had raised the issue in May. Now, with the results of the summit meeting available, it seemed clear to Sadat that the Soviets were not prepared to press his case with the Americans. Not only was their presence in Egypt of concern to the Americans and the Israelis, but his own officers were complaining about it. Then, in June, Saudi Arabia's minister of defense, Prince Sultan, reported on his conversations with Nixon and Kissinger. Until the Soviet presence in Egypt was eliminated, the Americans would not press Israel for concessions.[41]

Which of these factors was most compelling to Sadat is unknown, but in early July he decided to act. On July 8, Sadat informed the Soviet ambassador that he was requesting the departure of most of the Soviet advisers and technicians in Egypt. Sadat publicly announced his decision on July 18. More than ten thousand Soviet

40. The texts of both the basic principles and the joint communiqué are found in *United States Foreign Policy, 1972, A Report of the Secretary of State*, April 1973, pp. 598–603.
41. Heikal, op. cit., p. 183; *New York Times*, July 24, 1972.

personnel would leave Egypt, precisely as Kissinger and the Israelis had hoped.

REACTIONS TO THE EXPULSION OF SOVIET ADVISERS

If Sadat's primary motivation in announcing the expulsion of the Soviet advisers in Egypt was to open the way for an active United States diplomatic role, he had chosen a curious time for such a momentous step.[42] Nixon was in the midst of an election campaign and was not prepared to jeopardize his substantial lead over McGovern by embarking on a controversial policy in the Middle East. He and Kissinger, however, did recognize the importance of Sadat's move, and through the "back channel" they informed the Egyptian president that after the American elections were over, a new initiative would be launched. This time it would be under White House control.

A reelected president would presumably be immune to the normal pressures of domestic politics. Nixon's prestige was at its zenith, Kissinger's reputation was growing, and perhaps they could together fashion a settlement in the Middle East.

In midsummer 1972, few could have anticipated that Nixon's ability to conduct foreign policy, and eventually even his tenure in office, would be greatly affected by a seemingly minor incident on June 17. On that day, five men had been apprehended inside the offices of the Democratic headquarters in the Watergate complex in Washington, D.C. Investigation of the break-in revealed that the burglars had curious connections with the CIA and with the Committee to Reelect the President. Perhaps some overly motivated Republicans had broken the law, but no one suspected that the president himself might be involved. On June 23, 1972, however, in a conversation with his chief of staff, H. R. Haldeman, Nixon became enmeshed in the Watergate affair by ordering the CIA to block the FBI's investigation of the incident for political reasons. The conversation was recorded on the president's secret taping system. Its disclosure a little more than two years later proved fatal to Nixon's struggle to survive Watergate. For the moment, however, Nixon and

42. Uri Ra'anan, "The USSR and the Middle East: Some Reflections on the Soviet Decision-Making Process," ORBIS 17, no. 3 (fall 1973), has called into question whether Sadat took the initiative in asking the advisers to leave. Ra'anan raises some intriguing points, but seems to underestimate Sadat's anger at the Soviets.

his aides had little reason to fear that the Watergate affair would not be contained.

On the eve of his reelection, Nixon took pains to speak of his plans for the Middle East. ''The Middle East will have a very high priority because while the Middle East has been, over the past couple of years, in a period of uneasy truce or armistice or whatever you want to call it, it can explode at any time.''[43] The message to Sadat was intended to be that he should remain patient a bit longer. It would soon be his turn, once Vietnam was settled.

Nixon was reelected overwhelmingly on November 7, winning 60.8 percent of the popular vote and 97 percent of the electoral vote. But the ''peace at hand'' in Vietnam remained elusive a bit longer. It was only after an intensive bombing campaign against North Vietnam in December that negotiations resumed. At long last, on January 13, 1973, the Paris talks were successfully concluded; on January 27, the final agreement was signed.

THE KISSINGER STRATEGY

With the end of the fighting in Vietnam, Kissinger was ready to turn his attention to the Middle East. He had previously paid little attention to briefing materials prepared for him on that region; now he requested studies, perused long memoranda, and began to develop a detailed strategy of his own.

Kissinger wanted to avoid endless debates over the meaning of Resolution 242, the Rogers Plan, and the Jarring memorandum. A legalistic approach was bound to bog down rapidly. The key demands of both parties were phrased in totally incompatible terms. The Israelis wanted peace and recognition; the Arabs wanted territory and justice.

Rather than try for initial agreement on these ultimate goals, Kissinger hoped to move quickly to practical agreements, but he realized the importance of some formulation that would address the end result of the negotiating process. The Jarring formulation of ''peace'' for ''withdrawal'' did not appeal to him. Instead, he preferred the formulation recommended by his aides of establishing a balance between ''sovereignty'' and ''security.'' The virtue of such

43. Nixon interview with Garnett D. Horner of the *Washington Star*, Nov. 5, 1972; *New York Times*, Nov. 10, 1972.

a formula was that it opened the door to a wide range of negotiating outcomes. For example, it might be possible to recognize Egypt's sovereignty over Sinai at an early date, while establishing special security arrangements that would allow the Israelis to maintain a presence in key areas during a lengthy transitional period. If agreement could be reached on such a general formulation, then negotiations could begin on concrete issues, such as those identified during the interim-canal-settlement negotiations.

Kissinger had the chance to try out his ideas in February. King Hussein arrived in Washington for talks with Nixon and Kissinger on February 6. He had proposed the previous spring an unpopular plan to establish a United Arab Kingdom consisting of the East and West Banks of the Jordan, subject to approval in a referendum among the Palestinians. Little support had been found for the idea in the Arab world, and both Egypt and Syria had reacted hostilely. Nevertheless, Hussein was still interested in recovering the West Bank and was anxious, as always, for American help. In addition, he was in need of substantial increases in economic and military assistance. Nixon was prepared to accommodate him, for he liked and admired the king.

Still, little could be done to advance a settlement between Jordan and Israel without taking Egypt into account. Kissinger's next visitor, Sadat's national security adviser, Hafiz Ismail, was therefore unusually important. Ismail was the first high-level Egyptian official to meet with Nixon in some time. The visit had been arranged through the "back channel." The State Department was not informed until the last moment.

Nixon met with Hafiz Ismail on February 23, and appeared relaxed and self-confident. He outlined a strategy for negotiating on two levels: one would be handled in secret by Kissinger, as with Vietnam; the other would be public and would involve the State Department.[44] Nixon also mentioned the sovereignty and security formula.

Ismail's real purpose in coming to Washington, however, was to confer with Kissinger. During the next two days, February 24 and 25, Hafiz Ismail and his deputy, Ihab Wahba, met with Kissinger and Harold Saunders at a private estate in Connecticut.[45] Kissinger argued

44. Heikal, op. cit., pp. 200–02.
45. Ibid., pp. 202–03. The estate belonged to the chairman of the board of Pepsi-Cola,

for the necessity of accepting the idea of a settlement's being implemented over a prolonged period. He implied that Egyptian sovereignty over Sinai could be acknowledged at an early date, but that special security arrangements might be required for a long time. Ismail seemed interested and the talks went well. The Egyptian indicated that a normalization of relations with Israel might eventually be possible; that Jordan might have a role to play in solving the Palestinian issue; but he was adamant on full Israeli withdrawal.

They then discussed in detail the obligations that Egypt and Israel would undertake as part of a peace agreement; the relationship between an Egyptian-Israeli agreement and resolution of the Palestine problem; and concrete security arrangements for Israel in Sinai. Unable to resolve all of these issues, Kissinger and Ismail agreed to meet again at an early date. Kissinger was in no rush. He told Ismail that little could be accomplished before Israeli elections, scheduled for late October 1973.

Three days later, on February 28, Golda Meir arrived in Washington to meet with Nixon and Kissinger, and was told of the talks with Hussein and Ismail. As usual, she pressed the case for more military assistance to Israel. A decision on a new arms package was at that moment pending. Nixon urged her to be more forthcoming with ideas for an agreement on the Egyptian front.

As Hafiz Ismail was returning from his trip to Washington, an article appeared in the press implying, incorrectly, that the president had decided on new arms aid to Israel. The timing of the article seemed designed to embarrass Ismail and raised serious doubts in Cairo about United States intentions. Kissinger hastened to inform Ismail that the article was false. Yet a few weeks later Nixon did, in fact, make a decision on a new arms package for Israel.[46]

The diplomatic effort launched in February had as its goal the establishment of a "negotiating framework" between Egypt and Israel. Kissinger saw this as being complemented by a U.S.-Soviet agreement on principles of a settlement, based on those tentatively drawn up in Moscow the previous May. He realized that it would take time for all of the pieces to fall into place.

Donald Kendall, who was an ardent Nixon supporter and a proponent of improved U.S.-Egyptian relations.

46. The misleading story appeared in the *Washington Post*, Mar. 2, 1973; the correct story on Nixon's later decision appeared in the *New York Times*, Mar. 14, 1973.

During the spring, however, several events occurred that diverted the attention of the policy makers from the Egyptian-Israeli front. First was the assassination of the American ambassador in Khartoum, Cleo Noel, and his deputy, George Moore. CIA had received intelligence that Black September, the secret terrorist wing of Fatah, was responsible, and that Arafat might have ordered the killings.[47] In the wake of the Munich atrocity the previous September, when eleven Israeli athletes at the Olympic Games had been murdered by Palestinian terrorists, and the assassination in November 1971 of Jordan's Prime Minister Wasfi Tal by Black September, the Khartoum murders created an intense preoccupation with Palestinian terrorism. This was hardly the ideal environment in which to take initiatives aimed at improving U.S.-Arab relations.

A second preoccupation was the "energy crisis" that was increasingly apparent on the horizon. The price of oil had been rising rapidly since 1971. United States production was stagnating, American refinery capacity was insufficient to meet the demand, and shortages of gasoline and fuel oil might be felt by the end of the year. The oil companies were nervous. The president had no policy except to appear to be in control while he cast about for someone to take charge. Visitors to Saudi Arabia began to report that King Faisal, for the first time, was speaking of using the oil weapon to bring pressure on the United States unless Israel were forced to withdraw from Arab territory.

Against this background, tensions in the Middle East mounted sharply in mid-April. Lebanon was thrown into a crisis by an Israeli raid into downtown Beirut that killed three top PLO leaders. More dangerous still, toward the end of the month Egyptian war preparations along the Suez Canal took on an air of determination.[48] Intelligence reports were also received that Syria had completed a detailed war plan and was prepared to attack Israel on short notice. Israel took the signs seriously, ordered a partial mobilization, and eventually the crisis atmosphere passed by mid-May.

Meanwhile the smoldering Watergate issue had flared up. On March 21, a young lawyer working for the White House, John Dean,

47. Arafat and other top Fatah officials have always denied any direct involvement in the assassinations.
48. On Mar. 26, 1973, Sadat had formed a "war cabinet" with himself as prime minister. Three days later he told Arnaud de Borchgrave of *Newsweek* that war was imminent. De Borchgrave rushed the text of the interview to Kissinger prior to its publication on Apr. 9, 1973.

had informed Nixon of the extent of high-level involvement in the Watergate cover-up. He warned Nixon of a "cancer" growing on the presidency. Within weeks of this conversation, Dean was telling his story to the FBI investigators dealing with Watergate. Evidence was rapidly accumulating that implicated the president's closest associates—Mitchell, Haldeman, and Ehrlichman. Increasingly, Nixon was obliged to devote his time and energies to the Watergate crisis. On April 30, he accepted the resignations of Haldeman and Ehrlichman. Of his closest advisers, only Kissinger now remained.

Kissinger tried to keep Middle East policy on the track charted in February, but because Nixon's authority was being undermined, it was increasingly difficult. On May 3, Nixon's fourth "State of the World" message was sent to Congress. It spelled out clearly the Kissinger strategy. In a section entitled "The Situation Today," Nixon argued for serious negotiations between the local parties, insisting that an imposed settlement would not last. Sovereignty and security were identified as key issues. Nixon continued to develop the theme of negotiations:

> A step-by-step approach still seems most practical, but we fully recognize that one step by itself cannot bring peace. First, there is a relationship between any initial step toward peace and the steps which are to follow toward a broader settlement. We are open-minded on how that relationship might be established in a negotiating process, and on what role the United States might play. But the relationship cannot be ignored. Second, all important aspects of the Arab-Israeli conflict must be addressed at some stage, including the legitimate interests of the Palestinians. Implementation can occur in stages, and it should not be precluded that some issues and disputes could be resolved on a priority basis. But a comprehensive settlement must cover all the parties and all the major issues.
>
> The issues are formidable, interlinked, and laden with emotion. The solutions cannot be found in general principles alone, but must be embodied in concrete negotiated arrangements. The parties will not be tricked into compromise positions by artful procedures. But there is room for accommodation and an overwhelming necessity to seek it.[49]

Kissinger now began to think of how he might induce the Soviet Union to cooperate with his efforts to begin a negotiating process. He

49. *U.S. Foreign Policy for the 1970s, "Shaping a Durable Peace,"* A Report to the Congress by Richard Nixon, May 3, 1973, p. 138.

wanted Moscow to endorse publicly a set of principles that would serve as a set of guidelines for a settlement. Perhaps the Soviet Union would be more cooperative if they could be persuaded that the status quo was not working to their advantage in the Middle East. The expulsion of Soviet advisers from Egypt in 1972 had been a welcome development. Kissinger now toyed with the idea of trying to weaken the Soviets in Iraq and South Yemen as well, perhaps with the help of Iran and Saudi Arabia. In his view, such anti-Soviet moves in the Middle East would not be incompatible with his objective of enlisting Soviet support for negotiations, provided that United States involvement remain secret.

On May 4, Kissinger arrived in Moscow to prepare for the second Nixon-Brezhnev summit meeting. While there, he received a new document from Gromyko that set forth nine principles of an Arab-Israeli settlement. Gromyko's document, unlike that of the previous May, called for complete Israeli withdrawal to the June 4, 1967, lines. It also referred to the "legitimate rights" of the Palestinians. One new note was included: failure by either party to implement any part of the agreement would give the other party the right to refuse to fulfill its own obligations. On the whole, Kissinger much preferred the May 1972 document.[50]

The State Department was kept in the dark concerning these discussions, which added greatly to Secretary Rogers's frustration. Kissinger's domination of United States foreign policy was increasingly apparent as Nixon became engulfed in the Watergate crisis. His position did not go unchallenged, however. On May 15, 1973, Secretary Rogers proposed a new American initiative for settling the Arab-Israeli conflict. Rogers suggested an "exploratory" effort by the United States, which might help to stabilize the region even if it did not immediately produce results. He proposed a two-track approach, one public and one secret. The public effort would focus on a canal agreement, as in 1971. The secret effort would aim at direct Egyptian-Israeli talks on broader issues. To break the impasse that had been encountered earlier, he recommended that the United States try to persuade the parties to agree that Resolution 242 neither endorsed nor precluded return to the pre-June 1967 lines. Kissinger

50. After returning from Moscow, Kissinger consulted with Israeli officials on Israel's reaction to the May 1972 principles. He was told that Israel was opposed to the idea altogether, but that if such principles were announced they should call for negotiations and should only speak of Israeli withdrawal to secure and recognized borders.

was unenthusiastic, and at his suggestion Nixon gave Rogers no encouragement.

Rogers's exasperation was further increased when he learned by accident that Kissinger was planning to meet again with Hafiz Ismail. This time he insisted that one of his own representatives be present, and when Kissinger and Ismail met secretly outside of Paris on May 20, Roy Atherton, the deputy assistant secretary of state for Near Eastern affairs, was part of the United States team.

Ismail was less interested in substance during these talks than he had been in February. He concentrated his questions instead on the role that the United States intended to play. What kind of White House involvement could Egypt expect? Why was the United States continuing to arm Israel so lavishly? How could Egyptian sovereignty in Sinai be made real, not just a symbol? The unresolved issues from February were discussed, but inconclusively. Ismail insisted that a final peace between Egypt and Israel was contingent upon a solution to the Palestinian problem.

Kissinger described to Ismail his strategy of trying for a U.S.-Soviet agreement on principles, to be followed by secret negotiations between the parties. Kissinger spoke with Ismail privately for a few minutes and felt that he made some progress. He then suggested that further talks would be desirable. Ismail promised an early reply, but when it came on June 3, it was guarded and unenthusiastic. Perhaps the Egyptians were beginning to have their doubts about Nixon's ability to produce results, given his crumbling domestic base. In any event, the promising tone of the February talks was missing in May.

BREZHNEV'S VISIT

If U.S.-Egyptian relations seemed to be stagnating, the same could not be said for U.S.-Soviet ties. Kissinger had been treated with great courtesy and attention in May, and now, in June, Brezhnev arrived for his first visit to the United States. Talks on the Middle East were focused on the May 1972 document, with some additions from Gromyko's more recent draft. The Soviet language on full withdrawal and the "rights" of the Palestinians, however, was not accepted by the United States.

Nixon and Brezhnev, along with Kissinger and Gromyko and their staffs, discussed the Middle East at length. Brezhnev warned that the Egyptians and Syrians were intent upon going to war and

that the Soviet Union could not stop them. Only a new American
initiative and, in particular, pressure on Israel to withdraw, could
prevent war. The joint communiqué issued on June 25, 1973, gave
little idea of the content of the talks. The Soviets even refused to
allow Resolution 242 to be mentioned unless Jarring's February 1971
document was also included. The final language therefore merely
stated: "Both parties agreed to continue to exert their efforts to promote the quickest possible settlement in the Middle East. This settlement should be in accordance with the interests of all states in the
area, be consistent with their independence and sovereignty, and
should take into account the legitimate interests of the Palestinian
people."[51]

Following the June summit talks, United States Middle East
policy entered the summer doldrums. Nothing much could be done
until after the Israeli elections in any case, according to Kissinger. The
Arabs were clearly frustrated—Sadat called the United States the
"world's biggest bully" on July 23—and Faisal was publicly linking
oil and the Arab-Israeli conflict.[52] Sadat also seemed intent upon
forcing the United States into an anti-Arab posture by calling for a
UN debate on the Middle East crisis and then pressing for a vote on
a resolution strongly condemning Israel. For the fifth time in its
history, the United States cast a veto. The Arab world reacted angrily.
Kissinger wondered why Sadat was seeking a confrontation. Was he
merely trying to pressure the United States to take a more active role?

During the third week of July 1973, Kissinger devoted considerable time to the Middle East, particularly the question of Soviet involvement. He was concerned that the State Department's penchant
for solving conflicts led the United States to "lean on" its friends. His
preference was to build on those friendships to look after American
interests in the region.

In talks held during this period, Kissinger developed this perspective with regard to the Arab-Israeli conflict. He called the highly
publicized American peace initiatives in the Middle East "disastrous." When the United States had gone public with its views, it

51. U.S.-U.S.S.R. joint communiqué, June 25, 1973.
52. Kissinger was concerned by signs of Faisal's growing involvement in the Arab-Israeli
conflict. He feared that Saudi activism would ultimately bring down the monarchy, which
might then be replaced by a Qaddafi-like regime. Each time King Faisal made some reference
to the use of oil as a weapon against the West, however, one of his aides would hasten to inform
United States officials that this was meant only for domestic Arab consumption.

had been attacked by Israel, the Israeli lobby, and the Arabs, and was thus caught in the middle. In his view, the United States lacked the kind of leverage in the Middle East that it had in Vietnam. Before moving publicly with a new initiative, it should have one side lined up "so we can move against the other." In that way, the United States would not be attacked by both sides. In addition, it could not dissociate itself too greatly from Israel without displaying dangerous signals to the Soviet Union.

He thought of the Arab negotiating position as "impossible." The Arabs called for total Israeli withdrawal in return for an end of belligerency; then, according to the Egyptians, Israel would have to negotiate with the Palestinians for a final peace. Egypt's position on the difference between the end of belligerency and a final peace was very vague. The United States could not simply tell Israel to withdraw and then to talk to the Palestinians. Furthermore, Egypt was not clear on whether King Hussein could speak for the Palestinians.

Kissinger argued that Israel could not be forced to accept an overall solution all at once. It would be necessary to segment the negotiations into pieces that Israel could manage, after which the negotiations should proceed step by step. Egypt, he felt, was playing into the hands of the Israelis because Israel was primarily interested in wasting time. On the other hand, if a negotiating process could begin, history could work on the side of a settlement.

Kissinger continued to try to separate sovereignty and security. He knew that Sadat saw this as phony, but it was better for his interests than previous positions. He also thought that it might be self-defeating for the United States to adopt a more balanced policy. The Arabs wanted the United States to strike poses, but that would serve no useful purpose. Instead, this country wanted to preserve its influence with Israel until the time when taking a separate position could produce tangible results. The United States sought a balanced policy, but it needed a "fulcrum to move the situation." It could not support the maximum Arab position in negotiations, but if negotiations did start, Israel would begin to move back and a process would be under way. In Kissinger's view, it would be easier to dislodge the Israelis from almost anywhere else in Sinai than it would be from the cease-fire lines.

These thoughts summarize well Kissinger's views on the Arab-Israeli conflict as of mid-1973. The importance of the U.S.-Israeli relationship and his preoccupation with the Soviet Union stand out. The Jordan-crisis lessons were still alive and well nearly three years later.

On August 22, Nixon made a surprise announcement that he was nominating Henry Kissinger as secretary of state to replace William Rogers. Kissinger would keep his position as adviser to the president for national security affairs as well. No longer would Kissinger have to worry about the secretary of state undercutting his strategy.

Three days after becoming secretary of state, on September 25, Kissinger met with most of the Arab ambassadors to the UN. He tried to establish his credentials as a credible mediator, joking about his own Jewish background.[53] He promised to work for a settlement, but warned the ambassadors not to expect miracles. He would only promise what he could deliver, but he would deliver all that he promised. This became a common refrain in Kissinger's talks with the Arabs.

Over the next two weeks, Kissinger spoke several times with the Arab and Israeli foreign ministers attending the UN General Assembly in New York. He proposed, and they seemed to agree, that serious talks between Egypt and Israel, with the United States as mediator, should begin in November. On October 5, he met with Egypt's Foreign Minister Zayyat to confirm these arrangements. On the whole, he was satisfied with the results of his first foray as secretary of state into Middle East diplomacy.

The next day, Yom Kippur, Egypt and Syria launched a combined military offensive against Israeli forces in the Golan Heights and Sinai. Kissinger's policy lay in ruins, overtaken by a war that he had feared but that he had felt sure would be prevented by maintaining the military balance in Israel's favor and by inducing the Soviet Union to play a restraining role through the policy of détente. Those beliefs, forged in the midst of the Jordan crisis, had been dangerously deceptive.

CONCLUSIONS

The period between the Jordan crisis in September 1970 and the October 1973 war was deceptively calm. In the absence of acute crises, American policy makers paid comparatively little attention to the

53. Edward R.F. Sheehan. *The Arabs, Israelis, and Kissinger* (New York: Reader's Digest Press, 1976), pp. 27–28.

area. The basic frame of reference, set by Nixon and Kissinger, emphasized the U.S.-Soviet relationship in the area and the need to maintain the balance of power in Israel's favor. Periodically, the State Department tried to launch a new initiative—the Jarring talks, the interim canal settlement, proximity talks—but the White House was only mildly supportive at best, and on occasion was distinctly negative. Bureaucratic rivalries became personalized in the Rogers-Kissinger quarrel. On the whole, Nixon sided with Kissinger. As a result, United States policy during this period was particularly ineffective and inconsistent. During the interim canal-settlement talks, it was especially flawed; the Rogers-Sisco mediation and the Bergus memorandum left a bitter after-taste in Israel, Egypt, and the White House.

During this noncrisis period, domestic politics also began to intrude on policy making in noticeable ways. Because of election-year imperatives in 1972, no initiatives were undertaken, even in response to Sadat's expulsion of the Soviet advisers. Then, in 1973, Watergate began to divert the attention of the president from the region to which he had promised to devote highest priority in his foreign policy.

As Kissinger began to focus on the Middle East, he wavered between striving for U.S.-Soviet agreement on principles as the main thrust of his policy and the effort to begin step-by-step negotiations between Egypt and Israel. Curiously, both of these approaches had been tried by Rogers and had failed, but Kissinger had confidence that his skills as a negotiator would help prevent the tactical errors that he perceived in the previous American efforts.

The most impressive shift in policy during this period concerned U.S.-Israeli relations. Despite occasional disagreements over arms, the United States and Israel entered an unusually cooperative phase in their often troubled relationship. This was very much the result of the Jordan crisis and Kissinger's view of Israel as a strategic asset. In fiscal years 1968, 1969, and 1970 Israel had received from the United States military credits worth $25 million, $85 million, and $30 million respectively. After the Jordan crisis, in fiscal years 1971, 1972, and 1973 Israel received military credits of $545 million, $300 million, and $307.5 million respectively. This represented nearly a tenfold increase in aid.

Yet the military balance proved not to be the key to regional stability and the prevention of war. Nor did détente prevent the

Soviet Union from continuing to arm Egypt, Syria, and Iraq, despite the mounting signs of Arab intentions to resume hostilities. Nixon and Kissinger remained insensitive to the regional trends leading to war and ignored the growing importance of Arab oil as an element in the regional equation. The concepts that guided their policies were simply too broad to incorporate these developments; nor were they convinced of the need for a major United States initiative in the Middle East. It required the October war to change United States policy and to engage Nixon and Kissinger fully in the search for an Arab-Israeli settlement.

CHAPTER VI

The October 1973 War

THE ARAB-ISRAELI WAR of October 1973 had all the elements of a severe international crisis. It caught most of the world, including the United States and Israel, by surprise; it did not fit anyone's preconceptions of how a war in the Middle East was likely to develop; it threatened core values of the countries directly involved as well as those of outside powers; and it ended with a near-confrontation between the two nuclear superpowers, the United States and the Soviet Union.

Crises, by their very nature, expose prevailing assumptions about reality in particularly acute ways. Faced with surprise, danger and uncertainty, decision makers act on the basis of previously formulated conceptions of reality. When reality no longer conforms to these images, and under great pressures of time and events, policy makers are likely to restructure their perceptions with extraordinary speed. Impending failure or danger, much like a hanging, clears the mind. Pieces of the puzzle are quickly rearranged, and new policies are tried. If the crisis is resolved successfully, the revised or restructured image is likely to endure for some time; lessons will be drawn; and a new policy framework will emerge and will guide action until the next failure or crisis. The October war was therefore doubly important as an object of study, for it revealed the underlying assumptions of American policy toward the Arab-Israeli conflict from 1970 to 1973 and produced a major revision of those assumptions within a very short period.

WHY THE SURPRISE?

Shortly after 6:00 A.M. Washington time on October 6, 1973, a
flash cable from the American embassy in Tel Aviv was received in
the White House situation room. Israel finally had conclusive evidence that the Egyptians and Syrians planned to attack by 6:00 P.M.
Middle East time (noon in Washington). Prime Minister Meir assured
the United States that Israel did not intend to preempt and asked
that American efforts be directed at preventing war. Kissinger received the message while in New York; Nixon was in Key Biscayne,
Florida, worrying about recent evidence of corruption on the part of
Vice President Spiro Agnew.

In the less than two hours that remained before the war began,
Kissinger took charge, calling the Israelis to warn against preemption,
urging the Soviets to use their influence to prevent war, telephoning
the Egyptian ambassador to the UN with the Israeli message that
Israel would not preempt, and sending messages to King Hussein and
King Faisal to enlist their help on the side of moderation. Kissinger's
efforts were futile, and the first word of hostilities was received shortly
after 8:00 A.M.

Why was Washington caught off balance? Surely there was ample
evidence of Egyptian and Syrian frustration because of the status
quo, of their sizable military capabilities, and of their intention to
resort to force at some time to recover their territories lost in 1967.[1]
Sadat had publicly stated on several occasions his intention to go to
war, most explicitly in April 1973.[2] During the spring, Egyptian
military maneuvers had been unusually realistic and had prompted
a genuine war scare. State Department intelligence analysts, reflecting on the spring crisis, had predicted on May 31 that the chances
of Sadat's going to war by fall were "better than even" in the
absence of a credible political initiative toward a settlement.[3] Gen-
eral-Secretary Brezhnev, in his talks with President Nixon in San

1. Roberta Wohlstetter, *Pearl Harbor: Warning and Decision* (Stanford: Stanford University Press, 1962), provides a classic study of the misinterpretation of evidence indicating
an impending surprise attack.
2. In an interview with Arnaud de Borchgrave, published in *Newsweek,* Apr. 9, 1973.
3. See excerpts of the report of the House Select Committee on Intelligence, chaired by
Congressman Otis Pike, as reprinted in *The Village Voice,* Feb. 16, 1976, pp. 78–79. See
also the account written by the director of the Intelligence and Research Bureau of the State
Department, Ray S. Cline, "Policy Without Intelligence," *Foreign Policy* 17 (winter 1974–
75), pp. 121–35.

Clemente in June, had warned that the Arabs were planning for war and that this time they were determined. Only American pressure on Israel to make concessions would prevent hostilities.

Kissinger had been sufficiently alarmed by these signs of tension in the Middle East that he had asked that a new contingency plan on the Arab-Israeli conflict be drafted. What would happen if there were another war? What options would be available to the United States? The bureaucracy abhors contingency plans, so the task fell to a junior State Department official who thought the whole exercise was a waste of time. The Israelis were so powerful that the Arabs would never dare attack. When war broke out several months later, the contingency plan lay half-finished in his file drawer.

By fall, several new signs of danger were available to anyone who cared to watch. Soviet military shipments to Egypt and Syria, especially the latter, were going on at a high level. In mid-September, Egypt, Syria, and Jordan patched up their differences, just as tension flared on the Syrian-Israeli front.[4] Shortly thereafter, Syria began to redeploy some of its forces from the Jordanian border to Golan, and large numbers of surface-to-air missiles were moved into the region between Damascus and the Israeli front. This was known in Washington and was interpreted as a reaction to the September 13 air battle in which Israel had shot down twelve Syrian planes and the easing of tensions with Jordan. At about the same time, Egypt began its fall maneuvers. On September 26, Kissinger was awakened with news that Egyptian forces had gone on a high stage of alert. In response, United States intelligence-collection activities in the Middle East were increased and Kissinger requested that CIA and INR prepare an estimate of the likelihood of an Arab-Israeli war. The flow of information was staggering, but it was also inconsistent. Along with one "reliable" report that Egypt and Syria were planning a combined military offensive in the near future came dozens of equally reliable reports that painted a very different picture.

On October 4, a new element entered the equation. Soviet civilians were reportedly being evacuated from Syria and Egypt. Did the Soviets know something of which the Americans were ignorant?

4. On Sept. 12, Sadat, Asad, and Hussein met in Cairo. Syria and Jordan agreed to restore diplomatic relations. Jordan, without being told of specific war plans, committed itself to preventing Israeli troops from attacking Syria through northern Jordan in the event of future hostilities.

Or was this, like July 1972, a sign of a crisis in Arab-Soviet relations?[5] Neither interpretation could be confirmed initially, but the CIA daily report on October 6 tentatively concluded that the latter explanation seemed more plausible, inasmuch as there were no clear signs of impending hostilities.[6]

Why was the American intelligence community wrong? Why was Kissinger caught by surprise? Where were all the Middle East "experts"? Two basic conceptual biases led to the misperception of Egyptian-Syrian intentions. First, it was widely assumed that the "military balance" was the key to whether there would be another war in the Middle East. This had been a basic element in American policy since 1967. However strongly the Arabs might feel about the need to regain their territory, they would not go to war if they faced certain defeat. In view of Israel's qualitative advantages in the military realm, and the substantial flow of American arms after 1970, it would be an act of folly for the Arabs to initiate a war. Nor was it expected that Israel would feel the need to preempt. A deliberate, rationally planned war was simply implausible in the light of military realities. An unintended war, caused by each side's reacting to defensive moves of the other, seemed more likely, but this would be difficult to anticipate or predict.[7] Finally, war as an irrational act might occur, but again could not be predicted with accuracy.

Second, war seemed to make sense for the Arabs only if a political alternative for recovering their territory was precluded. Although most of the bureaucracy remained uninformed, top officials were aware that Kissinger, in his talks with Israelis and Egyptians at the UN, had arranged for preliminary talks on a settlement to begin in November, after Israeli elections. The continuation of Israeli military superiority and the option of a political alternative made an Arab-initiated war implausible. The maneuvers, threats, and warnings could all be explained away as part of a Soviet-Arab campaign to force the United States to lean on Israel to make concessions.

5. Following the air battles on Sept. 13, Arab newspapers, especially in Beirut, carried stories about Syria's dissatisfaction with Soviet military equipment and the Soviet advisers.

6. The Watch Committee, whose task it is to evaluate intelligence for signs of impending hostilities, reached the same conclusion. See the Pike Committee report, loc. cit, p. 78.

7. Some analysts at CIA deliberately played down evidence of preparations for hostilities, fearing that each side might overreact to the moves of the other, thereby producing an unintended war. They may well have had the 1967 war in mind, where this process did lead to escalation and eventual hostilities.

Perhaps as important as these conceptual errors was a sense that Israel had the greatest incentive and the best capabilities for determining whether war was likely or not. After all, Israel, not the United States, would be the target of any Arab military threat; Israeli intelligence had an excellent reputation, drawing on sources unavailable to the United States; therefore, if the Israelis were not overly worried, why should Americans be? Repeated checks with Israeli sources showed a comparatively relaxed attitude. Even on October 5, when Israel was close to putting the pieces together accurately, a message to Kissinger from Golda Meir included the assessment that neither Egypt nor Syria was planning to go to war. But just in case they feared Israel's intentions, Meir asked Kissinger to reassure the Arabs that Israel had no plans to attack.[8]

Despite all of the technically accurate information available in Washington about Arab war preparations, Egypt and Syria did manage to observe high standards of secrecy and deception. Well-placed Israeli intelligence agents in Egypt had been captured early in 1973.[9] Sadat and Asad confided in virtually no one concerning the precise moment of the attack. Communications security in the days preceding the attack was unusually good, and deliberate deception tactics were used successfully. Even so, Israel had nearly ten hours' warning.[10] This was not enough, however, to take any steps to prevent war, and very little could even be done to limit the damage of the initial Arab attack.

Some have argued that if Israel had launched a preemptive air strike, the course of the war would have been significantly different. And in some quarters, the United States has been blamed for preventing Israel from preempting. It is true that Kissinger and Nixon had consistently warned Israel that she must not be responsible for initiating a Middle East war. Kissinger repeated this admonition immediately before the outbreak of hostilities, but by then Prime

8. Matti Golan, *The Secret Conversations of Henry Kissinger* (New York: Quadrangle Books, 1976), pp. 37–39, contains a detailed account of the Israeli message, which he claims did not reach Kissinger till the next day. Marvin and Bernard Kalb, *Kissinger* (Boston: Little, Brown, 1974), p. 458, give a partial text of the message and state that Kissinger received it at 8:00 P.M. but did not take it very seriously.

9. Interview with high-ranking Israeli intelligence official, December 1975.

10. Israel received confirmation that the Arabs planned to attack at about 4:00 A.M. Israeli time, Oct. 6. It was expected that hostilities would begin about 6:00 P.M. See Chaim Herzog, *The War of Atonement, October 1973* (Boston: Little, Brown, 1975), pp. 52–54.

Minister Meir had already stated that Israel would not preempt. The Israeli decision was not made in Washington, at least not on October 6.

INITIAL REACTIONS

For several hours after the outbreak of war, it was not clear in Washington whether the Israelis or the Arabs had fired the first shots. During the rump session of the Washington Special Action Group (WSAG), convened at 9:00 A.M., the prevailing view was that Israel had probably struck first.[11] CIA Director Colby judged that, in any event, neither side had premeditated military action, but rather that the war was the result of mutual fears of actions and reactions that had escalated to hostilities.[12] The United States, it was felt, should not make accusations against either side. A multiplicity of interests was at stake—U.S.-Soviet détente, U.S.-Israeli relations, American credibility with the Arabs, and the weakened authority of the president. The initial American reaction was therefore one of caution.

It soon became clear that the Egyptians and Syrians had indeed begun the hostilities, but at no point during the next three weeks did any United States official make an issue of this. The public record will be searched in vain for references to Arab "aggression."[13] Unlike

11. This meeting was chaired by Kissinger's deputy, General Brent Scowcroft, and was attended by Defense Secretary James Schlesinger, Chairman of the Joint Chiefs of Staff Admiral Thomas Moorer, Deputy Secretary of State Kenneth Rush, CIA Director William Colby, Deputy Assistant Secretary of State for the Near East Alfred Atherton, Deputy Assistant Secretary of Defense for International Security Affairs James Noyes, and several staff members. As a member of the National Security Council staff during this period, I attended most of the WSAG meetings. The accounts of these sessions included here are based on memory, interviews with participants, and brief notes on the main substantive topics discussed at each meeting. The full record of the meetings is, of course, still classified, and the sources I have been able to use are in no way definitive. I have tried to concentrate on recording the themes that recurred in the discussions, on the major concepts that participants relied upon in reaching judgments, and on the mood that existed on each day of the crisis.. Decisions were not usually made at WSAG meetings. Their real value lay in keeping top-level decision makers on the same wavelength. There was very little controversy or argument during any of the meetings.

12. See the same version in the Watch Committee report, Oct. 6, 9:00 A.M., printed in *The Village Voice*, Feb. 16, 1976, p. 78, footnote 305. "We can find no hard evidence of a major, coordinated Egyptian/Syrian offensive across the canal and the Golan Heights area. Rather, the weight of evidence indicates an action-reaction situation where a series of responses by each side to preconceived threats created an increasingly dangerous potential for confrontation."

13. Kissinger made a point of this in his discussion with Mohamed Heikal, Nov. 7, 1973, as translated from *Al-Anwar*, Nov. 16, 1973, in *Journal of Palestine Studies* III, no. 2 (winter 1974), p. 213.

President Johnson, who held Nasser responsible for the 1967 war, despite Israel's opening fire on June 5, Nixon and Kissinger ignored the issue of who was at fault. Among the reasons for this "even-handed" perspective was the feeling that U.S.-Arab relations were growing in importance because of oil and this was no time for a confrontation; that an Arab attack on Israeli forces in occupied Arab territory was not quite the same as an attack across recognized borders; and that the status quo that prevailed prior to the war had, in fact, given the Arabs ample incentive to try to break the "no war, no peace" stalemate by engineering an international crisis. For several days it was widely considered that the Arab action had been foolish, but not that it had been immoral.

Toward the end of the first day of fighting, a second WSAG meeting was convened, this time under Kissinger's chairmanship. For all practical purposes, he and Nixon made policy during the next several weeks, with occasional inputs from Defense Secretary Schlesinger. Kissinger's initial views are therefore of particular interest.

When Kissinger entered the situation room at 7:22 P.M., one cabinet member was calmly reading the comic strips in the local newspaper. Other WSAG participants were bantering lightly about the crisis. With Kissinger's arrival, the serious discussion began. He reported that he had just been on the telephone to Nixon, Dobrynin, and Eban. The president wanted the Sixth Fleet moved east and held near Crete as a visible sign of American power. One aircraft carrier was ordered to leave port in Athens; other moves would be considered later.

Kissinger was concerned about the Soviet Union. If the Arabs suffered a real debacle, he thought, the Soviets would have a hard time staying out. United States military moves should be restrained so as not to give the wrong impressions to the Soviet Union. Reminded that future American military steps might require use of the Azores base, Kissinger quipped that the Portuguese would be happy to grant permission, because he had just refused to see their foreign minister in New York!

Discussion ensued on the diplomatic contacts taken to date. In the UN, the United States would try to work with the Soviet Union to reestablish the cease-fire on the basis of the status quo ante. The Arabs, in their "demented state," presently opposed this, but they would beg for it once the Israeli counteroffensive got under way. The

United States strategy would be to prevent the diplomatic debate
from going to the UN General Assembly, where an automatic pro-
Arab majority would be available. The Soviets, it was acknowledged,
would have a problem accepting a cease-fire based on the status quo
ante, for this would mean Arab forces would have to withdraw from
Arab territory. A Soviet response would nonetheless be forthcoming
the next day.

Israel would undoubtedly reject any cease-fire not based on a
return to the status quo ante. The president did not want a situation
where Israel, the victim of the attack, would be condemned for rejecting a cease-fire appeal. The United States goal was to adopt a
position that would remain consistent throughout the crisis. The war
would quickly shift in Israel's favor, and what appeared to be a pro-
Israel position of a cease-fire on the post-1967 lines would soon look
pro-Arab. If Israel went beyond the previous lines, the United States
would oppose this, thereby regaining some credit with the Arabs.
Consequently, the United States would propose a cease-fire status
quo ante, but would not push it hard until the military realities made
both parties want to accept it.

Everyone felt that the crisis would be crucial for U.S.-Soviet relations. If collaboration worked, détente would take on real meaning;
if it failed, the Soviets could "kiss MFN goodbye."[14] It was realized
that the Soviets might have been duplicitous in helping the Arabs
plan the war, but still held the hope of working with them to end it.

U.S.-Israeli relations were also on many minds. By sticking close
to the Israelis during the war, the United States should be able to
enhance the credibility of a future guarantee as part of a peace settlement. Eventually, American and Israeli positions on a settlement
would diverge, and the only way to get the Israelis to withdraw from
Arab territory would be to offer some kind of formal United States
guarantee. The president felt strongly about this. The Israelis must
see the United States as a reliable partner during the crisis for the
sake of postwar diplomacy. Arms and oil were briefly mentioned.
Kissinger concluded with the thought that the worst outcome for

14. Granting the Soviets "most-favored nation" trading status was a key issue in the fall
of 1973. Senator Henry Jackson had introduced an amendment that would withhold most-
favored-nation treatment (MFN) for the Soviet Union unless Soviet Jews were allowed to
emigrate freely. Nixon and Kissinger opposed the amendment, arguing that "quiet diplomacy" would be more effective and that the Soviets would not accept such interference in
their internal affairs. Ultimately, the Soviets refused MFN tied to free emigration.

the United States would be to appear crippled by the domestic crisis over Watergate. Kissinger then left for an evening meeting with Soviet Ambassador Dobrynin.

A basic strategy was already set. The United States, expecting a short war in which Israel would quickly prevail, hoped to be in a strong position with Israel and the Soviets for postwar diplomatic moves. In addition, Kissinger wanted to avoid a confrontation with the Arabs. For the moment, the United States would adopt a low profile, developing a position on a cease-fire that would soon be seen as balanced. The viability of this policy depended upon a quick Israeli reversal of the military situation and Soviet restraint. For the next two days, these conditions seemed to hold.

On Sunday, October 7, Kissinger kept in close touch with the Soviets, Egyptians, and Israelis. Nixon sent Brezhnev a letter urging mutual restraint and calling for a meeting of the Security Council. Brezhnev's reply was conciliatory and encouraging.[15] Together with the movement of Soviet ships away from the zone of combat, this was a promising sign.

Supplementing Kissinger's talks with Foreign Minister Zayyat, the Egyptians began to send messages through the "back channel" which had been established after July 1972. Although rejecting the idea of a cease-fire that was not linked to Israeli withdrawal to the pre-1967 lines, Sadat made it clear that he did not want a confrontation with the United States.[16]

The Israelis were in a grim mood, but in communications with the United States they still appeared confident of success. Ambassador Dinitz, just arrived from Israel, met with Kissinger in the evening and presented a list of arms that Israel needed, but the sense of urgency was not particularly great, or at least so it seemed to Kissinger and Schlesinger.[17]

By the time the WSAG met shortly after 6:00 P.M. on October 7,[18]

15. Golan, op. cit., p. 64; M. and B. Kalb, op. cit., pp. 462–63.
16. Kissinger subsequently told Egyptian officials that he was very impressed when they began to send messages through the "back channel" shortly after the war began; interview with high-level Egyptian diplomat, April 1976. Nixon and Kissinger attached considerable importance to the possibility of improving U.S.-Arab relations after the war was over.
17. Golan, op. cit., p. 45.
18. Membership at WSAG meetings varied, but the following members usually were present: Kissinger, Schlesinger, Moorer, Colby, Scowcroft, Rush, Sisco, Clements, and several staff assistants. When oil was discussed, Deputy Secretary Simon, Governor John Love, and Charles di Bona might participate.

the best estimate of the CIA was that Israel would regain the initiative the following day and would go on to win the war by the end of the week. Initial concentration would be on the Syrian front, then on the Egyptian front.

Kissinger voiced his perplexity as to why the Arabs, if their situation was really so precarious, were refusing a cease-fire that would protect their initial gains.[19] Schlesinger felt they were being illogical; Kissinger replied that the Egyptian strategy would be to cross the canal and then sit tight. The Arabs, he thought, had attacked to upset the status quo, because they feared there would be no diplomatic movement unless there was a crisis.

After a brief discussion of oil, possible evacuation of American citizens from Libya[20] and other Arab countries, and the Israeli request for arms, the meeting ended. Kissinger indicated that he would ask the president, who was arriving at 10:00 P.M. from Florida, about further American military moves and Israeli requests for arms. For the moment, he felt the United States was in a good position to come out of the crisis with its essential interests intact.

The following day, October 8, the UN Security Council was convened. John Scali, the American representative, mentioned in his speech that a cease-fire based on the status quo ante would be the "least damaging" solution to the crisis, but he did not formally propose a resolution for a vote.[21]

Israel was now beginning to encounter military difficulties on both fronts. In Golan the Syrian air-defense system was taking a high

19. Kissinger apparently was aware that the Soviets, six hours after the war had begun, had suggested to Sadat that he accept a simple cease-fire at an early date. The Soviets had repeated the request on Oct. 7. See William B. Quandt, *Soviet Policy in the October 1973 War,* R–1864, The RAND Corporation, May 1976; and Sadat's own account in *Al-Hawadith,* Mar. 19, 1975, and *Al-Jumhurriyah,* Oct. 24, 1975. Also, Mohamed Heikal, *The Road to Ramadan* (New York: Quadrangle Books, 1975), pp. 209, 212–15.

20. Libya had recently decreed that American oil-company personnel were not free to leave the country without government permission. President Qaddafi's erratic behavior led some United States officials to fear that he would order attacks against American interests and citizens. Instead, Libya cooperated in allowing Americans departing Egypt to transit Libya, for which Qaddafi received a message of thanks.

21. The United States position favoring a cease-fire based on the status quo ante was opposed by a number of American ambassadors in Arab countries. Kissinger replied that if the United States were to call for a vote on any cease-fire resolution that was not linked to a full Israeli withdrawal, the resolution would be defeated; then a vote would be called on a cease-fire tied to withdrawal, which the United States would have to veto. This, in his view, would hurt U.S.-Arab relations worse than Scali's tentative call for a cease-fire based on the post-1967 lines. Above all, Kissinger wanted to avoid a vote in the Security Council until he could be sure of its desirable outcome. This required U.S.-Soviet agreement; Soviet agreement seemed to require Arab acquiescence.

toll of Israeli Skyhawks and Phantoms. In Sinai, an Israeli effort to break through Egyptian lines with armor had been thwarted. Demands for resupply of equipment from the United States mounted. Dinitz spoke to Kissinger several times and was reportedly told that Israeli El Al planes could begin to pick up supplies the following day, provided they painted over their Israeli markings.[22] "In principle," Israeli losses would be replaced. When Dinitz complained about the slow American response, Kissinger blamed it on the Defense Department, a ploy he used repeatedly with the Israeli ambassador over the next several days.[23] In fact, the United States position was still based on the expectation of an early end to the fighting and a desire to maintain a low profile. The arms issue was therefore handled discreetly.

The WSAG met again at 5:30 P.M. on October 8 to review the day's events.[24] CIA reported that Israel was making rapid progress and had virtually retaken the Golan Heights. One member offered the opinion that if the Soviets did not resupply the Arabs, perhaps the Americans should not resupply Israel. Kissinger again expressed puzzlement as to why the Arabs were refusing a cease-fire. The Soviets, by contrast, were being very conciliatory. With their help, it was felt, a cease-fire could be achieved by Wednesday night. The Soviets would respond on Tuesday. Even if Israel were to cross the canal, the United States would be in a good position by sticking to a call for a cease-fire based on the status quo ante. Military realities would shortly make the American proposal acceptable to Egypt, Syria, and the Soviet Union. When the meeting ended at 6:30 P.M., Kissinger immediately went to his White House office to confer with Dinitz. He then delivered a previously scheduled speech to the Pacem in Terris conference in Washington in which he alluded to the Middle East and the need for Soviet restraint there if détente were to survive.[25]

22. M. and B. Kalb, op. cit., p. 465.
23. Ibid., p. 466. See also Edward N. Luttwak and Walter Laqueur, "Kissinger and the Yom Kippur War," *Commentary* 58, no. 3 (September 1974), p. 36.
24. Kissinger arrived at 5:55 P.M. and was already well briefed on the course of the day's fighting.
25. Henry A. Kissinger, "The Nature of the National Dialogue," address delivered to the Pacem in Terris III Conference, Washington, D.C., Oct. 8, 1973. In the speech, Kissinger, who discussed détente at some length, said:

Coexistence to us continues to have a very precise meaning:
—We will oppose the attempt by any country to achieve a position of predominance either globally or regionally. . . .

The basic United States policy, rooted in the initial assumptions of a short war with an Israeli victory, was still on the tracks, but it would not be for much longer. In the jargon of Washington, it was about to be "overtaken by events."

THE CRISIS DEEPENS

From the perspective of Washington, the war entered a new and acute phase on October 9. Reality was refusing to conform to the comparatively optimistic forecast upon which initial United States policy had been based. Between October 9 and October 12, the possibility of a swift and conclusive Israeli military victory on both fronts faded; Soviet restraint began to erode; and pressures began to build for an urgent military resupply of Israeli forces. The American response was to modify gradually two aspects of policy: the call for a cease-fire based on the status quo ante was replaced by a search for a cease-fire-in-place, and arms for Israel began to flow in modest quantities, first aboard El Al aircraft, then increasingly with direct American involvement. In one of the most controversial decisions of the war, the president used the supply of arms to Israel to obtain Israeli acceptance of the principle of a cease-fire-in-place. By late evening October 12, this had been successfully accomplished; within hours, President Sadat's refusal of a cease-fire-in-place led to a drastic change in American policy.

This second stage of the crisis opened on Tuesday morning, October 9, with an urgent Israeli appeal for arms.[26] Dinitz informed Kissinger of heavy Israeli losses, especially of aircraft on the Syrian front. Shortly thereafter, Kissinger convened the WSAG principals for two emergency sessions before noon. Only Schlesinger, Moorer, Rush, Colby, and Scowcroft met with Kissinger to consider the new Israeli request. To date, this was the most difficult moment of the war. The two recommendations that emerged from these sessions were presented to Nixon by Kissinger at noon. First, some arms must

—We will react if relaxation of tensions is used as a cover to exacerbate conflicts in international trouble spots. The Soviet Union cannot disregard these principles in any area of the world without imperiling its entire relationship with the United States. Our policy with regard to détente is clear: We shall resist aggressive foreign policies. Détente cannot survive irresponsibility in any area, including the Middle East.

26. M. and B. Kalb, op. cit., pp. 466–67.

begin to reach Israel quickly, without violating the principle of maintaining a low American profile in the conflict. Second, a new formula for a cease-fire should be explored.[27]

While these deliberations were going on, word began to reach Washington that Israel had launched a major counteroffensive on the Syrian front. On the ground, Israeli troops had recovered virtually all of the territory lost during the first three days of fighting and in some areas were pushing beyond the former cease-fire line. Nonetheless, the fighting was still difficult. The Syrians were not breaking, and Iraqi reinforcements were on their way. In the air, the Israelis, thwarted in their efforts to use the air force for close support of ground troops, initiated a campaign of strategic bombing deep within Syria. The oil refinery at Homs was attacked; the defense ministry and air-force staff headquarters in Damascus were bombed; and, by mistake, the Soviet cultural center in Damascus was hit, causing at least one Soviet fatality.

As the Syrian front began to weaken, King Hussein of Jordan came under great pressure to enter the war, if not by opening a new front, then at least by sending some of his troops to Syria. Israel conveyed an extremely harsh message to Hussein on October 9, warning of the consequences of opening a front along the Jordan River. Kissinger also urged Hussein to stay out of the fighting, stressing that a diplomatic effort was under way that, it was hoped, would succeed in ending the war within a few days.

This diplomatic effort consisted of sounding out the Egyptians, Soviets, and Israelis on the possibility of a cease-fire-in-place. Dinitz was the first to convey his government's refusal, stressing the need for any cease-fire to be tied to the restoration of the status quo ante.[28]

Egypt's position was equally negative. Any cease-fire must be directly linked to a concrete plan calling for full Israeli withdrawal from all territories captured in 1967. Kissinger had raised the issue of a cease-fire-in-place through his "back channel" to Hafiz Ismail on October 9, stressing that Egypt had "made its point." Ismail's reply, reportedly drafted by Sadat, reached him the following day:[29]

27. According to Golan, op. cit., p. 49, Nixon subsequently took credit with the Israelis for the decision to start sending arms to Israel.

28. The London Sunday Times Insight Team, *The Yom Kippur War* (New York: Doubleday, 1974), p. 279.

29. Heikal, op. cit., pp. 223–24.

—There should be a cease-fire followed by a withdrawal within a specified period, under UN supervision, of all Israeli forces to the pre–June 5, 1967, lines.

—Freedom of navigation in the Strait of Tiran should be guaranteed by a UN presence at Sharm al-Shaykh for a specified period.

—Following the complete withdrawal of Israeli forces, the state of belligerency with Israel would be ended.

—Following the withdrawal of Israeli troops from Gaza, the area would be placed under UN supervision pending its self-determination.

—Within a specified period after the ending of the state of belligerency, a peace conference would be convened under UN auspices, to be attended by all interested parties, including the Palestinians, and all members of the Security Council. The conference would deal with all questions concerning sovereignty, security, and freedom of navigation.

Egypt promised also that once Israeli evacuation began, diplomatic relations with the United States would be resumed, and work on clearing the Suez Canal would start.

This was hardly the simple cease-fire-in-place that Nixon and Kissinger now envisaged. Under no circumstances were they prepared to link a cease-fire to the terms of a final settlement. Not only would the Israelis adamantly refuse, but also it was entirely contrary to Nixon's and Kissinger's negotiating strategy. Sadat was aiming far too high. Either the Soviets or Israeli military successes would have to bring him to a more realistic sense of what was possible.

The Soviets seemed less of a problem than Sadat. They, after all, had indicated a willingness earlier to accept a cease-fire, but had been rebuffed by Sadat. Although they were unlikely to oppose Egypt and Syria publicly on the issue of a cease-fire, they might be prepared to use their influence in Cairo. By October 10, the Soviets were indeed indicating that they would cooperate in the search for a cease-fire-in-place. They implied that Sadat was now prepared to accept such a cease-fire.

THE CEASE-FIRE INITIATIVE

Offsetting this conciliatory gesture, however, was the first evidence that the Soviets were beginning an airlift of arms to the Middle East. On that day, twenty-one AN-12s flew to Damascus with over

200 tons of military equipment.[30] Late that Sunday in Washington, it was learned that seven Soviet airborne divisions had been placed on a high state of alert. It was obvious that the Soviets were worried about the deteriorating situation on the Syrian front. Whether their solution to the danger posed to their interests would emphasize diplomacy or force was an unanswered question on October 10. Elements of both were visible.

Meanwhile, the United States resupply of Israel was beginning on a modest scale. On October 9, Dinitz was informed that a number of F-4 Phantoms would soon be on their way.[31] In addition, El Al planes were allowed to pick up preassembled cargoes at Oceana Naval Station near Norfolk, Virginia.[32] The first resupplies had reached Israel by October 10, the same day on which the first Soviet resupplies by air reached Damascus.

The intensity of the fighting was such, however, that Israeli requests for arms could not be met simply by El Al flights. Consistent with the principle of avoiding direct official American involvement in the transport of arms to Israel, Kissinger and Schlesinger began on October 10 to explore the possibility of chartering civilian transports for that purpose. Ten to twenty flights per day were envisaged. That same day Kissinger spoke with Dinitz several times about arms, a possible Jordanian movement of troops to Syria, and, most important, Moscow's renewed interest in a cease-fire-in-place. Dinitz relayed the Soviet position to the prime minister, who still refused to consider it.[33]

At this point the American and Israeli positions began to diverge. The United States wanted an early cease-fire. Israel wanted arms in sufficient quantity to ensure a military victory. Over the next two days, the United States moved slowly on arms for Israel as a form of pressure to induce the Israelis to accept a cease-fire-in-place and in the conviction that the fighting was nearly over in any case. President Nixon, in one of his rare public remarks about the crisis while it was under way, summed up the American position on October 10 as

30. W. Quandt, "Soviet Policy in the October 1973 War," summarizes available data on the Soviet delivery of military equipment by air and sea during the war.

31. On Oct. 9, Israeli Defense Minister Dayan told an audience: "We have a positive reply for many Phantoms. I hope we will also get tanks, but that situation is less acute." *Jerusalem Post Weekly*, Feb. 19, 1974, p. 11.

32. M. and B. Kalb, op. cit., pp. 466–67.

33. Ibid., pp. 468–70; Golan, op. cit., p. 65.

follows: "The U.S. is trying its best to play a mediating role and bring the fighting to an end, and then, beyond that, to help to build not just a temporary, but a lasting peace for the people in that very troubled section of the world."[34]

October 11 was a day of regrouping and consolidation. Nothing extraordinary happened on the battlefield or in Washington. Israel began to transfer troops from the Syrian to the Egyptian front in order to push Egyptian forces back to the canal. United States diplomacy aimed at restraining King Hussein, now under pressure from Asad, Sadat, and Faisal, from joining the war, and at reassuring the Israelis that the charter flights and F-4s would soon be on their way.

Israel's refusal to consider a cease-fire-in-place was now beginning to weaken somewhat. Having made new gains on the Syrian front, Israel was prepared to consider a cease-fire coupled with a subsequent exchange of Israeli control over captured Syrian territory for a restoration of Israeli positions in Sinai.[35] Syria might see some merit in this, but Sadat would not, hence the U.S. continued to press for a simple cease-fire-in-place. By October 12, it seemed within grasp.

The day began with Israeli queries about the charter flights that had been promised but that had not yet begun. In an effort to retain credibility with the Israelis, Kissinger tried to accelerate the process. A message was sent at 11:09 A.M. to the Portuguese requesting the use of Lajes airbase in the Azores for chartered civilian aircraft flying military consumables to Israel. Ten to twenty flights, chartered by the Defense Department, would pass through Lajes each day. The flights were to begin that same evening. The Portuguese, no doubt resenting that the United States seemed to take their assent for granted, delayed their response.

Meanwhile, the Defense Department, having failed to arrange the charter of civilian transport, was exploring the possibility of using American military transports to carry equipment to Lajes, where it would then be transferred to Israeli transports. The United States was still reluctant for its own military aircraft to be seen flying into Tel Aviv.

At a press conference called at 11:00 A.M., Kissinger tried to clarify

34. Richard M. Nixon, remarks at a Medal of Science ceremony, Oct. 10, 1973.
35. *The Yom Kippur War*, p. 279. This has been confirmed by a highly placed Israeli source.

the various, sometimes conflicting, strands of United States policy as of October 12:

> After hostilities broke out, the United States set itself two principal objectives. One, to end the hostilities as quickly as possible. Secondly, to end the hostilities in such a manner that they [sic] would contribute to the maximum extent possible to the promotion of a more permanent, more lasting solution in the Middle East . . . We have not gratuitously sought opportunities for confrontations in public forums which might harden dividing lines. . . .
>
> . . . [T]he Middle East may become in time what the Balkans were in Europe before 1914, that is to say, an area where local rivalries . . . have their own momentum that will draw in the great nuclear powers into a confrontation. . . .

Kissinger went on to "urge all the parties in the conduct of their diplomacy now to keep in mind that, whatever momentary advantages might be achieved in this or that forum, our principal objective should be to maintain relationships that can move the area and the world towards a more lasting peace."

Kissinger then referred to the "traditional friendship" of the United States for Israel and to the continuing military relationship with that country. He termed the Soviet airlift "moderate," "more than light. It's a fairly substantial airlift." Then, in something of a forewarning to the Arabs of the impending United States role in aiding Israel militarily, Kissinger stated: "We have made a very serious effort, in this crisis, to take seriously into account Arab concerns and Arab views. On the other hand, we have to pursue what we consider to be the right course; we will take the consequences in pursuing what we consider to be the right course."[36]

Kissinger was apprehensive that, in the absence of a rapid end to the war, the United States would have to rearm Israel; then the Arabs would react by embargoing oil and attacking American interests throughout the region. There was all the more reason, therefore, for one additional try at a cease-fire.

Prime Minister Meir, under pressure from the United States to accept a cease-fire-in-place, apparently appalled by the mounting casualties, and realizing that American arms might not be readily

36. Kissinger press conference, Oct. 12, 1973, *Department of State Bulletin*, Oct. 29, 1973.

forthcoming if she refused, finally agreed to accept a cease-fire-in-place. Her acceptance was accompanied by an urgent personal appeal to President Nixon to order an immediate resupply of arms to Israel. She went so far as to raise the specter of an Israeli military defeat.[37]

On October 12, late in the evening, Ambassador Dinitz met with Kissinger at the White House. He conveyed Israel's acceptance of the principle of a cease-fire-in-place and Golda Meir's urgent request for arms. Kissinger was gratified at the Israeli change of position, but he had just heard a preliminary report from the British that Sadat was not willing to accept a simple cease-fire.[38] Therefore Great Britain would not introduce such a resolution in the UN. Nor would the Soviets, for fear of being seen as anti-Arab. Kissinger then suggested that the United States might take the initiative, if Israel agreed. The Israelis demurred.[39]

Kissinger had expected a cease-fire during the night of October 12–13. He had worked hard to obtain Israel's acceptance. The British were supposed to take the initiative in the UN, not to ask Sadat, who was bound to say no when queried directly. The resupply of arms to Israel had been deliberately delayed as a form of pressure on Israel and in order not to reduce the chances of Sadat's acceptance of the cease-fire proposal.[40] Now everything was coming unstuck. Kissinger

37. M. and B. Kalb, op. cit., p. 474; Golan, op. cit., pp. 53, 61, 66–67; *The Yom Kippur War*, pp. 279–80. According to Defense Secretary Schlesinger, "Kissinger called me Friday night. . . . He indicated Israel was running short. To say the least, he was a little bit concerned." Interview with James Schlesinger, Jewish Telegraphic Agency Daily Bulletin, July 1, 1974, p. 4. In his Oct. 26, 1973, news conference, Schlesinger stated that on Oct. 13 "there were some who believed that the existence of the state of Israel was seriously compromised."

38. Earlier in the day, Kissinger, in the presence of Dinitz, had called the British ambassador to ask that Great Britain introduce a resolution for a cease-fire-in-place. The idea had grown out of talks with the Soviets, who felt that Sadat would refuse a U.S.- or Soviet-sponsored resolution, but would go along with a resolution supported by the other members of the Security Council. Under those circumstances, both the United States and the Soviet Union would have abstained. Sadat could then bow to the consensus of the international community, without its appearing that he had capitulated to a superpower *diktat*. Some of this is discussed in Kissinger's talk with Heikal on Nov. 7, 1973, translated from *Al-Anwar*, Nov. 16, 1973, in *Journal of Palestine Studies* III, no. 2 (winter 1974), pp. 210–15. There he refers to his proposal for a cease-fire-in-place, conveyed to the Soviets and the Egyptians, on Oct. 10, and the subsequent Egyptian refusal, communicated through the Soviets and the British. He describes the Israelis as furious, "but eventually they yielded" to his proposal. See also *The Yom Kippur War*, pp. 280–82, where it is reported that the British ambassador met with Sadat a second time at 4 P.M., Oct. 13, at which time Sadat gave his final word refusing the United States proposal. This news reached Washington prior to Nixon's morning meeting where he ordered the full-scale airlift to Israel. The *Washington Post*, Oct. 14, 1973, p. 1, also mentions the link between the arms-supply decision and Israel's acceptance of a cease-fire.

39. M. and B. Kalb, op. cit., p. 67.

40. In a press conference on Oct. 26, 1973, Schlesinger stated: "The U.S. delayed,

was angry at Sadat, at the British, and at the Soviets, and he was worried by the tone of Prime Minister Meir's message. A new strategy had to be devised, and quickly.

THE AIRLIFT

President Nixon's role in the shaping of American policy during the October war is difficult to assess accurately. He was obviously preoccupied by his own domestic political difficulties and with the resignation in disgrace of his hand-picked vice president, Spiro Agnew, on October 10. The president showed little interest in the details of policy, leaving the task of day-to-day diplomacy to Kissinger. Nixon did make the key decisions, however, and it was his authority that could be invoked to influence other governments. On the morning of October 13, having received confirmation of Sadat's refusal of a cease-fire-in-place, President Nixon took the responsibility of ordering a full-scale airlift of military equipment to Israel.[41]

The Portuguese, who had still not granted permission to use Lajes, received a harsh note from Nixon dispatched from Washington at 8:00 A.M. At this point, consideration was still being given to the plan to fly equipment to the Azores where it would be picked up by the Israelis. Portuguese permission was finally received at 3:40 P.M. that same day.

Meanwhile, Nixon met later in the morning with his senior advisers—Kissinger, Schlesinger, Moorer, Haig, and Colby—and reiterated his instructions that United States military aircraft should fly equipment directly into Israel, using Lajes only for refueling. The delivery of F-4s was also accelerated, and as many as fourteen were scheduled to arrive on Sunday and Monday.[42] Finally, an SR-71 reconnaissance plane was ordered to photograph the battle area in order to provide an independent basis for judging losses on both sides. This was the first such flight during the hostilities.[43]

---

deliberately delayed, the start of its resupply operation, hoping that a cease-fire would be implemented." *Department of State Bulletin*, Nov. 19, 1973, p. 624.

41. Dinitz was reportedly informed at 1:45 A.M. on Oct. 13 that Nixon had ordered the immediate delivery of ten F-4s and that U.S. Air Force planes would fly direct to Israel. At 3:30 A.M., orders were issued for the giant C-5 transports to leave for Israel. Luttwak and Laqueur, op. cit., p. 37.

42. M. and B. Kalb, op. cit., p. 477.

43. The only other SR-71 flight took place on October 25. See the Pike Committee report, loc. cit., p. 79.

The main considerations underlying this stage of the Nixon-Kissinger strategy were to convince Sadat that a prolonged war of attrition, fueled by Soviet arms, would not succeed, and to demonstrate to the Kremlin that the United States was capable of matching Soviet military deliveries to the Middle East. Above all, for the sake of the future American position globally and in the region, Soviet arms must not be allowed to dictate the outcome of the fighting. This did not mean that the United States now favored a total Israeli military victory, but it did mean that Israeli success on the battlefield had become an important factor in persuading the Arabs and the Soviets to bring the fighting to an end.[44]

Nixon and Kissinger were aware of the likelihood of adverse Arab reaction to the airlift of arms to Israel. Up to this point in the crisis, there had been no confrontation between the United States and the Arab world. The "oil weapon" had not yet been brandished, as many had feared; American lives were not endangered in any Arab country, including Libya, which had been a source of early concern; no Arab country had broken diplomatic relations; and Sadat was in continuing contact with Nixon through the "back channel." United States influence with King Hussein had helped keep Jordan out of the war, although a token Jordanian force was now being sent to Syria. All of this might change as a result of the airlift, but Nixon and Kissinger were prepared to take the risk. The airlift, they would argue, was a response to prior Soviet intervention on the Arab side. Global political realities dictated that the United States respond. This was not an anti-Arab move, for it was not designed to ensure Israeli supremacy over the Arabs or to rob the Arabs of their recaptured dignity. Rather, it was a simple fact of international political life. In any event, the United States would use its influence with Israel, gained through the provision of arms, on behalf of an equitable peace settlement. This, at least, was how the policy would be explained to

44. It is extremely difficult to ascertain the degree to which the United States airlift affected Israeli strategy. From interviews with top Israeli officials, I have concluded that the impact of the airlift on strategic decisions was minimal on the Syrian front and only slightly more significant on the Egyptian front. The crossing of the canal had been seriously recommended by Bar Lev on Oct. 12. (See Herzog, op. cit., pp. 202–07.) After the Israeli victory in Sinai on Oct. 14, it would have been ordered even without the assurance of United States resupplies. However, the crossing might not have been exploited as aggressively if arms had not been on their way. Some items, such as TOW and Maverick missiles, were being used to good effect in the last few days of the fighting and may have raised the prospect of a full defeat of the Third Army Corps. Ironically, the United States resupply put Israel in a position to do something that Kissinger was determined to prevent.

the Arabs[45] and to the rest of the United States bureaucracy. In Washington, there was little dissent, even from allegedly "pro-Arab" elements.

By 12:30 P.M., Washington time, on October 14 (6:30 P.M. in Israel), the first giant C-5 transport plane arrived at Lod airport. An air bridge capable of delivering nearly one thousand tons per day was now in operation, consisting of four to five flights of C-5s and twelve to fifteen flights of C-141s. El Al planes also continued to carry military supplies to Israel. In addition, twelve C-130 transports were flown to Israel and were turned over to the Israeli air force.[46]

With the airlift in full swing, Washington was prepared to wait until the new realities on the battlefield led to a change of Egyptian and Soviet calculations. In the meantime, the United States began to plan for an anticipated Arab oil embargo. Only 12 percent of United States oil consumption, or 5 percent of total energy, consisted of crude oil and refined products received directly or indirectly from the Arab world. Through reduction of demand for oil and some re-direction of imports, the overall impact of a selective Arab oil em-bargo against the United States would hardly be felt. If, however, an embargo was combined with severe cutbacks in production, then not only the United States, but also Europe and Japan, would feel the pinch. Consequently, plans for sharing of oil among allies, as well as a domestic energy plan, were required. At a minimum, the Middle East crisis might provide an incentive for Congress and public opinion to support a major energy project. Governor John Love, energy co-ordinator for Nixon, his aide, Charles di Bona, and Deputy Secretary of the Treasury William Simon were given primary responsibility for working out a plan in the event of an embargo.

By the time the first C-5 had set down in Israel on the afternoon

45. Faisal and Sadat were sent messages explaining the airlift in those terms before it became publicly known. Kissinger later used the same argument with Heikal; see *Journal of Palestine Studies,* loc. cit. The Soviets were also informed in advance of the airlift and were told that the United States would stop if they ended their resupply to the Arabs.

46. From Oct. 14 until the Oct. 25 cease-fire, the United States resupply effort delivered approximately 11,000 tons of equipment, forty F-4 Phantoms, thirty-six A-4 Skyhawks, and twelve C-130 transports. Included were only four tanks on the early C-5 flights, and fewer than twenty were sent during the entire airlift. From Oct. 26 until the airlift ended on Nov. 15, another 11,000 tons of equipment were delivered. In all, 147 sorties were flown by C-5s, with 10,800 tons aboard, and 421 sorties by C-141s with 11,500 tons. During the same period, El Al aircraft carried about 11,000 tons of military supplies to Israel in over 200 sorties. By Nov. 15, the first ships were beginning to reach Israel with resupplies, and the airlift became superfluous. *Aviation Week and Space Technology* 99 (no. 24), Dec. 10, 1973, pp. 16–19, contains information on the airlift.

of October 14, the decisive battle of the war on the Egyptian front
had been fought and won by Israel. An Egyptian offensive toward
the Mitla and Giddi passes had failed, at a cost to Egypt of over 200
tanks. It had been for the sake of this battle that Sadat had rejected
the cease-fire-in-place offered by the British ambassador the previous
day.[47] Now, with this victory behind them, the Israelis showed little
interest in the cease-fire they had been prepared to accept two days
earlier.[48] Instead, Israel, assured of continuing American supplies,
decided to undertake a risky military operation to cross the Suez
Canal. If successful, this might result in the destruction of Egyptian
missile fields, thereby exposing Egyptian ground troops to bombing
by the Israeli air force. In addition, Egyptian forces in Sinai ran the
risk of being cut off from their lines of communication and surrounded by the Israelis. A critical moment was approaching. The
Israeli operation was scheduled for the night of October 15–16.

Kissinger convened morning sessions of the WSAG on both October 14 and 15. Besides discussing oil, the group assessed the evolving military and diplomatic situation. By October 15, the American
airlift to Israel had been publicly acknowledged and widely reported.
Kissinger was surprised at the moderation of the Arab response.
Although he did not expect the Arab oil ministers' meeting in Kuwait the following day to cut off oil to the United States, he did feel
that a plan for counterpressure on the Arabs was necessary if they
did. An administration already weakened by its domestic political
problems could not afford to appear susceptible to "blackmail" by
Arab oil producers.

On the Soviet role in the conflict, Kissinger still reflected a certain
ambivalence. The noted Washington columnist Joseph Alsop had
published an article on the morning of October 15 accusing the
Soviets of collusion and extensive foreknowledge concerning the Arab
war effort. Kissinger was suspicious, but, at the same time, he felt
that the Soviets were still interested in a diplomatic settlement. Perhaps because of the American airlift, or perhaps because of the outcome of the October 14 battle in Sinai, the Soviets early on October
15 had indicated that they were actively trying to persuade the Arabs
to accept a cease-fire. Kosygin, the secretary was told, would go to
Cairo the next day.

47. Heikal, op. cit., p. 224.
48. Golan, op. cit., p. 67.

Kissinger planned to see Egyptian Foreign Minister Zayyat on October 16 and President Nixon would meet with four Arab foreign ministers on October 17. Diplomatic channels would thus remain open with both the Arabs and the Soviets, despite the growing superpower involvement in the conflict.[49]

THE TIDE BEGINS TO TURN

October 16 was a crucial day for the war and the diplomacy. Both President Sadat and Prime Minister Meir gave important public speeches outlining their policies. Israeli forces had managed to cross the Suez Canal in small numbers and were moving into the missile fields, causing havoc among the Egyptian forces. Soviet Premier Kosygin was en route to Cairo to try to persuade Sadat to stop fighting, and Kissinger had reason to feel that the United States strategy was working well. Sadat's speech was comparatively moderate in tone and contained an "open message" to Nixon on Egypt's peace terms. Kosygin's mission had been foreshadowed in Soviet communications during the previous day. As yet, no Arab embargo of oil had been announced. And the Israeli military successes, although not specifically designed or intended by Washington, were consistent with Kissinger's view that Sadat had to be persuaded by battlefield developments to accept a cease-fire. It was of prime importance that the fighting should be ended at the moment when all parties could still emerge from the conflict with their vital interests and self-esteem intact.

At the WSAG meeting on Tuesday morning, October 16, Kissinger further elaborated on the objectives of the airlift. He minimized its importance in the context of the Arab-Israeli conflict. Rather, he stressed, the Soviets must see that the United States could deliver more than they could. Each day until a cease-fire, the United States

49. Impromptu comments by Nixon on Oct. 15 at a Medal of Honor ceremony caused some consternation in Arab diplomatic circles. United States policy, he stated, is "like the policy that we followed in 1958 when Lebanon was involved, it is like the policy we followed in 1970 when Jordan was involved. The policy of the United States in the Mideast, very simply stated, is this: We stand for the right of every nation in the Mideast to maintain its independence and security. We want this fighting to end. We want the fighting to end on a basis where we can build a lasting peace." *Weekly Compilation of Presidential Statements*, Oct. 22, 1973.

The president's reference to Lebanon and Jordan raised the specter of United States military intervention. Nixon was presumably simply mentioning the two other Middle East crises in which he had been personally involved.

should send by air 25 percent more equipment than the Soviets did. The Soviets should be "run into the ground," "forced down." American arms in Israeli hands would outmatch Soviet arms in Arab hands.

As Kissinger was expounding on the U.S.-Soviet aspects of the crisis, the door to the situation room opened and a message was passed in. The time was 10:55 A.M. General Scowcroft read the message and passed it to Kissinger, who broke into an embarrassed laugh and then a proud grin. He had just received word that he would share a Nobel peace prize with North Vietnam's Le Duc Tho, his negotiating partner during the Paris talks.

Turning their attention again to the Middle East, the WSAG addressed the question of aid to Israel to finance the arms being sent. To some, it was time to get maximum credit with Israel, because during the subsequent diplomatic effort, United States and Israeli positions were bound to diverge. Kissinger therefore argued for a very large aid bill for Israel—as much as $3 billion—as well as another $500 million for Cambodia and other countries, thrown in for good measure. In his view, the United States had already paid its price with the Arabs, and a massive aid bill for Israel would do little further damage. By noon, he may have had some second thoughts upon receiving a letter from King Faisal in response to his message on the airlift to Israel. The king was "pained" by the American action. The United States should stop sending arms and should call on Israel to withdraw. Otherwise, U.S.-Saudi relations could become "lukewarm." (Nonetheless, the aid bill went forward, and on October 19, President Nixon formally requested $2.2 billion in aid for Israel. The following day, King Faisal announced an embargo of oil to the United States as well as substantial production cuts. In retrospect, Kissinger wondered whether he had pushed too hard on the Arabs with the $2.2-billion-aid request just as the military situation was turning to Israel's advantage.)

The following day, October 17, was largely devoted to talks with four Arab foreign ministers, Benhima of Morocco, Bouteflika of Algeria, Saqqaf of Saudi Arabia, and Sabah of Kuwait. Shortly after 10:00 A.M., Kissinger met with the four ministers in his White House office.[50] He listened while the Saudi ambassador spelled out their

50. Heikal, op. cit., pp. 232–34, gives a somewhat distorted version of these talks, but covers most of the main points.

concerns: an immediate settlement of the conflict based on complete Israeli withdrawal from Arab territory seized in 1967 and restoration of Palestinian rights in accordance with UN Resolution 242. Kissinger then explained that the basic American policy was now to end the current fighting and to prevent its spread. After the war, the United States would engage in a diplomatic effort for a just and lasting peace. U.S.-Arab relations should therefore remain as strong as possible. The Arabs had created a new reality in the Middle East and the time had come for a diplomatic effort. The United States had initially expected the Arabs to be defeated and this was why the October 6 lines had been proposed for a cease-fire. Now a cease-fire would have to take into account new realities, but it would be a mistake to try to link a cease-fire to a total settlement. A better strategy would be to get a cease-fire quickly, and then to launch a diplomatic effort. The guarantee that such an effort would be made resided in Arab strength. The United States had more influence with Israel, the Arab military and diplomatic positions had improved, and the time was therefore ripe for diplomacy. The United States would not promise to do what it could not accomplish, but it would do everything it promised.

Kissinger concluded by remarking that he did not like big plans, and preferred quiet diplomacy. He recounted how his talks with the Chinese had progressed and urged the same step-by-step procedure on the Arabs. He warned that the Middle East should not become involved in the U.S.-Soviet global rivalry. Then he excused himself, remarking lightly that he was not used to dealing with "moderate Arabs" and that he needed to talk to the president for a few minutes before their appointment in the Oval Office.

At 11:10 A.M. President Nixon began his talks with the four Arab foreign ministers. Saqqaf again presented their collective position, emphasizing the American responsibility to force Israel to withdraw to the 1967 lines. He evoked the long history of Arab friendship for the United States and appealed to the United States to uphold the principle of the territorial integrity of all states in the area. Nixon replied by referring to his visits to the Middle East, his meetings with various Arab leaders, and his desire to travel again to the area once a peace settlement had been achieved. Echoing Kissinger's themes, he said that the United States was now working for a cease-fire, after which it would engage in active diplomacy. He denied that domestic politics would influence United States Middle East policy and urged the Arabs to trust Kissinger, despite his Jewish background. He concluded by promising to work for the "implementation of Resolution 242" after a cease-fire, but emphasized that he could not promise that Israel would withdraw to the 1967 lines.

After the talks, Ambassador Saqqaf spoke briefly with the president alone, then proceeded to the Rose Garden to tell the press that the talks had been constructive and friendly. Kissinger then returned to the State Department with the ministers for further talks in the early afternoon.

On the whole, Kissinger felt that the meetings had gone well. At the afternoon WSAG meeting, he stated that he no longer expected the Arabs to cut off oil to the United States. Ironically, just as he was drawing this optimistic conclusion, the Arab oil ministers meeting in Kuwait were announcing that oil production would be cut by 5 percent each month until Israel had withdrawn from all Arab territories. Three days later, King Faisal pushed even further, calling for a 10 percent cut immediately and an embargo of shipments of oil to the United States and the Netherlands.

On the diplomatic front, the only sign of progress from the Kosygin visit to Cairo was a Soviet request for the United States view of a cease-fire-in-place linked to Resolution 242.[51] The American response was positive, but asked for a concrete proposal. The Soviet position was conveyed to Ambassador Dinitz, who passed it to Israel, where Golda Meir found it unacceptable. Rather than linking a cease-fire-in-place to Resolution 242, the Israelis favored a link to direct negotiations between the parties.[52] The next day brought little change. Sadat was still not ready to stop.

As Kissinger had expected, the diplomacy opened up on October 19, shortly after Kosygin's return to Moscow from Cairo.[53] During the morning, a message from Brezhnev reached the White House requesting urgent consultations on the Middle East crisis. Either Kissinger could come to Moscow or Gromyko would fly to the United States. Time was of the essence. Kissinger now felt that a cease-fire could be achieved quickly. In talks with Dinitz, he implied that by agreeing to go to Moscow, he would be able to gain Israel a few more

51. Golan, op. cit., p. 70.
52. Ibid., p. 72.
53. Kosygin left Cairo at 2:55 A.M., Washington time, on Oct. 19.

days to complete her military operations.[54] Dinitz emphasized the need for a link between a cease-fire and negotiations.[55]

Later that afternoon, the administration sent to Congress its $2.2-billion-aid request, which stated that the United States was trying to reach "a very swift and honorable conclusion, measured in days, not weeks." Then, shortly after midnight, having dined with the Chinese representative in Washington, Kissinger left for Moscow.[56] Before his departure, he congratulated the WSAG members on "the best-run crisis ever."

THE MOSCOW TALKS

Whatever he had told Dinitz, Kissinger did not go to Moscow primarily to gain time for Israel's battlefield success, but rather, to obtain Soviet and Arab agreement to a cease-fire resolution that could serve as the basis for a subsequent diplomatic effort. If the Soviet and Arab position remained locked into an unacceptable formulation, then Kissinger was prepared to wait, assuming that Israeli advances on the west bank of the canal would eventually bring about a change. On the other hand, if Brezhnev and Sadat were prepared for a simple cease-fire, then Kissinger would press for a quick end to hostilities. He had no interest in seeing Sadat humiliated, especially in view of the encouraging tone of U.S.-Egyptian exchanges over the past two weeks. Nor did he want to force the Soviets to choose between standing aside to watch their clients be defeated by Israel with American arms or intervening militarily on the Arab side, with the attendant risks of nuclear confrontation. The trick would be to get a cease-fire at just the right moment. Until then, Israel should continue to advance on the ground; but Kissinger felt that Israel must be prepared to stop once the superpowers reached agreement on a cease-fire. After all, the stakes were no longer confined to the Middle East; they were also global. If necessary, Kissinger was prepared to lean hard on the Israelis.

During his flight to Moscow, Kissinger received two important messages. One informed him of the Saudi decision to embargo oil

54. Golan, op. cit., p. 75.

55. M. and B. Kalb, op. cit., pp. 481, 483; Zeev Schiff, *October Earthquake* (Tel Aviv: University Publishing Project, 1974), p. 264.

56. He was accompanied by Joseph Sisco, Alfred Atherton, William Hyland, Winston Lord, and Peter Rodman. Helmut Sonnenfeldt joined the party during a refueling stop in Copenhagen. Ambassador Dobrynin also flew to Moscow aboard the secretary's aircraft.

shipments to the United States. Another, from Nixon, gave Kissinger full authority to negotiate the terms of a cease-fire agreement without Nixon's further approval.[57] At the time, Kissinger was unaware of the depth of the domestic crisis surrounding Nixon. The appeals court had ruled against him on his bid to withhold nine Watergate tapes. The special prosecutor, Archibald Cox, was requesting tapes that Nixon did not want released, so he decided to fire Cox. However, Attorney General Richardson and his deputy, William Ruckelshaus, refused to carry out Nixon's orders to dismiss Cox, preferring instead to resign. All of this culminated in the "Saturday night massacre," just as Kissinger's first talks with Brezhnev were getting under way in the Kremlin.[58] Little wonder that Nixon had decided to leave the cease-fire negotiations to Kissinger or that Kissinger had preferred to negotiate in Moscow, where he, rather than the harassed Nixon, could present the United States position.

The crucial U.S.-Soviet talks began in Moscow on October 21 at about 11:00 A.M. and lasted only four hours. The Soviets, who had initially tried to link a cease-fire to some type of call for Israeli withdrawal from all Arab territory and to guarantees by the superpowers, were swift to change their negotiating position. Time was at a premium, and their client's position was in jeopardy. Ultimately, Brezhnev agreed to a simple cease-fire-in-place, together with a call for the implementation of Security Council Resolution 242 and, at American insistence, to negotiations between the parties under appropriate auspices. In addition, both sides agreed that they would serve as cochairmen of an eventual peace conference and that prisoners should be immediately exchanged by the parties after the cease-fire.

By noon, Washington time, on October 21, the United States and the Soviet Union had agreed upon the text of a cease-fire resolution. It was now up to Kissinger to persuade Israel to accept it. In mid-afternoon, General Alexander Haig, Nixon's chief of staff and former deputy to Kissinger, telephoned Ambassador Dinitz with the proposed text of the resolution. Dinitz was told that time was short and that no changes could be made. The Security Council would meet that evening. Dinitz was given a message from President Nixon to Prime Minister Meir asking that she immediately agree to the resolution. Arms would continue to flow to Israel. Dinitz immediately

57. M. and B. Kalb, op. cit., p. 489.
58. See Theodore White, *Breach of Faith* (New York: Dell, 1975), pp. 328–42.

called Prime Minister Meir with the text of the resolution and Nixon's message. She was irritated that she had not been consulted in advance and was now being confronted with a *fait accompli*. At about 8:00 P.M., Washington time, Prime Minister Meir reportedly tried calling Nixon direct to seek a delay in the cease-fire,[59] but he was unyielding. At 9:00 P.M., shortly before the UN Security Council was to convene, the Israeli cabinet decided to accept the cease-fire resolution. In her message informing Nixon of Israel's decision, Mrs. Meir requested that Kissinger stop in Tel Aviv on his return from Moscow for consultations.

At 10:00 P.M., the Security Council met. Two hours and fifty minutes later, at 12:50 A.M. October 22, Resolution 338 was adopted by the Security Council.[60] Within twelve hours, the fighting was to stop on all fronts.

Kissinger left Moscow in the morning of October 22 for Tel Aviv,[61] where he arrived shortly after noon, Middle East time (6:45 A.M., Washington time). The cease-fire was still not in effect, but in his talks with Prime Minister Meir, Kissinger was insistent that Israel move into defensive positions and not violate the cease-fire. He later claimed that he was very tough with the Israelis on this point, and that Prime Minister Meir, Defense Minister Dayan, and Foreign Minister Eban, if not the Israeli military, agreed that Israel had nothing further to gain from fighting.[62] Kissinger emphasized that the resolution called for the first time for negotiations between Israel and the

59. *The Yom Kippur War*, p. 380.
60. The text of UN Security Council Resolution 338 is as follows:

The Security Council:
1. Calls upon all parties to the present fighting to cease all firing and terminate all military activity immediately, no later than 12 hours after the moment of adoption of this decision, in the positions they now occupy.
2. Calls upon the parties concerned to start immediately after the cease-fire the implementation of Security Council Resolution 242 in all of its parts.
3. Decides that, immediately and concurrently with the cease-fire, negotiations will start between the parties concerned under appropriate auspices aimed at establishing a just and durable peace in the Middle East.

61. Upon learning that Kissinger was stopping in Israel, Sadat invited him to come to Egypt as well. Kissinger declined, but expressed hope that he would be able to visit Cairo soon. Heikal, *Ramadan*, pp. 248–49.

62. Golan, op. cit., pp. 84–87, states that Kissinger hinted that Israel would not be held to strict observance of the cease-fire. No other source maintains this, and I find it unlikely. Joseph Sisco, testifying before the Committee on Foreign Affairs of the House of Representatives, Dec. 3, 1973, stated that "The Israelis were anxious for a cease-fire at the time [Oct. 22] the cease-fire was concluded as were the Egyptians." "Emergency Security Assistance Act of 1973," *Hearings Before the Committee of Foreign Affairs of the House of Representatives,*

Arabs. He also assured Mrs. Meir that there were no secret U.S.-Soviet understandings. Resolution 242 remained as ambiguous as ever as a guideline for the subsequent diplomacy. Israel's bargaining position was not being undercut in advance. Arms would continue to be sent. Kissinger left Israel five hours after his arrival with a feeling that Israel would abide by the cease-fire.[63] One hour after his departure, at 6:50 P.M., Middle East time, the guns fell silent, but not for long.

TOWARD CONFRONTATION

With the achievement of the cease-fire on October 22, Nixon and Kissinger had reason to feel satisfied. A long and dangerous crisis had been brought to an end without a U.S.-Soviet military confrontation. The parties to the conflict had each made some gains to offset their heavy losses, so perhaps the prospects for peace negotiations would be good. Even the oil embargo seemed manageable, if irritating.

Soon after he reached his office on Tuesday morning, October 23, Kissinger was contacted by the Soviets with charges that Israel was violating the cease-fire.[64] Kissinger was worried. He had sensed the bitterness among the Israeli military at being deprived of victory. He had assured the Soviets that Israel would respect the cease-fire, hence when he called Dinitz to report the Soviet charges, he made it clear that Israel should not try to destroy the nearly surrounded Egyptian Third Army Corps. From the onset of the crisis, Kissinger had realized that American credibility with the Arabs might ultimately be tested in circumstances like these. If the United States were now to stand idly by and watch the Third Army Corps be destroyed with newly delivered American weapons, Kissinger's future role as peacemaker would be gravely jeopardized. It did not now matter which side was technically responsible for firing the first shot after the cease-fire was to have gone into effect. What was clear was that it was the Israeli forces that were advancing beyond the October 22 cease-fire lines. Despite his concern, however, Kissinger was not yet unduly alarmed.

93d Congress, Nov. 30 and Dec. 3, 1973 (Washington: Government Printing Office), p. 56. See also Walter Laqueur, *Confrontation* (New York: Bantam Books, 1974), p. 194, and *Maariv,* Oct. 26, 1973.

63. During a stopover in London, Kissinger called the Soviets, urging them to press the Syrians to call off an offensive planned for the following day.

64. M. and B. Kalb, op. cit., p. 481.

During the afternoon of October 23, the UN Security Council passed Resolution 339 calling for immediate cessation of hostilities, a return to positions occupied on October 22 when the cease-fire went into effect, and the dispatch of UN observers to supervise the cease-fire on the Egyptian-Israeli front. Syria had still not accepted the cease-fire, but finally did so later that evening.

Wednesday, October 24, began for Kissinger with a series of exchanges with the Egyptians, Israelis, and Soviets. Sadat was now in frequent communication with Nixon, even on small matters.[65] He asked for the president's help in getting the Israelis to allow medical and food supplies through to the nearly entrapped Third Army Corps. He requested that a United States military attaché from Tel Aviv proceed to the front lines to verify Israel's observance of the cease-fire. Kissinger was prepared to cooperate. He called Dinitz and requested that Israel respect the cease-fire and allow supplies through to the Third Army Corps.[66]

At 10:20 A.M. he met with the WSAG. He expressed his feeling that the United States was now in the "catbird seat. Everyone is looking to us," but he would not act under the threat of the Arab oil embargo. Egypt, he thought, understood this point and would be helpful. The next phase would involve direct Arab-Israeli negotiations under U.S.-Soviet auspices.

In midafternoon, word reached Washington that President Sadat had publicly appealed to the United States and the Soviet Union to send forces to the Middle East to oversee the cease-fire. The White House immediately issued a statement rejecting the idea of forces from the superpowers being sent to the area. Shortly thereafter, Kissinger met with Dobrynin at the State Department to discuss the convening of a peace conference. They agreed on Geneva as the site and considered other procedural matters. Dobrynin denied that the Soviets were interested in sending a joint U.S.-Soviet force to the Middle East in response to Sadat's appeal. The meeting ended on a cordial note, and there was no hint of impending crisis.[67]

65. Heikal, op. cit., pp. 251–52, prints the text of two of Nixon's letters to Sadat of Oct. 24. In addition, Nixon wrote Sadat on Oct. 23 to clarify that the United States had only committed itself to engage in a process designed to make possible a political settlement, but had not guaranteed any specific outcome of that process.
66. M. and B. Kalb, op. cit., p. 488.
67. Ibid.

Three hours later, at 7:05 P.M., Dobrynin called Kissinger to tell
him that the Soviets would support the idea of a joint U.S.-Soviet
peacekeeping force if the nonaligned members of the UN were to
call for one, and shortly thereafter called again to say the Soviets were
considering introducing such a resolution. This caused concern in
Washington, but did not provoke any United States reaction. Then,
at 9:25 P.M. (or at 10:30 P.M., in Kissinger's recollection), Dobrynin
called Kissinger with a "very urgent" message from Brezhnev to
Nixon. He slowly read the text over the telephone. It began by noting
that Israel was continuing to violate the cease-fire, thus posing a
challenge to both the United States and the Soviet Union. Brezhnev
stressed the need to "implement" the cease-fire resolution and
"invited" the United States to join Moscow "to compel observance
of the cease-fire without delay." Then came the threat: "I will say
it straight, that if you find it impossible to act with us in this matter,
we should be faced with the necessity urgently to consider the question of taking appropriate steps unilaterally. Israel cannot be permitted to get away with the violations."[68] Kissinger quickly relayed
the message to Nixon, who reportedly empowered him to order a
military alert if necessary.[69] Kissinger then convened an ad hoc session
of the National Security Council, which at that point consisted only
of himself and the secretary of defense as ex-officio members. In
addition, Colby, Moorer, Haig, and Scowcroft participated in the
deliberations.

There could be no question that the situation was dangerous. No
one knew what the Soviet Union intended to do, but Brezhnev's
note conveyed unmistakably his determination not to let Israel destroy the Egyptian Third Army Corps. Kissinger understood the dilemma that would be posed for the Soviets and the pressures they
would be under to act. Their prestige as a superpower was on the line.
This was something with which Kissinger could empathize. But did
the Soviets have the capability to intervene, whatever their intentions? The answer seemed definitely to be yes. The transport aircraft
that had been flying arms to the Middle East had all returned to
the Soviet Union and could be used as troop carriers. At least seven

68. Part of the text of the Brezhnev letter appears in the *New York Times*, Apr. 10, 1974,
p. 9; and in M. and B. Kalb, op. cit., pp. 489–90. The chronology used here follows that of
the Kalb book.
69. M. and B. Kalb, op. cit., p. 490.

airborne divisions were on a high state of alert.[70] Two amphibious landing craft were in the eastern Mediterranean with the Soviet squadron.

Although a massive Soviet intervention was still difficult to imagine, even with this combination of motives and capabilities, it was not implausible that Moscow might resort to impressive displays of military power that could have explosive political, and perhaps even military, consequences. For example, a small "peace-keeping" contingent might be sent to deliver supplies to the entrapped Third Army Corps. Would the Israelis fire on Soviet forces in such circumstances? If so, then the Soviets might feel compelled to react on a larger scale. If not, Soviet prestige would have gained a significant boost, precisely at a critical moment in U.S.-Arab relations.

Kissinger and the other participants in the NSC meeting reached two conclusions. The Soviet Union, which had seemingly not taken seriously United States warnings about the introduction of their forces into the area, must be under no illusion that the United States did not have the will and the ability to react to any move they might make. To underline this, United States military forces would be placed on a Def Con 3 alert, which meant that leaves would be canceled and an enhanced state of readiness would be observed. The Strategic Air Command would be on a higher state of alert than the normal Def Con 4. No change would be needed for the Sixth Fleet, which was already on a stage 3 alert. Although considerably short of a decision to go on a war footing, this would be a visible move that should convey to the Soviets the American determination to act if necessary. If the crisis were quickly resolved, it would be easy to change the alert status. As had been the case earlier in the crisis, Kissinger was concerned that the Watergate scandal not appear to impede the conduct of American foreign policy. Intentional overreaction would be better than underreaction. To underscore the meaning of the alert, Nixon sent a message to Brezhnev saying that the sending of Soviet troops to the Middle East would be considered a violation of article II of the agreement on the prevention of nuclear war of June 22, 1973.

Besides recommending the alert to the president, Kissinger felt that Israel must stop its advances on the Egyptian front. The Israelis

70. An enhanced alert status of seven Soviet airborne divisions was first noted on Oct. 11; the alert status was altered on Oct. 23. See Schlesinger's press conference, Oct. 26, 1973.

were therefore told in no uncertain terms that the United States would not permit the destruction of the Third Army Corps.[71]

Around midnight, the first orders for the alert were issued, and at 1:30 A.M. on October 25, its scope was widened. Nixon had not participated in the deliberations of the NSC, but he had approved the orders. Now he and his advisers would await the Soviet reaction.

During the morning of October 25, while most Americans were first learning of the alert and wondering about its meaning, Kissinger met with Nixon for a long talk.[72] Several new bits of information were now available. Further messages had been received from Sadat, denying that Egypt was violating the cease-fire and emphasizing again that United States and Soviet forces were needed to enforce the cease-fire. More ominously, intelligence reports had just been received to the effect that a suspicious Soviet ship had arrived in Alexandria. While transiting the Bosporus on October 22, the ship had given off neutron emissions, indicating the possible presence of nuclear weapons on board.[73] Moreover, several ships from the Soviet squadron, including the amphibious landing craft, were steaming toward Egypt. A fragmentary piece of intelligence had been received referring to the imminent arrival of Soviet troops in Cairo. In fact, these proved to be the seventy observers and their interpreters that the Soviets did send to Cairo, but at the time the number was unknown. All in all, the Soviets seemed to be moving toward a confrontation, and the Egyptians seemed to be encouraging it. The president ordered Kissinger to develop a plan for sending United States troops to the Middle East in case the Soviets did intervene. This would, at a minimum, provide some leverage to get the Soviet troops out of

71. Dayan was subsequently quoted as saying that Kissinger threatened to send United States forces to resupply the Third Army Corps. Other Israelis, including Eban, have contended that Kissinger stated that the Soviets might try to resupply the Egyptian forces. The latter seems more plausible, perhaps with the addition of an implied threat not to help them if they found themselves in confrontation with the Soviets over the fate of the Third Army Corps. This issue is discussed by Theodore Draper, "The United States and Israel: Tilt in the Middle East," *Commentary* 59, no. 4 (April 1975), and the exchange of letters in *Commentary* 60, no. 3 (September 1975). Moshe Dayan, *Moshe Dayan: Story of My Life* (New York: William Morrow, 1976), p. 544, says the Americans "more or less" gave Israel an ultimatum to allow supplies through to the Third Army Corps, but does not go into details.

72. M. and B. Kalb, op. cit., pp. 493–94.

73. Ibid., p. 493; Schlesinger press conference, Oct. 26, 1973, loc. cit. If the Soviets intended to send nuclear warheads to Egypt, they presumably would not send them by ship. If, however, they were engaging in a dangerous form of psychological warfare aimed at making the Americans worry about the possibility of nuclear weapons in the area, they might have chosen to send such weapons through the heavily monitored Turkish strait.

the region after the crisis subsided. He also told Kissinger to give a press conference explaining the United States moves.

At 10:15 A.M., Kissinger convened the WSAG once again, and explained the steps leading to the crisis and the president's latest instructions. Kissinger was worried by the behavior of the Soviets, who did not seem interested in finding a solution and who, instead, were exploiting the situation. Schlesinger suggested that they might be genuinely fearful of a collapse on the Egyptian front and might even suspect American duplicity in urging the Israelis on. The meeting ended at 10:50 with Kissinger requesting a contingency plan for sending United States forces to the Middle East, including Arab countries if possible.

Shortly after noon, Kissinger appeared before the press in the State Department auditorium. In a somber but restrained tone, he described the various stages of the crisis and the evolution of United States policy. It was a brilliant performance, one of his most impressive.

After reviewing the diplomatic efforts of the first two weeks, he spoke of the cease-fire and the alert. In the president's name, he reiterated United States opposition to the sending of U.S.-Soviet forces to the Middle East. He was even more strongly opposed to a unilateral Soviet move into the area. He then reviewed the prospects for a peace settlement, which he termed "quite promising," and had conciliatory words for Israel, the Arabs, and even the Soviets. Afterward, he took questions.

In response to several questions about U.S.-Soviet détente, Kissinger emphasized the complex adversary nature of the relationship, but he refused to condemn the Soviets for violating the spirit of détente. Asked whether the alert had been called because of the American domestic crisis, Kissinger, more in sorrow than in anger, dismissed the idea, although he went on to say that the Soviets might have acted as boldly as they did because of the weakened position of the American president. "[O]ne cannot have crises of authority in a society for a period of months without paying a price somewhere along the line."

In his concluding remarks, Kissinger spelled out the principles of a new American policy toward the Arab-Israeli conflict.

> Our position is that . . . the conditions that produced this war were clearly intolerable to the Arab nations, and that in the process of

negotiations, it will be necessary for all sides to make substantial concessions.

The problem will be to relate the Arab concern over—for the sovereignty over the territories—to the Israeli concern for secure boundaries. We believe that the process of negotiations between the parties is an essential component of this.

And, as the president has stated to the four Arab ministers, and as we have stated repeatedly, we will make a major effort to bring about a solution that is considered just by all parties. But I think no purpose would be served by my trying to delimit the exact nature of all of these provisions.[74]

One hour later, the UN Security Council passed Resolution 340, calling for an immediate and complete cease-fire, return to the October 22 lines, dispatch of an augmented UN observer force, creation of a UN Emergency Force composed of nonpermanent members of the Security Council, and implementation of Resolution 338. This time the cease-fire did take hold, and the fourth Arab-Israeli war finally ended. A new chapter in American diplomacy was about to open, with Kissinger as the star performer.

CONCLUSIONS

American policy toward the Arab-Israeli conflict was fundamentally affected by the events of the October 1973 war. Prior to the outbreak of hostilities, it was widely believed that stability in the Middle East was ensured by Israeli military predominance; that Arab oil could not be effectively used to pressure the West; and that Soviet influence in the region had reached its limit. The situation in the area caused concern, but not anxiety. Diplomatic initiatives were contemplated, but not with a sense of urgency or with expectations of success.

It would be wrong to maintain that the United States shifted from

74. See Kissinger's press conference of Oct. 25, *Department of State Bulletin*, Nov. 12, 1973, for the complete text. The following day, Oct. 26, Nixon held a press conference in which he discussed the alert: "We obtained information which led us to believe that the Soviet Union was planning to send a very substantial force to the Mideast, a military force. . . . When I received that information, I ordered, shortly after midnight on Thursday morning, an alert for all American forces around the world. This was a precautionary alert. The purpose of it was to indicate to the Soviet Union that we could not accept any unilateral move on their part to move military forces into the Mideast. . . . [T] he outlook for a permanent peace is the best that it has been in twenty years. . . . [W] ithout détente, we might have had a major conflict in the Middle East. With détente, we avoided it." *Weekly Compilation of Presidential Statements*, Oct. 29, 1973.

a pro-Israeli to a pro-Arab policy as a result of the October war. The changes that did occur were more nuanced and multidimensional than the simple Arab-versus-Israel dichotomy suggests. The war did, however, challenge several basic assumptions of United States policy makers that had been central to prewar policy. Israeli military power had not ensured stability, as had been expected after 1967. That "lesson," reinforced in the September 1970 crisis, was shattered on October 6. This did not mean, of course, that the military balance was seen as having no importance. The latter stages of the war clearly showed that military power counted for a great deal. Israeli strength alone, however, would not lead to a political settlement, as Johnson had hoped it would in 1967.

A second assumption that was undermined by the October war was that U.S.-Soviet détente would serve to minimize the danger of regional conflicts. Although Nixon, Kissinger, and Schlesinger all emphasized that détente had been helpful in resolving the crisis, they were acutely aware that the two superpowers had not been able to remain aloof from the Middle East conflict. Each side was too deeply committed to allow its friends to be sacrificed for the spirit of détente. Concrete local interests won out over global abstractions when put to the test. This did not mean that détente was illusory or dangerous, but rather that it was limited in scope. Superpower confrontation was still a possibility in the era of détente and negotiations, and it was this, above all, that preoccupied the senior decision makers. The events of October 24–25 confirmed their worst fears.

Thirdly, the prevailing attitude toward the Arab world held by policy makers was challenged by the October war. Despite the remarkable Israeli military achievements on both fronts, it appeared that the Egyptians and Syrians had fought comparatively well. They had also achieved surprise in the initial attack; the degree of Arab solidarity was impressive; the use of the oil weapon was well coordinated with the diplomatic and military moves; and the tone of restraint in private and public communications was a welcome contrast to 1967. Sadat, in particular, was emphatic in his desire to work with Nixon and Kissinger for a posthostilities diplomatic settlement. This was a very important new element in the picture.

Three days passed before United States policy makers began to revise their previously held assumptions. The initial call for a cease-fire based on the status quo ante, and the restraint in rearming Israel, were products of prewar views. Between October 9 and 13, these perceptions underwent steady modification, culminating in a revised position on both a cease-fire and arms for Israel. The new policies, which contributed to the cease-fire on October 22, resulted from a reordering of a few elements in the views of the decision makers, rather than from an entirely new appreciation of the situation. The Israelis were encountering more difficulties than anticipated; the Arabs were both more effective at arms and more skillful at diplomacy. These incremental changes in perception, combined with the reality of a prolonged and dangerous war, produced a shift in American policy that was both quantitative and qualitative. The United States would henceforth devote much more attention to the Middle East. It would be a top-priority concern for Nixon and Kissinger. Moreover, the United States would consciously try to improve its relations with the major Arab countries, especially Egypt. This would be a primary element in the new American diplomatic strategy, an element that had been conspicuously lacking before October 1973. Nixon and Kissinger felt that this could be done without sacrificing the U.S.-Israeli relationship. In fact, as they saw it, it was the strength of the U.S.-Israeli tie, with the obvious influence this gave Washington over Israeli policy, that would impress the Arabs and convince them that the United States held most of the diplomatic cards once the fighting was over. The Soviets could provide arms; the United States could help produce territory, provided the Arabs were prepared to make appropriate concessions of their own in the context of peace negotiations.

The shift in policy brought about by the October war was at least as important as that produced by the Jordan crisis of 1970. In the latter case, the result had been an inactive, status-quo-oriented policy; in the case of October 1973, the new approach was much more active and aimed at bringing about substantial change. For the first time, the United States committed its top diplomatic resources to a sustained search for a settlement of the Arab-Israeli conflict.

In view of the importance of the policy change during October 1973, one is tempted to seek explanations in domestic or bureaucratic politics, or in the psychological makeup of the individuals involved. After all, Watergate and the energy crisis were persistent themes throughout the crisis. And both Nixon and Kissinger had strong and unusual personalities.

Domestic politics is often linked in complex ways to foreign policy, and there is little doubt that Nixon and Kissinger took it into account as they considered policy choices. The key decisions of the crisis, however—the cease-fire proposals, the airlift to Israel, and the alert—were not responses to domestic politics. Pro-Israeli groups were not responsible for the decision to rearm Israel, mostly because Kissinger skillfully persuaded the Israeli ambassador not to "unleash" Israel's supporters. Pro-Arab groups and oil companies played no role in Nixon's decision to press Israel to accept a cease-fire on October 12 or to save the Third Army Corps. Nor does Watergate explain the military alert of October 24–25.

Crisis periods, especially, tend to isolate policy makers from domestic pressures. Decisions are often made rapidly, before public opinion can be mobilized. Information is closely held, depriving interest groups of the means for effective action. The stakes are high and the public tends to be deferential to presidential authority, even when that authority has been weakened, as Nixon's had been.

One theme that did recur in Kissinger's comments was that the rest of the world must not draw the conclusion that the Watergate crisis had weakened the president's ability to conduct foreign policy. The size of the United States airlift to Israel, once begun, the magnitude of the aid bill for arms to Israel, and the scope of the American military alert may have been partly related to this desire to appear strong and decisive. In each case, however, the basic decision was not rooted in the fear that Watergate had led other nations to underestimate the United States. Rather, the decisions were responses to external events that seemed to require urgent action. With or without the Watergate affair, the same course almost certainly would have been taken.

Other explanations of United States policy during the war have emphasized bureaucratic or personality factors. In some accounts, Schlesinger and Clements are portrayed as opposing the airlift to Israel; in others, Kissinger is painted as the villain.[75] The reasons

75. The debate over Kissinger's role in the October war has spawned a remarkably partisan body of writing. Marvin and Bernard Kalb, op. cit., are favorable to Kissinger and erroneously portray Schlesinger as the obstacle to the airlift to Israel. Tad Szulc, "Is He Indispensable? Answers to the Kissinger Riddle," *New York*, July 1, 1974, points the finger at Kissinger instead. Luttwak and Laqueur, op. cit., try to set the record straight, but overlook the importance of the cease-fire effort of Oct. 10–13. Gil Carl Alroy, *The Kissinger Experience* (New York: Horizon Press, 1975), is a bitterly anti-Kissinger polemic. Golan, op. cit., is better

given may be institutional—military men resented seeing arms taken from active United States units and sent to Israel; they may be linked to economic interests—Clements had ties to the oil industry; or they may be traced to personality—Kissinger and Nixon had deluded themselves with the success of détente and therefore failed to appreciate ways in which the Soviets were manipulating the situation to their advantage.

The problem with these perspectives is that they do not account for the fact that individuals from widely different backgrounds agreed on each of the major decisions. Whatever their subsequent relationship, Kissinger and Schlesinger did not argue over basic policy in the October war. Whatever their personal feelings toward Israel, Deputy Secretary Clements and Air Force General Brown helped organize a remarkably efficient airlift to Israel once the orders were given. Bureaucratic politics was barely in evidence, so tight was Kissinger's control over the policy-making machinery. Nor did the policy changes result from the replacement of individuals with one set of views by those of contrasting persuasions. The same officials were in place, with about the same relative power, before and after the war. The difference was that they now saw the situation differently.

The key to the consensus among top officials was the ability of Kissinger to draw on President Nixon's authority. On occasion, Nixon directly gave orders, but even when he was not present, Kissinger was clearly speaking in his name. In each of the major decisions, the president was involved. When Kissinger would say ''The president wants'' or ''The president has ordered,'' few of the other key officials were inclined to argue. Moreover, only Kissinger had direct, continuing access to the president.

American policy during the October 1973 war demonstrated once again the centrality of the president in the making of foreign policy, particularly in crises. In this case, Kissinger must be considered an extension of the president, for he was given an unusual margin of responsibility. It was his tie to Nixon, however, not his position as

---

informed, but equally hostile to Kissinger. Edward R. F. Sheehan, *The Arabs, Israelis, and Kissinger* (New York: Reader's Digest Press, 1976), is sympathetic to him. Very few writers have been able to discern Nixon's role in the formulation of United States policy during the war, or to distinguish between those aspects of policy designed to preserve détente and those aimed at promoting a new relationship with Egypt.

secretary of state, that ensured the acceptance of his formulations. Perhaps if the policies had been less nuanced, less complex, there might have been some overt dissension within the bureaucracy. The Nixon-Kissinger policy, however, could be seen as pro-Israel, pro-Arab, pro-détente, or anti-Soviet, depending on what one was looking for. Those who disagreed with one element of policy were likely to support other aspects. This left the president and Kissinger in a commanding position.

As the crisis came to an end, the Middle East undoubtedly had top priority in American foreign policy. American relations with allies had been damaged by the crisis; détente was under attack; the energy crisis was likely to become more acute. Progress toward an Arab-Israeli settlement would not necessarily solve these problems, but failure to defuse the Middle East situation could only complicate them. Perhaps equally important, for the first time Nixon and Kissinger sensed the opportunity to make progress toward a settlement. The Arabs were looking to Washington now, not to Moscow. The Israelis were heavily dependent on American arms and financial support, which could be translated into influence in the proper diplomatic setting. Public opinion would be supportive of a major United States initiative, provided that it did not become anti-Israeli or appear to be responsive to the Arab oil embargo.

By the time the cease-fire had gone into effect, the United States was already preparing for a new diplomatic effort. It would not be like the Rogers Plan, formal, legalistic, and worked out in U.S.-Soviet negotiations. Instead, the Soviets would be kept out of the substance of the negotiations. Their record during the war had not inspired confidence that they were prepared to play an "even-handed" role in settling the conflict. Nor did Sadat seem to want them involved. Furthermore, no American plan would be presented to the parties. Instead, the United States would try to play the role of mediator, eliciting propositions from the parties, trying then to modify them, and eventually pressing for a compromise. The process would move slowly, beginning with concrete issues of particular urgency, and proceeding later to more fundamental problems, such as the nature of a final peace settlement. Above all, each step must remain independent of the next; otherwise the process would never get under way, as the United States had discovered in the interim-settlement effort of 1971. As the war came to a close, Kissinger had already decided on his new strategy—"step-by-step" diplomacy. Now he merely needed to persuade Israel, the Arabs, the Soviets, Congress, and the American public to give him a chance to prove his success where others had failed. For the next six months, Kissinger was accorded the opportunity to demonstrate both the strengths and limitations of his conception of how to solve the Arab-Israeli conflict.

CHAPTER VII

Step-by-Step Diplomacy: The Disengagement Agreements

THE EIGHT MONTHS that followed the October 1973 war witnessed an unprecedented American involvement in the search for a settlement of the Arab-Israeli conflict. Henry Kissinger, before becoming secretary of state, had devoted little energy to the seemingly intractable issues dividing Israel and her Arab neighbors. Nor had he progressed far in his understanding of the "energy crisis" and the part played by Middle East oil in the international economy. Only the danger of confrontation between the superpowers growing out of tensions in the Middle East seemed capable of arousing in him, and in President Nixon, a sustained interest in the affairs of the region. Now, with the October war a vivid example of the volatility of the Arab-Israeli conflict, Kissinger, with Nixon's full backing, set out to become the peacemaker, orchestrator, mediator, and catalyst in a new diplomatic initiative that would take him repeatedly to countries he had never before visited to deal with statesmen he had previously not taken seriously.

Although President Nixon was eager for the United States to play an active part in resolving the Arab-Israeli conflict, he was also increasingly preoccupied with his crumbling domestic base of support as the Watergate scandal continued to unfold. Kissinger therefore was allowed extraordinary latitude in shaping the details of American diplomacy, calling on Nixon to invoke presidential authority as necessary, while keeping the president well informed at each stage.

Above all, Nixon wanted results. Internationally, he worried about the consequences of other nations concluding that the American domestic crisis had weakened the president's ability to act in foreign affairs. Domestically, he hoped that foreign-policy successes would help him through the crisis of confidence in his judgment and leadership stemming from his handling of Watergate.

SHAPING AN AMERICAN STRATEGY

During the October 1973 hostilities, Kissinger and Nixon had both promised an active American diplomatic initiative aimed at "implementing Resolution 242" after the war ended, but they steadfastly refused to promise any specific results, despite Sadat's pleas. The United States, they repeated, was committed to a process, not an outcome. It guaranteed that it would make a major effort, but it could not guarantee that Israel would withdraw from all Arab territory or that Palestinian rights would be restored. To do so would be to invite severe domestic criticism and to raise Arab hopes to an unrealistic level. Kissinger frequently mentioned that he feared the Arabs' "romanticism," their impatience, their desire for quick results.[1]

These initial perceptions, shaped by the October crisis, became the foundations of postwar policy. With the achievement of the shaky cease-fire of October 25, Nixon and Kissinger began to define what the contours of that policy would be. Two key elements quickly emerged. First, the United States would play an active role in trying to resolve the Arab-Israeli conflict. Unlike Johnson after 1967 and their own policy after 1970, Nixon and Kissinger now felt that the situation in the Middle East was too dangerous in terms of American interests to be ignored, and, perhaps even more important, an opportunity for a successful American initiative existed.[2] As Kissinger had sensed during the war, everyone was looking to the United States. He held the cards, or at least so the principal actors believed, which

1. He expressed this concern to Mohamed Heikal in Cairo on Nov. 7, as reported by Heikal in a lengthy account of his talk with Kissinger in *Al-Ahram*, Nov. 16, 1973.

2. Ibid. Kissinger told Heikal that he had not dealt with the Middle East crisis before October 1973 because of his fear of failure. Not enough elements of the situation were under his control to ensure success.

was what mattered. The Israelis, more isolated internationally than ever before, were in the awkward position of being heavily dependent on Washington for arms, for economic aid, and for diplomatic support. The Arabs, realizing the potential for United States influence with Israel, were anxious to turn that potential to their own advantage. As Kissinger and others had hinted, the Soviets could provide arms to the Arabs, but only the United States could produce Israeli territorial concessions through negotiations.[3]

The second element of the new American strategy was to try to avoid linking initial diplomatic steps with the nature of a final peace agreement. Kissinger had disliked the Rogers Plan of 1969, and was not even particularly keen on UN Resolution 242. Such public statements of principles might provide psychic gratification to one side or the other, but, in his view, they did little to advance the diplomatic process. Instead, they allowed each side to focus on what it rejected in the abstract plan instead of concentrating on tangible issues in the present. If an active United States role in the diplomacy was meant as a signal to the Arabs of a more balanced American policy, Washington's refusal to link first steps with final outcomes was meant to reassure Israel that a settlement would not be imposed against her will.

In order to sustain an active and effective United States role in the evolving diplomacy of the Arab-Israeli conflict, Kissinger felt that it was necessary to break up the international pressures created by the October 1973 war. The Arab offensive had succeeded in mobilizing European, Japanese, and Third World support for a rapid settlement on essentially Arab terms. The UN could be counted on to support Egypt, Syria, and the Palestinians. The Soviets were committed to the Arab position, even at some risk to détente and U.S.-Soviet relations. The Arab oil embargo was an added source of tension, as was the continuing danger that the cease-fire would break down. Kissinger, although he admired the way in which Sadat had succeeded in marshaling his forces, was not prepared to act under these combined pressures. He would therefore try to persuade the American allies to leave him a free hand; he would isolate the Soviets from the substance of the negotiations; he would endeavor to get the oil embargo lifted;

3. Ibid. "The Soviet Union can give you arms, but the United States can give you a fair solution by which your lands will be returned to you, particularly since [the Arabs] have actually been able to change the situation in the Middle East. . . . [P]olitics in our present age is not a matter of sentiment, but facts of power."

he would build support for "moderate" Arab positions at the expense of "radical" ones; he would try to avoid a public quarrel with Israel that might have serious domestic repercussions; and he would attempt to win over the United States Congress and press to support his role in the diplomacy. Much of Kissinger's tactical maneuvering of succeeding months was aimed at ensuring that the United States could act free of the multiple pressures, domestic and international, generated by the October war. On the whole, he was remarkably successful.

Kissinger felt that previous administrations had erred in seeing their choices as being pro-Israel or pro-Arab. In his view, it was precisely the special American relationship with Israel that obliged the Arabs to deal with the United States in the diplomatic arena. Power, not sentiment, was what counted. The difficulty, of course, was that in order to keep the Arabs looking toward the United States, the diplomatic process had to hold out more hope than another round of war. If war were seen as the answer, the Soviet Union could always provide more than the United States. Consequently, progress toward a settlement was an absolute prerequisite for maintaining the confidence of the Arabs. At a minimum, this meant the return of territory, and eventually some move in the direction of addressing Palestinian grievances. For the United States, it meant that Israel would have to make concessions in order to keep the diplomacy alive. Where possible, the United States might try to extract comparable Arab concessions, but, given the nature of the issues, this would be difficult. An additional dimension of United States diplomacy would therefore be offers of aid to Israel—with the implied threat of withholding it if circumstances so dictated—and promises of assistance to Egypt, Syria, and Jordan to strengthen bilateral relations through other means than delivering Israeli concessions.

U.S.-Egyptian relations were seen as the linchpin of the new American policy in the Arab world, with Jordan and Saudi Arabia playing key supportive roles in favor of Arab "moderation."[4] Only gradually did Syria's importance come to be perceived by Kissinger; he was even more reluctant to acknowledge the Palestinians as par-

4. Edward R.F. Sheehan, *The Arabs, Israelis, and Kissinger* (New York: Reader's Digest Press, 1976), p. 51, refers to a coherent Arab policy based on a "quasi-alliance" between Washington and Cairo and the promotion of American technology as a means of increasing American influence in the Arab world.

ticipants in the settlement process. For the moment, the new U.S.-Egyptian relationship, already in evidence during the war, was to receive most of Nixon's and Kissinger's attention.

The role of the Soviet Union in the Middle East had long preoccupied Nixon and Kissinger. Having at one time overrated Soviet influence in the Arab world, they were now inclined to minimize the Soviet role in the settlement process. Soviet behavior in the October war, though not viewed as totally contrary to the spirit of détente, was nonetheless not particularly encouraging.[5] Nor had previous U.S.-Soviet efforts to reach agreement on the terms of settlement been successful. The two superpowers not only had different interests in the region, but also a different concept of what a peace settlement should entail. Perhaps most important of all, the key participants in the regional conflict were not anxious to see the Soviets deeply involved in the diplomacy. Certainly the Israelis were unenthusiastic, given Soviet hostility and the lack of diplomatic relations. Jordan was still prepared to work with the United States instead of with the Soviet Union. Sadat was also ready to play his American card, and Soviet-Egyptian relations suffered as a result. Even President Asad of Syria indicated a willingness to let Kissinger try his hand, although his skepticism was considerably greater than Sadat's. Finally, there was enough of the cold warrior left in both Nixon and Kissinger to produce a sense of real pleasure in demonstrating the limits of Soviet influence in the Middle East.[6]

To maintain an effective American role in the resolution of the Arab-Israeli dispute, domestic public opinion would have to be mobilized. Most Americans were sympathetic to Israel, a sentiment that was particularly strong in Congress and in the press.[7] The Arab oil boycott was doing little to change this; in fact, it seemed more likely that an anti-Arab backlash might result, making it difficult to pursue the policy of building the new ties to the Arab world that were central to the Nixon-Kissinger strategy. American policy could

5. See William B. Quandt, *Soviet Policy in the October 1973 War*, R-1864, The RAND Corporation, May 1976.

6. Nixon and Kissinger may also have been irritated by Moscow's unwillingness to live up to the commitment it undertook on Oct. 20–21 to work for the immediate release of Israeli prisoners held in Egypt and Syria.

7. William B. Quandt, "Domestic Influence on US Foreign Policy in the Middle East: The View from Washington," in *The Middle East: Quest for an American Policy*, ed. Willard A. Beling (Albany: State University of New York Press, 1973).

not appear to be dictated by Arab oil pressures. Domestically and internationally, that would be an untenable posture for the administration. Consequently, the new diplomatic initiatives would have to be explained to the American public and to Congress in terms of the overall objective of seeking peace in the Middle East, of strengthening United States ties with the Arab world without sacrificing Israel, and of minimizing the ability of the Soviets to threaten Western interests, including oil. Broad support for these objectives could be expected, especially if aid to Israel continued to flow at high levels and if the oil embargo were lifted.

If an active United States diplomatic role in the search for an Arab-Israeli settlement was the first principle of the new American policy, the second was the pursuit of a settlement through a "step-by-step" process. This soon came to be the hallmark of the Kissinger diplomacy. Kissinger's negotiating experiences with the Chinese, the Vietnamese, and the Soviets had convinced him that the process of negotiation had a dynamic of its own.[8] It was important to create the proper balance of incentives first; then to reach limited results at an early stage without making commitments to the final goal; eventually, when a mutuality of interests had emerged, more substantial areas of agreement would be possible. Kissinger was skeptical of the American penchant for the "quick fix," the technical solution to a political problem, of negotiations carried on in the blaze of publicity, of bureaucratic compromises, and of good will as a substitute for tangible concessions. Although he would later be charged with some of these mistakes in his own conduct of diplomacy, he was at least conscious of these pitfalls, of the weakness of his own role as mediator, and of the sizable gap that separated the parties. Unlike other negotiations he had engaged in, the Arab-Israeli arena was one where the United States faced the challenge of persuading adversaries to make commitments to one another. It was not enough for the United States to develop its own policies; the key to success would be to induce the parties to modify their irreconcilable positions.

Timing would be an important element of the Kissinger step-by-step diplomacy. He envisaged negotiations that very probably would go on for several years. The Arabs were pressing for immediate Israeli withdrawal; the Israelis were pleading for time. Kissinger was anxious

8. William B. Quandt, "Kissinger and the Arab-Israeli Disengagement Negotiations," *Journal of International Affairs* 29, no. 1 (spring 1975).

to pace the negotiations so that some results could be produced at an early date, while still allowing time for all parties to adjust to a gradual, phased approach to a settlement. Most immediately, the Israelis had a national election scheduled for the end of December, and until then no serious negotiations could be expected. Somehow the Arabs would have to be persuaded to wait until early 1974 for the first Israeli withdrawals.

In the meantime, it would be important to establish a negotiating framework, a forum that would provide the symbolic umbrella under which various diplomatic moves might be made. This forum would be a multilateral conference, with United States and Soviet participation, to be held at Geneva under UN auspices. Its primary value would be to legitimize the settlement process, to give the Soviets enough of a sense of participation to prevent them from disrupting the peace effort, and to provide a setting where agreements could be ratified, talks could be held, and delegations could meet. Kissinger fully expected, however, that progress toward agreements would not be made in such a cumbersome forum.

Instead of counting heavily on Geneva, Kissinger planned to deal with concrete issues through bilateral channels. Most urgent were the problems on the Egyptian-Israeli front. There the armies were entangled in a dangerous fashion, constantly tempting one side or the other to resume hostilities. The Egyptian Third Army Corps was nearly cut off from supplies, a situation that was intolerable for Sadat to accept. International pressure was building for Israel to pull back to the October 22 lines, which would release the Third Army. Prisoners of war had to be exchanged, an issue of very great sensitivity to the Israelis. The Egyptian semiblockade of Bab al-Mandab at the southern entrance of the Red Sea was preventing the movement of Israeli shipping to and from Aqaba. Taken together, these issues might be negotiated in a first step that would stabilize the cease-fire through a "disengagement" of military forces.

The conceptual underpinnings of the new American policy in the Middle East, initially forged in the midst of the October war, were quickly established. Nixon and Kissinger, with virtually no opposition from the bureaucracy, were committing the United States to an unprecedented active role in mediating the Arab-Israeli conflict, to a "step-by-step" diplomatic process, and to a "disengagement" of Egyptian-Israeli military forces at an early date.

One result of the improvement in the relationship between Cairo and Washington was President Sadat's frequent and urgent appeals to the United States to help the entrapped Third Army Corps. The Israelis, by contrast, were determined to use pressure on the corps as a means of obtaining release of prisoners of war and the end of the naval blockade at Bab al-Mandab. The stalemate threatened to destroy the precious cease-fire. Kissinger therefore quickly set two urgent goals: first, to stabilize the cease-fire; second, to bring about a separation of military forces. By October 27, the State Department was able to announce that Egyptian and Israeli representatives had agreed to meet to implement the cease-fire agreement. Even before the talks began on October 30, temporary arrangements had been made for the nonmilitary resupply of the Third Army Corps.

The Egyptian and Israeli positions on the terms of a cease-fire and on a military disengagement proved to be far apart. Ismail Fahmy, Egypt's new foreign minister, met with Kissinger on October 29.[9] Two days later he again met Kissinger, as well as President Nixon. In addition to discussing the secretary's forthcoming trip to Egypt, Faymy was authorized to present an eleven-point proposal. Most urgently, Egypt insisted that Israel withdraw unconditionally to the October 22 lines, as called for in UN Resolutions 339 and 340. Once that was done, Egypt would agree to release all prisoners of war. Then Israel should withdraw to a line inside Sinai that would lie east of the passes, and Egyptian forces would remain in place. UN forces would man a zone between Egyptian and Israeli forces. The blockade of Bab al-Mandab would be lifted once Israeli forces began to withdraw toward the disengagement zone, and the clearing of the Suez Canal would begin after this stage was completed. Within an agreed time period, Israel would withdraw in one more step to the international frontier, at which point the state of belligerency would end. Similar steps should be planned for Syria and a peace conference should be convened during the implementation of the disengagement phase. Finally, U.S.-Egyptian diplomatic relations would be restored at an early date.

Kissinger told Fahmy that the plan contained constructive ideas,

9. In his first meeting with Kissinger, Fahmy agreed that the Third Army Corps would only be resupplied with nonmilitary items if Israel agreed to pull back to the Oct. 22 lines. Fahmy at the time was acting foreign minister. He was named foreign minister on Oct. 31.

but that it seemed too ambitious at that stage. In discussions during the next two days, Kissinger raised the issue of the October 22 lines, emphasizing that it would be difficult to persuade Israel to withdraw to them and that a broader step as part of the disengagement of forces would make the October 22 lines irrelevant in any case.[10] Reflecting the new tone in U.S.-Egyptian relations, President Sadat, in a speech delivered that same day, termed the American role "constructive."

Next it was Kissinger's and Nixon's turn to talk with Prime Minister Meir, who arrived in Washington on October 31. Kissinger met with her on the morning of November 1. She was particularly concerned with the fate of Israeli prisoners in Egypt. Continued resupply of the Third Army Corps, she argued, was conditional upon the return of wounded POWs, a complete list of all prisoners, and Red Cross visits to them. Israel would agree to permanent nonmilitary supply of the Third Army Corps once the prisoners were returned and the naval blockade was lifted. Only then would Israel agree to talk to Egypt about the October 22 lines. Kissinger was authorized to convey these terms to Sadat, with the understanding that the United States would not take a position on the location of the October 22 lines and would not pressure Israel on this issue, leaving it instead to negotiations between the two parties.

Shortly after noon, President Nixon met with Prime Minister Meir. Nixon offered the opinion that Sadat really wanted peace, and then laid out the American strategy for the months ahead. He would try to break up the problems so that they could be dealt with through a step-by-step process. The United States would stand up to the Soviets, as it had done in the October war. It would try to improve its relations with Egypt and Syria, which would also help Israel. His goal would be to assure "secure borders" for Israel. Meir was undemonstrative, emphasizing only that Israel did not want to be pressed on the October 22 lines. That evening Kissinger dined with Mrs. Meir and a few others. The atmosphere was chilly, if not hostile. The Israeli Prime Minister barely spoke to Kissinger, and when she did, her tone was reserved. There was no expression of gratitude for United States aid, only anger at being deprived of victory by "friends." No toasts were drunk.

10. Kissinger did promise, however, that Israel would not launch a military offensive from its position on the west bank of the Suez Canal. He also agreed to send a high-level representative to Cairo at an early date.

The following morning Kissinger convened a meeting of the WSAG. Still incensed over the previous day's talks with the Israelis, he implied that Israeli leaders had deliberately misled him on several occasions during the war. Now United States foreign policy would be determined by the United States, not Israel. By working for a moderate peace proposal, the United States would reduce Soviet influence and end the oil embargo. If this effort failed, the Arabs would be driven back to the Soviets, the oil crisis would worsen, and the United States and Israel would be isolated internationally. The Arabs must see that they would be better off dealing with the United States than with the Soviet Union. The view was expressed that Egypt's position on accepting nonmilitary resupply of the Third Army Corps and an exchange of POWs once Israel returned to the October 22 lines was reasonable. If necessary, Israel would be forced to accept it. Eventually the tone of the discussion moderated, but anger at Israeli intransigence was genuine and would be displayed repeatedly in succeeding months.[11]

KILOMETER 101

With these initial talks behind him, Kissinger set off for the Middle East on November 5. His first stop, which also marked his first visit to an Arab country, was in Morocco, partly to symbolize the long tradition of friendly U.S.-Arab relations, and partly to open channels through King Hassan to Syria and the Palestinians.[12] Cairo, not Rabat, however, was the real goal of Kissinger's travels. There, on November 7, he met President Sadat for the first time. In private talks that day, Kissinger began to develop a genuine admiration for the Egyptian leader.[13] The turning point came in discussing the issue of the October 22 lines. Kissinger was in an awkward position, for he knew the Israelis could not easily be pressured and yet he felt that Sadat was right that Israeli forces should not be allowed to keep the Third Army Corps at their mercy.

By the time Kissinger arrived in Cairo, the Israeli cabinet had

11. Kissinger met again with Prime Minister Meir. The following day, the prime minister was reportedly called by Nixon's chief of staff, Alexander Haig, and by Nelson Rockefeller, both of whom conveyed Nixon's displeasure at her attitude. Matti Golan, *The Secret Conversations of Henry Kissinger* (New York: Quadrangle Books, 1976), p. 111.

12. Kissinger had seen the Syrian representative to the United Nations on Nov. 2, but there was still no channel for continuing contacts between Washington and Damascus.

13. See Sheehan, op. cit., pp. 48–51.

approved the positions presented to Kissinger by Prime Minister Meir on November 3. He was thus able to tell Sadat that Israel would respect the cease-fire; that nonmilitary resupply of the Third Army Corps would be allowed, with UN and Israeli inspection of convoys; that the town of Suez would receive food, water, and medicine; concurrently with the agreement on nonmilitary supplies, POWs should be exchanged and the naval blockade lifted; and the October 22 lines could be discussed in the framework of the disengagement of forces. In addition, Israel had indicated that, in return for the POWs in Syria, Syrian civilians could return to areas controlled by Israel and two outposts on Mt. Hermon could be turned over to the UN.

Sadat was prepared to accept most of these points, although he was still anxious for Israel to pull back to the October 22 lines. Kissinger replied that if Egypt insisted, he would agree to try to persuade the Israelis. But he offered his opinion that it might be just as easy, although it might take more time, to work out a substantial disengagement of forces that would by-pass the issue of the October 22 lines. Meanwhile arrangements could be made to resupply the Third Army Corps. To Kissinger's surprise, Sadat agreed with this line of argument. He urged Kissinger to strive to obtain rapid agreement on the Israeli points. At the conclusion of the talks it was agreed that diplomatic relations between Egypt and the United States would be restored "in principle" immediately.[14]

Kissinger promptly decided to send two of his aides, Joseph Sisco and Harold Saunders, to Israel to work out the details of an accord. Upon learning that Sadat had agreed to drop the issue of the October 22 lines, the prime minister termed this a "fantastic achievement," but quickly she found fault with the Egyptian position. Sadat did not want Israel to control the road used to supply the Third Army Corps, nor was he prepared publicly to acknowledge that Egypt would lift the naval blockade. After several rounds of discussion of these two points, Israel agreed to accept United States assurances that the blockade would be ended. On November 9, agreement on a cease-fire plan and the exchange of POWs was announced, and two days later a six-point agreement modeled on the original Israeli proposal was signed by Israeli and Egyptian military representatives at a point along the

14. An experienced career diplomat, Herman Eilts, was named as American ambassador to Egypt, and American-educated Ashraf Ghorbal became Egypt's ambassador to the United States.

Cairo to Suez road known as Kilometer 101.[15] The settlement process was off to a start, albeit a shaky one.

Meanwhile, Kissinger flew to Jordan to talk with King Hussein, and encouraged the king to participate in the peace negotiations. Without making firm commitments, he expressed sympathy with the king's opposition to a West Bank Palestinian state dominated by the Palestine Liberation Organization. For the moment, however, Kissinger was still concentrating on the Egyptian-Israeli front. Jordan and the Palestinians would be left for later.

In Saudi Arabia, Kissinger appealed to King Faisal for support of his diplomatic effort, referring to the oil embargo as an obstacle to the American efforts. He argued the logic of the step-by-step approach, and appealed to Faisal for help in opening channels of communication with the Syrians.[16] Faisal gave Kissinger his standard rendition of the Zionist-Communist conspiracy, but also promised to help, including an easing of the boycott once progress began on Israeli withdrawal.[17]

On balance, Kissinger felt pleased with the results of his first trip. He had established a personal relationship with Sadat, and U.S.-Egyptian relations seemed off to a good start. The cease-fire had been stabilized. An important agreement had been signed by Israel and Egypt, with United States help. Faisal had promised to ease the oil embargo. Now it was necessary to develop the broad negotiating framework at Geneva as a prelude to disengagement talks. Kissinger was in no rush, being still committed to a gradual pace under close United States control.

THE GENEVA CONFERENCE

The first Egyptian and Israeli prisoners were exchanged on November 15. The next day, General Yariv of Israel and General Gamasy of Egypt began talks at Kilometer 101 aimed at implementing the six-point agreement, particularly its second point, concerning

15. The text of the agreement can be found in *Arab Report and Record*, Feb. 1–14, 1974, p. 60.
16. Sheehan, op. cit., pp. 70–73, contains a partial transcript of the Kissinger-Faisal meeting.
17. Several days later, in Peking, Kissinger spoke of Israeli "withdrawals" as part of a settlement, in a deliberate effort to signal his good intentions to the Saudis. The Israelis were not particularly pleased; they worried about Kissinger's mention of United States guarantees, fearing that external guarantees would become a substitute for Arab concessions. See Kissinger's news conference of Nov. 12, 1973, *Department of State Bulletin*, Dec. 10, 1973, p. 713.

"return to October 22 lines in the framework of agreement on the disengagement and separation of forces." On November 18, Kissinger reminded Foreign Minister Fahmy that disengagement should be the first order of business of the upcoming Geneva peace conference, but it could not become a precondition for the convening of the conference. Nor could the issue of Palestinian participation in the peace conference be settled at this stage. Only at the peace conference would the United States be able to use its full influence. In short, Kissinger was trying to build up Geneva as an important step in the process of negotiations and to keep the United States role central to substantive progress.

Meanwhile, Israeli and Egyptian positions were being discussed at Kilometer 101. Israel initially proposed that both sides should pull back from territory gained in the October war, and that UN forces should take over these areas. The Egyptian reply was to insist that Egyptian forces would stay in place and that Israeli forces should withdraw to a line running from Al-Arish to Ras Muhammad in the southern tip of Sinai. Gamasy then proposed Israeli withdrawal in a more modest disengagement phase to the vicinity of the Mitla and Giddi passes, with designated zones for both the Egyptian and the Israeli main forces, lightly armed forces, and a UN buffer between them. On November 22, General Yariv replied that Israel would withdraw from the west bank of the canal provided that Egyptian forces on the east bank were thinned out.[18]

Negotiations continued for several days, with Israel offering deeper withdrawals in return for a substantial reduction of Egyptian armored strength. On November 26, Yariv suggested that Israel would even withdraw east of the passes if Egypt would reduce its level of armor in Sinai to token strength. Egypt showed interest in the proposal, but insisted on mutual force reductions; then on November 29, Gamasy discovered that Yariv had gone back to his original proposal that both sides should withdraw from territory gained in the war. This reversal of position angered the Egyptians and led to the breakdown of the talks.

Kissinger has been charged with responsibility for aborting this promising experiment in direct Egyptian-Israeli negotiations.[19] There

18. Moshe Dayan, *Moshe Dayan: Story of My Life* (New York: William Morrow, 1976), p. 556, refers to Yaviv's Nov. 22 proposals.
19. Golan, op. cit., pp. 120–21. He states that Kissinger did not use direct pressure, but made his preferences known to the Israelis.

is some truth in the charge. Kissinger felt that the talks were proceeding too rapidly. He was beginning to think of the Syrian front, and feared that if Egypt and Israel reached a disengagement agreement before Geneva, Asad would insist on the same, and this might mean an indefinite delay in convening the Geneva conference. Then, too, Kissinger did want to demonstrate that a United States role was essential for sustained diplomatic progress. Perhaps Egypt and Israel could reach agreement without his help, but would the same be true when it came to Syria, the Palestinians, or even a second Egyptian step? He doubted it. If the oil boycott was to be lifted, it would also be in return for American success in promoting agreement. And if Soviet prestige was to remain low, the United States must remain in control of the negotiations. Kissinger therefore advised the Israelis to slow down at Kilometer 101 and to reserve their position on disengagement until Geneva. To some observers, this seemed cynical, but it fitted into Kissinger's broader diplomatic scheme. And it should be added that Israel did not resist this piece of advice, as it so often did on other occasions. In retrospect, it appears as if General Yariv was considerably ahead of the Israeli cabinet in his willingness to offer concessions in the disengagement stage.[20]

Kissinger now turned his attention to organizing the Geneva conference.[21] On December 6, he announced that it was "extremely probable" that a conference would be convened at Geneva on December 18. But who would attend? Egypt would go, and Sadat had implied that Syria would as well.[22] Jordan could be counted on, but since the Arab summit meeting in Algiers the previous month, the PLO had been recognized by all Arab countries except Jordan as the sole legitimate representative of the Palestinian people. If the PLO attended the Geneva conference, Israel would not, nor would Israel sit with Syria unless a list of Israeli prisoners held in Syria were forthcoming.

To help overcome Israeli reluctance to attend the conference, Kissinger talked to Defense Minister Dayan in Washington on December 7. A long list of arms requests was presented, and Kissinger

20. Dayan, op. cit., p. 548, states that he opposed the Kilometer 101 talks because he felt the United States should be involved in the negotiation.

21. Nixon wrote to Sadat on Dec. 1, proposing that Egypt attend a conference in Geneva on Dec. 18.

22. Sadat's reply to Nixon's invitation, dated Dec. 8, confirmed Egypt's willingness to go to Geneva, but did not mention Syria.

implied that the United States would give it favorable consideration. In return, Dayan stated that disengagement need not await Israeli elections. Dayan proposed a disengagement based on Israeli withdrawal to a line west of the passes, combined with substantial demilitarization of forward areas and an Egyptian commitment to reopen the Suez Canal. Once again, however, Kissinger urged the Israelis not to move too quickly in negotiations. Israel should not look weak. It was important for the Arabs to see that it was difficult for the United States to influence Israel, otherwise their expectations would soar.

Kissinger set off on his second trip to the Middle East on December 12, stopping in London en route to deliver an important speech.[23] He proceeded to Algiers for talks with President Boumedienne, and was successful in gaining his support for the Geneva conference. Boumedienne would thereafter be kept well informed on the peace negotiations, for Kissinger felt that Algeria's endorsement of his strategy would make it easier for both Sadat and Asad to resist radical Arab pressures.

During the next several days, Kissinger traveled to Cairo, Riyadh, Damascus, and Tel Aviv. Only the talks with Sadat were devoid of difficulty. Sadat had already accepted a short delay in opening the Geneva conference, and now agreed to postpone the substantive phase of disengagement negotiations until mid-January, after the Israeli elections.[24] With King Faisal the next day, December 14, Kissinger won Saudi endorsement for Sadat's approach and a promise that the oil embargo would be ended and production restored once agreement had been reached on the first stage of a settlement.

While Kissinger was lining up support for Geneva among key Arab countries, Israel was making its participation in a peace conference conditional on a number of important points. Israel opposed a strong role for the UN Secretary General; it refused to discuss the issue of eventual Palestinian participation at the conference, as Sadat had proposed; nor would Israel's representatives sit in the same room

23. Kissinger's speech before the Pilgrims of Great Britain on Dec. 12 discussed the October war and the energy crisis. It contained the revealing admission that "it is fair to state . . . that the United States did not do all that it might have done before the war to promote a permanent settlement in the Middle East."

24. Kissinger spent four hours with Sadat on Dec. 13 and five hours on Dec. 14. They discussed what they might do if Israel refused to attend the Geneva conference. Sadat also promised to work for the lifting of the oil embargo in early January.

with the Syrians until Syria complied with Israeli demands for a list of POWs and Red Cross visits to them. It began to appear that Israel might boycott Geneva.

At this point Nixon and Kissinger began to exert heavy pressure on Israel. At 6:45 P.M. on December 13 in Washington, Israeli Minister Shalev was handed a letter from Nixon to Prime Minister Meir. She had objected to the draft of a joint U.S.-U.S.S.R. letter to the UN Secretary General on convening the Geneva conference. Nixon indicated that he was disturbed by her attitude, and denied that the UN Secretary General would have more than a symbolic role. Regarding the Palestinians, Nixon argued that the mention of Palestinian participation in the conference did not prejudice the outcome and that, in any case, the participation of additional members of the conference would require agreement of all the initial participants. In short, Israel would not be forced to negotiate with the Palestinians. Nixon concluded his letter by warning the prime minister that the United States would not understand Israel's refusal to attend the Geneva conference and that he would no longer be able to justify support for Israel if Israel did not send its representatives to Geneva.

The next day, upon learning that the Israeli cabinet had not been able to reach a decision as to attending Geneva, Nixon sent another message. The United States was prepared to delay the conference to December 21. Nixon referred to Israel's long-standing goal of negotiations with the Arabs, and termed it inconceivable that Israel would not now take this step. In any event, the president had ordered Kissinger to attend the opening session of the Geneva conference whether Israel were present or not.[25]

While an effort was being made to obtain Israeli agreement to the Geneva conference through a combination of pressures and promises, the latter formalized in another memo of understanding,[26] Kissinger set off for his first meeting with Syria's President Hafiz al-Asad.[27] Kissinger found Asad to be intelligent, tough, personable, and possessed of a sense of humor. He was also the least conciliatory

25. Nixon's tone in these letters was reflected in remarks he reportedly made to a group of seventeen Governors on Dec. 13. "The only way we're going to solve the crisis is to end the oil embargo, and the only way we're going to end the embargo is to get the Israelis to act reasonable. I hate to use the word blackmail, but we've got to do some things to get them to behave." *Washington Post*, Dec. 22, 1973.

26. Described in *Jerusalem Post*, Dec. 18, 1973, and by Harif in *Maariv*, Dec. 21, 1973.

27. Sheehan, op. cit., pp. 95–97, includes transcripts of portions of these talks.

of all the Arab leaders Kissinger had met to date. Asad implied that
he did not object to the convening of the Geneva conference on
December 21, but Syria would not attend unless a disengagement-of-
forces agreement was reached first. And disengagement, he thought,
should involve the entire Golan Heights. Neither was he prepared to
yield to Kissinger's pleas to turn over a list of Israeli POWs. After six
and one-half hours of talks with Asad, Kissinger left for Israel empty-
handed.[28]

During the next two days, December 16 and 17, Kissinger used
all of his persuasive abilities to convince the Israelis that they should
attend the Geneva conference. He met with Golda Meir alone and
with members of her cabinet, painting for them a grim picture of the
consequences of a breakdown in the diplomatic process. Much more
than the Middle East was at stake. Global stability, international
economic order, the coherence of the NATO alliance, and virtually
every other major issue in world politics was linked to Israel's decision.
During a private dinner with most of the Israeli cabinet at Foreign
Minister Eban's house on December 16, Kissinger was at his most
persuasive.[29] The Israelis held out for one more change in the letter
of invitation—no mention by name of the Palestinians—and, subject
to that condition, the cabinet met late at night to approve of Israel's
attending the Geneva conference on December 21.

Kissinger now made one last try to obtain Syrian attendance. In
return for a list of POWs, Israel would allow Syrian villagers to return
to their homes in Israeli-controlled areas. Egypt's foreign minister,
Fahmy, discussed the proposal with Asad at Kissinger's request, and
the American ambassador in Beirut traveled to Damascus to take up
the matter again with the Syrian leader. On December 18, Kissinger
received Asad's reply, to the effect that Syria would not attend this
phase of the Geneva talks, but might participate later.

On December 21, the Geneva conference finally convened under
the auspices of the UN secretary general, with the United States and
the Soviet Union as cochairmen, and with the foreign ministers of
Egypt, Jordan, and Israel in attendance. A table with Syria's name-
plate on it remained unoccupied. Each foreign minister spoke, but it

28. Asad did agree to the opening of an American-manned interests section in Damascus.
Thomas Scotes was sent to head the mission.
29. Marvin and Bernard Kalb, *Kissinger* (Boston: Little, Brown, 1974), pp. 526–27.
Kissinger also told Mrs. Meir that Sadat was moving toward moderate views and that by talking
of disengagement Israel could put off negotiations on final borders.

was mostly for the public back home, not for one another. Kissinger tried to articulate his step-by-step strategy, stating that the goal of the conference was peace, but that the urgent need was to strengthen the cease-fire by accomplishing a disengagement of forces as the "essential first step" on the path of implementing UN Resolution 242. With these formal remarks, the Geneva conference recessed, not to be convened in plenary session again for an indefinite period. A symbol now existed, however, a useful fiction perhaps, and a forum where working groups might discuss aspects of a settlement was available if needed. It had not all been in vain, but one might wonder if the results were commensurate with the effort.

EGYPTIAN-ISRAELI DISENGAGEMENT

Having successfully convened the Geneva conference, Kissinger now faced the challenge of producing early results on the Egyptian-Israeli front. Several related problems stood in his way. The Syrians were on a high level of military alert in late December and a resumption of fighting seemed possible. The oil embargo was continuing, and, equally important, OPEC had decided to double oil prices on December 23. The fact that the Shah of Iran played the leading role in the price rise did not make it any more palatable. More than ever, the energy crisis hung over the Arab-Israeli negotiations.

Apart from difficulties with Syria and the frustration of the continuing oil embargo, Kissinger had to confront again the fact that the positions of Egypt and Israel on disengagement were still far apart. In Israel on December 17, he had discussed disengagement with Mrs. Meir and her top aides. The Israeli position was that a small Egyptian force would be allowed to remain on the east bank of the canal up to a distance of ten kilometers. A lightly armed Israeli force would control the main north-south road beyond the Egyptian forces, and the Israeli main forces would be stationed east of the Mitla and Giddi passes, beyond Egyptian artillery range. Israel would not yield the passes in the disengagement phase. On other points there was less Israeli consensus. Some cabinet members felt that Egypt should end the state of belligerency in return for the pullback of Israeli forces and should allow free passage for Israeli ships in the Suez Canal and at Bab al-Mandab. Some limits on Egyptian forces on both banks of the Suez Canal were also desired. Egypt should begin work on reopening the canal and rebuilding cities along it as a sign of peaceful intentions.

Egypt's position, as conveyed to Kissinger during his pre-Geneva talks in Cairo, began with the proposition that neither Egypt nor Israel should gain military advantage in the disengagement phase. In other words, any force limits would have to be mutual, as Gamasy had insisted at Kilometer 101 in November. Egypt would keep its forces east of the canal on existing lines in numbers not to exceed two divisions, a reduction of three divisions from existing levels. No heavy artillery and no surface-to-air missiles would be placed across the canal. Israel would retain control of the eastern ends of the passes. A demilitarized zone would be established between the Egyptian and Israeli lines, to be patrolled by UN troops. Egypt would begin work on clearing the canal and would rebuild the cities once Israeli troops had withdrawn. Israeli cargoes would be allowed to pass through the canal after it reopened.

Two gaps separated the Egyptian and Israeli positions. Egypt wanted Israeli forces to withdraw east of the passes; Israel refused. Israel wanted only a token Egyptian force on the east bank; Sadat was thinking of two infantry divisions with 100 tanks each. It would be difficult for him to accept publicly substantial force limitations in territory returned to his control. Nonetheless, the conceptual underpinnings of the two sides' positions were not very far apart, and agreement seemed possible.

Israeli elections for the Knesset were held on December 31. The opposition to Prime Minister Meir's Labor Alignment coalition was somewhat strengthened, but not to the point of requiring a new cabinet and prime minister. For the next six months, despite her own loss of popularity and the public disenchantment with her defense minister, Moshe Dayan, Prime Minister Meir carried the heavy burdens of government, fighting hard against American and domestic pressures to win agreements that protected Israel's vital interests. Kissinger found her to be tough and often emotional, and their talks were at times stormy, but there is little doubt that the two developed a genuine respect for one another during the difficult disengagement negotiations.

With Israeli elections out of the way, Moshe Dayan was sent to Washington for talks with Kissinger on January 4 and 5. He presented a five-zone concept for disengagement, in which each party would have two limited-force zones, separated by a UN buffer. He also specified the type of force limitations that Israel could accept. Basically, each side's forces should be beyond the artillery range of the other side, and SAMs should not be able to reach each other's air-craft. In addition, the number of tanks in the limited zones should be kept very small.

During their talks, Dayan urged Kissinger to return to the Middle East to aid in reaching an agreement. This proved to be acceptable to Sadat, and Kissinger left late on January 10. Kissinger originally expected to help establish the framework for an agreement, the de-tails of which would be worked out by the parties at Geneva, but Sadat was anxious for results and asked Kissinger to stay in the region until an agreement was reached. Kissinger thus embarked on his first exercise in "shuttle diplomacy," flying between Egypt and Israel with proposals.

On January 13, the Israelis handed Kissinger a map of the pro-posed disengagement line and authorized him to show it to Sadat, which he did the following day. Sadat had already accepted, in his first talk with Kissinger, the idea of force limitations in three zones, and had promised to work for the end of the oil embargo once an agreement was reached. Now he also indicated that he would accept Israeli forces west of the passes, but he had trouble with the extent of force limits.[30] To overcome Sadat's reservations, Kissinger suggested that the United States might take the responsibility for proposing the limitations on forces. Perhaps it would be easier for Sadat to accept an American plan than an Israeli one. And instead of publicly an-nouncing the limits in the formal documents, these could be defined in letters exchanged by Sadat and Nixon. In addition, Sadat's private assurances on Israeli cargoes transiting the canal could be handled in a secret memo of understanding. Sadat agreed.

In Israel the next day, January 15, Prime Minister Meir dropped the demand for an end of belligerency as part of the disengagement agreement. A few changes in force levels and the line of disengage-ment were made, wherein Dayan played an especially constructive role. With a new map in hand, Kissinger returned to Aswan to see Sadat on January 16, and Sadat agreed to scale down the Egyptian presence on the east bank to eight battalions and thirty tanks.[31] Kis-singer then went back to Israel, and the next day, at 3:00 P.M., Presi-dent Nixon announced that the two parties had reached an agreement on the disengagement of their military forces. The following day the

30. M. and B. Kalb, op. cit., pp. 534–35.
31. Ibid., p. 539.

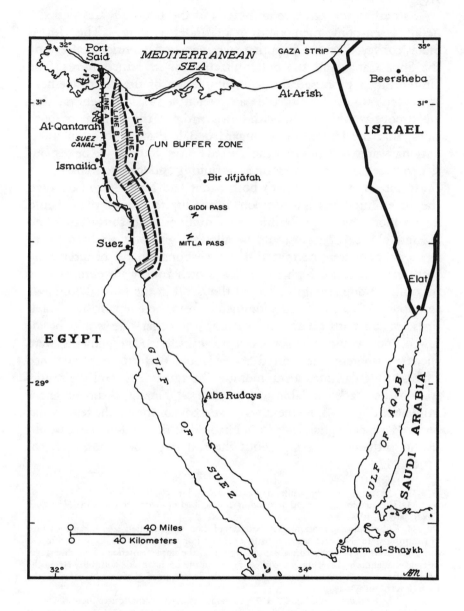

First Sinai Disengagement Agreement.

agreement was signed by the chiefs of staff of Israel and Egypt at Kilometer 101.[32]

As part of the agreement, Israel and the United States signed a detailed ten-point memorandum of understanding.[33] The United States conveyed several Egyptian statements of intention concerning the Suez Canal and the demobilization of its armed forces. The United States promised that the completion of the disengagement agreement would take precedence over new steps at Geneva; that UN troops would not be withdrawn without the consent of both sides; that the United States regarded Bab al-Mandab as an international waterway; and that the United States would try to be responsive to Israel's defense needs on a continuing and long-term basis.

In letters exchanged with both Sadat and Meir, Nixon detailed the force limitations agreed upon. In the limited zones, there would be no more than eight reinforced battalions with thirty tanks; no artillery above 122 mm would be allowed, and only six batteries of these weapons were permitted.[34] No weapons capable of interfering with reconnaissance flights over one's own zone were permitted; a maximum troop strength of seven thousand in the limited zone was set; up to a distance of thirty kilometers from the Egyptian and Israeli lines, no weapons capable of reaching the other side would be allowed, nor would any surface-to-air missiles. Arrangements were specified whereby the United States would perform reconnaissance flights at regular intervals to monitor the agreement, and the results were to be made available to both sides.[35] Finally, a timetable for implementing the agreement was made part of the public text. Sadat received a special guarantee from Nixon that the United States would use its influence to bring about the full implementation of Resolution 242.

32. The text and map appear in the *Jerusalem Post*, Jan. 20, 1974.

33. The memorandum of understanding is described in general terms in the *New York Times*, Jan. 22, 1974.

34. The stipulation concerning six batteries of short-range artillery later became a source of controversy. In the Israeli army, a battery consisted of six guns; in the Egyptian army, it contained twelve. The first reconnaissance flights after the implementation of the disengagement agreement found seventy-two artillery pieces on the Egyptian side and thirty-six on the Israeli. After angry Israeli complaints in late March, Sadat agreed to reduce his forces to the Israeli level of thirty-six guns.

35. The *Jerusalem Post*, Jan. 20, 1974, contains a generally accurate account of the secret provisions of the agreement. See also Kissinger's news conference of Jan. 22, 1974, *Department of State Bulletin*, Feb. 11, 1974.

With the signing of the disengagement agreement on January 18, Nixon and Kissinger had entered into important and unprecedented commitments for the United States. American prestige in the Arab world was on the rise, and more than ever the United States seemed to hold the key cards. The Israelis might complain of excessive pressure, but the agreement was not bad for Israel and United States aid was still flowing in large quantities. A mood of optimism, a rare occurrence, could be sensed in much of the Middle East.

INTERLUDE BETWEEN DISENGAGEMENTS

Kissinger's next task was to preserve this mood by translating it into new agreements that would help develop momentum toward a settlement. To do this, he set off immediately from Aswan for talks with King Hussein of Jordan and President Asad of Syria. Meanwhile, President Sadat, as promised, flew to Saudi Arabia to try to persuade King Faisal to take the lead in lifting the oil embargo against the United States, an act which Kissinger had termed "increasingly less appropriate" earlier in the month.[36]

Agreement on the Egyptian-Israeli front did little to dampen expectations or ease tensions elsewhere in the Middle East. Now Syria, Jordan, and perhaps even the PLO were ready to get in on the act. Israel, however, was hardly anxious to face a new set of negotiations, fearing that once more American pressures would be brought to bear to extract territorial concessions as the price of keeping diplomacy alive. Much as improved U.S.-Arab relations might be desirable in the abstract, Prime Minister Meir feared that they would be purchased in Israeli coin. Timing of a second step therefore was bound to be a problem. Kissinger decided to use the unavoidable interval to consolidate gains of the first round and to lay the basis for a next step between Syria and Israel.

Before returning to Washington after the signing of the Egyptian-Israeli disengagement agreement, Kissinger flew to Jordan for talks with King Hussein. This was basically a holding action, since no movement on the Jordanian front was likely until after Syrian-Israeli disengagement. Kissinger told the king that Israel opposed the idea

---

36. Kissinger's Jan. 3, 1974, news conference, *Department of State Bulletin*, Jan. 28, 1974, p. 78. On Jan. 6, 1974, Defense Secretary Schlesinger raised for the first time the possible use of force if the oil embargo should continue indefinitely.

of territorial withdrawal from the Jordan River, preferring to allow King Hussein to assume gradual administrative responsibility on the West Bank without immediate Israeli withdrawal. Kissinger posed the issue as one of reinstating the king's authority on the West Bank. Israel would either deal with Jordan now or with Arafat later. Despite Kissinger's efforts to convince Hussein of the merits of "administrative disengagement," the king insisted on recovering some territory, delineated clearly on a large map given to the American party before their departure. The Jordanian plan would have Israel withdraw to a line parallel to the Jordan River at a distance of approximately eight to ten kilometers.[37] Given the Israeli insistence on keeping control of the Jordan Valley, it seemed like a nonstarter, but at least an exchange of positions had begun. At this point Kissinger was not thinking so much of an early agreement as he was trying to devise a strategy for keeping the more radical PLO out of the picture for a bit longer. It would be difficult enough having to deal with Asad, as he discovered the next day in Damascus.

In talks with President Asad on January 20, Kissinger managed to obtain a new Syrian disengagement proposal. In December, Asad had spoken of Israeli withdrawal from all of the Golan Heights as part of a disengagement agreement. Now Syria was holding out for half of the territory conquered by Israel in 1967, as well as all of that gained in 1973, in a disengagement agreement. Asad also clung tenaciously to his one bargaining card—the Israeli prisoners. Kissinger left Damascus with the feeling that Asad did want an agreement and with a map showing two straight lines running north-south through the Golan Heights. These, presumably, would be the disengagement lines under the Syrian proposal.[38] Later that day Kissinger flew to Israel to brief the Israeli leadership on Asad's thinking, then returned to Washington to explain the details of the Egyptian-Israeli agreement to a generally supportive Congress and public.

Kissinger next began to try to end the oil embargo, while simultaneously laying the groundwork for a Syrian-Israeli agreement. Nixon was anxious to be able to announce the end of the embargo in his State of the Union message to Congress at the end of the month, and the Egyptians and Saudis were bombarded with messages

37. The *New York Times*, Feb. 10 and 15, 1974, contained details of the Jordanian proposals.
38. Golan, op. cit., p. 182.

to that effect.[39] Kissinger also began to try out an idea that he had tentatively discussed during his recent trip to Syria and Israel. If Syria would give the United States a list of Israeli POWs, Israel would agree to make a concrete proposal on disengagement. This vague procedure was conveyed to Sadat for his information and approval. Several days later, on February 3, King Faisal, who had just conferred with President Asad in Saudi Arabia, informed President Nixon that the oil embargo could not be lifted until a disengagement agreement had been reached on the Syrian-Israeli front. Nixon replied on February 6, saying that unless the embargo were lifted, the United States would not be able to continue its diplomatic efforts.

Nonetheless, the United States did propose a five-point plan to Asad on February 5. Syria would tell the United States the number of Israeli POWs, and this would then be conveyed to Israel. Syria would give a list of POWs to the United States Interests Section in Damascus, and in exchange for the list, Israel would make a concrete proposal. After Red Cross visits with the Israeli prisoners in Syria, Kissinger would transmit the Israeli proposal to Asad and would invite an Israeli delegation to Washington for further talks. Negotiations would then begin at Geneva in the context of the already existing Egyptian-Israeli military working group. On February 9, Asad accepted this procedure.

The following week, Presidents Asad, Sadat, and Boumedienne, and King Faisal, met in Algiers for two days. They agreed not to lift the embargo until further progress toward Syrian-Israeli agreement had been made, and Foreign Ministers Fahmy and Saqqaf were sent to Washington to inform Kissinger. Nixon and Kissinger were angry, but realized that they could not go through with their threat to withdraw from the diplomacy. That would clearly link American policy to the oil embargo, and Kissinger was anxious to convince Asad and the American public that United States action in the Middle East was not primarily a function of oil interests. If the United States had reasons of its own to want peace in the Middle East, it would continue its efforts despite the embargo. On February 18, Nixon and Kissinger

39. These messages, which seemed to imply that Nixon wanted the embargo lifted for domestic political reasons, later proved an embarrassment to him. When the Saudis failed to live up to their promises to lift the embargo, Kissinger hinted that he might be obliged to release the texts of the commitments undertaken by Faisal. The Saudis responded by suggesting that they, too, might have some embarrassing messages to release. The issue was quickly dropped.

decided to drop the issue of the embargo for the time being. The following day, Nixon announced that Kissinger would make another visit to the area, and on February 25 Kissinger departed on his fourth trip in as many months.

SHUTTLE DIPLOMACY

Kissinger met with Asad for four hours the night of February 26 and again the following morning. The discussions were complex but basically friendly, Asad showing flexibility on procedural issues and toughness on substance. As previously agreed, Kissinger was authorized to transmit to the Israelis the list of POWs, which he had actually been given prior to his departure from Washington.[40] Red Cross visits would begin, and Israel would be expected to make a concrete proposal on disengagement. Asad made it clear that if Israel offered nothing more than a pullback to the post-1967 cease-fire lines, he would break off the talks. Kissinger was inclined to think he was serious and so told the Israelis during his stop on February 27. He then left the Israelis to develop their proposal over the next twenty-four hours prior to his return visit.

Meanwhile Kissinger flew off to Egypt for talks with Sadat. U.S.-Egyptian ties were developing well and rapidly, and full diplomatic relations were restored on February 28. Sadat extended an invitation to Nixon to visit Egypt. Bilateral issues, including aid and the long-term prospects for United States arms sales to Egypt, financed by Saudi Arabia, were also discussed. By that time, Kissinger was relying heavily upon Sadat's advice on how to deal with other Arab leaders. The Libyans wanted to purchase American radar. What was Sadat's opinion? Asad was insisting on Israeli withdrawal beyond the 1967 cease-fire lines. What were Sadat's views? When would the oil embargo be lifted? How could Soviet influence in Iraq be weakened? Kissinger and Sadat began to develop what amounted to a joint strategy in the Middle East.

As for the specific problem of disengagement on the Syrian front, Sadat argued for a line just west of the town of Quneitra. He offered to send his chief of staff to Syria prior to Kissinger's next visit to press for an agreement based on such a line. If Asad refused, Sadat would

40. *New York Times*, Mar. 3, 1973. There were sixty-five names on the list, which was more than some observers had expected.

nonetheless support it publicly and would continue to try to build Arab backing for a moderate disengagement agreement between Syria and Israel. Kissinger was pleased with his talks with Sadat and began to count heavily on Egypt's leadership in the Arab world. Having once erred in the direction of underestimating Sadat and Egypt, Kissinger now seemed on the verge of making the opposite mistake.

From Egypt, Kissinger flew to Israel where he received the Israeli proposal. Basically the Israeli plan was for disengagement to be modeled on the Egyptian-Israeli agreement of January, with three zones—one Israeli, one UN, and one Syrian—all within the territory captured by Israel in October 1973. Not only would Quneitra remain entirely under Israeli control, but also Israeli forces would remain well beyond the October 6 lines.

Kissinger feared that Asad would reject the proposal and the talks would end then and there. Therefore, when in Damascus on the evening of March 1, Kissinger did not give Asad the details of the Israeli plan. Instead, he concentrated on the concept of limited-force zones and a UN buffer. He also pinned down Syrian agreement to send a representative to Washington for talks later in the month, following a similar visit by an Israeli official. Kissinger left Damascus with little in the way of substantive progress, but agreement on a further exchange of views over the next several weeks. Asad, not to be outdone by the more effusive Sadat, embraced the secretary in Arab fashion for the first time. An improbable but genuine personal relationship was beginning to develop between these two very different men.

Kissinger's next stop was Saudi Arabia, his goal there being to urge again the removal of the oil embargo and to solicit support for a Syrian-Israeli disengagement. The secretary also discussed with the Saudis ways of strengthening bilateral economic and security relations. The idea of creating several joint commissions was put forward and eventually was implemented, symbolizing in a tangible way Kissinger's desire to use American technology and arms as complementary to his diplomatic efforts with the aim of building a strong United States presence in key Arab countries.

On March 2 and 3, Kissinger met with King Hussein of Jordan for lengthy strategy talks. Hussein was growing impatient. The Arab leaders who had met in Algiers in February had agreed upon the need to create a Palestinian state headed by PLO leader Yasir Arafat. Pressures were building for the creation of a Palestinian government-in-exile. Hussein asked whether the United States would recognize such a government. Kissinger denied any such intention. The king went on to stress his need for a good agreement with Israel to justify his participation in future negotiations. Ultimately, he said, he would have to obtain all of the West Bank of the Jordan and Arab Jerusalem. Anything less would expose him to charges of being a traitor. If Israel was not prepared to go that far, then perhaps Jordan should step aside and let the PLO try to negotiate a better deal than he was able to get. They would, of course, fail, which might bring the Israelis and Palestinians back to reason and open new possibilities for Jordan. Kissinger urged the king to give the Israelis another chance to come up with a more meaningful proposal than "administrative disengagement." Meanwhile, both Jordan and the United States should work to forestall the creation of a Palestinian government-in-exile. Hussein would be visiting Washington shortly, hence further talks would take place soon. Meanwhile, Kissinger would contact Sadat on the Palestinian issue, and Jordan should try to learn whether Israel was prepared to make a serious offer. If not, Jordan should threaten to pull out of the negotiations.

As Kissinger flew back to Washington on March 4, the Egyptian-Israeli disengagement agreement was completed, with all parties in their new positions. Simultaneously, tensions increased on the Syrian front, as Asad began to raise the danger of renewed hostilities. In the course of the next two months, negotiations on Syrian-Israeli disengagement were to be accompanied by heavy shelling and numerous casualties on the Syrian front. Asad was clearly going to be more difficult to deal with than Sadat had been, nor were the Israelis in a particularly conciliatory frame of mind.

Upon his return to Washington, Kissinger consulted with Nixon on the results of his trip. By that time, the president was deeply preoccupied with his Watergate defense. His closest aides had been indicted by a grand jury on March 1 for perjury, obstruction of justice, and illegal payments to suppress evidence. Tapes had come to light that seemed to suggest that Nixon himself had been involved in the payment of hush money to one of the Watergate burglars. Demands for the full transcripts of the tapes of presidential conversations were being made. With all of these worries, Nixon turned to foreign policy as a form of release and escape, but only to deal with the large issues. Details were still left to Kissinger.

One of the questions requiring presidential decision concerned the terms on which Israel would receive the $2.2 billion in emergency assistance to cover the purchase of military equipment. Nixon was not averse to pressuring Israel; he was unhappy with the recent Israeli proposal on disengagement. He and Kissinger therefore agreed that for the moment all $2.2 billion would be extended as credit. The president would have the option until July 1 of waiving repayment of as much as $1.5 billion. If Israel were forthcoming, she could expect favorable presidential action. Meanwhile an aid package was being put together for fiscal year 1975 which would, for the first time in years, contain a substantial sum, $250 million, for Egypt, and an unprecedented $207.5 million for Jordan.[41] Only $350 million would be requested for Israel, in the knowledge that Congress would increase that sum significantly in any event. Aid was clearly going to be an important adjunct of the Nixon-Kissinger diplomacy.

Kissinger recognized that it would be difficult to reach an agreement between Israel and Syria on disengagement. The United States alone might be able to persuade Israel to make the necessary concessions, using a combination of pressures and positive inducements, but how could Syria be brought to a more workable position? Could Sadat and other Arab leaders play a role? What about the Soviets, who seemed so anxious to be involved in the negotiations? Would Asad be influenced by the offer of American aid? Kissinger needed time to explore each of these possibilities and to let each of the parties reconsider its opening stance on disengagement.

The first order of business was to end the oil embargo. Nixon referred to this again in a press conference on March 6. The Arab oil producers would soon be meeting in Tripoli. If the embargo was not then lifted, the American diplomatic effort would be undermined. After some delays, most Arab oil producers announced on March 18 that the embargo against the United States was ended, at least on a

41. During his visit to Washington on Mar. 12, King Hussein had requested $130 million in budget support, in addition to other sums for military assistance. The administration at the time was considering $100 million, which was about twice the amount provided the previous year. The formal aid request for the Middle East for fiscal year 1975 was sent to Congress on Apr. 24 and contained an uncommitted $100 million, presumably to be used as aid for Syria if diplomatic relations were resumed.

provisional basis. Privately, Faisal stressed the importance of achieving a Syrian-Israeli disengagement agreement within two months to avoid reimposition of the embargo.

Syria had opposed the lifting of the embargo. Kissinger was now anxious to bring inter-Arab pressure to bear on that country to accept a disengagement agreement. Egypt, Saudi Arabia, and Algeria could all play a role. If Syria refused a reasonable offer, Kissinger wanted to make sure that Asad would be isolated rather than supported by a bloc of rejectionists. Only Iraq might be able to strengthen Asad's resolve to resist making concessions. Iraqi forces could help reinforce the Syrian front, as they had done in October. If fighting were to be resumed, Asad might be obliged to turn to Iraq and the Soviets for more military help. Fortunately, Iraq was becoming preoccupied with its border with Iran, where serious clashes had occurred in February, and with the Kurds, who had entered into armed opposition to the Baghdad regime in late February. Some wondered if Iraq's preoccupation were entirely coincidental.

Kissinger now needed a reasonable Israeli offer to lure Asad toward an agreement. On March 15 and 19, Kissinger met with Foreign Minister Eban. He explained his strategy of trying to isolate Syria from the radical Arabs, and stressed the need for continued movement in the diplomatic arena. Israel would have to pull back to the October 6 lines if not farther, and would have to give up Quneitra. Israel should not, however, be expected to abandon any settlements on the Golan Heights at this stage. Dayan should bring an Israeli proposal along these lines when he visited Washington later in the month.

On March 24, Kissinger set off for the Soviet Union, where, among other things, he would try to keep the Soviets from obstructing his efforts at disengagement on the Syrian-Israeli front. During a three and one-half hour meeting on March 26, described as the "toughest and most unpleasant" he had ever had with Brezhnev and his top aides, Kissinger resisted Soviet pressures to return the negotiations to Geneva. Brezhnev hotly accused Kissinger of violating agreements that the talks would be held under joint U.S.-U.S.S.R. auspices, and referred to assurances given to Gromyko in February that the negotiations would be conducted at Geneva. Kissinger defended his actions as being taken at the request of the regional parties. In any case, they were only paving the way for talks on a final settlement which would be held at Geneva. Brezhnev referred to the good relations existing between Iraq and the Soviet Union, and also mentioned Asad's forthcoming visit to Moscow, observing that he would surely ask for more arms. Kissinger replied that he was sure that Asad would ask the Soviet Union for arms, because he had just made such a request of the United States. Brezhnev noted that he was withholding arms from Egypt, then returned to Syria, asking Kissinger why the United States did not give Asad arms. Kissinger replied with a straight face that he did not want to fuel the arms race! Obviously irritated at the growing American involvement in the Arab world, Brezhnev accused Kissinger of trying to keep the Soviet Union out of the substance of the negotiations. He argued that Syria wanted the Soviets to be present.

Kissinger quickly checked with Asad on whether he did in fact want the Soviets involved at this stage. Asad obliquely replied that the agreed procedure was that Dayan would go to Washington, followed by a Syrian representative. Then Kissinger would come to the Middle East, after which a military working group could conclude the details of an agreement in Geneva with the Soviets present.

Shortly after his return from Moscow, the secretary of state met with Dayan in Washington on March 29.[42] Dayan brought a large arms request—for one thousand tanks, four thousand armored personnel carriers, and much more—as well as an Israeli proposal for a disengagement line that would run east of the October 6 line. Israeli forces would emphatically remain in Quneitra. Kissinger was irritated by the Israeli proposal, whose only value, in his view, was the concept of a buffer zone flanked by two limited-force zones to the east and west. Kissinger warned the Israelis that Asad would not accept the line and termed their proposal inadequate, but he repeated that Israel should not give up any settlements at this stage.

Against the background of intensified fighting on the Syrian-Israeli front, Syrian Brigadier General Hikmat Shihabi flew to Washington for talks with Kissinger on April 13. Shihabi brought with him a revised map showing a disengagement line running west of Quneitra. It was far from being Dayan's proposal, but an improvement over the Syrian position of January. Kissinger showed Shihabi

42. Dayan's visit had nearly been called off by the Israelis in protest over what they viewed as Egypt's violations of the terms of the disengagement agreement. The dispute over the violations is mentioned in the *Washington Post*, Mar. 26, 1974.

the line proposed by Dayan, terming it unacceptable but emphasizing the desirability of the three-zone concept. The secretary implied that he would try to persuade the Israelis to go back to the October 6 line and to leave Quneitra, but that would be the most that Syria could hope for at this stage. Two days later, Kissinger passed the Syrian map to Israeli Ambassador Dinitz.

While Kissinger was trying to induce Israel and Syria to modify their respective proposals, Sadat spent the month of April in a strident press campaign against the Soviet Union. He publicly mentioned that he had nearly canceled the treaty between the two countries. On April 18, he declared his intention of ending his exclusive dependency on the Soviets for arms, and said he would seek arms in the West, including the United States. His foreign minister, Ismail Fahmy, was at that moment talking to Nixon and Kissinger in Washington, presumably on the same topic. Surprisingly, a long-time ardent supporter of Israel, columnist Joseph Alsop, responded to Sadat's bid by calling on April 26 for an American policy of becoming the main arms supplier of Egypt. This would confirm the "complete reversal of alliances that President Sadat has been publicly talking about" and would constitute "the most dazzling feat of diplomacy in the twentieth century."[43]

This tone in Sadat's speeches and in Alsop's column could scarcely be expected to place the Soviets in a conciliatory mood. Kissinger did, however, meet with Gromyko several times during April, and seemed to succeed in at least neutralizing Soviet opposition to his diplomatic efforts with Syria and Israel. Having achieved enough during March and April to justify another round of shuttle diplomacy, Kissinger departed for the Middle East on April 28. Little did he realize at the time how long and difficult the negotiations would be.

SYRIAN-ISRAELI DISENGAGEMENT

It was clear to Kissinger and his colleagues that a disengagement agreement between Syria and Israel would be much more difficult to attain than that between Egypt and Israel. In the latter case, both sides wanted an agreement and had come close to an accord on basic issues before Kissinger began his shuttle. In the Syrian-Israeli case, the positions of the two parties were far apart, the incentives for an

43. *Washington Post*, Apr. 26, 1974.

agreement were lacking, and the objective situation on the ground lent itself less well to an agreement than was true in Sinai. In addition, both Syria and Israel were governed by somewhat shaky coalitions. Neither could afford to appear soft in the negotiations.

If the local parties had less of a stake in an agreement, the United States had more than before. Among other things, it must protect the Egyptian-Israeli agreement, and beyond that, the flourishing U.S.-Egyptian relationship. If Syria refused to reach a comparable disengagement agreement, Sadat's position would be threatened in the Arab world and a radical, rejectionist bloc might gain influence. War might resume on the Syrian front, and Egypt might well be pulled in. Apart from the intrinsic danger of another war, that situation would provide the Soviet Union with new opportunities of reasserting its presence in the region. Finally, without an agreement there might be another troublesome oil embargo.

Kissinger realized that he would have great problems with the Syrians and the Israelis. To deal with the former, he counted on building strong Arab support for his efforts. With the Israelis, he would, as usual, have to combine carrot and stick. Prior to Kissinger's departure for the Middle East, Nixon had waived repayment on $1 billion of the $2.2 billion in aid to cover arms purchases. In normal times, that might have won Kissinger a cordial reception in Israel, but these were not normal times. Besides, the United States had just voted in the UN to condemn Israel for a retaliatory raid in southern Lebanon. Whatever credit Kissinger may once have had with the Israelis was rapidly being dissipated. Nixon's authority would have to be invoked when the going got rough, but that authority was itself in question. The day after Kissinger's departure, Nixon released edited texts of a large number of taped conversations concerning Watergate. They did not make for edifying reading. Slowly but surely, the judicial process seemed to be leading to Richard Nixon's impeachment. For this very reason, Nixon seemed extremely anxious for Kissinger to succeed on his mission. During the ensuing weeks, a severely weakened president repeatedly threw his weight behind his secretary of state, in what proved to be some of the bluntest exchanges with the Israeli leadership ever to take place.

Kissinger's itinerary took him first to Geneva, for talks with Gromyko, and then to Algeria and Egypt. Boumedienne and Sadat were key Arab leaders, whose support Kissinger sought. The Algerians had close relations with the Syrians and had good credentials as revolutionaries.[44] No one would accuse them of being stooges of the Americans. In Alexandria, the next day, Kissinger received Sadat's blessings and a prediction that "my friend, Dr. Henry" would succeed in his mission. With that, Kissinger braced himself for the arduous business of talking with the Israelis and Syrians.

Kissinger felt that Israel would have to make concessions on the line of disengagement and that the Syrians, who rejected any force limitations other than a narrow buffer zone, would have to back down as well. First he would try to win consensus on an acceptable line. Then, it might be hoped, the other elements of agreement would begin to fall into place.

His talks in Israel on May 2 did nothing to make Kissinger optimistic. The Israelis were angry at the United States for its UN vote, and were obdurate about any alteration of the position that Dayan had presented in late March. Why should Asad be rewarded for having gone to war against Israel and lost? Why now should he get a better offer than the more reasonable Sadat? Was it good for United States interests to appease the most militant of the Arabs? What would the world think if Israel and the United States submitted to such blackmail? And so the arguments went, until in despair Kissinger turned to Nixon for help. A letter from Nixon to Mrs. Meir on May 4 warned her not to allow Israeli actions to jeopardize the favorable trends in the area. Otherwise the United States, out of friendship for Israel and a sense of responsibility, would have to reexamine the relationship between the two countries.

In Damascus the next day, Kissinger avoided precise discussion of the Israeli line of disengagement. Instead he emphasized to Asad the weakness of Prime Minister Meir's domestic position and the linkages between Israeli domestic politics and her foreign policy. He raised the issue of United States aid to help Syria with reconstruction. Asad remained adamant that the disengagement line would have to be west of the October 6 lines, but seemed to show flexibility on other issues, such as force limitations. The following day, however, he repeated to Kissinger his "nonapproval" of the idea of limited-force

44. Nixon had met with Boumedienne at the White House on April 11 and had offered a small private dinner for him in the evening. The talks had gone well, although Boumedienne pressed Nixon hard on the Syrian-Israeli disengagement and the Palestinians.

zones. Kissinger, for his part, then tried to stimulate Egyptian, Algerian, and Saudi pressure on Asad to moderate his views.[45]

In the course of the next several days, Israel began to modify its proposal on the disengagement line.[46] Part of Quneitra would now be returned to Syria, but the western part of the city must remain under Israeli control. Kissinger told the Israelis that Asad would not accept such an arrangement. On May 7, Kissinger flew to Cyprus to brief Gromyko on the talks, and found that the Soviets were prepared to remain neutral.[47]

Despite some progress in Israel on May 6 and 7, Kissinger was not optimistic. In Damascus on May 8, he disclosed some of Israel's concessions to Asad, but withheld others so that he would have something to show on later trips. The tactic was a risky one, but Kissinger felt that he had to avoid whetting Asad's already substantial appetite for Israeli concessions, while at the same time being able to show continued progress.[48] In any event, on May 8 Asad began to talk seriously about a line in the vicinity of that proposed by Israel.[49] Quneitra and the three surrounding hills now loomed as the major obstacle.

Kissinger continued to seek Egyptian, Algerian, and Saudi help. He kept these leaders well informed on the negotiations and asked for their support. At the same time, he tried to persuade the Israelis to make more concessions, but to little avail. On May 9, he reported to President Nixon that he was organizing forces for what he expected to be his "climactic meeting" with President Asad on May 11.

Instead of the hoped-for breakthrough, Kissinger encountered a stalemate. Asad insisted on all of Quneitra as well as the three surrounding hills. Israel would simply not yield on the hills, the "Himalayas of General Gur," as Kissinger termed them. On May 13, however, he did get Israeli agreement to a Syrian civilian presence in all of Quneitra, along with two other minor concessions.[50] He decided on one last trip to Damascus on May 14; then he would return

45. Kissinger sent Saunders to Saudi Arabia and Algeria to brief Faisal and Boumedienne on the talks and to ask for their support.
46. Sheehan, op. cit., pp. 36–41, covers this period, including texts of some of the conversations between Kissinger and Mrs. Meir. See also Golan, op. cit., p. 194.
47. *Pravda*, May 20, 1974, did, however, warn Asad not to settle for half-measures.
48. Sadat fully endorsed this approach to Asad.
49. Golan, op. cit., p. 196; *New York Times*, May 9, 1974.
50. Nixon had sent Mrs. Meir a letter on May 10 expressing his concern that an agreement be reached.

to Washington. In Damascus he found that Asad was not satisfied with the last Israeli proposal, insisting that the line must lie along the peak of the hills and that UN troops, not Israelis, must man the peaks. By now the bargaining concerned a few hundred meters, but neither side seemed prepared to yield.[51]

At this point President Nixon weighed in with Kissinger, urging him to continue to work for an agreement and promising his full support. If Israel was intransigent, he was prepared to go very far if necessary. On May 14, he asked for a list of all military and economic aid promised to Israel, as well as the total of tax-free private contributions to Israel. He also asked for ideas on aid to Syria as a possible incentive.

This was what the Israelis had long feared—pressure on them and offers of aid to the Arabs. In this instance, however, Nixon did not threaten to cut aid to Israel. Instead, the negotiations inched forward, as Kissinger shuttled back and forth. Encouraged by some members of the Israeli cabinet, Kissinger decided on May 15 to begin to introduce his own ideas in talks with Asad and the Israelis. As he had done in January once the gap had been narrowed, he would try to find a compromise that left each side's basic interests intact. Perhaps the Syrians would find his ideas easier to accept than Israel's.

On May 16, Kissinger succeeded in inducing the Israelis to pull back to the base of the hills. He immediately flew to Damascus to try out ideas of his own.[52] The next day he reported to Nixon that he was close to agreement on a disengagement line. In Damascus on May 18, however, it seemed as if the remaining gap could not be bridged. Kissinger decided to leave, began drafting a departure statement, and had his luggage sent to the plane. At the last moment, Asad dropped his insistence on controlling the hills west of Quneitra and urged Kissinger to keep trying for an agreement. Israel could keep the hills if Kissinger would guarantee that no heavy weapons

51. The Americans had anticipated difficult negotiating around Quneitra and had come armed with large aerial photographs of the area. The photographs were actually used for drawing the final lines instead of maps because of their extraordinarily accurate detail.

52. After four hours with Prime Minister Meir and eight with President Asad, Kissinger reported to Nixon that this had been his toughest day yet. The previous day Israel had been traumatized by a terrorist attack against the town of Maalot, which had resulted in the deaths of numerous schoolchildren. This contributed to the defiant mood in Israel concerning concessions to Syria and added to the difficulty of Kissinger's task.

capable of firing into Quneitra would be placed there. On May 19, Kissinger was able to obtain Israel's assent to Asad's request, and on May 20 he returned to Damascus with a map of the agreed line.

With agreement on the line of disengagement virtually assured, the problem arose of force limitations and the size of the restricted-armaments zones.[53] In addition, Asad wanted Israel to give up all the positions on Mt. Hermon. Syria also wanted only a small UN force in the buffer zone, whereas Israel preferred at least two to three thousand UN troops.

After two more days of haggling over these issues, on May 22 Kissinger began to lose heart. Once again, he drafted a departure statement and planned to leave the following day. Egypt, however, had sent General Gamasy to Syria, and by the time of Kissinger's next visit to Damascus, on May 23, Asad had changed his position to accept a large UN force and a wider buffer zone of ten kilometers and limited-force zone of fifteen kilometers. He was still insisting, nevertheless, on fairly sizable armaments in the limited zones, while accepting the concept developed on the Egyptian front of keeping SAMs and heavy artillery out of range of the other side's lines.

Kissinger returned on May 24 to Israel, where he faced demands that Asad commit himself to preventing terrorist attacks from his side of the lines. In addition, Israel asked for a United States commitment that the UN force would not be withdrawn without the consent of both parties to the agreement. Israel also wanted reassurances on long-term military supplies. From this point on, Prime Minister Meir and Defense Minister Dayan were extremely helpful and flexible in working out the final details of an agreement.

On May 26, the drafting of the final documents began. To Kissinger's consternation, issues that he thought had been settled were now reopened by Asad. Once more it seemed as if the talks would collapse.[54] On May 27, Asad backed down and, after ten hours of talks, Kissinger agreed to make one more trip to Israel to work out compromises on several more points. Then, on May 28, in four hours of private conversation, Asad gave Kissinger his oral commitment that he would not allow the Syrian side of the disengagement line to become a source of terrorist attacks against Israel. With that

53. *New York Times,* May 23, 1974.
54. Sheehan, op. cit., p. 126.

concession in hand, Kissinger flew to Israel, and on May 29 the announcement was made that Syria and Israel had reached agreement
on the terms of a disengagement agreement. Two days later Syrian
and Israeli military representatives signed the necessary documents
in Geneva.[55]

The agreement consisted of a public document, a map, a protocol
on the status of the UN forces, and several secret letters between the
United States and the two parties detailing the understandings on
force levels and other issues.[56] The force-limitation agreement specified a UN buffer zone paralleling the post-1967 line and including
the city of Quneitra. In zones of ten kilometers east and west of the
buffer zone, each party could station two brigades, with no more
than six thousand men, 75 tanks, and 36 short-range (122 mm)
artillery pieces. In adjacent zones of ten kilometers, no artillery with
a range of more than twenty kilometers, and no more than 162 artillery pieces, would be allowed. No SAMs could be closer than
twenty-five kilometers to the front lines. UN Disengagement Observer Forces (UNDOF) would have the right to inspect these zones,
and United States aircraft would carry out reconnaissance flights as in
the January Egyptian-Israeli accord. Agreement was reached on the
exchange of prisoners, and both sides declared that disengagement
was only a step toward a just and durable peace based on UN Resolution 338.

Nixon wrote to Asad on May 29 to confirm that Israel would
observe the cease-fire on the hills around Quneitra; that no Israeli
forces or weapons would be stationed on the eastern slopes of the
hills; and that no weapons would be placed on the hills that would
be capable of firing into Quneitra. Nixon also informed the Israelis
that the last paragraph of the public agreement was to be interpreted
to mean that guerrilla raids were contrary to the cease-fire and that
the United States recognized Israel's right of self-defense in the event
of violations. As usual, the Israelis also insisted on a memorandum
of understanding dealing with such contingencies as a breakdown in
the cease-fire at Syria's initiative and on the pacing of the negotiations. To the Syrians, the United States committed itself to work for
the full implementation of UN Resolution 338.

55. As late as June 2, Syria was still trying to make changes in the disengagement line.
Israel refused.
56. For the text of the agreement, see *Arab Report and Record,* May 16–31, 1974, p. 214.

With the signing of the agreement between Syria and Israel, together with all of the side agreements conveyed through the United States, Kissinger and Nixon could point to another outstanding achievement in their Middle East diplomacy. By itself, the step was modest, but in light of the recent history of Syrian-Israeli relations it was substantial indeed. The lingering question, of course, was whether it was a step toward a more comprehensive peace agreement, or whether it would prove to be merely a pause before another round of fighting at a later date. Was Kissinger determined to continue his efforts, or, after spending one month of murderously difficult negotiations for limited results, would he conclude that no further progress was possible? Would "step-by-step" remain his preferred tactic, and if so, where would the next step be? All of these questions would have to be dealt with in the near future, but first President Nixon wanted to reap the rewards of Kissinger's efforts by staging a whirlwind tour of the Middle East. The adulation of the Egyptian crowds might take his mind off Watergate.

NIXON TO THE MIDDLE EAST

President Nixon's trip to the Middle East was an odd affair. Inevitably, he was accompanied by an enormous retinue of aides, security men, and journalists. Every detail of the visit had been worked out by advance men. The local governments were nearly overwhelmed by the onslaught of American technicians, public-relations experts, TV crews, and assorted hangers-on.

Nixon himself was not in good health, his leg being inflamed and sore as a result of a mild attack of phlebitis. Presumably his emotional state was less than serene as well. He reportedly spent his free time listening to the possibly incriminating Watergate tapes. The House Judiciary Committee was holding hearings on whether there was sufficient evidence to warrant his impeachment. Subpoenas for evidence had been issued, Nixon had refused to comply, and the Supreme Court would have to decide the matter.

Even Kissinger was under attack, not for his Middle East efforts, for which he had won overwhelming praise, but rather for his alleged role in ordering the wiretapping of members of his own staff in 1969. In Salzburg, the first stop of the presidential party, Kissinger had emotionally denied any wrongdoing and had threatened to resign if his name were not cleared. The one man who could instantly have cleared his name by assuming responsibility for the wiretapping, President Nixon, remained silent.

For the next several days, Kissinger seemed to sulk in the background as Nixon received an incredibly enthusiastic reception in Cairo and Alexandria. Sadat went to great lengths to emphasize the new chapter in U.S.-Egyptian relations that he had helped to open. In public, the two men were friendly, and the immense crowds almost succeeded in raising Nixon's flagging spirits. After all, it was the first official visit of an American president to Egypt, and Nixon liked firsts. Moreover, he could be proud of the results of his foreign policy. He saw himself as one working for peace against adversaries at home and abroad, and as a man misunderstood by those who were seeking to bring him down. A touch of the martyr in Nixon showed through as he disobeyed his doctor's orders and needlessly tired himself to remain on display before the cheering Egyptian crowds.

In private, Nixon was uncommunicative. Conversations were stilted and marked by frequent pauses.[57] He did, however, make promises of future American assistance. Egypt would be allowed to purchase a nuclear reactor for energy production;[58] economic aid would continue; Nixon even turned over his personal helicopter to Sadat. In regard to the diplomatic front, Nixon promised that he would work for the restoration of the international frontier as Egypt's border in a final settlement, a position that had not been taken since the ill-fated Rogers Plan in 1969. The president also agreed that the Palestinians should be brought into the negotiations at an early date. Sadat suggested that the United States should secretly talk to the PLO leaders, and Nixon seemed receptive, if noncommittal. The talks concluded with the issuance of a joint statement of principles.

Nixon then flew to Saudi Arabia for two days of talks on June 14 and 15. Here the focus was primarily on strengthening bilateral relations and on oil. He then went on to Damascus, for a somewhat restrained reception and cordial talks with President Asad. Full diplomatic relations were restored on June 16. In addition, Nixon and Asad discussed next steps in the peacemaking process. The president

57. Sheehan, op. cit., p. 132.
58. Nixon had never quite overcome his belief in the Eisenhower-Strauss plan of bringing peace to the Middle East by making the deserts bloom through the provision of desalted water produced by nuclear-powered desalting plants. Like many bad ideas, this one was difficult to kill, and the offer of nuclear power plants to Egypt and Israel was a variant of it.

Syrian-Israeli Disengagement Agreement, May 1974.

indicated that the Geneva conference should be reconvened in September. Then to an astonished and delighted Asad, he explained that the purpose of step-by-step diplomacy was to persuade the Israelis to pull back gradually on the Syrian front until they reached the edge of the Golan Heights, tumbled over, and returned to the old borders. The imagery was fanciful, but the Syrians took it as a commitment to work for full Israeli withdrawal. As he departed from Damascus, Nixon drafted a long list of possible aid projects that might be offered to Syria. He feared that Asad might require substantial inducements to remain on good behavior.

The president was more at home on his next stop, Israel, than earlier. His counterpart, however, was no longer the worthy friend and adversary of former crises, Golda Meir, but rather Yitzhak Rabin, the new prime minister of Israel and something of an unknown quantity, despite his years in Washington as ambassador. The Israelis, who had not been informed in advance, were less than pleased with the American offer of nuclear reactors to Egypt, and to soothe them, Nixon made them the same offer. He also talked at some length about the importance of dealing quickly with King Hussein on the fate of the West Bank. Better Hussein now, he observed, than Arafat later.[59] When discussing terrorism with the Israelis, Nixon startled his hosts by leaping from his seat and declaring that there was only one way to deal with terrorists. Then, Chicago-gangland-style, he fired an imaginary submachine gun at the assembled cabinet members. Strange behavior, strange president. Best friend or dangerous enemy of Israel? It was hard to tell.

Nixon concluded his swing through the Middle East by visiting Jordan.[60] Determined to proceed with talks concerning disengagement on the Jordan-Israel front, Nixon invited Hussein to Washington in late July.

On June 19, the president returned to Washington. Three days later, the Judiciary Committee completed its hearings, which had been watched by a fascinated television audience while Nixon was winging his way through the Middle East. On June 24, the committee issued four more subpoenas to Nixon. The next day he departed for Moscow. Affairs of state continued to provide him with some relief

59. Golan, op. cit., pp. 214–17.
60. Kissinger did not accompany Nixon to Jordan. He flew instead to Canada for a NATO meeting.

from Watergate, and he could be sure that the Soviet leaders would not take seriously the charges against him of obstructing justice and misusing his office.

THE FINAL DAYS

Back in Washington, Nixon agreed on the last day of the fiscal year to waive Israel's repayment of $500 million in credit for arms, a bit more carrot in anticipation of negotiations between Jordan and Israel. Throughout the month of July, Nixon and Kissinger kept up the pressure for an agreement.[61] Sadat was prepared to reverse his previous stand and endorse King Hussein as the spokesman for the Palestinians living in the Hashemite Kingdom of Jordan.[62] The Israeli cabinet, which had been toying with a formula providing that Israel would talk with the PLO if the PLO ended acts of terrorism and accepted Israel's existence, quickly reversed itself and went back to the position that Jordan was the spokesman for the Palestinians.[63] On July 21, however, the cabinet rejected the concept of disengagement along the Jordan River, and in talks with Foreign Minister Allon the next week Kissinger was unable to persuade the Israelis to change their position.[64]

American involvement in the search for an agreement between Jordan and Israel was temporarily deflected by another Middle East crisis, this one in Cyprus. For several weeks, Kissinger and his top aides were engaged in trying to prevent Greece and Turkey, two NATO allies, from going to war. The Arab-Israeli conflict, for the first time in months, was eclipsed by a crisis elsewhere in the world.[65]

But the gravest crisis, in certain respects, was in Washington. On July 24, the Supreme Court unanimously ruled that Nixon must turn

61. Golan, op. cit., pp. 220–21, claims that arms shipments were delayed as a form of pressure on Israel.

62. As announced by Sadat in Alexandria in mid-July 1974, after talks with King Hussein.

63. Yariv stated in July 1974 that "Negotiations with the PLO would be possible should the PLO . . . declare its readiness to enter into negotiations while acknowledging the existence of the Jewish state in Israel and calling off all hostile actions against it."

64. Golan, op. cit., pp. 220–22.

65. During July 1974, however, Secretary of the Treasury Simon did travel to Egypt, Israel, and Saudi Arabia to discuss economic cooperation. He had little to offer, but learned that the Egyptians were developing a very large appetite for American aid and technology, and that the Israelis were contemplating a five-year military-modernization program that would cost $4 billion per year, of which at least $1.5 billion was earmarked as American grant aid. Peace in the Middle East would not come cheaply.

over the records of sixty-four subpoenaed tapes. Three days later, the House Judiciary Committee began voting the first of three articles of impeachment. Nixon seemed committed to fighting to the last moment to save his presidency and his reputation, but on August 5 the final bit of evidence that alienated even his most ardent supporters was made public. In a taped conversation on June 23, 1972, shortly after the Watergate break-in, Nixon was clearly heard ordering that the CIA be used to prevent the FBI investigation into the case. Two days later, the president reluctantly reached the conclusion that he would have to resign, a decision that he announced at 9:00 P.M. on August 8. At noon on August 9, Richard Nixon ceased to be president. His successor, Gerald Ford, was sworn into office as the country's first nonelected president. He quickly assured a troubled nation that Secretary of State Henry Kissinger would remain in the cabinet to conduct the foreign policy of the country. It would be some time before Middle East affairs would become the new president's strong suit. And Kissinger himself would have other preoccupations in the weeks ahead. Step-by-step diplomacy seemed to have reached an end, at least for the moment.

CONCLUSIONS

It is impossible to know with certainty whether American policy toward the Middle East after October 1973 would have been substantially different without the deleterious effects of the Watergate scandal. On the whole, it seems as if the answer is no. The policy that grew out of the October crisis had little to do with Watergate. It was aimed at ending the multiple pressures generated by the war and bringing the United States to a position of influence over the peacemaking process between Israel and her Arab neighbors. The level of commitment and the amount of energy expended in pursuit of this policy could not have been greater. Nor does it appear as if the pace of diplomacy could have been quickened, or that more substantial agreements might have been reached. After all, the Israelis, Egyptians, and Syrians were operating under severe constraints. Even the modest disengagement agreements strained their political systems almost to the breaking point.

Kissinger has been criticized for specific decisions that he took during the negotiations, such as discouraging the Israelis and Egyptians from reaching agreement at Kilometer 101 in November. He has been accused of exerting too much pressure on Israel, of being less than straightforward in his dealings with the parties, and of being more of a tactician than a strategist. Yet his critics have rarely presented a viable alternative to his gradualist, step-by-step diplomacy, and few would maintain that more could have been achieved in the first seven months after the October war.

Serious doubts do arise, however, as to whether Kissinger conceived of his diplomacy as a step toward a comprehensive political settlement or whether, pessimist that he often was accused of being, he saw his efforts as aimed at buying time and reducing pressures on the United States and Israel. To the Arabs, Kissinger consistently stressed the former goal, while reassuring the Israelis with the latter.

If step-by-step diplomacy as carried out by Kissinger is to be judged on its own merits, it rates high as a tactic but fails to convey any sense of long-term purpose. For a few kilometers of Sinai or Golan, it was surely not worth repeated crises of confidence with Israel and substantial offers of aid to all parties. Kissinger's justification for his efforts was that without the disengagement agreements there would be another war, accompanied by another oil embargo and by a resurgence of Soviet influence in the Arab world. To prevent this was ample justification for his endless travels and his deep involvement in the disengagement negotiations.

Kissinger knew what he wanted to avoid better than he knew what positive goals he might be able to achieve. The October war was his immediate point of reference. The simple lesson from that crisis was that the status quo in the Middle East was volatile, dangerous, and could disintegrate with serious consequences for American global and regional interests. Consequently, the status quo must be stabilized through a combination of diplomacy and arms shipments. A political process must begin that would offer the Arabs an alternative to war, but it must be carried on at a pace that the Israelis could accept. This was the extent of Nixon's and Kissinger's initial conceptualization. There was no American peace plan—that had been tried in 1969 and had failed.

Without a convincing picture, however, of where step-by-step diplomacy was heading, would the parties to the negotiations ever be able to address the core issues of peace, security, and the Palestinians? And would the United States indefinitely be able to remain uncommitted to outcomes? The answer was unmistakably no, and by mid-1974 Nixon found himself making private commitments to Sadat, Asad, Rabin, and Hussein on where American diplomacy was heading.

With strong presidential leadership, it might have been possible to transcend step-by-step diplomacy and move on to a more comprehensive negotiation, including the Palestinians. Instead, the United States was involved in an unprecedented crisis of authority, and Nixon's successor was unlikely to convey a clear sense of purpose in foreign policy. Step-by-step diplomacy therefore remained as a tactic for buying more time, a tactic cut off from a larger political concept of peace in the Middle East. Unable to move beyond step-by-step diplomacy, yet fearing the loss of momentum if no results were achieved, Kissinger was obliged to continue the search for partial solutions, either on the Jordanian or the Egyptian front, whichever seemed more feasible. The chance for a more ambitious policy was lost when Nixon was forced to resign, and considerable time would have to pass before a strong American initiative in the Middle East would be resumed.

CHAPTER VIII

Beyond Disengagement?
Ford's Middle-East Policy

GERALD FORD was an unlikely president. He had not sought the office. As a long-time member of the House of Representatives, his political ambition had been to become Speaker of the House—until Richard Nixon selected him as vice president in October 1973. Less than a year later, in early August 1974, the final act of the Watergate scandal brought Ford to the White House.

There is a strong presumption in American politics that it does matter who occupies the Oval Office. Immense sums are spent on presidential election campaigns. And in no other area is presidential discretion thought to be so great as in foreign policy, or at least so it seemed in the pre-Vietnam, pre-Watergate era.

This president, however, was different from his predecessors. He had not been elected. His initial popularity stemmed from his apparent honesty and openness, not from confidence in his ability or leadership, and even that popularity began to wane after his pardon of Richard Nixon. Foreign policy was obviously not his field of expertise, and it appeared likely that he would defer to his prestigious secretary of state and national security affairs adviser, Henry Kissinger. But could Kissinger be as effective as he had been in the past without a strong president to back his initiatives? Although Kissinger may have harbored misgivings about Nixon, he had admired his

253

decisiveness and his willingness to take risks. Would Ford have the same attributes?

Little was known of Ford's views on foreign policy generally. As a congressman, he had supported a strong defense and had backed Nixon in his Southeast Asian policy. He was known to be a good friend of Israel, but otherwise his ideas on the Middle East were uncertain. It seemed probable that it would be some time before a distinctive Ford foreign policy would take shape. For the moment, Kissinger would remain in charge.

Kissinger had adopted step-by-step diplomacy as the means to deal with the problems created by the October war and to establish the United States as the key diplomatic broker between Israel and the Arabs. Despite some reservations, Egypt, Syria, and Israel had all gone along with Kissinger's approach, and he had even been able to enlist the support, or tacit agreement, of Saudi Arabia, Algeria, and Jordan. By mid-1974, two disengagement agreements stood as testimony to the success of Kissinger's efforts. But the issues between Israel and her Arab neighbors went well beyond disengagement of military forces, and subsequent diplomatic moves would have to address a much more complex range of political considerations than had been true in the first round of step-by-step diplomacy.

Kissinger may well have had his doubts about the wisdom of continuing to seek political agreements on each Arab front separately. But what were the alternatives? A global negotiation at Geneva was sure to fail unless carefully prepared in advance. The Israelis were wary of Geneva, and Kissinger himself was not anxious to bring the Soviet Union back into the peacemaking moves. A U.S.-Soviet-imposed settlement would require both a higher degree of superpower agreement than existed and a strong American president. A suspension of United States diplomacy was a possibility, but ran the risk of weakening the "moderate" Arab coalition that Kissinger had been trying to encourage.

By a process of elimination, Kissinger came back to step-by-step diplomacy, with all of its obvious limitations, as the best means to keep the settlement process alive. But where to begin? The answer, never fully thought through, was the Jordan-Israel front. The unstated belief was that it was worth trying to bring Jordan into the diplomacy as a way of undercutting the more radical PLO. Kissinger would also continue to press for a second step between Egypt and Israel.

A JORDANIAN-ISRAELI SETTLEMENT?

Negotiations on the Jordanian-Israeli front presented Kissinger with unprecedented problems. "Disengagement" was hardly an appropriate concept here, since there had been no military engagement in the October war. Rather than separating military forces along cease-fire lines, Kissinger would have to deal with sensitive political issues such as sovereignty and the status of the Palestinians. Despite the tacit cooperation that existed on some levels between Jordan and Israel, the prospects for reaching agreement were unusually dim, largely for reasons of domestic Israeli politics and inter-Arab pressures on King Hussein. Israel was now led by an untried and untested leader, Prime Minister Yitzhak Rabin. On foreign-policy matters, he was obliged to work closely with his popular defense minister, Shimon Peres, and his foreign minister, Yigal Allon. Unfortunately for Rabin, these two key figures in his cabinet did not often see eye to eye. The only consensus Rabin was able to develop regarding the West Bank was essentially a negative one: he would call elections before agreeing to anything affecting the former Jordanian territory.

The pressures on Hussein were equally confining, but less focused. His own sense of responsibility, and his understandable fear of being accused of selling out to the Israelis, led him to insist on negotiating terms that he could defend before other Arabs and before the Palestinians. Despite Hussein's own "moderate" inclinations, and his genuine acceptance of Israel's right to exist, he was not in a position to capitulate to Israeli demands. He needed to prove to his people and to the Arab world that he, like Asad and Sadat, could recover Arab territory held by Israel. Above all, he could not accede to the Israeli position of administering the populated areas of the West Bank while Israel retained military control of the area.

Kissinger recognized the danger that negotiations might fail on the Jordan-Israel front. If they did, the momentum that he had hoped to develop through step-by-step diplomacy might be dissipated; precious time might be lost; Kissinger's own reputation might suffer. An alternative strategy did exist, namely, to concentrate on another quick step on the Egyptian-Israeli front, and then to move on to more comprehensive negotiations at Geneva during 1975. Kissinger wavered, then finally opted for a half-hearted attempt at a Jordanian-Israeli agreement.

Within days of becoming president, Ford was conferring with Middle East diplomats and leaders, while Kissinger tried to bring him up to date on the intricacies of the Arab-Israeli negotiations. First to arrive for talks with Ford was Egyptian Foreign Minister Fahmy. A few days later, King Hussein met with Ford, Kissinger, and Schlesinger. The king was told that the United States would accord priority to the search for a Jordanian-Israeli agreement, while also exploring possibilities for another step in Sinai. It was then the turn of Syrian Foreign Minister Khaddam to see Kissinger, on August 23. Not to be outdone, Prime Minister Rabin arrived in Washington on September 10 for discussions with the new President.

The upshot of all these preliminary consultations was another Kissinger trip to the Middle East. Israel was still reluctant to pull back from the Jordan River, and Hussein would accept nothing else. The alternative of Israeli withdrawal from the town of Jericho, and perhaps even from the important Nablus area, had been suggested, but neither side was enthusiastic. Kissinger therefore began his travels with little chance of success. In talks with Sadat, he tried to press for Egyptian support of Jordan at the forthcoming Arab summit conference in Rabat. That support had slipped somewhat during September, and the dynamics of inter-Arab politics might well produce a ringing endorsement of the PLO, to the exclusion of Jordan, which Kissinger wanted to prevent. As bait, he discussed with Sadat the outlines of another agreement between Egypt and Israel. Sadat's position was firm: in a second step, he must recover the Mitla and Giddi passes and the oil field at Abu Rudeis. Nothing less would justify the risks for Egypt of entering into a second agreement with Israel.

In Amman, Kissinger and Hussein reviewed the bleak prospects for an agreement and discussed the possibility that at Rabat the PLO would be endorsed as the sole negotiator for the West Bank and as the only spokesman for the Palestinians. If that were to happen, the king would withdraw from the negotiations entirely. There were many Jordanians who would be delighted to wash their hands of the whole Palestinian problem. It would be far better to concentrate on developing the East Bank and on building ties to Syria and Saudi

Arabia than to run the risk of isolation and violent opposition that might result if the king signed an unpopular agreement with Israel. For the time being, Hussein and Kissinger agreed to await the outcome of the Arab summit in Rabat. With support from Sadat, Kissinger felt sure that Hussein would emerge with a mandate to negotiate for the West Bank.

To Kissinger's considerable annoyance and dismay, the Arab heads of state who assembled in Rabat during the last week of October did not behave as he anticipated. On October 28, the conference unanimously endorsed the PLO as the sole legitimate representative of the Palestinian people. Hussein had no more right in the eyes of the Arab world to negotiate for the West Bank than any other Arab leader. Faced with such an overwhelming consensus, even Hussein had accepted the final resolution. Sadat had tried to bring about a more ambiguous outcome, but had failed. Saudi Arabia, ostensibly a moderate Arab state, and Syria had been among the most vocal champions of the PLO.

The Rabat summit, followed shortly by the appearance of PLO Executive Committee Chairman Yasir Arafat at the United Nations on November 13, suddenly propelled the Palestinians to the front and center of the Arab-Israeli conflict. Kissinger was unprepared for this. He had hoped to put off the Palestinian issue until later, while trying to strengthen King Hussein at the expense of the PLO. He had expected Egypt, Saudi Arabia, and perhaps even Syria to recognize the practical necessity of keeping Jordan in the negotiations. Now his carefully constructed policy had been derailed. American public opinion, which had strongly supported his efforts until then, began to express skepticism of step-by-step diplomacy, as well as firm opposition to pressure on Israel to deal with the PLO. Some felt that Rabat symbolized the failure of Kissinger's diplomacy, that Egypt and Syria were now preparing to back Arafat in his demands for dismantling the Zionist state, and that the proper response of American policy was to throw all its weight behind Israel, while invoking any sanctions available against the Arabs.[1]

In fact, the Rabat action was much less decisive than it appeared at the time, but it did cause problems for Kissinger. To salvage his

---

1. See, for example, William Safire's column in the *New York Times,* Oct. 31, 1974, p. 41. A more thoughtful analysis can be found in Richard H. Ullman, "After Rabat: Middle East Risks and American Roles," *Foreign Affairs* 53, no. 2 (January 1975).

policy and his reputation, he needed another success. It could not be on the Jordan front, so it would have to be in Sinai. Egypt, however, was not the strong leader of the Arab world that it had been under Nasser—the Rabat meeting had shown that to be true—and would have to move carefully in any next step. At the same time, Israel was hardly in the mood to make concessions, nor did the new government seem to have any clear diplomatic strategy. Golda Meir may have been tough and difficult to deal with, but at least she was in control of the government. It was less clear that Rabin could guide the divided country through a complex set of negotiations, particularly with his defense minister, Shimon Peres, eager to take his place if he should falter. To reach any agreement would definitely take time. Meanwhile, other Middle East issues demanded attention.

OIL PRICES AS AN ISSUE

Issues have a curious way of coming and going in American politics, and this is especially true of complex problems such as the energy crisis. Few people understand the economics and politics of oil and energy, or the nature of the international petroleum market. The Arab oil embargo was at least a concrete act that could be isolated from other issues and dealt with accordingly. It had a clear beginning and end. Yet the crisis did not seem to go away when the embargo was lifted in March 1974. In fact, it seemed as if the embargo per se had not really had much impact on the U.S. economy. But then what about the price of oil?

Oil prices became a major issue in the latter part of 1974. With the price of Persian Gulf oil near $10 a barrel, this was no surprise. At that price, the United States would be spending approximately $20 billion per year on petroleum imports. Even if the United States might be able to afford such a drain on its economy, it seemed questionable whether Europe and Japan could. It seemed likely that the sheer magnitude of the financial transactions between oil importers and exporters might overwhelm the international financial system.

New terms such as "petrodollars" and "recycling" began to make their appearance. The rush to sell goods to Saudi Arabia, Iran, Iraq, and other oil-rich countries was on. Despite pious calls for cooperation among oil consumers and between consumers and producers, the reality was one of fierce competition. How long could it go on?

Kissinger began to worry about the international economic repercussions of the high price of oil sometime in the fall of 1974. The continued sluggishness of the western economies, combined with high rates of inflation and unemployment, were apparently linked to oil prices. American public opinion tended to blame the Arabs for these economic ills, failing to note that other OPEC members such as Iran and Venezuela were more militant on prices than Saudi Arabia. The net effect of this shift in mood was to make it even more difficult for Kissinger and Ford to pursue a diplomatic strategy aimed at promoting an Arab-Israeli settlement. After all, why do favors for the Arabs when they were threatening to bring down the economies of the western democracies by their irresponsible behavior?

Several efforts were made by Kissinger to try to persuade the Saudis and the Iranians to take the lead in lowering oil prices. At the same time, the United States worked out an agreement with the OECD countries of Europe and Japan for the sharing of oil in an emergency.[2] In addition, a producer-consumer dialogue was begun. Behind these efforts was the realization that in the event of another war between Israel and the Arabs, there might be another embargo, followed by oil-price increases. No one was quite sure, but it seemed plausible that progress toward a settlement of the Arab-Israeli conflict might at least reduce the chances of an embargo and even lead to more moderate action on prices by the Arab oil producers.[3]

Meanwhile, the public concern over oil prices and possible embargoes was weakening the support for Kissinger's diplomacy, and an alternative strategy of counterpressure against the Arabs, including the use of force, began to receive a hearing.[4] A number of rather lurid

2. In November 1974, the International Energy Agency was established under OECD auspices. It agreed upon a program to build up oil stocks, to plan for reducing demand in the event of oil-supply interruptions, and to share oil if any member of the group were subjected to a selective embargo. By agreeing to these terms, the United States in theory became as vulnerable to an embargo as Europe or Japan.

3. For a discussion of the link between the Arab-Israeli conflict and the energy crisis, see William B. Quandt, "U.S. Energy Policy and the Arab-Israeli Conflict," in *Arab Oil: Impact on the Arab Countries and Global Implications*, ed. Naiem A. Sherbiny and Mark A. Tessler (New York: Praeger, 1976). In a major address on energy at the University of Chicago on Nov. 14, 1976, Kissinger maintained that the price of oil would come down only when the objective situation changed. In other words, market forces, not political favors, would be the means of reducing prices.

4. Kissinger was pressed by an aggressive interviewer to state that the use of force against oil producers could not be excluded in the event of actual "strangulation" of the western economies; *Business Week*, Jan. 13, 1975. Detailed discussions of the circumstances in which force might appropriately be used appeared in Robert Tucker, "Oil: The Issue of American

pictures of impending financial chaos were painted. If OPEC did not collapse, the economies of the industrialized west were bound to do so. Neither, of course, happened, but throughout the next phase of Kissinger's diplomacy, petroleum and its financial ramifications were very much part of public and official preoccupation. Only gradually did the intense concern over the issue wane, as prices stabilized at a high level, adjustments were painfully made, and economic recovery began in the latter part of 1975.[5] By 1976, the issue had all but disappeared as a topic of public debate.

A SECOND EGYPTIAN-ISRAELI STEP

Kissinger's technique for arranging limited agreements between Israel and the Arabs was by now well developed. It began by eliciting proposals from each side, getting preliminary reactions, identifying obstacles, and then starting the diplomatic process that would eventually bridge the substantive gaps. This process would include a heavy dose of reason and persuasion, as Kissinger would explain the dire consequences internationally of failure to reach an agreement; it involved marshalling forces that might influence the parties, such as other Arab countries or the United States Congress; then Kissinger would commit his own prestige to bringing about an agreement, shuttling back and forth between the two sides. At this last stage, Kissinger was likely to involve the president if additional pressure on Israel or commitments on future aid were needed.

Even before the Rabat meeting, Kissinger had obtained a fairly good idea of the Egyptian and Israeli objectives in a second step. Egypt wanted Israel to withdraw beyond the strategically important Mitla and Giddi passes and to relinquish control over the Abu Rudeis and Ras Sudr oil fields, which were providing Israel with about 50 percent of its total oil needs. Sadat wanted this step to be treated as another military disengagement, with only minimal political overtones. He felt that he could not afford to be seen in the Arab world as having withdrawn from the conflict with Israel.

Israel's objectives in a second agreement with Egypt were quite

---

Intervention," *Commentary* 59, no. 1 (January 1975), pp. 21–31; and Miles Ignotus (presumably Edward Luttwak), "Seizing Arab Oil," *Harper's,* March 1975, pp. 45–62.

5. An article by Hollis Chenery, vice-president of the World Bank, marked an important turning point in the debate over oil prices. See "Restructuring the World Economy," *Foreign Affairs* 53, no. 2 (January 1975).

different. Israel hoped to split Egypt from Syria, thereby reducing the prospects of a combined Arab offensive such as had occurred in October 1973. This would require Egypt to make substantial political concessions as the price of further Israeli withdrawals. Israel would demand that Egypt renounce the state of belligerency, that the new agreement be of long duration, and that Israeli withdrawal would not include the passes or the oil fields.

During November and December 1974, Kissinger was able to clarify each side's position. He was convinced that Sadat would settle for nothing less than Mitla, Giddi, and the oil fields and that he would not formally renounce the state of belligerency. He so informed the Israelis and urged them to concentrate instead on the "functional equivalents" of nonbelligerency, such as the end of the economic boycott.

As Egypt and Israel began to show readiness for a second agreement, two potentially dangerous sources of opposition appeared. The Syrians were well aware that Israel was trying to isolate Egypt, which would then leave Syria alone to confront the militarily superior Israeli forces. Asad therefore was opposed to a second step on the Egyptian front. To underscore his attitude, Asad ordered his armed forces on high alert in mid-November, just on the eve of the renewal of the mandate of the UN forces. The crisis subsided, but not before Asad had made his point.

The second source of opposition to Kissinger's strategy was the Soviet Union. By now the Soviets saw clearly that one of Kissinger's primary goals was to weaken Soviet influence in the Middle East, especially in Egypt. Ford and Brezhnev met in Vladivostok on November 23–24, 1974, primarily to discuss a second strategic-arms agreement, but also to consider the Middle East. The two sides remained far apart, the Soviets insisting on Geneva and Ford favoring a continuation of step-by-step diplomacy, at the request, of course, of Egypt and Israel.[6] On the whole, U.S.-Soviet relations were cooling, as would become clear on January 14, 1975, when the Soviet Union rejected the offer of most-favored-nation trading status on terms that would have required a liberalization of emigration for Soviet Jews.

6. The joint communiqué issued on Nov. 24, 1974, said that the search for peace in the Middle East should be based on UN Resolution 338, "taking into account the legitimate interests of all the peoples in the area, including the Palestinians, and respect for the right to independent existence of all states."

Meanwhile, despite Syrian and Soviet opposition, Kissinger pressed forward, his task complicated by the curious unfolding of the Israeli negotiating position. On December 3, 1974, in an interview with *Haaretz,* Prime Minister Rabin openly stated that Israel's goal was to separate Egypt from Syria and to delay negotiations until after the American elections in 1976. He spoke of seven years during which the oil crisis would mean that Israel would be subjected to heavy pressures for concessions, but after which alternatives to petroleum would have been found, thus weakening the power of the Arab world. Finally, Rabin added that it was unrealistic to expect Egypt to offer nonbelligerency at this stage of the negotiations.[7]

A few days after the Rabin interview, Foreign Minister Allon arrived in Washington for talks with Kissinger. For several hours on December 9, they discussed a ten-point proposal that Allon had brought with him.[8] The points included an end to the state of belligerency, demilitarization of evacuated territory, an end to economic and propaganda warfare by Egypt against Israel, a duration of twelve years for the agreement, and a number of other demands similar to those written into the January disengagement accord. In return for this, Israel would withdraw thirty to fifty kilometers, but would remain in control of the passes and oil fields.

Kissinger and Ford were unimpressed by Israel's offer. Allon hinted that it was only a bargaining position and might be changed. For example, the duration of the agreement could be five years instead of twelve. Kissinger's main problem with the Israeli proposal, however, was the demand for nonbelligerency, which Rabin himself had termed unrealistic, and the refusal to cede on the passes and oil fields. The Israeli points were nonetheless transmitted to Sadat, and Sadat's expected rejection was duly received. Kissinger then asked the Israelis to make a new proposal.

As is frequently the case in Arab-Israeli affairs, external events impinge upon the local parties in unanticipated ways. In late December, an important development took place in Soviet-Egyptian relations. After a short visit to Moscow by Egypt's foreign minister and its chief of staff, it was announced on December 30 that the expected visit by Brezhnev to Cairo had been canceled. Kissinger had been

7. Matti Golan, *The Secret Conversations of Henry Kissinger* (New York: Quadrangle Books, 1976), p. 229.
8. Ibid., pp. 229–30, and *Haaretz,* Dec. 17, 1974.

planning to await the results of the Brezhnev visit before pressing ahead with his own strategy. Now it seemed as if Egyptian-Soviet relations were indeed very poor; more than ever, Sadat needed to demonstrate that his turning to the United States had not been a foolish move. Without Soviet arms, he would not easily be able to make war; but with American support, he might recover his territory anyway and get on with the urgent task of developing the Egyptian economy.

When Allon arrived in the United States for another round of discussions with Kissinger, he acknowledged that the cancellation of the Brezhnev visit had created a new situation, but during his talks with Ford and Kissinger on January 15-16, 1975, he had nothing new to offer except an invitation to Kissinger to return to the area. Kissinger repeated his warning to Allon that an agreement could not be reached on the basis of the Israeli proposal. He would nonetheless make another trip to see if the gap could be narrowed. After an exploratory round of talks in February, he would return in March to complete the negotiations, but Israel would have to drop the demand for nonbelligerency and be more forthcoming as to territory.

Prior to Kissinger's departure, Sadat publicly endorsed his efforts, adding that the United States now held virtually all of the trump cards.[9] This was precisely what Kissinger wanted to hear from Sadat. From the Syrians and the Soviets, however, he was continuing to encounter resistance to his efforts. As Sadat seemed to move forward toward another agreement, Syria began to band together with Jordan and the Palestinians in opposing him, with growing support from the Soviet Union.[10]

Even though Syria and the Soviet Union were aligning against Sadat, Israel at least seemed to be softening somewhat in its demands. On February 7, Rabin gave an interview to John Lindsay, former mayor of New York, in which he stated that "in exchange for an Egyptian commitment not to go to war, not to depend on threats of use of force, and an effort to reach true peace, the Egyptians could get even the passes and the oil fields."[11] Kissinger was appalled at Rabin's carelessness in revealing Israel's position in such a forum—he

9. *Le Monde*, Jan. 21, 1975.
10. On Feb. 1, 1975, Syria and the Soviet Union issued a joint communiqué calling for the reconvening of the Geneva conference.
11. Golan, op. cit., p. 232.

would no doubt have preferred to appear responsible for achieving such an Israeli concession—but at least the chance for an agreement now seemed brighter. On this somewhat optimistic note, Kissinger left for the Middle East on February 9.

Kissinger's February trip was admittedly exploratory. He did not expect to reach agreement, but he did hope that Egypt and Israel would each recognize the constraints the other was operating under and modify some elements of their proposals. Instead, he found little new. The Israelis seemed to ease up a bit on the issue of nonbelligerency, and Sadat indicated a willingness to end some hostile actions against Israel, but a substantial gap remained. Nor did Kissinger succeed in persuading the Syrians to drop their opposition to a second step in Sinai.[12] The only positive note of the trip came from Kissinger's talks with the Shah of Iran in Zurich on February 18, where the Shah indicated that he would be prepared to provide Israel with oil if she gave up Abu Rudeis and Ras Sudr.

For the next several weeks, Kissinger continued to urge the parties to moderate their positions, for he wanted an agreement, and soon. But he did not want to embark upon a third "shuttle" until he was virtually certain of success. Assuming that the parties now understood the minimum terms required for a successful negotiation, Kissinger departed for the Middle East once again on March 18.[13]

Kissinger's task was complicated by a number of domestic and international developments. Both he and Ford were experiencing a decline in their popularity. Congress was becoming more assertive in its demands to guide foreign policy. Indochina was progressively coming under communist domination. A leftist coup in Portugal had created a potentially dangerous situation in the western Mediterranean. U.S.-Turkish relations were at a low point because of a congressional ban on arms to Turkey. Only on the Egyptian-Israeli front was there the chance of another Kissinger spectacular. The Israelis seemed apprehensive that Kissinger was a bit too anxious for success. It would be they, after all, who would be asked to make the major concessions, and that was more than Rabin's weak government was anxious to do.

Kissinger did succeed in obtaining new Egyptian proposals during

12. Asad's position on a second step in the Golan Heights remained ambiguous. He did not appear particularly anxious for such an agreement, but neither did he preclude it.
13. That same day, Syria and the PLO announced the formation of a joint political-military command.

the March shuttle. Sadat was prepared to say that the conflict with Israel would not be solved by military means; that Egypt would not resort to force; that it would observe the cease-fire and would prevent all military and paramilitary forces from operating against Israel from Egyptian territory; that a new agreement would remain in effect until superseded by another agreement; that hostile propaganda against Israel in Egyptian-controlled media would be reduced; and that the economic boycott would be selectively eased.[14]

Israel's position, as first conveyed informally by Rabin to Kissinger on the evening of March 9, consisted of seven points entitled "Proposal on Main Elements of Agreement Between Israel and Egypt." Israel sought a separate agreement with Egypt that would not be dependent upon agreements with other Arab parties. The agreement must be a step toward peace in some practical aspects, such as the free passage of Israeli cargoes through the Suez Canal, the end of the economic boycott, and the free movement of persons between Egypt and Israel. Egypt must agree to the end of the use of force through a "renunciation of belligerency clearly and in its appropriate legal wording." A real buffer zone must be created between the military forces of both sides. Some solution must be found for the "dilemma of vagueness" about the duration of the agreement. An understanding must be reached on the relationship between an interim agreement in Sinai and what might happen later at Geneva. Finally, Israel would agree to discuss the question of the line of withdrawal only after Egypt had responded to the first six points.[15]

Kissinger was dismayed that Israel was still holding out for nonbelligerency. Sadat was prepared to meet some of Israel's demands, but insisted on knowing whether Israel would remain in the passes. He also flatly refused to agree to nonbelligerency, but would consider a formula based on the "nonuse of force." After several days of shuttling, Kissinger managed to persuade the Israelis to accept the "nonuse of force" formulation, but Rabin and his negotiating team were adamant that Israel would not withdraw from the passes for anything less than nonbelligerency. At best they might consider pulling back to a line halfway through the passes, but at no point in the negotiations did the Israelis provide Kissinger with a map showing a

14. *Jerusalem Post*, May 13, 1975.
15. Edward R.F. Sheehan, *The Arabs, Israelis, and Kissinger* (New York: Reader's Digest Press, 1976), p. 156.

line that they would accept. Complicating the bargaining further was Israel's insistence on maintaining control over an electronic intelligence station at Umm Khisheiba at the western end of the Giddi pass. Sadat would not agree to Israel keeping the station, even if it were formally placed in the UN zone. Consequently, the negotiations deadlocked on the issues of nonbelligerency and its functional equivalents, on the extent of Israeli withdrawal in the passes and the oil fields, and on the status of the Umm Khisheiba facility.

After ten days of shuttling between Egypt and Israel, with side trips to Syria, Jordan, and Saudi Arabia, Kissinger was still not able to get the Israelis out of the passes. Israel agreed to cede the oil fields, but refused to give Egypt control over a road connecting the fields to the Egyptian zone. On Friday, March 21, Kissinger arrived in Israel with Sadat's final word: Israel could not keep the intelligence station, and the mandate of the UN forces would be renewed only for a second year. Without further Egyptian concessions, the Israelis would not budge. Even a tough letter from President Ford, which reached Israel on March 21, was unable to change the situation.[16] It may, in fact, have stiffened Israel's will to resist. In any event, the cabinet met Friday night and rejected virtually all of Sadat's demands.

Kissinger conveyed Israel's rejection to Egypt and awaited Sadat's reply. Meanwhile he spent the day of March 22 touring the historic site of Masada, where, nearly two thousand years earlier, the Jews had taken their own lives rather than surrender to the Romans. The symbolism of Masada hung over the talks later that evening when Kissinger met with Rabin and other top Israeli officials.[17] Kissinger was deeply concerned. According to the notes of his remarks, he stated that:

> The Arab leaders who banked on the United States will be discredited. . . . Step-by-step has been throttled, first for Jordan, then for Egypt. We're losing control. We'll now see the Arabs working on a united front. There will be more emphasis on the Palestinians, and there will be a linkage between moves in the Sinai and on Golan. The Soviets will step back onto the stage. The United States is losing control

16. Golan, op. cit., pp. 236–38, although he incorrectly gives the date of the letter as Mar. 19.

17. Sheehan, op. cit., pp. 160–62, contains parts of the transcripts of these talks. It should be noted that the transcripts are not verbatim records, but reconstructions of the conversations in dialogue form based on notes taken during the sessions by one of Kissinger's aides.

over events. . . . Our past strategy was worked out carefully, and now
we don't know what to do. There will be pressure to drive a wedge between Israel and the United States, not because we want that but
because it will be the dynamics of the situation. Let's not kid ourselves.
We've failed. . . . An agreement would have enabled the United States
to remain in control of the diplomatic process. Compared to that, the
location of the line eight kilometers one way or the other frankly does
not seem important. And you got all the military elements of nonbelligerency. You got the "nonuse of force". . . .

This is a real tragedy. . . . We've attempted to reconcile our support
for you with our other interests in the Middle East, so that you wouldn't
have to make your decisions all at once. . . . Our strategy was to save
you from dealing with all those pressures all at once. . . . If we wanted
the 1967 borders, we could do it with all of world opinion behind us.
The strategy was designed to protect you from this. We've avoided
drawing up an overall plan for a global settlement. . . . I see pressure
building up to force you back to the 1967 borders—compared to that,
ten kilometers is trivial. I'm not angry at you, and I'm not asking you to
change your position. It's tragic to see people dooming themselves to a
course of unbelievable peril.

This was vintage Kissinger. He could have made the same remarks at
any point from October 1973 on. The emphasis on United States
control of the diplomacy, on breaking issues into manageable parts,
and on avoiding an overall peace plan were all basic elements of the
strategy developed in the midst of the October war. Now that strategy
seemed to have failed. The following day Kissinger left Israel, having
announced that his negotiating effort was being suspended.[18] Upon
Kissinger's return to Washington on March 24, President Ford
ominously announced that there would now be a reassessment of
United States policy toward the Middle East.

REASSESSMENT

Kissinger's disappointment at the Israelis for thwarting his efforts
to arrange a second agreement in Sinai was genuine. He felt that the
Israeli leadership was shortsighted, incompetent, and weak. In his
view, Israel had no foreign policy, only a domestic political system
that produced deadlock and stalemate. A David Ben Gurion or a

18. Before his departure, Kissinger called on Golda Meir. While she publicly supported
Rabin, she privately implied to Kissinger that Rabin had mishandled the negotiations and
that she would have known how to get the cabinet and the Knesset to support an agreement.

Golda Meir might be able to lead Israel, but not the Rabin-Peres-Allon triumvirate, each of whom pulled in a different direction. In his less guarded moments, Kissinger suggested that the Israelis were trying to bring him down. Reassessment, however justified, became in part an instrument for Kissinger to vent his exasperation toward Israel.

President Ford, whatever his sentimental attachment to Israel might have been in the past, was also irritated at Israel, and publicly blamed Rabin for his lack of flexibility.[19] He lent his weight to a serious reassessment of policy during which new military and economic agreements with Israel were suspended. Like each of his predecessors, Ford found that his sympathies for Israel and his perception of American global and regional interests did not always mesh. When the two seemed to come into conflict, Ford was as capable as Nixon of pressuring Israel for concessions. The test, however, would be whether this could produce the desired results—and whether Israeli counter-pressure might not raise the cost of the effort.

Israel, after all, was not without influential friends and supporters in the United States, nor did it lack effective spokesmen who could defend it before the American public against the charge of inflexibility. If the administration insisted on withholding needed aid, Israel could appeal to Congress to support its requests. The Israeli case did seem plausible: in return for making important economic and territorial concessions, Israel was merely asking that Egypt renounce belligerency. Why was that unreasonable or inflexible? Should Israel risk its security for anything less? Kissinger's case against Israel was less convincing to many Americans. He claimed that the Israeli leaders had misled him into undertaking the shuttle when they knew that nonbelligerency could not be achieved, and yet they continued to insist on it. Israel had refused to make the minimal territorial concessions in the passes and around the oil fields. Kissinger argued that an agreement was necessary to preserve the delicate balances that he had brought into being after the October 1973 war. On occasion, he implied that the alternative to an agreement might be war and another Arab oil embargo.

During the nearly three months of reassessment that followed the collapse of the Egyptian-Israeli talks on March 22, American foreign

19. Ford interview with the Hearst newspaper chain, Mar. 27, 1975. See *New York Times*, Mar. 28, 1975.

policy witnessed the final dénouement of the Southeast Asia conflict and the beginning of a tragic civil war in Lebanon. In both cases, the United States seemed powerless to act constructively. The Cambodian capital of Phnom Penh fell to communist forces on April 17. Shortly thereafter, on April 29, Saigon also came under communist control. So much for the peace with honor in Indochina that Nixon and Kissinger had proudly proclaimed in January 1973.

Events in the Middle East, also, did not hold out the hope of peace. On March 25, one of the mainstays of American policy in the area, King Faisal of Saudi Arabia, was assassinated. A period of uncertainty began. Was Saudi Arabia on the verge of revolution? Would the new rulers continue the same foreign policy of friendship for the United States and support for Sadat? It would be some time before anyone would know. Meanwhile, the always tense situation in Lebanon was about to explode. On April 13, right-wing Christian gunmen had opened fire on a busload of Palestinians, killing twenty-two of them. It was not long before a vicious cycle of reprisals and counterreprisals was underway.

Against this disquieting background, Kissinger carried out the promised policy reassessment. On April 1, he met with a group of prominent men from the foreign-policy establishment—Dean Rusk, McGeorge Bundy, George Ball, Douglas Dillon, Cyrus Vance, George Schultz, Robert McNamara, David Bruce, Peter Peterson, John McCloy, William Scranton, and Averill Harriman. Some of the group, such as Ball, had been openly critical of Kissinger's step-by-step policy. Ball favored a more comprehensive agreement in which the United States and the Soviet Union would work out the guidelines for a settlement, which would then be negotiated by all the parties at Geneva. He had criticized Kissinger for ignoring the Soviets and trying to divide the Arabs. He did not shy away from the notion of an imposed settlement.[20] Others at the meeting also favored a return to the Geneva conference and a major effort to work out an American peace plan.

Over the next several weeks, Kissinger heard essentially the same recommendations from his closest aides, from eminent academics, and from American ambassadors to the key Middle East countries.[21]

20. *Atlantic Monthly*, January 1975, pp. 6–11.
21. During this period Stanley Hoffmann brilliantly argued the case that it was in Israel's own interest to come up with a comprehensive peace initiative. The major flaw in his argument

The time for step-by-step diplomacy was past. A more ambitious strategy was needed. The Palestinians could no longer be ignored. The Soviets would have to be brought into the negotiations. It all sounded reasonable in the abstract, but Kissinger was haunted by the fear that this approach, too, would fail. No one could detail the steps that would be required to ensure success. And it would be costly in domestic political terms, since it would surely require heavy and sustained pressure on Israel. Ford and Kissinger were not at all certain that they wanted to take on that battle unless the results were sure to warrant the effort.

By the third week of April, reassessment had produced three basic options for the president. The first, supported by many in and outside the government, was a return to Geneva with a detailed American peace plan. The United States would call for Israeli withdrawal, while offering strong guarantees of Israel's security. The Soviets would be invited to cooperate. A second option would aim for a virtually complete settlement, especially on the Egyptian-Israeli front, but would fall short of calling for full withdrawal and final peace. The third option was to resume step-by-step diplomacy where it had left off in March.[22] Ford referred publicly to these three options in a general way on April 21.[23]

For several weeks it seemed as if a new American approach to peace in the Middle East might emerge, but gradually the realization set in that nothing of the sort could be expected. Kissinger's consultations with Allon, Hussein, and the Soviets had not given him any reason to be optimistic about a new policy. American public support for a global initiative was not strong, and Congress was beginning to respond to arguments that Kissinger was exerting too much pressure on Israel. On May 21, seventy-six senators sent a letter to President Ford, urging him to be "responsive to Israel's economic and military needs." This was a clear sign that continued pressure on Israel would be politically counterproductive. Ford and Kissinger realized that the only viable strategy, in light of these realities, was to resume step-by-step diplomacy. Ford himself would participate

---

was that such a policy would require a strong Israeli government backed by a broad public consensus. That apparently was lacking. See "A New Policy for Israel," *Foreign Affairs* 53, no. 3 (April 1975).

22. Sheehan, op. cit., p. 166.
23. He also referred to United States policy as "even-handed."

in talks with Sadat and Rabin to explore the prospects for an agreement. Sadat helped to improve the atmosphere by unexpectedly announcing that the Suez Canal would be reopened on June 5 and that the mandate of UNEF would be extended. The Egyptian president still seemed to want to reach an agreement.

On June 1 to 2, President Ford and Sadat met for the first time in Salzburg. The two men got on well together, feeling relaxed in each other's company and finding it easy to talk. Sadat appealed for a public statement from Ford that Israel should withdraw to the 1967 lines, but Ford demurred, reportedly repeating instead Nixon's private commitment of the previous year to work for that goal.[24] Ford then sounded out Sadat on his willingness to try again for a limited agreement in Sinai. Sadat was favorably disposed, but his terms were still those of the previous spring: Israel must leave the passes and the oil fields and must not demand nonbelligerency. Sadat was still opposed to the idea of the Israelis' keeping the intelligence-gathering facility at Umm Khisheiba, but did indicate that he might accept an American presence there.[25] The idea of an American military contingent in the buffer zone had been raised earlier in the spring, but Kissinger had been unenthusiastic. The more modest concept of an American civilian presence, however, soon began to emerge as the solution to one of the problems in the negotiations.

SINAI II

By the time Prime Minister Rabin reached Washington for talks with President Ford and Secretary Kissinger on June 11–12, the decision to continue with step-by-step diplomacy had basically been made. The alternative of Geneva, of a U.S.-Soviet imposed settlement, or of a withdrawal from the peacemaking effort, had all been rejected. Ford and Kissinger viewed the situation in the Middle East as requiring continued diplomatic progress; as had been shown early in 1974, that could best be done through United States mediation. If progress toward a settlement were not made during the next few months, it might not be possible to launch a new initiative until 1977. After all, 1976 was an American election year, and Middle East politics could hardly hope to compete for attention with a presidential campaign.

24. Sheehan, op. cit., pp. 176–77.
25. Golan, op. cit., p. 59.

Ford asked Rabin to be more forthcoming in the negotiations, and pressed for a new Israeli line of withdrawal to the eastern ends of the passes. Rabin was anxious to end the painful and costly confrontation with the United States. His refusal of Kissinger's demands in March had greatly contributed to his prestige within Israel. Now he might be able to negotiate with more confidence. A new line therefore was drawn to demonstrate Israel's good will, and this was a modest step in the right direction. However, Rabin had not been authorized by the cabinet to make any such concessions, and a week later he was obliged to return to Israel's previous offer of withdrawal halfway through the passes.[26] Once again, Ford and Kissinger were angry at Rabin for his apparent inflexibility and his awkwardness.

During the next six weeks, Kissinger remained in Washington while Israeli and Egyptian positions were refined and transmitted through him to the other side. Dinitz was his channel to the Israeli government, and the American ambassador to Egypt, Herman Eilts, shuttled back and forth between Cairo and Washington with messages and clarifications.

Sometime in the last half of June, the Israeli leaders apparently decided that it would be impossible to obtain the desired political concessions from Sadat and undesirable to resist the United States indefinitely. If Egypt would not make peace, then at least Israel could bargain with the United States on issues involving her security. If the Americans wanted an agreement so badly, they could pay for it. Israel would agree to withdraw to the eastern slopes of the passes, but would maintain control over the high ground above the passes. At the urging of Defense Minister Peres, Israel also sought to make the buffer zone between the two sides into a genuine barrier to military surprise attack by stationing American civilians there to monitor early-warning stations. The Americans could also serve as a cover for continued Israeli use of the intelligence facility. If Sadat objected, the Americans could offer to build a comparable facility for him as well.

Sadat was also prepared to be somewhat more forthcoming. He would agree to three annual renewals of the mandate of the UN forces, and to the continued Israeli use of the intelligence facility, provided he was given one facing the Israeli lines. He accepted the

26. Ibid., p. 245; *New York Times*, June 25, 1975.

idea of easing the boycott of some companies dealing with Israel and promised to tone down anti-Israeli propaganda. And finally, he would be willing to have most of the terms of the agreement published.

It remained for the United States and Israel to work out their own understanding of the American commitments necessary to gain Israel's consent to a new agreement. Early in July, Dinitz met with Kissinger in the Virgin Islands to present the full package of Israeli proposals and requests.[27] In addition to a promise of about $2 billion in aid, the United States agreed to drop the idea of an interim step on the Jordan-Israel front and to accept that only "cosmetic" changes could be expected on the Golan Heights in another step. Israel also wanted a clear commitment that the United States would prevent Soviet military intervention in the Middle East.

In the course of the next several weeks, further discussion of these and other points took place.[28] By the time Kissinger departed for Israel on August 20, an agreement was within reach. Only the exact location of the Israeli line, the levels of United States aid, and the technical aspects of the American civilian presence in the passes remained to be negotiated.

Kissinger was received in Israel with unprecedented hostility, mainly from the right-wing opposition parties, and demonstrators accosted him at each stop. Nevertheless, his discussions with the leadership progressed. This time Rabin wanted an agreement. Kissinger continued to harbor misgivings about the American presence in Sinai, which by now was an essential ingredient of the Israeli package, but he was prepared to go along with the idea. Sadat was willing to accept this condition, but some quibbling still went on over the exact location of the line.[29]

27. Golan, op. cit., p. 248, although he mistakenly gives the date of this meeting as early August. New York Times, July 4, 1975.
28. Rabin and Ford met in Bonn on July 12, after which the Israeli cabinet authorized a new negotiating position. See Arab Report and Record, July 1–15, 1975, p. 401; and New York Times, July 13, 15, 1975. Egypt's reply was forthcoming on July 21, but was rejected by Israel on July 27. Israel then presented an "absolutely final" position to Kissinger, who transmitted it to Sadat via Eilts on July 31. The Egyptian response reached Kissinger in Belgrade on Aug. 3, and by Aug. 7 Dinitz had responded with the Israeli position. During the next few days, further exchanges took place, and by mid-August United States and Israeli officials had completed work on a draft agreement. Ford then instructed Kissinger to undertake another trip to the Middle East to pin down the details of an agreement.
29. Sheehan, op. cit., p. 184.

By August 25, Kissinger was working with the Israelis on the language of a draft agreement. Gradually Israel began to soften its position on the line of withdrawal, finally agreeing to give Kissinger a map for Sadat's consideration late in the second week of talks. Squabbling over withdrawal in the Giddi pass continued, as well as in regard to the oil fields. Only at the very last minute did Israel agree to complete withdrawal from Giddi. Very detailed discussions on force limits and on the American presence were also required. Then, in a nonstop session in Jerusalem lasting from 9:30 P.M. August 31 to 6:00 A.M. the following day, the United States and Israel worked out the fine points of their bilateral military relationship, assurances on Israel's supply of oil, and an understanding on the need for consultations in the event of Soviet military intervention in the Middle East. Israel was disappointed with the weak language on Soviet intervention, but otherwise could point to a very impressive list of American commitments. Later that afternoon, both Egypt and Israel initialed the text of the agreement. It was formally signed in Geneva on September 4, 1975.

Unlike the January 1974 accord, Sinai II was greeted with a sigh of relief, but with little real enthusiasm by the parties to the negotiations. Within both Israel and the Arab world, many were violently opposed to the agreement, although for entirely different reasons.

The agreement itself was modeled in part on the previous disengagement pacts.[30] The two parties committed themselves to resolve the conflict between them by peaceful means and not to resort to the threat or use of force against each other. The UN force would continue its function and the lines for each side's military deployments were designated on a map. Egypt agreed to allow nonmilitary cargoes destined for or coming from Israel to pass through the Suez Canal, which had been reopened to traffic the previous June. The agreement itself would remain in force until superseded by a new agreement.

Attached to the agreement was a detailed annex dealing with military deployments and aerial surveillance. At Sadat's insistence, the forces allowed in the limited zone under the agreement were

30. The text of the agreement can be found in a news release from the Bureau of Public Affairs, Department of State, Sept. 1, 1975. The secret part of the agreement was published by the *New York Times*, Sept. 17 and 18, 1975. The map was also released by the Department of State.

slightly larger than those permitted in January 1974: up to eight thousand men in eight battalions, with seventy-five tanks and seventy-two short-range artillery pieces. Neither party, however, was permitted to locate any weapons in areas from which they could reach each other's lines.

The arrangements for United States manning and supervision of the early-warning systems in the buffer zones were also spelled out in detail. Israel and Egypt would be allowed to have up to 250 technical and administrative personnel at their respective surveillance stations. United States civilians would operate three other smaller watch stations and would establish three unmanned sensor fields as well. Israel's willingness to implement the terms of the agreement was contingent upon U.S. congressional approval of the United States role in Sinai.

The United States also signed four secret agreements, three with Israel and one with Egypt. A sixteen-point U.S.-Israeli memorandum of understanding dealt with military assistance, oil supply, economic aid and a number of political points. The United States and Israel agreed that the next step with Egypt should be a final peace agreement. The same should be true on the Jordan front. In addition, the United States agreed to consult promptly with Israel in the event of any threat to Israel from a "world power," e.g., the Soviet Union. In an addendum on arms, the United States gave a vague commitment to provide a "positive response" to Israeli requests for F-16 aircraft and the Pershing missile with a conventional warhead.[31] In effect, the freeze on new arms agreements, which had begun the previous April, was ended. A special memo dealing with Geneva was signed, which reconfirmed the policy of the United States with respect to the Palestinians: no recognition of and no negotiation with the PLO until the PLO recognizes Israel's right to exist and accepts UN Resolutions 242 and 338. The United States would also carefully coordinate its strategy at Geneva with Israel and agree to keep the negotiations on a bilateral basis. To Egypt, the United States merely committed itself to try to bring about further negotiations between Syria and Israel, to provide assistance for the Egyptian early-warning

31. Kissinger had kept Sadat informed of most of the commitments he was making to Israel, but did not mention the Pershing missile. This irritated the Egyptians and raised doubts about other secret agreements that Kissinger might not have mentioned.

system in the buffer zone, and to consult with Egypt on any Israeli violations of the agreement.

REACTIONS TO SINAI II

In his more optimistic moments, Kissinger had justified step-by-step diplomacy as a process by which parties to a negotiation would gain confidence, would become committed to achieving results, and would be carried along by the momentum of peacemaking to resolve issues that previously had seemed intractable. But Sinai II came closer to confirming his more somber vision of the Arab-Israeli conflict. The issues were so complex, the emotions so deeply involved, that peace between the two sides was unattainable in this generation. This did not mean that no agreements could be reached, but they would be modest and imperfect at best. The diplomat aspiring to mediate between Israel and the Arabs would have to be content with small achievements. These, at least, were better than nothing. Stabilization of the region, reduction of the chances of war, and the end of the oil embargo were far preferable to renewed hostilities and superpower confrontation. Egypt, in any case, seemed firmly committed to a moderate course.

Kissinger had not consciously sought to provoke dissension among the Arabs. On the contrary, he was deeply concerned that Saudi Arabia continue to back Sadat's policies. He also recognized that Syria played a vital role in inter-Arab politics, and he genuinely wanted to draw Syria toward a moderate settlement with Israel.[32] The objective situation, however, thwarted his efforts. Golan was not Sinai, and a second step there would be difficult to manage unless Israel were prepared to give up the settlements along the post-1967 cease-fire lines. Israel had just demonstrated a remarkable capacity to hold out against American pressures and to exact a high price for eventual compliance. Was it worth the effort for a few kilometers on Golan? Sadat had very much wanted a second agreement, whereas Asad, by contrast, was lukewarm to the idea. He did not entirely reject the concept of a second step, but he made it clear that he was not prepared to pay much of a price for it. Instead, Asad began to

32. On Sept. 29, 1975, Kissinger spoke to the Arab representatives at the UN. He said that the United States was prepared to work for a Syrian-Israeli second step, if that was wanted; that the United States would consider ways of working for an overall settlement; and that he would begin to refine his thinking on how the legitimate interests of the Palestinian people could be met. Press release, Department of State, Bureau of Public Affairs, Sept. 29, 1975.

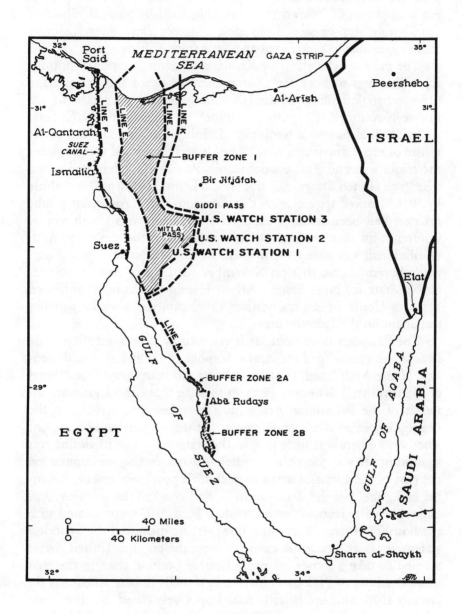

Egyptian-Israeli Sinai Agreement, September 1975.

attack Sadat for having abandoned the struggle against Israel and to press for international recognition of the PLO. Inter-Arab politics has a dynamics of its own that was unleashed by Sinai II. Short of abandoning step-by-step diplomacy, it is not clear what Kissinger could have done to keep Egypt and Syria from drifting apart.

The most serious effort by Kissinger to demonstrate his continuing willingness to work for a comprehensive peace agreement came prior to Syria's renewal of the UN disengagement observation force in late November 1975. On November 10, 1975, the UN General Assembly had passed a resolution defining Zionism as "a form of racism or racial discrimination." The United States had voted against the resolution, and Ambassador Daniel Patrick Moynihan had stated that "the United States . . . does not acknowledge, it will not abide by, it will never acquiesce in this infamous act." American public reaction had been strongly supportive of Moynihan's tough words. Contempt for those nations who had presumably succumbed to Arab oil blackmail was strongly expressed. In this atmosphere, it was particularly remarkable that on November 12, Deputy Assistant Secretary of State for Near Eastern Affairs Harold H. Saunders appeared before a House of Representatives subcommittee to make a policy statement on the Palestinians.

The Saunders document, as it came to be called, infuriated the Israelis and encouraged the Arabs. It spoke of the Palestinian dimension of the Arab-Israeli conflict as being, in many ways, the "heart of the conflict." Saunders went on to state that "the legitimate interests of the Palestinian Arabs must be taken into account in the negotiating of an Arab-Israeli peace." It was a question of how, not whether.[33] There was little new in the statement, but its timing was significant. It was meant to symbolize a continuing willingness on the part of the administration to work for a peace settlement. Kissinger had gone over the draft carefully, had checked the wording, and had reportedly cleared it with President Ford. When confronted with the hostility of Israel's reaction, however, he dismissed the Saunders statement as an academic exercise. Nonetheless, the United States seemed to take a somewhat more flexible position than in the past when the issue of PLO participation in the UN debate scheduled for January 1976 came up. Briefly, Arab hopes were raised, but they were

33. The Saunders statement can be found in a Current Policy release put out by the Department of State, Bureau of Public Affairs, November 1975.

soon to be disappointed. Behind the symbolic shift in American policy, there was no real substance.

Public opposition to dealing with the PLO was only one aspect of a broader disenchantment with Kissinger's foreign policy. Détente, once the hallmark of the Nixon-Kissinger policy, was increasingly being attacked, not only by such inveterate cold warriors as Henry Jackson, but also by former Defense Secretary James Schlesinger and by Moynihan, once he had ceased to be UN ambassador.[34] In addition, the Nobel-prize-winning Russian author who had been forced into exile by the Soviet government, Alexander Solzhenitsyn, was drawing considerable attention by his gloomy warnings about the dangers of détente with the Soviet Union. All of these opponents of détente proved to be ardent supporters of Israel: Israel was anti-Soviet; Israel was in the forefront of defending the human rights of Soviet Jews; Israel was democratic. American pressure on Israel for the sake of détente or Arab oil was especially to be deplored, in the eyes of these critics.

Congress, for its part, was not very pleased with Sinai II as an example of Kissinger's diplomatic prowess. At a minimum, United States aid to the Middle East in fiscal year 1976 would exceed $3 billion, $2.25 billion of which would go to Israel, thereby cutting deeply into aid funds available for the rest of the world.[35] Moreover, Congress initially balked at the idea of sending American civilians to man the buffer zone between Egypt and Israel. The Vietnam analogy was raised, although it was not sufficiently compelling to cause Congress to reject the idea. Then, too, even the most ardent supporters of Israel were dismayed to find Pershing missiles among the military items requested by Israel. It seemed doubtful that Congress would authorize the sale of Pershings to Israel, and in December 1975 Israel withdrew her request, at least for the time being.

As the election year 1976 began, it became apparent that President Ford would be preoccupied with domestic politics. His position

34. Schlesinger was dismissed by Ford on Nov. 2, 1975, to be replaced by Donald Rumsfeld; CIA Director Colby was replaced by George Bush; and Kissinger was relieved of his position as national security affairs adviser, to be replaced by Brent Scowcroft. Moynihan resigned on Feb. 2, 1976.

35. Even without Sinai II, of course, the level of aid for Israel and Egypt would have been substantial. The marginal cost of Sinai II should be measured as several hundreds of million dollars, not several billion. For an account of the congressional debate on Sinai II, see the *New York Times,* Oct. 1, 1975. The House and Senate voted in favor of United States technicians in Sinai by large majorities, on Oct. 8 and 9 respectively.

within his own party was precarious, and it was not at all certain that
he would even be nominated at the Republican convention in August. Ronald Reagan, former governor of California, was mounting a
strong challenge, with support of the most conservative elements in
the party. Kissinger and his foreign policy were emerging as a campaign issue for the Reagan Republicans as well as the Democrats. And
although the Middle East was not initially one of the issues in the
campaign, the criticisms aimed at Ford and Kissinger did drive them
to a tougher stance toward the Soviet Union, as symbolized by American policy in Angola, and precluded an ambitious new initiative in
the Arab-Israeli arena.

Despite these election-year pressures, however, President Ford
persevered in the attempt to improve U.S.-Egyptian relations. In
October 1975, Sadat had been the first Egyptian president to pay an
official visit to the United States. During that visit, Sadat had appealed for American economic and even military assistance. A complex debate between Congress and the administration ensued, with
Ford reducing requested aid for Israel in fiscal year 1977 from $2.25
billion to $1.8 billion and simultaneously urging Congress to consider
approval of a limited sale of six C-130 transport planes to Egypt.

Congress not only favored higher levels of aid to Israel, but also
felt that Israel should receive a supplemental grant to cover the "transitional quarter" from July 1976 to October 1, 1976, the beginning
of the new fiscal year. In one of the rare instances of public disagreement between Ford and Kissinger, Ford opposed on budgetary
grounds additional aid to Israel for the transitional quarter, while
Kissinger stated that the administration would not mind if Congress
chose to vote an additional $500 million.

The consideration of arms for Egypt took a new turn in mid-March
1976, when President Sadat announced the abrogation of the fifteen-
year treaty of friendship and cooperation with the Soviet Union.
Against the background of the news that CIA analysts had concluded
that Israel possessed from ten to twenty operational atomic weapons,[36] opposition to the sale to Egypt faded, although Congress
preferred that it be handled purely as a commercial transaction.
Eventually Egypt got the planes, worth about $50 million, and Israel
received the supplementary aid, worth many times more.

36. *New York Times*, Mar. 15, 1976.

Ford's willingness to take a hard line on aid to Israel and to oppose in the United Nations the Israeli policy on settlements in the occupied territories lasted through the first part of the election campaign. By the fall, however, when Governor Jimmy Carter of Georgia, the Democratic candidate, was enjoying a huge lead in the polls, the president began to play up his credentials as a strong supporter of Israel. In the last month of the campaign, the Middle East became a topic of occasional debate, wherein Carter and Ford tried to outdo each other as the better friend of Israel, and Carter in particular hinted at very severe action against any future Arab oil embargo.

Carter's narrow victory over Ford on November 2, 1976, settled the issue of who would be the next president, but neither the Israelis nor the Arabs had any clear idea of what the next president's policies would be. Both expected new initiatives, and both were apprehensive.

THE LEBANON CRISIS

Throughout the early part of 1976, as the Americans turned their attention inward, inter-Arab relations continued to deteriorate in the absence of progress toward a settlement. Egypt was trying to emerge from the isolation produced by Sinai II, but only Saudi Arabia offered support. Syria and Jordan were moving together, and the Palestinians were still denouncing Sadat as a traitor to the cause.

In January 1976, the ongoing crisis in Lebanon grew more acute as hundreds of casualties were registered every day. Conspiratorial interpretations of the events in Lebanon abounded, producing a particularly suspicious and mistrustful mood in the Arab world. The only party that seemed to be profiting from the Lebanon crisis, in the eyes of many Arabs, was Israel. Some would also add the United States and Egypt. Lebanon was deflecting attention from Sinai II and was ensuring that combined Arab pressure could not be brought to bear on Israel or the United States. In addition, the right-wing Christian groups in Lebanon, armed and supported by the West and even Israel, were inexplicably pressing their attacks against the Lebanese left, and the Palestinians in particular. Some saw this as part of a master plan, orchestrated in Washington, to destroy the PLO. Then Egypt, Syria, and Jordan could make peace with Israel under United States auspices.

Syria's objective in Lebanon appeared to be to bring the fighting to an early end. Initially Syria allowed several battalions of the Palestine Liberation Army to enter Lebanon. The tide of the battle seemed to turn in ensuing months, to the point where the left, headed by Kamal Jumblatt, spoke of an impending military victory over the right. This concerned the United States, because a leftist Lebanon might allow Palestinian guerrilla attacks against Israel, which could lead to war eventually. Syria, and perhaps even Egypt, would be drawn in. During this period, then, the United States played a very active role in urging restraint on Israel and Syria.[37] Above all, the United States feared that large-scale Syrian intervention on the side of the Palestinians would provoke an Israeli military reaction, thus threatening to upset the fragile stability of the agreements so laboriously negotiated by Kissinger.

The warnings to Syria may have struck home. Asad was perfectly aware that a leftist- or Palestinian-dominated Lebanon would cause him problems. It might invite Israeli attacks, drawing Syria into premature military action against Israel, or it might align itself with Syria's bitter rival, Iraq. What Asad most wanted was a Lebanon that was responsive to Syria's leadership, but as the fighting went on, it became clear that the left and Palestinians were not about to take orders from Damascus. The American assessment of Syria's interests in Lebanon began to change, and by May the United States, with the encouragement of Jordan's King Hussein, was indicating that a limited Syrian military intervention in Lebanon might help to stabilize the situation and restore security. Inasmuch as the United States, and presumably Israel as well, no longer opposed a Syrian move, Asad ordered his armed forces into Syria on a large scale in early June to protect the embattled Christians and rightists against the left and the Palestinians.

Soon most of Lebanon was under Syrian control, but the fighting

37. In late March, the State Department repeatedly warned Syria against military intervention in Lebanon. On Mar. 31, the former ambassador to Jordan, Dean Brown, was sent to Lebanon to try to promote a political settlement. Shortly thereafter, a modest number of Syrian troops did enter Lebanon. The United States and Israel both augmented their military capabilities as precautionary measures. Throughout April, while Syria was working to achieve agreement that Elias Sarkis should replace President Frangieh, riots broke out on the West Bank after the victory on Apr. 12 of nationalists in the municipal elections. Despite the increase of tensions, however, both the United States and Israel began to perceive the Syrian role in Lebanon as potentially stabilizing. Sarkis was elected as Lebanon's new president on May 8, but was not scheduled to take office until September. As fighting continued, Syria increased its military involvement in Lebanon in late May and early June. On June 5, Syria and Egypt withdrew their diplomatic representatives in each other's capitals.

raged on, especially in Beirut. Syria's intervention in Lebanon was roundly condemned by other Arab states, especially Egypt, which joined forces with Iraq, Libya, and the PLO to thwart the Syrian moves. New conspiracy theories began to emerge, linking Syria's action to Kissinger's diabolical policies: Syria would crush the PLO and would be rewarded by the return of the Golan Heights. Jordan would recover the West Bank. A Pax Americana would then descend over the area. Radical forces and Soviet influence would be banished. Saudi oil money would finance the flow of American technology.

The only flaw in the theories was that they bore little resemblance to reality. The United States, rather than having a grand policy for dealing with the Lebanon crisis or the Palestinians, was confused and perplexed by the internecine war in Lebanon. Kissinger dealt with the crisis chiefly as an extension of the Arab-Israeli conflict; hence the warnings to both Israel and Syria not to intervene during the spring of 1976. The conflict had a dynamic of its own, however, as did Syrian policy, once the commitment to Lebanon was made early in 1976. Asad was not playing the American or Israeli game in Lebanon, whatever the superficial appearances. Kissinger and Ford, quite simply, had no game in mind, other than to prevent a full-scale Arab-Israeli war. Apart from urging the evacuation of Americans in Lebanon, the United States did little.[38]

The fighting in Lebanon continued into the fall, and the Christians consolidated their control over a small coastal strip between Beirut and Tripoli. For all intents and purposes, this became an autonomous region with its own government and armed forces. Even the newly elected President Elias Sarkis had little sway over the Christians. Syria helped them by removing the Palestinians from the mountainous areas to the east of the Christian-held areas, gradually and methodically pushing them toward their stronghold around the port of Sidon. The Palestinians, with help from the Iraqis, Libyans,

38. A new ambassador, Frank Meloy, replaced Brown in late April. Subsequently, Brown criticized Kissinger for having discouraged Syria from sending troops into Lebanon. "We reined in the Syrians too much in order to please the Israelis. It resulted in a lot more killing." *Arab Report and Record,* May 16–31, 1976, p. 321. Meloy was kidnapped and assassinated, presumably by dissident Palestinians, on June 16, 1976. He was replaced by an experienced Arabist, Talcott Seelye, but in short order the American diplomatic community in Beirut was reduced to a token force and Seelye returned to Washington. Two evacuations by sea were successfully carried out on June 20 and July 27, 1976, with the cooperation of the PLO. Throughout this period, discreet contacts between the United States and the PLO were undertaken in the interests of arranging for local security.

and Egyptians, fought against great odds, but could not withstand the Syrian offensive.

At the moment of impending Syrian victory, Saudi Arabia flexed its diplomatic and financial muscles, summoning President Asad and Sadat, along with PLO Chairman Arafat, to Riyadh in late October 1976 for an urgent conference to end the bloodshed in Lebanon. Asad conducted himself with considerable sophistication, seeking a reconciliation with Sadat in return for Egypt's endorsement of Syria's predominant role in Lebanon. Within hours, the course of events in the Arab world reversed direction. A hastily convened Arab summit meeting in Cairo a few days later ratified the agreements reached in Riyadh, the key element of which was the creation of an Arab peacekeeping force, consisting mainly of Syrians, which would restore law and order in Lebanon. The PLO, reading the new Arab consensus correctly, concluded that it had no alternative but to acquiesce. By November, most of Lebanon was under effective Syrian control and the eighteen-month-long civil war seemed to be at least at a temporary end. Only in southern Lebanon, where Syrian troops were constrained by Israeli threats, was the situation still explosive, but even there, neither Syria nor Israel seemed to be anxious for a confrontation.

The Arab coalition, which had fallen apart over Sinai II, now seemed to be resurrecting itself. With Saudi encouragement, Egypt and Syria were back on speaking terms, Jordan maintained good relations with Syria, and the PLO, chastened by its severe setbacks in Lebanon, gave off signals that some interpreted as a willingness to pursue more moderate policies in the future. Perhaps not coincidentally, the Arabs appeared to be putting their own house at least partly in order to be better able to confront the new American president with a coherent position. The divisions that had so crippled them throughout the American election year were apparently forgotten, although in other times and in other circumstances they would almost certainly come to the surface again. For the moment, however, the renewed sense of Arab solidarity could be a valuable asset in a new round of diplomacy, just as it could raise the risks of war if diplomacy were to fail.

THE KISSINGER LEGACY

Henry Kissinger's impact on American foreign policy will be debated endlessly. Of the accomplishments credited to him, few were not also in part the product of circumstances or the actions of others. But Kissinger will undoubtedly be regarded as one of the most powerful and most successful of American statesmen in the post-World War II era. How he managed to achieve such prominence is a story in its own right, revealing Kissinger's remarkable talents as a bureaucratic maneuverer and politician. His more enduring legacy, however, will be his policies and the concepts behind them.

After several false starts, Kissinger finally developed a coherent approach to the Arab-Israeli conflict after the October 1973 war. He started from the premise that the United States need not choose between a pro-Arab or pro-Israeli policy. In fact, it was the American special relationship to Israel that compelled the Arabs to deal with Washington instead of Moscow when it came to diplomacy. Consequently, if an alternative to war could be offered to the Arabs, their interests, quite apart from their sentiments, would lead them to deal with the United States. A credible diplomatic process was therefore essential to the weakening of Soviet influence in the Middle East. This view, once stated, seems unexceptional, perhaps obvious, but one should recall that it has often been ignored, on occasion by Kissinger himself.

Kissinger's second contribution to American diplomacy in the Middle East was the development of specific negotiating techniques designed to produce limited agreements between Arabs and Israelis. If Kissinger's grand strategy often seemed fairly conventional, his tactical skills as a negotiator and mediator were unsurpassed. Here his originality, his sense of timing, his intelligence, and even his personality served him especially well. Whether or not any successor can model himself on Kissinger's style, several points will endure. In practice, successful negotiations require an ability to break issues into manageable pieces which can then be imaginatively recombined into viable agreements. Mastery of detail is essential to success, as is a sense of context and nuance. A sustained, high-level effort, fully supported by the president, is the only American approach to negotiations that seems likely to produce results. Kissinger has shown that it can succeed, as well as how difficult it can be.

Finally, Kissinger translated into practice his belief that power and diplomacy must always go hand in hand. The United States can never rely solely on force or on negotiations in the Middle East. The test of statesmanship is to find the critical balance of the two. Arms supplies to the Israelis or the Arabs must be viewed as part of the diplomatic process, not as a technical military issue. Whatever troubles Kissinger may have had in practice with this principle, he clearly saw political considerations outweighing narrowly military ones in decisions of this sort.

Kissinger's successors will no doubt ponder the value of these views and reflect on both the strength and the limits of the Kissinger approach. Kissinger was unable to decide how to deal with the Soviets in the Middle East. He wavered between exaggerating their role and then minimizing it. Similarly, his views on a comprehensive approach to negotiations seemed to fluctuate between a recognition that some form of framework was essential and a belief that each step could and should be taken in isolation from the others. Behind this ambiguity seems to have been a doubt whether peace between Arabs and Israelis could really be established in this generation. At times he acted as if he believed it could be, whereas on other occasions he seemed to be prepared to settle for a stable status quo. Lastly, Kissinger had a blind spot toward the Palestinian issue. He knew that at some point it would have to be confronted. He even appeared to be tempted by the idea of dealing directly with the PLO leadership. But he geared much of his diplomacy to trying to circumvent this crucial issue, to putting off the moment of truth, to weakening the appeal of the Palestinian movement, all the while hoping that some alternative would appear. Perhaps with time, with better luck, and with a strong president behind him, Kissinger would have helped find acceptable solutions to all of these unanswered problems. But Ford's defeat brought his public career to an end and left to the Carter administration the unenviable task of shaping an American policy toward the Arab-Israeli conflict.

CHAPTER IX

Conclusions

IN THE TEN YEARS that followed the Arab-Israeli war of June 1967, American presidents remained remarkably consistent in their broad objectives in the Middle East, but at the same time they were unable to find a successful formula for achieving those goals. No one questioned the desirability of peace and stability in the region; no one ignored the basic American commitment to Israel's survival; no one was unmindful of the dangers of U.S.-Soviet military confrontation in the area; and no one, especially since 1973, was unaware of the value of uninterrupted supplies of oil at moderate prices from the Middle East.

Despite this unanimity on goals and substantial agreement on the nature of the issues, presidents and their advisers have shown great uncertainty concerning the most effective means to pursue the often divergent interests of the United States in the Middle East. They have also differed over the priority to be accorded the Arab-Israeli conflict compared with other pressing international and domestic issues. Since 1967, American policy makers have alternately treated the Middle East as a region of great importance in its own right and as a secondary theater in the global rivalry with the Soviet Union. Virtually every imaginable policy has been considered or tried at some point. The United States has pursued package settlements, interim settlements, and no settlement. It has tried to work with and against the Soviet Union, sometimes simultaneously. It has been remarkably generous in providing economic and military aid to Israel, but on occasions it has withheld aid as a calculated form of pressure. It has sought to isolate, to punish, and then to court Egypt and other Arab states. If there has been any consistent note, it has been an extreme reluctance to deal directly with the sensitive Palestinian issue, and even there a few tentative forays into the unknown can be detected.

It seems clear that policy does not flow simply from a cool, rational calculation of American national interests in the Middle East. Nor do domestic or bureaucratic politics dictate policy. Presidents do have choices to make, even when all the external and domestic constraints have been taken into account. Nothing is more important in determining American policy toward the Arab-Israeli conflict than the definition of the situation held by the president. His perception and understanding of issues will set the tone, establish the framework, and determine the rules by which policy will be carried out. This is not to say that the president is omnipotent, but he is certainly more than merely first among equals.

Too often in the past, it has taken a major crisis to engage the attention of the president; and too often, the policies set in times of crisis have persisted well beyond their usefulness. We therefore have seemed to lurch from one crisis to the next, improvising responses to deal with today's dangers, but often failing to follow up with policies suited to more normal times. Both our friends and adversaries tend to misread such unsteadiness of policy as an uncertainty of purpose.

THE AMERICAN ROLE

The one posture toward the Arab-Israeli conflict that the United States seems unlikely to adopt is that of disinterested bystander. Whether we wish to be or not, we are far too deeply involved in the Middle East to pretend that we are not crucially concerned by what happens there. Even without an active diplomatic stance, the United States influences events through the provision of billions of dollars in aid, through its energy policies, through the activities of its private sector, and through its policies elsewhere in the world. Involvement flows from being a superpower. The contours of that involvement, the ways in which American influence will be used, and the strategy to be adopted remain uncertain.

It is of utmost importance to the United States to try to prevent the outbreak of another full-scale Arab-Israeli war. That goal can be pursued in two ways. One is through the deterrence of war by maintaining a military balance in the area that discourages the resort to force; the other is to provide a diplomatic channel for resolving disputes short of war. Peace between Arabs and Israelis would greatly ease some of the acute dilemmas of United States policy, but the seemingly more attainable objective of stability is also tempting, especially as a short-run goal. The problem is that the stability of the status quo is likely to be illusory, and maintaining the military balance in Israel's favor is not necessarily a deterrent to war and to the use of oil as a political weapon.

The United States therefore is likely to find itself cast in two simultaneous, and at times conflicting, roles. The need to ensure the stability of the military balance in the short run, to reduce the risks of war, and to maintain the confidence of the Israelis in particular causes the United States to assume the role of supplier of very substantial amounts of economic and military aid to Israel. The Arab states resent this aspect of American policy, although they seem to be resigned to it to some extent. The Arabs are told that United States support for Israel is the precondition for an effective American diplomatic role, but they fear that the true purpose is to underwrite the status quo until they are forced to capitulate to Israeli demands. Their bitterness is only somewhat assuaged by the provision of arms and aid to selected Arab regimes as well as to Israel.

Without a corresponding diplomatic strategy, an American policy of arming and supporting Israel risks polarizing the region and driving the Arabs to seek comparable support from the Soviet Union. The United States therefore has generally tried to counterbalance its arms policy with diplomatic initiatives that offer the prospect to the key Arab states of achieving at least their minimum goals by peaceful means. In this role, the United States has offered its services as mediator, and possibly even arbitrator, of the conflict. The part has been played in several ways, ranging from self-restraint and the modest provision of a channel of communication between suspicious parties to a more energetic and substantively directed peacemaking effort.

The United States is invariably caught in a bind because of the very different perceptions and purposes of the regional parties. Israel welcomes American arms and aid, hopes for diplomatic support, and yet fears pressure and abuse. In Israel's view, the United States should not involve itself in the substance of negotiations, but should limit its efforts to bringing the parties together and encouraging a negotiating process. The Arabs, on the other hand, have been led to expect a more active role from the United States. Arms to Israel have been explained as providing necessary "leverage" over Israel, hence the Arabs await evidence that the United States will bring pressure to bear on Israel to relinquish captured territory. An American president has promised to work for the full implementation of UN Resolution 242, which sounds like more than a modest mediation effort, and Kissinger's remarkable "shuttles" stand as testimony to the degree of involvement that the United States is capable of generating when it decides to do so.

A FRAMEWORK FOR PEACE

Somewhat unexpectedly, it is less difficult to discover an American consensus on the content of an eventual Arab-Israeli settlement than on the process by which it might be achieved. In official and nonofficial American circles concerned with the Middle East, one finds a recognition that a genuine, negotiated peace between Arabs and Israelis will have to conform to a number of fairly well understood basic principles if it is to have any chance of success. The details of a peace agreement may vary greatly, but not the general outline.

One attempt to sketch the broad terms of an Arab-Israeli peace agreement that reflects this American consensus is the report issued by a study group convened at the Brookings Institution in late 1975 entitled "Toward Peace in the Middle East."[1] Academics, congressmen, journalists, State Department officials, and prominent politicians have endorsed much of the content of the "Brookings Report."

That report begins with the assumption that the United States has a strong interest in peace between Israel and her Arab neighbors and that peace can best be achieved through negotiations leading toward a comprehensive settlement. It is the content of such a settlement, however, that receives most attention. These points might be considered as agenda items for a future Geneva peace conference.

---

1. "Toward Peace in the Middle East," Report of a Study Group, The Brookings Institution, 1975. The members of the study group who signed the report were Morroe Berger, Robert R. Bowie, Zbigniew Brzezinski, John C. Campbell, Najeeb Halaby, Rita Hauser, Roger W. Heyns, Alan Horton, Malcolm Kerr, Fred Khouri, Philip Klutznick, William Quandt, Nadav Safran, Stephen Spiegel, A. L. Udovitch, and Charles W. Yost.

1. *Mutual Acceptance and Peaceful Relations:* A peace agreement will have to contain commitments by each of the parties to respect the sovereignty, independence, and territorial integrity of the others and to refrain from the use or threat of force. Other hostile actions, such as boycotts and obstacles to the free movement of goods and peoples, should be ended. The long-term objective of a full normalization of relations should be endorsed in the agreements, with progress toward this goal defined as a part of the phased process of settlement.

2. *Palestinians:* The Palestinians, provided they are prepared to accept the right of Israel and Jordan to self-determination, should be accorded that same right. In addition, Palestinian refugees should be helped to resettle in a newly formed Palestinian entity if they so choose and to be compensated for lost property. (Jewish claims for lost property in Arab countries should also be addressed.) Credible Palestinian representatives who are prepared to accept the existence of Israel should participate in the peace settlement negotiations.

3. *Boundaries:* In accordance with principles laid down in UN Resolution 242, Israel, in exchange for the establishment of peaceful relations and suitable security arrangements, should agree to withdraw to the pre–June 5, 1967, lines with only such modifications as might be mutually accepted. No boundary incorporating irredenta will be secure, nor can security be assured without peaceful relations across those boundaries.

4. *Jerusalem:* Any settlement devised for Jerusalem should meet at least the following criteria: unimpeded access to all holy places; no physical barriers to free circulation within the city; substantial political autonomy for each national group within the city in those areas where it predominates.

5. *Stages of Implementation:* The peace agreement should define stages for carrying out the elements of the overall settlement. In particular, withdrawal and the establishment of peaceful, normal relations might proceed in matched phases, along with the implementation of special security measures. The objective would be to avoid pressures for one-sided implementation of the agreement.

6. *Safeguards, Guarantees, and Assistance:* To reinforce the commitments made by the parties, there should be specific security arrangements, such as demilitarized zones and perhaps UN forces, in sensitive areas. Specific multilateral or bilateral guarantees might be considered as supplements to the basic agreement among the parties.

These broad principles, which are somewhat more precise than those incorporated in UN Resolution 242, still leave several questions unsettled. Most ambiguous, from the Israeli point of view, is the so-called "quality of peace" issue. Israelis often say that for "real peace" they would be prepared to make substantial concessions. But they fear that the Arabs are thinking merely of a formal arrangement that will allow for the recovery of their territories, but will leave the underlying hostility alive. Before withdrawing completely, therefore, Israel wants signs that Arab attitudes have fundamentally changed, that the Arabs are thinking of a "peace of reconciliation," not just a momentary pause in the longer-term struggle against the Jewish state in Palestine. Israelis put forward several guidelines by which to measure a change of Arab attitudes. What do Arab leaders say to their own people about Israel? Have propaganda attacks decreased? Will Arabs meet with Israelis without third-party mediation? Can Israelis freely travel to Arab countries? How are Jewish communities in Egypt, Syria, and Iraq treated? Is anti-Semitism a feature of official Arab statements? Would peace include an end to discriminatory actions against Israel and to the establishment of full diplomatic relations? Are the Arabs prepared to talk about regional economic cooperation?

The customary Arab response to this list of Israeli demands is that Israel must first show the Arab world that it does not have expansionist designs and must take steps to restore the rights of the Palestinians. This would necessitate full Israeli withdrawal to the 1967 lines, including withdrawal from east Jerusalem, and some tangible progress in the direction of allowing Palestinians the choice of repatriation to their original homes or of compensation for lost properties, along with the right to form a state of their own. Only when Israel has shown its good faith by these acts would the Arab world be prepared to go beyond a minimal *de facto* recognition of Israel and a formal commitment to peace.

THE GAP BETWEEN ISRAELI AND ARAB VIEWS OF PEACE

The gap in perceptions of peace between Israel and the major Arab states is thus very substantial. The United States doubtless prefers the Israeli vision of "real peace," but some observers question whether an Arab change of heart can be negotiated. They would argue for a less ambitious agreement based on solemn international undertakings to recognize borders and to abstain from the use of force, leaving for the process of implementation the linkage between stages of withdrawal and concrete manifestations of peaceful intent. They would also try to hedge against uncertainty by emphasizing security arrangements as being of at least as great importance as some of the symbols of normalization. Although the United States will certainly not want to discourage any moves toward reconciliation, it might have to play a role in compensating Israel for Arab reluctance to make some concessions by emphasizing bilateral and multilateral security arrangements, as was the case in the Sinai II agreement of September 1975.

A second area of inevitable controversy involves the Palestinians and the Palestine Liberation Organization (PLO). Self-determination is an appealing idea, as is the notion of a just settlement of the status of the Palestinian refugees. Nevertheless, both raise many questions. First, within what territory would Palestinians be given the right to self-determination? Presumably the West Bank and Gaza are the primary areas, but this will have to be defined precisely at some point. Then there is the issue of how to determine the desires of the Palestinians. Some have suggested a UN-sponsored referendum, but the attractiveness of the idea fades on closer examination. Others have urged following the French-Algerian precedent, whereby France negotiated an agreement with the leading nationalist group and then submitted the agreement to a referendum for ratification.[2]

Many Palestinians are concerned that behind the screen of self-determination they will be asked to give up what they consider to be their basic rights. Moreover, the entity that may emerge is likely to be squeezed between powerful, suspicious neighbors to both the east and the west. Almost certainly such a state will have to accept limits on its military capabilities, and will thus be vulnerable to the pressures of its neighbors. Economically, such a state will find it difficult to absorb large numbers of resettled Palestinians and provide them with productive work. All in all, few Palestinians are genuinely enthusiastic about the prospective ministate and some are deeply opposed to it.

Then, too, most Israelis are not happy with the idea of a Palestinian state, although their concerns are quite different. A Palestinian state, they fear, might turn to the Soviet Union for arms, thus becoming a serious threat to Israel's security. Furthermore, Israel's Arab

2. See Gidon Gottlieb's interesting discussion of the Evian agreements and their possible relevance to the Palestinian situation in "Palestine: An Algerian Solution," *Foreign Policy*, no. 21 (winter 1975–76).

population might be attracted to such a state, causing severe internal problems for Israel. And if large numbers of Palestinians are allowed to return to pre-1967 Israel, they might become a dangerous fifth column. Finally, Israel refuses to deal with the PLO so long as it adheres to its official slogan of establishing a united, secular, democratic state in all of the former area of the British mandate in Palestine.

The United States has refrained from taking a clear position on the issues regarding the Palestinians. In view of their complexity, this may have been a reasonable posture in the short term, but at some point the United States will have to confront the question of Palestinian participation in peace negotiations. Beyond that lie the substantive issues, on which great disagreement exists. Egypt, Syria, and Jordan will presumably have to develop with the Palestinians an agreed negotiating position consistent with the terms of reference for the Geneva peace talks. Then a judgment would have to be made on whether negotiations can proceed.

Israel has been reluctant to define "secure and recognized borders" in any precise fashion, and official statements suggest that Israel hopes for substantial changes in the lines that existed before June 5, 1967. The United States has not given any specific encouragement to the Israelis on this point. President Johnson noted that final borders should not reflect the weight of conquest and that there could be only insubstantial changes in the pre-1967 lines. President Nixon endorsed this same view, adding that on the Egyptian-Israeli front the old international frontier should be restored in a peaceful settlement, provided adequate security arrangements could be devised. Nixon, however, also spoke of "defensible borders" for Israel, which Israelis interpreted as an endorsement of some changes in the pre-1967 lines.

Because of the concreteness of the territorial issue, any statement of an American position will immediately be identified as favoring Israel or the Arabs. The United States has no reason to prefer one set of borders to any other, provided the parties themselves can reach agreement. It does seem, however, that Egypt and Syria have no intention of ceding sovereignty over any significant portion of the Sinai or the Golan Heights. Only concerning the West Bank have Arab leaders spoken of negotiated minor mutual adjustments in the armistice line, a position which is totally unacceptable to the Israelis.

Jerusalem stands as the most complex of the issues involving territory. It has long been felt that Jerusalem can be dealt with only when agreement has been reached on most other issues.

Israeli settlements in the Golan Heights, in the West Bank, around Jerusalem, and in Gaza and northern Sinai are particularly troublesome to the Arabs. As a matter of principle, Israel will be extremely reluctant to abandon any settlements. Some are viewed as important for defense; others stand as affirmation that Jews have the right to live anywhere in their historic homeland. The United States is on record as opposing Israeli settlements in occupied territories but it has done little to dissuade Israel from "creating facts" in the West Bank, the Golan Heights, and Gaza.

PEACE BY STAGES

The principle of staged implementation of a peace agreement seems to be of crucial importance. Both sides have in practice accepted it, and the need for the future will be to find equivalent concessions for each stage. In addition, some agreed concept on how long the period of implementation will be is essential. Israel will prefer a very prolonged period, whereas the Arabs will hope that Israeli troops will be withdrawn at an early date. A certain amount of flexibility exists here which a skillful mediator may use to good advantage.

Ultimately, regardless of how conciliatory and moderate the parties themselves may be, substantial differences on the terms of agreement are bound to remain. Third parties, and especially the United States, may try to bridge these differences through concrete security measures and outside guarantees. Understandably, Israelis are fearful that these will become substitutes for Arab concessions, but, if past practice is any guide, Israel will insist on some form of security measures and guarantees regardless of the nature of Arab concessions. After all, the Arab regime that makes peace with Israel may one day be replaced, and Israel will want some hedge against such uncertainties.

Security measures can be of three essential types. First are measures designed to reduce inadvertent clashes between opposing forces. Zones of separation and demilitarization may be helpful, along with such devices as UN or joint patrols to ensure against violations. At best, these arrangements may help to reduce tensions. Second are measures designed to make aggressive military action difficult or costly. These include limitations on certain types of equipment and military infrastructure, physical barriers to troop deployments, and interposition forces. It is sometimes thought that the mere presence of UN forces will help to deter war because of the presumed onus of attacking an international force. There is little reason, however, to suppose that any of these measures can be a guarantee against a determined aggressor. They may, however, raise the costs of war marginally and thus could contribute to deterrence and stability.

Third, and extremely important in the Middle East, are arrangements which can provide early warning against surprise attack. In 1956, 1967, and 1973, war began with little or no advance warning. Technology, along with agreed force deployments, can lessen the possibility of surprise attack, can extend the period of warning, and can thus minimize the incentive for launching preventive or preemptive wars. Early-warning stations, along with regular reconnaissance, can help to reduce the likelihood of war and might well be incorporated into future agreements. Because of its advanced technology, the United States can play a major role in this area.

In addition to these specific security measures, Israel will want to reach an understanding with the United States on continuing supplies of arms and on possible intervention in the event of flagrant violations of the agreement by the Arabs or by the Soviet Union. Some Arab states may seek similar understandings, although the U.S.-Israeli relationship will be the most crucial. If Israel seeks to formalize its ties to the United States by some form of treaty, the United States may seriously consider the idea, although other forms of expressed commitment might be equally acceptable.

LESSONS OF THE PAST

The hard choices for any American administration in formulating a coherent Arab-Israeli policy lie beyond merely supporting a negotiated peace agreement. Although the specific decisions that will have to be confronted in the future are unpredictable, one can anticipate that they will involve questions of how the United States will choose to use its influence to break the diplomatic deadlocks that are likely to arise from time to time. In deciding how to deal with these issues, policy makers may find it useful to ponder the experience of the decade that followed the 1967 war.

First, policy makers should be wary of those who claim that time is on the side of peace. There may be perfectly valid reasons for the United States to adopt a restrained attitude toward the Arab-Israeli conflict, but this is not one of them. The past decade yields little evidence that time has reduced hostility, has changed basic attitudes, or has strengthened moderate views in Israel, Egypt, Syria, Jordan, or among the Palestinians. At best, one can detect a greater degree of realism, an important ingredient in peacemaking, but also useful in planning another war. Both Arabs and Israelis at times tend to believe that time is on their side, but there is no reason for the United States to fall into such dangerous complacency. President Johnson treated the problem from this perspective in 1967–68; Nixon and Kissinger did likewise from 1971 to 1973. Events suggest that they profoundly misjudged the situation.

A second belief is that war can be prevented primarily by maintaining the military balance clearly in Israel's favor. Again, there are strong arguments for keeping Israel adequately armed. Yet the war of attrition in 1969–70 and the October 1973 war show that Arab leaders are quite capable of deciding on military operations for essentially political reasons. The near certainty of defeat on the battlefield is not by itself enough to deter war at Arab initiative. Nixon and Kissinger after September 1970 were insensitive to this point, with the consequence that they were caught by surprise in October 1973.

A third lesson from recent experience seems to be that the Soviet Union is unwilling or unable to play either the role of spoiler or peacemaker. There is no evidence that the Soviet Union has been able to force the Arab states to act against their own perceived interests. The Soviets cannot be held ultimately responsible for either the September 1970 crisis in Jordan or the October 1973 war, although in May 1967 they did contribute to the early stages of escalation by supplying misinformation to the Egyptians about Israeli intentions. Although it is true that the Arabs could not have fought in 1967 or 1973 without Soviet weapons, the Soviet Union did not make the decision for war in either case. Nor have the Soviets ever taken significant steps to bring the Egyptians, Syrians, Iraqis, or Palestinians to accept moderate positions toward Israel. Occasionally they have urged restraint on practical grounds, such as military unpreparedness, but they have not brought pressure to bear on their military clients to change their basic diplomatic posture. Nixon's concept of linkage assumed that the Soviets could be pried away from their friends in the Middle East in the interests of superpower détente. When he learned that they could not, he made a second error of holding them responsible for much of what happened in the area from 1970 to 1972. At the core of his misperception was an excessive concentration on superpower relations to the detriment of regional trends in the Middle East.

A fourth misconception was to view the area primarily in terms of radical versus moderate regimes. To some degree, of course, such labels make sense, but generally, when used in Washington, they simply meant pro- or anti-American. By relying on such categories, policy makers inadvertently adopted a whole series of associated, and often misleading, concepts: polarization, erosion, confrontation. To be sure, these were not meaningless terms, but they came to be used as shorthand for describing considerably more complex trends in the Middle East. The net effect was to keep the focus on the U.S.-Soviet dimension of the crisis at the expense of understanding developments in Israel, in the Arab world, and in the region as a whole.

The fifth mistake that appears to have been made at various times in the past has been to assume that signs of inter-Arab cooperation are necessarily dangerous for Israel, and hence for the United States. Some seem to feel that only a fragmented Arab world in which regimes are at odds with one another can be managed in terms of Israeli security, and would therefore urge a conscious strategy of trying to divide the major Arab regimes. While it is true that a modicum of Arab solidarity is essential to make war, the same is needed if the Arabs are ever to make peace. At a minimum, a coalition of Arab regimes including Egypt, Syria, and Saudi Arabia must remain intact for either war or peace. Jordan, the Palestinians, and perhaps even Algeria, may be associated with this coalition. The United States has no interest in trying to divide these regimes, and policies that are likely to have such consequences, such as the pursuit of Sinai II, must be very carefully considered.

A corollary to the preceding point involves the Palestinians. It is often argued that the Palestinians can or should be excluded from the diplomatic process. Jordan is seen as a possible spokesman for Palestinian interests. By now, however, it should be clear that the Palestinians cannot be so easily ignored. To a large degree, the war of 1967, the Jordan crisis of 1970, and the Lebanese civil war of 1975–76 can be traced to the Palestinians. At the same time, it is a mistake to believe that a peace settlement can start with the Palestinians. They are neither strong enough nor well enough organized to take the first steps toward peace with Israel. They remain heavily dependent on Arab regimes, and will ultimately follow their lead to some extent. They have one major concession to make—recognition of Israel—but this is a card that can be played only once, and therefore is likely to be played late in the game, if at all.

GUIDELINES FOR THE FUTURE

With these experiences from the past in mind, a few general guidelines for future policy can be suggested:

—A comprehensive approach to peace should not evolve toward the "package settlement" concept whereby complete agreement on all issues must be reached before any part is implemented. Within a framework of agreed principles, it is perfectly reasonable to expect that some problems will be resolved before others and that implementation of some points will come in stages.

—If the United States really aims to promote an Arab-Israeli peace, nothing short of a sustained, high-level initiative with full presidential backing can hope to succeed.

—An effective policy must be adapted to the realities of the Middle East rather than simply reflecting superpower relations. Decisions on war and peace will be made primarily in Cairo, Damascus, Riyadh, and Jerusalem, not in Moscow or Washington. We would do well to know as much as possible about the constraints operating on each of the regional actors and to convey our understanding of those forces to the other parties to the negotiations.

—The president must be prepared to devote considerable time and energy to building domestic support in Congress and in public opinion for his Middle East policy. It is here that the quality of leadership will be tested. Without domestic support, no policy is likely to succeed.

—Once a course of action is decided upon, there is considerable virtue in consistency, assuming the premises of the policy are sound. Often we have been too reactive, too vacillating, and have not done what we said we would do. This has confused adversaries and friends, a confusion which becomes especially acute when we explain our policies in substantially different terms to each party.

Although these guidelines will do little to help the president and his advisers determine the specifics of American policy toward the Arab-Israeli conflict, they can serve as a checklist against which to evaluate proposals for action. In the end, however, it will be the president, with his particular view of the stakes involved in the Middle East and of the opportunities for effective American diplomacy, who will establish the framework for our policies. Lest he become a captive of a limited definition of the situation, the president should invite a variety of perspectives and should periodically review the premises on which our policies are based.

Ultimately, the test of leadership is to combine vision with understanding of concrete issues. Nowhere in the world is leadership more essential to the achievement of peace than in the Middle East. And no one, perhaps unfortunately, is better suited for the role of peacemaker between Arabs and Israelis than the American president. The challenge is clearly an immense one, the risks are very great, and the likelihood of failure is substantial. The lessons of the past decade suggest that peace will not be easily achieved, but they also suggest that without American leadership in the search for peace, another war is inevitable, and that such a war could gravely threaten American interests. The president of the United States will have many difficult choices to make in dealing with the Arab-Israeli conflict. But he will not have the choice of remaining indifferent.

Bibliography

I. SOURCES ON AMERICAN FOREIGN POLICY AND THE POLICY-MAKING PROCESS

Allison, Graham. *Essence of Decision.* Boston: Little, Brown & Co., 1971.

Almond, Gabriel. *The American People and Foreign Policy.* New York: Praeger, 1960.

Aron, Raymond. *The Imperial Republic: The United States and the World, 1945–1973.* Englewood Cliffs, N.J.: Prentice-Hall, 1974.

Art, Robert. "Bureaucratic Politics and American Foreign Policy: A Critique." *Policy Sciences* 40 (1973).

Axelrod, Robert. "Argumentation in Foreign Policy Decision Making: Britain in 1918, Munich in 1938, and Japan in 1970." Paper delivered to the 1976 Annual Meeting of the American Political Science Association, Chicago, September 2–5, 1976.

Bauer, Raymond A.; de Sola Pool, Ithiel; and Dexter, Lewis A. *American Business and Public Policy: The Politics of Foreign Trade.* New York: Atherton Press, 1963.

Bauer, Raymond; and Gergen, Kenneth, ed. *The Study of Policy Formulation.* New York: The Free Press, 1968.

Bentley, Arthur. *The Process of Government: A Study of Social Pressures.* Chicago: University of Chicago Press, 1908.

Braybrooke, David; and Lindblom, Charles E. *A Strategy of Decision.* New York: The Free Press, 1970.

Cohen, Bernard C. *The Public's Impact on Foreign Policy.* Boston: Little, Brown & Co., 1973.

Davis, Lynn E. *The Cold War Begins: Soviet-American Conflict Over Eastern Europe.* Princeton: Princeton University Press, 1974.

Destler, I.M. *Presidents, Bureaucrats and Foreign Policy.* Princeton: Princeton University Press, 1972.

Friedrich, Carl J. *Man and His Government.* New York: McGraw-Hill, 1963.

George, Alexander L. "The Case for Multiple Advocacy in Making Foreign Policy." *American Political Science Review* 66, no. 3 (September 1972).

Halperin, Morton. *Bureaucratic Politics and Foreign Policy.* Washington: Brookings Institution, 1974.

301

Hoffmann, Stanley. *Gulliver's Troubles, or The Setting of American Foreign Policy.* New York: McGraw-Hill, 1968.

Janis, Irving L. *Victims of Groupthink: A Psychological Study of Foreign Policy Decisions and Fiascoes.* Boston: Houghton-Mifflin Co., 1972.

Kissinger, Henry A. "The Viet Nam Negotiations." *Foreign Affairs* 47, no. 2 (January 1969).

Lindblom, Charles E. "The Science of 'Muddling Through.'" *Public Administration Review* 19 (spring 1959).

May, Ernest. *"Lessons" of the Past: The Use and Misuse of History in American Foreign Policy.* New York: Oxford University Press, 1973.

Miller, Merle. *Plain Speaking: An Oral Biography of Harry S. Truman.* New York: Berkeley Publishing Corporation, 1973.

Mueller, John E. *War, Presidents and Public Opinion.* New York: John Wiley, 1973.

Nixon, Richard M. "Asia After Viet Nam." *Foreign Affairs* 46, no. 1 (October 1967).

Steinbruner, John D. *The Cybernetic Theory of Decision.* Princeton: Princeton University Press, 1974.

Szulc, Tad. "Behind the Vietnam Ceasefire Agreement." *Foreign Policy* 15 (summer 1974).

Truman, David. *The Governmental Process.* New York: Alfred A. Knopf, 1951.

Wicker, Tom. *JFK and LBJ.* New York: William Morrow & Co., 1968.

Wildavsky, Aaron. *The Politics of the Budgetary Process,* 2d ed. Boston: Little, Brown & Co., 1974.

Wohlstetter, Roberta. *Pearl Harbor: Warning and Decision.* Stanford: Stanford University Press, 1962.

II. SOURCES ON AMERICAN POLICY IN THE MIDDLE EAST

Adelman, M.A. "Is the Oil Shortage Real? Oil Companies as OPEC Tax Collectors." *Foreign Policy* no. 9 (fall 1972).

Akins, James E. "The Oil Crisis: This Time the Wolf Is Here." *Foreign Affairs* 51, no. 3 (April 1973).

Alroy, Gil Carl. *The Kissinger Experience.* New York: Horizon Press, 1975.

Bar Zohar, Michel. *Embassies in Crisis.* Englewood Cliffs, N.J.: Prentice Hall, 1970.

Brandon, Henry. *The Retreat of American Power.* New York: Doubleday & Co., 1973.

Brecher, Michael. *Decisions in Israel's Foreign Policy.* New Haven: Yale University Press, 1975.

Chenery, Hollis. "Restructuring the World Economy." *Foreign Affairs* 53, no. 2 (January 1975).

Cline, Ray S. "Policy Without Intelligence." *Foreign Policy* 17 (winter 1974–75).

Dayan, Moshe. *Moshe Dayan: Story of My Life.* William Morrow & Co., 1976.

Draper, Theodore. "The United States and Israel: Tilt in the Middle East." *Commentary* 59, no. 4 (April 1975).

Erskine, Hazel. "The Polls: Western Partisanship in the Middle East." *Public Opinion Quarterly* (winter 1969–70).

Garnham, David. "The Oil Crisis and US Attitudes Toward Israel." In *Arab Oil: Impact on the Arab Countries and Global Implications.* Edited by Naiem A. Sherbiny and Mark A. Tessler. New York: Praeger, 1976.

Gilboa, M. *Six Years, Six Days* (in Hebrew). Tel Aviv: Am Oved, 1968.

Golan, Matti. *The Secret Conversations of Henry Kissinger.* New York: Quadrangle Books, 1976.

Gottlieb, Gidon. "Palestine: An Algerian Solution." *Foreign Policy* no. 21 (winter 1975–76).

Heikal, Mohammed. *The Cairo Documents.* New York: Doubleday & Co., 1973.

———. *The Road to Ramadan.* New York: Quadrangle Books, 1975.

Herzog, Chaim. *The War of Atonement, October 1973.* Boston: Little, Brown & Co., 1975.

Hoffmann, Stanley. "A New Policy for Israel." *Foreign Affairs* 53, no. 3 (April 1975).

Howe, Jonathan Trumbull. *Multicrises.* Cambridge, Mass.: MIT Press, 1971.

Johnson, Lyndon Baines. *The Vantage Point.* New York: Holt, Rinehart, & Winston, 1971.

Kalb, Marvin and Bernard. *Kissinger.* Boston: Little, Brown & Co., 1974.

Lall, Arthur S. *The UN and the Middle East Crisis, 1967.* New York: Columbia University Press, 1968.

Laqueur, Walter. *Confrontation.* New York: Bantam Books, 1974.

London Sunday Times Insight Team. *The Yom Kippur War.* New York: Doubleday & Co., 1974.

Luttwak, Edward N., and Laqueur, Walter. "Kissinger and the Yom Kippur War." *Commentary* 58, no. 3 (September 1974).

Quandt, William B. "Domestic Influences on U.S. Foreign Policy in the Middle East: The View from Washington." In *The Middle East: Quest for an American Policy.* Edited by Willard A. Beling. Albany: State University of New York Press, 1973.

———. "Kissinger and the Arab-Israeli Disengagement Negotiations." *Journal of International Affairs* 29, no. 1 (spring 1975).

——— et al. *The Politics of Palestinian Nationalism.* Berkeley: University of California Press, 1973.

———. *Soviet Policy in the October 1973 War.* R–1864, The RAND Corporation, 1976.

———. "U.S. Energy Policy and the Arab-Israeli Conflict." In *Arab Oil: Impact on the Arab Countries and Global Implications.* Edited by Naiem A. Sherbiny and Mark A. Tessler. New York: Praeger, 1976.

———. "United States Policy in the Middle East: Constraints and Choices." In *Political Dynamics in the Middle East.* Edited by Paul Y. Hammond and Sidney S. Alexander. New York: American Elsevier, 1972.

Ra'anan, Uri. "The USSR and the Middle East: Some Reflections on the Soviet Decision-Making Process." *ORBIS* 17, no. 3 (fall 1973).

Rostow, Eugene. *Law, Power and the Pursuit of Peace.* Lincoln: University of Nebraska Press, 1968.

———. *Peace in the Balance.* New York: Simon & Schuster, 1972.

Schiff, Zeev. *October Earthquake.* Tel Aviv: University Publishing Project, 1974.

Sheehan, Edward R.F. *The Arabs, Israelis, and Kissinger.* New York: Reader's Digest Press, 1976.

Szulc, Tad. "Is He Indispensable? Answers to the Kissinger Riddle." *New York,* 1 July 1974.

"Toward Peace in the Middle East." Report of a Study Group. The Brookings Institution, 1975.

Trice, Robert H. "Domestic Political Interests and American Policy in the Middle East: Pro-Israel, Pro-Arab and Corporate Non-Governmental Actors and the Making of American Foreign Policy, 1966–1971." Ph.D. thesis in political science, University of Wisconsin, 1974.

Tucker, Robert. "Oil: The Issue of American Intervention." *Commentary* 59, no. 1 (January 1975).

Ullman, Richard H. "After Rabat: Middle East Risks and American Roles." *Foreign Affairs* 53, no. 2 (January 1975).

U.S. Foreign Policy for the 1970s, "Building for Peace." A Report to the Congress by Richard Nixon, February 25, 1971.

U.S. Foreign Policy for the 1970s, "The Emerging Structure of Peace." A Report to the Congress by Richard Nixon, February 9, 1972.

U.S. Foreign Policy for the 1970s, "Shaping a Durable Peace." A Report to the Congress by Richard Nixon, May 3, 1973.

Van der Linden, Frank. *Nixon's Quest for Peace.* New York: Robert B. Luce, 1972.

Whetten, Lawrence L. *The Canal War: Four Power Conflict in the Middle East.* Cambridge, Mass.: The MIT Press, 1974.

Index

Agnew, Spiro, 166, 183
Algeria, 221, 236, 239–240, 241, 254, 298
Allon, Yigal, 249, 255, 262, 268, 270
Alsop, Joseph, 186, 238
American Israel Public Affairs Committee (AIPAC), 19
American Jews, 18, 23, 37, 94–95, 97
Americans for Near Eastern Refugee Aid, 21
Amit, Meir, 56, 57, 58, 59
Anderson, Robert, 55, 57, 91
Angleton, James, 75n
Angola, 280
Anticipated reaction, law of, 20
Aqaba, Gulf of, 42, 44, 59, 86, 213
Arab-American University Graduates, 21
Arabists, 25–26, 62, 75n
Arab states, 209; Rabat conference, 256–258; solidarity of, 201, 202, 276, 278, 281, 283, 284, 298; U.S. aid and arms to, 6, 66, 209, 279, 280, 286, 289; U.S. policy toward, 5, 18, 32, 129, 160, 168, 174, 181, 205, 208, 209, 210, 216, 259–260, 288, 289
Arafat, Yasir, 119, 156, 230, 234, 248, 257, 284
Arms limitation, Middle East, 66n, 67n, 96–97. *See also* Strategic arms limitation
Asad, Hafiz, 123, 124, 220, 221, 231, 234, 235, 237, 240, 246, 248, 255, 261, 264n, 276; inter-Arab relations, 167n, 169, 180, 231, 255, 278, 282–283, 284; Kissinger talks with, 222–223, 229, 230, 232, 233, 236, 240, 241–244
As-Samuᵖ, 38

Aswan high dam, 17
Atherton, Alfred (Roy), 75, 159, 170n, 191n
Atlantic Charter (1941), 34

Bab al-Mandab, 213, 214, 224, 228
Ball, George, 51, 65n, 269
Barbour, Walworth, 43, 55, 61, 107n
Battle, Lucius, 48, 51
Bauer, Raymond, 30
Beam, Jacob D., 88n
Ben Gurion, David, 267
Benhima, Ahmed, 188
Berger, Morroe, 290n
Bergus, Donald, 133–134, 139, 140, 141–142, 143, 144, 163
Bipolarity, erosion of, 5
Black September, 156
Blockade, Egyptian, 43–44, 58
Boumedienne, Houari, 221, 231, 239–240, 241n
Bouteflika, Abdalaziz, 188
Bowie, Robert R., 290n
Boycott, economic, 261, 262, 265, 272
Brezhnev, Leonid, 149, 158, 159, 166–167, 173, 190, 191, 192, 196, 197, 236–237, 261, 262–263
British proposal. *See* Multilateral naval force
Brookings Institution, 290–291
Brown, Air Force General George, 204
Brown, L. Dean, 116, 118, 282n, 283n
Bruce, David, 269
Brzezinski, Zbigniew, 290n
Bundy, McGeorge, 71n, 269

DATE DUE

DATE DUE			
FEB 15 2008			
JUN 0 4 2018			
GAYLORD			PRINTED IN U.S.A.

Political Science

O N FOUR OCCASIONS since 1967 the Middle East has been the scene of acute international crises: the June 1967 Arab-Israeli war, the Jordan crisis of September 1970, the October 1973 war, and the Lebanese civil war of 1975-1976. Except for the latter case, in each instance the United States was deeply drawn into the crisis, with serious consequences for US-Soviet relations as well as for the Middle East.

Mr. Quandt analyzes the formulation of American policy toward the Arab-Israeli conflict, with emphasis on the role of crisis in shaping the views of policy makers and the importance of Presidential leadership in translating general principles into concrete decisions. Both the process of decision making and the substance of policy during the decade following the 1967 war receive central attention.

One conclusion drawn from the study is that American policy makers have at times overestimated the centrality of the global setting in dealing with Middle East crises, often at the expense of an accurate understanding of regional developments. If the United States is to play an effective part in promoting a resolution of the Arab-Israeli conflict, careful attention will have to be paid to the views and policies of the parties most directly involved.

William B. Quandt is Associate Professor of Political Science at the University of Pennsylvania. In January 1977, he took leave to join the National Security Council Staff as Office Director for Middle Eastern Affairs.

UNIVERSITY OF CALIFORNIA PRESS
Berkeley 94720

ISBN: 0-520-03536-4

LOOK FOR BARCODE